SEVENTH EDITION

Southeast Asia
in the New International Era

ROBERT DAYLEY

The College of Idaho

WESTVIEW
PRESS

Copyright © 2017 by Westview Press
Published by Westview Press, an imprint of Perseus Books,
a Hachette Book Group company
2465 Central Avenue
Boulder, CO 80301
www.westviewpress.com

Library of Congress Cataloging-in-Publication Data

Names: Dayley, Robert, author.
Title: Southeast Asia in the new international era / Robert Dayley.
Description: Seventh edition. | Boulder, CO : Westview Press, [2016] |
    Includes bibliographical references and index.
Identifiers: LCCN 2016007236 (print) | LCCN 2016007751 (ebook) |
    ISBN 9780813350110 (pbk.) | ISBN 9780813350462 (e-book)
Subjects: LCSH: Southeast Asia—Politics and government—1945– | Southeast
    Asia—Politics and government—21st century. | Southeast Asia—Foreign
    relations.
Classification: LCC DS526.7 .N45 2016 (print) | LCC DS526.7 (ebook) |
    DDC 959.05/4—dc23
LC record available at http://lccn.loc.gov/2016007236

10 9 8 7 6 5 4 3 2 1

Contents

Preface and Acknowledgments
to the Seventh Edition

When Professor Clark Neher first invited me to take over *Southeast Asia in the New International Era*, I accepted without hesitation. My deep sense of gratitude to him alone would not allow me to decline. As his student and research assistant at Northern Illinois University, where I completed doctoral work in the 1990s, I was the recipient of his superior academic guidance and his fatherly interest in the well-being of my young family. Professor Neher is the consummate scholar and gentleman. For many of his former students, he was a model professor. Accepting the challenge to extend the life of this text beyond his retirement is a small token of my personal appreciation for his years of mentorship.

The final edition of *Southeast Asia in the New International Era* authored solely by Clark Neher was the fourth edition, which went to press shortly after the events of September 11, 2001. Since that time, I have been solely responsible for revising subsequent editions. Although much content has remained the same, there have been substantial changes to the text beyond updated material since the fourth edition. These changes include an entirely revised Chapter 1, the addition of comparison figures and country maps, the rearrangement of chapters according to standard mainland and insular divisions of Southeast Asia, a section titled "State-Society Relations and Democracy" for each country chapter, and the addition of new chapters on Timor-Leste and the Association of Southeast Asian Nations (ASEAN). The chapters of the book can be read in any order, and their arrangement in no way infers the relative importance of Southeast Asia's countries or their regional significance.

In addition to a new chapter on ASEAN, the seventh edition includes fully updated material for each country chapter through, roughly, the end of 2015. To make space for updates, some existing material has been revised, truncated, or removed. With hindsight always expanding, modest revision to existing text is necessary with each edition, but core themes and essential content remain intact. Necessary length restrictions may understandably leave some area experts troubled by relevant material not included in the book. As best as possible, the book's information and analysis is pitched for readers new to the region—it is most effectively used as a tool for students, professors, and professionals orienting themselves to Southeast Asia. It is not intended to be a comprehensive survey. In my own undergraduate classes at The College of Idaho, I supplement this text with other books and articles to ensure greater depth and breadth than a single text or perspective allows.

With respect to general acknowledgments, past teaching opportunities at Davidson College, St. Lawrence University, Oglethorpe University, China Agricultural University, and Payap University allowed me to exchange intellectually with wonderfully curious colleagues and students. The Asian Studies programs at Weber State University, the University of Oregon, and Northern Illinois University similarly deserve acknowledgment for supporting my area studies training as a student. My students at The College of Idaho are a constant source of inspiration to me.

I wish to thank The College of Idaho, Northern Illinois University, Payap University, the National Institute of Development Administration (Thailand), the Fulbright Program, ASIANetwork, the Freeman Foundation, the Mellon Foundation, and National Endowment for the Humanities (United States) for supporting my research and exploratory endeavors in Asia, where I have lived, taught, and researched for more than four years. This new edition benefited in particular from new research and field experiences in Cambodia, Indonesia, Myanmar, Thailand, Timor-Leste, and Singapore. I wish to thank the many scholars, professionals, government officials, experts, and other informants who gave me their time for briefings, interviews, and ongoing conversations. For their repeated hospitality and generous support in facilitating opportunities for me as well as many of my students, I wish to particularly thank Dr. Attachak Sattayanurak (Chiang Mai University), Dr. Siti Siyamsiyatun (Islamic State University–Indonesian Consortium for Religious Studies), Bunsak Thongdi (Upland Holistic Development Program–Thailand), Bonnie Brereton (Chiang Mai), and the community leaders at Huay Mak Liam (Thailand), Wat Khlong Sila (Thailand), and Sre Prey village (Cambodia).

For useful feedback on this and previous editions I extend special thanks to John Brandon (Asia Foundation), Zhiqun Zhu (Bucknell University), Selma Sonntag (Humboldt State University), William E. Carroll (Sam Houston State University), Trevor Morris (Texas Wesleyan University), Maria Ortuoste (California State University, East Bay), Thomas J. Bellows (University of Texas at San Antonio), Ming Xia (City University of New York–College of Staten Island), Steven G. Jug (Baylor University), Pek Koon Heng (American University), James DeShaw Rae (California State University, Sacramento), LaiYee Leong (Southern Methodist University), and multiple anonymous reviewers. Thanks are extended to my colleagues at The College of Idaho in the Department of Political Economy as well as to Lucinda Wong and Dr. Jeff Snyder-Reinke. For this edition, my students Courtney Indart, Ben Sutton, and Gabe Osterhout made contributions in researching current figures and events. Carolyn Sobczak, Katharine Moore, Grace Fujimoto, Sierra Machado, Kelli Fillingim, and Brooke Maddaford of Westview Press have provided excellent advice and support for the seventh edition. I appreciate their unwavering professionalism. Most importantly, I recognize the love of my life, Carrie, and our three children, Mara, Molly, and Eliot, for sharing with me a love of Southeast Asia.

Robert Dayley

Acronyms

ACFTA	ASEAN-China Free Trade Agreement
ADB	Asian Development Bank
ADMM	ASEAN Defense Ministers' Meeting
AEC	ASEAN Economic Community
AFP	Armed Forces of the Philippines
AFPFL	Anti-Fascist People's Freedom League (Burma/Myanmar)
AFTA	ASEAN Free Trade Area
AICHR	ASEAN Intergovernmental Commission on Human Rights
AIIB	Asian Infrastructure Investment Bank
APEC	Asia-Pacific Economic Cooperation
APSC	ASEAN Political-Security Community
APT	ASEAN Plus Three / ASEAN+3
APU	Angkatan Perpaduan Umnah (United Movement of the Faithful, Malaysia)
ARF	ASEAN Regional Forum
ARMM	Autonomous Region in Muslim Mindanao (Philippines)
ASA	Association of Southeast Asia
ASCC	ASEAN Socio-Cultural Community
ASEAN	Association of Southeast Asian Nations
BN	Barisan Nasional (National Front, Malaysia)
BSPP	Burmese Socialist Program Party
CAVR	Commission for Reception, Truth, and Reconciliation
CEPT	Common Effective Preferential Tariff
CGDK	Coalition Government of Democratic Kampuchea (Cambodia)
CLMV	Cambodia, Laos, Myanmar, Vietnam
CMI	Chiang Mai Initiative
CMIM	Chiang Mai Initiative Multilateralization
CNRP	Cambodia National Rescue Party
CNRT	National Congress for Timorese Reconstruction Party

CNS	Council on National Security (Thailand)
CPP	Cambodian People's Party
CPV	Communist Party of Vietnam
CSO	civil society organization
DAP	Democratic Action Party (Malaysia)
DPD	Dewan Perwakilan Daerah (Regional Representative Council, Indonesia)
DPR	Dewan Perwakilan Rakyat (People's Representative Council, Indonesia)
EAEC	East Asia Economic Caucus
EAS	East Asian Summit
ECCC	Extraordinary Chambers in the Courts of Cambodia
ENC	Ethnic Nationalities Council (Burma/Myanmar)
ERVI	election-related violent incident
Falantil	Forces Amadas de Libertação Nacional de Timor Leste
Fretilin	Revolutionary Front for an Independent East Timor
FTA	free trade agreement
FUNCINPEC	United National Front for an Independent, Peaceful, and Cooperative Cambodia
GATT	General Agreement on Tariffs and Trade
GDP	gross domestic product
GNP	gross national product
GRCs	Group Representation Constituencies (Singapore)
ICJ	International Court of Justice
ICMI	Indonesian Association of Muslim Intellectuals
ILO	International Labour Organization
IMF	International Monetary Fund
INTERFET	International Force for East Timor
ISI	import-substitution industrialization
ISIS	Islamic State of Iraq and Syria
JI	Jemaah Islamiyah (Islamic Congregation)
JPDA	Joint Petroleum Development Area (Timor-Leste)
JSOTF-P	Joint Special Operations Task Force–Philippines
KBL	Kilusang Bagong Lipunan (New Society Movement, Philippines)
KPNLF	Khmer People's National Liberation Front (Cambodia)
Lao PDR	Lao People's Democratic Republic
LDC	least developed country
LFNC	Lao Front for National Construction
LPRP	Lao People's Revolutionary Party
MCA	Malayan Chinese Association
MDG	Millennium Development Goals

MIB	Malay Islamic Beraja (Malay Muslim Monarchy, Brunei)
MIC	Malayan Indian Congress
MILF	Moro Islamic Liberation Front (Philippines)
MMR	maternal mortality rate
MNC	multinational corporation
MNLF	Moro National Liberation Front (Philippines)
MP	Member of Parliament
MPR	People's Consultative Assembly (Indonesia)
NAFTA	North American Free Trade Agreement
NCPO	National Council for Peace and Order (Thailand)
NDF	National Democratic Front (Burma/Myanmar)
NEP	New Economic Policy (Malaysia)
NGO	nongovernmental organization
NIC	newly industrialized country
NLA	National Legislative Assembly (Thailand)
NLD	National League for Democracy (Burma/Myanmar)
NLF	National Liberation Front (Vietnam)
NLHS	Neo Lao Hak Sat (Lao Patriotic Front, Laos)
NMP	Nominated Member of Parliament
NPA	New People's Army (Philippines)
NPKC	National Peace Keeping Council (Thailand)
NTB	non-tariff barrier
NU	Nahdlatul Ulama (Renaissance of Religious Scholars, Indonesia)
NUP	National Unity Party (Burma/Myanmar)
OECD	Organisation for Economic Co-operation and Development
OIC	Organization of the Islamic Conference (Philippines)
OPEC	Organization of Petroleum Exporting Countries
PAD	People's Alliance for Democracy (Thailand)
PAP	People's Action Party (Singapore)
PAS	Parti Islam Se-Malaysia (Pan-Malaysian Islamic Party)
PAVN	People's Army of Vietnam
PCA	Permanent Court of Arbitration
PDI	Partai Demokrasi Indonesia (Indonesia Democracy Party)
PDI-P	Partai Demokrasi Indonesia Perjuangan (Indonesian Democracy Party of Struggle)
PDRC	People's Democratic Reform Committee (Thailand)
PGNU	Provisional Government of National Unity (Laos)
PKB	Partai Kebangkitan Bangsa (National Awakening Party, Indonesia)
PKI	Partai Komunis Indonesia (Communist Party of Indonesia)
PKS	Partai Keadilan Sejahtera (Prosperous Justice Party, Indonesia)

PPP	Partai Persatuan Pembangunan (United Development Party, Indonesia)
PPP	Phak Palang Prachachon (People's Power Party, Thailand)
PR	Pakatan Rakyat (People's Front, or People's Pact, Malaysia)
PRK	People's Republic of Kampuchea (Cambodia)
RAM	Reform the Armed Forces Movement (Philippines)
RBAF	Royal Brunei Armed Forces
RCEP	Regional Comprehensive Economic Partnership
RSF	Reporters sans Frontiéres (Reporters Without Borders)
SARS	Severe Acute Respiratory Syndrome
SBY	Susilo Bambang Yudhoyono (Indonesia)
SEATO	Southeast Asia Treaty Organization
SLORC	State Law and Order Restoration Council (Burma/Myanmar)
SNC	Supreme National Council (Cambodia)
SOE	state-owned enterprise
SPDC	State Peace and Development Council (Burma/Myanmar)
SRP	Sam Rainsy Party (Cambodia)
TAC	Treaty of Amity and Cooperation
TPP	Trans-Pacific Partnership
TRT	Thai Rak Thai Party (Thais Love Thais)
UDD	United Front of Democracy against Dictatorship (Thailand)
UMNO	United Malays National Organization (Malaysia)
UMNO Baru	New UMNO (Malaysia)
UNAMET	United Nations Assistance Mission in East Timor
UNCLOS	United Nations Convention on the Law of the Sea
UNCTAD	United Nations Conference on Trade and Development
UNDP	United Nations Development Program
UNESCO	United Nations Educational, Scientific, and Cultural Organization
UNICEF	United Nations Children's Fund
UNIDO	United Nationalist Democratic Organization (Philippines)
UNLD-LA	United Nationalities League for Democracy–Liberated Areas (Burma/Myanmar)
UNMISET	United Nations Mission of Support in East Timor
UNMIT	United Nations Integrated Mission in Timor-Leste
UNOTIL	United Nations Office in East Timor
UNTAC	United Nations Transitional Authority in Cambodia
UNTAET	United Nations Transitional Administration in East Timor
USAID	United States Aid for International Development
USDA	Union Solidarity and Development Association (Burma/Myanmar)

USDP	Union Solidarity and Development Party (Burma/Myanmar)
USSFTA	United States–Singapore Free Trade Agreement
UXO	unexploded ordnance
VFF	Vietnam Fatherland Front
WTO	World Trade Organization
ZOPFAN	Zone of Peace, Freedom, and Neutrality

1

INTRODUCTION

L earning about contemporary Southeast Asia can be a challenge because the
region is no longer a primary focus of international attention. Weeks go by
without any major news stories about countries that used to dominate the discussions of government officials and ordinary citizens. Because of the end of
the Cold War, as well as events put in motion on September 11, 2001, international observers now focus their attention on other parts of the world. Moreover, the lingering trauma, disillusionment, and cynicism associated with the
Vietnam War have also kept many journalists, political scientists, and policymakers from focusing on Southeast Asia.

International news coverage of Southeast Asia today remains dominated by
the superficial and sensational. Images of sunny beaches, soccer-playing elephants, and "exotic" cuisine are standard fare for both viral videos and reporters of the globalization era. When serious stories from the region manage to
enter the global news cycle, the images are typically of tragedy, violence, and
exploitation—of cyclone victims, bandanna-clad kidnappers, or underage
workers in sweatshops. In-depth commentaries about Southeast Asia might
center on the region's transformation "from a battleground to a marketplace"
or on problems of environmental degradation but, generally speaking, Southeast Asia's story is persistently overshadowed by conflict in the Middle East, the
movements of US troops, and the rise of China.[1]

Southeast Asia's recent story is more complex than sensational headlines
and stereotypical images suggest. In fact, as the world turns its attention elsewhere, the 600 million people who live in the region are experiencing unprecedented socioeconomic change. New forms of wealth and poverty are emerging
across the region. Wrenching conflicts over rights, identity, social justice, and
power have become the everyday experience of many Southeast Asians. Although it no longer draws the international attention it once did, perhaps no
region in the world is more dynamic.

2

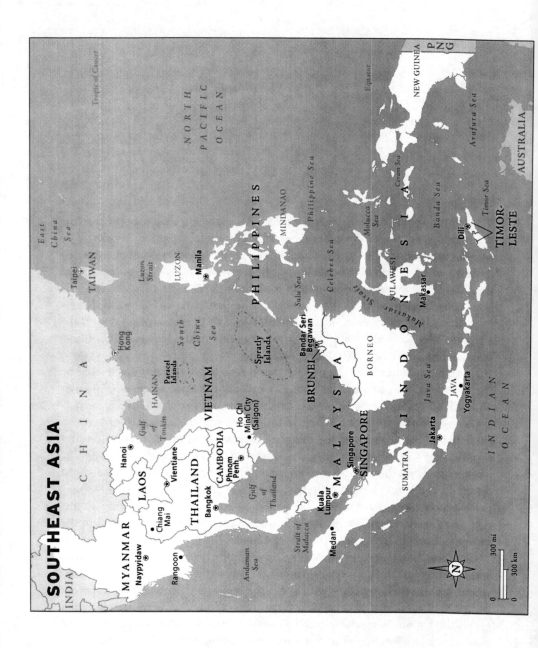

SOUTHEAST ASIA

A new era in international relations has arisen in the past several decades with lasting repercussions for Southeast Asia. Political, economic, and social forces of unprecedented scope are currently transforming the entire region. *Southeast Asia in the New International Era* analyzes contemporary politics in the context of these new international and domestic realities from both the Southeast Asian and the international perspective. This chapter introduces the region, describes changes accompanying the new international era, and explains how standard regime labels fall short in characterizing the richness and complexity of Southeast Asian politics. Eleven country chapters follow that evaluate each country in terms of basic political history, major institutions and social groups, state-society relations and democracy, economy and development, and foreign relations. A new chapter on the Association of Southeast Asian Nations (ASEAN) critically assesses regional integration and its future prospects.

INFLUENCES AND EXPERIENCES

Southeast Asia, a region of remarkable diversity, consists of eleven countries with differing histories, cultural traditions, resource bases, and political-economic systems.[2] Except for geographic proximity and a somewhat similar tropical environment and ecology, few characteristics link all these nations into a coherent whole. Nevertheless, before the international era arrived, a broad shape to a Southeast Asian political economy had developed from a few generalized influences, experiences, and social patterns described in this chapter. These influences and experiences include religious penetration by Hinduism, Buddhism, Islam, and Christianity; colonialism and introduction of political ideas from the West; the rise of nationalism associated with the struggle for independence; Japanese occupation; Cold War trauma; and regional economic transition. Shared social patterns, also outlined below, include a strong sense of the village as the primary unit of traditional identity; agricultural economies overtaken by urban-based manufacturing and service economies; and patron-client systems that influence sociopolitical interaction.

An important force shaping Southeast Asia from ancient to modern times has been the arrival and expansion of nonnative religions across the region. By supplanting local belief systems—or more often blending with them— exogenous religious influences evolved into today's seemingly endogenous value systems, which contribute to the region's diverse cultural milieu. Hinduism and Theravada Buddhism, arriving from South Asian sources, brought to the region Brahmanical notions of *deva-raja* (god-king); classical literature, such as the *Ramayana* and the *Jataka* tales; and karmic notions of rightful authority. Throughout the region, these cultural imports profoundly shaped the concept of power and the royal structures that wielded it. Mahayana Buddhism, brought from India via China, also influenced political ideals in the region, particularly in Vietnam. There, social order was believed to stem from hierarchal

(Confucian) relations, Buddhist cosmology, and (Taoist) naturalism. Centuries of overseas Chinese migration also spread the influence of Chinese religion and folk beliefs throughout the region, especially in urban areas where migrant communities established themselves.

Subsequent to Hinduism and Buddhism, Islam arrived from merchants and traders from South Asia. Islam did not enjoy a wide presence in Southeast Asia until the fifteenth century, about the time Europeans first began to arrive with Christian traditions. Islam spread throughout insular Southeast Asia from island to island and then from coastal ports to interior settlements. Christianity did not spread deep roots in the region, except for in the predominantly Catholic Philippines and East Timor, as well as among some enduring communities in Vietnam and Indonesia. Over the centuries of religious interaction, the eclectic, religio-royal traditions of Hinduism and Buddhism have sometimes clashed with the universalist, law-based religions of Islam and Christianity. However, tolerance and syncretism rather than conflict characterizes most of Southeast Asia's history of religious practice. Taken together, the diverse practices and beliefs of these religions, and their interactions, generate an array of cultural claims on how to organize societies politically and economically across the region.

Adding yet more complexity to this milieu of beliefs and practices was the gradual penetration of Western ideas of modernity, including "civilization," nationalism, capitalism, republicanism, democracy, and communism. Most of these foreign notions and ideologies emerged in the region during the nineteenth and early twentieth centuries, that is, during the latest phase of nearly five centuries of European influence in the region. Many of the problems of political and economic development facing Southeast Asian leaders today can be traced to colonialism.[3] The grand strategic games of imperial competition and colonial rule brought the formation of internationally recognized boundaries. These new "states" replaced the region's nonintegrated dynastic principalities that only loosely governed rural populations and upland minority groups. Foreign attempts to integrate these disparate populations often proved difficult. The imperialists eventually guaranteed new boundaries and imposed a Western sense of geographic and political order on the region.[4]

By the late nineteenth century, national boundaries had been demarcated and the entire area of Southeast Asia was in European hands except Thailand, which ceded much territory to remain independent. Over time, a money economy was introduced and resource extraction created large-scale industries that required skilled and unskilled laborers. Because the rural populations of Southeast Asia found industrial labor antithetical to traditional values, the colonialists imported Chinese and Indians to work in factories, tin mines, and rubber plantations. The Chinese and Indian communities were often employed as a buffer between Europeans and local populations. In many cases, laws prevented the immigrants from owning land and pushed them into the commercial sector. Urban life in colonial Southeast Asia was, in many respects, more Chinese and Indian than local or European. A discernible immigrant communalism evolved in tandem with urbanization. Hindu, Confucian, and European influences affected trade, urban architecture, art, as well as societal tastes and norms. From the nineteenth century forward, overseas communities (the Chinese in particular) enjoyed economic power in Southeast Asia disproportionate to their numbers.

Among other changes, European colonists were responsible for the growth of the region's first economic infrastructure of modern ports, railways, and roads. Although they staffed their bureaucracies with local elites, offering education to the most gifted, the colonists failed to develop institutions of accountable governance. Serving European rather than local interests, imperial administrators exploited natural resources for export and introduced new industries and economies related to mercantilist trade in tin, rubber, tapioca, opium, spices, tea, and other valued commodities. As they extracted from mines and expanded plantations, European governors wholly neglected local socioeconomic development. Over time the cruelty, exploitation, and injustice of colonial rule bred popular resentment and put into motion a new force in the region: nationalism.

The rise of anti-imperial nationalism was the most consequential product of colonialism in Southeast Asia. Although deliberate movements against European control punctuated the entire colonial history of Southeast Asia, it was the ideological battles of the twentieth century that fed the transformative nationalism that came to define the region's future.

A traumatic experience under Japanese occupation during World War II further fueled aspirations for self-rule and independence across the region. Following Japan's surrender in 1945 to Allied forces, Europe's postwar leaders disregarded attempts by Southeast Asian leaders to declare formal independence. Eager for resources to rebuild their own war-torn economies, the colonists audaciously returned to extend control over their previously held territories: the British in Burma and Malaya; the French in Indochina (Vietnam, Cambodia, and Laos); the Dutch in Indonesia; and the Portuguese in East Timor. To legitimize their ambitions, European administrators received international recognition for their actions through postwar treaties that excluded Southeast Asians from negotiations. In 1946, the Philippines, vacated by its American occupiers of forty-seven years, joined Thailand as one of the two independent Southeast Asian countries in the early postwar period.

Resolve for independence hardened. In Burma, Indonesia, and Vietnam, nationalism became an especially potent and unifying force that led to fierce struggles for self-determination. In Malaysia and Singapore, the struggle for *merdeka* (independence) was less violent but every bit as formative in cultivating a new sense of nationalist purpose. Across the region, experiences with colonialism differed but the nationalist rhetoric for genuine self-governance emerged as a political lingua franca among anticolonial revolutionaries. Thailand, having escaped direct colonial rule, attempted to construct its own sense of nationhood. Hoping to bind the various peoples within the borders of its constitutional monarchy, modernizing Thai elites suppressed local identities and cultivated a nationalist creed, "Nation, Religion, King."

Relentless anti-imperial political activity and painfully violent episodes of conflict with colonial forces gradually produced two significant consequences for the region: the overdue withdrawal of the Europeans and the rise of a handful of charismatic, larger-than-life independence leaders, including Ho Chi Minh in Vietnam, Sukarno in Indonesia, Aung San in Burma, Tungku Abdul Rahman in Malaysia, and Prince Sihanouk in Cambodia. But even as decolonization and courageous independence leaders offered fresh hopes under sovereign statehood, a new dimension of geopolitical struggle, the Cold War, enveloped the region.

For Southeast Asians, the ironically named Cold War thoroughly destabilized the region with occupation, warfare, and even genocide. From 1945 to 1989, the effects of superpower politics led to the deaths of more than 10 million soldiers and civilians. Countless bombs and bullets from conventional warfare and unimaginable atrocities caused by zealous ideologues and murderous despots, not to mention the appalling use of chemical defoliants by US forces, produced long-term tragedy for many Southeast Asians. The political and economic chaos of the Cold War not only delayed the independence of Southeast Asian states but retarded their early development by politically dividing societies, peoples, and communities.

The Cold War was fought in Southeast Asia along three interrelated dimensions: internal ideological struggle, superpower rivalry, and interstate conflict. Leftist movements embracing communist visions for state control existed in every major Southeast Asian country during this period. In theory, competing ideological visions pit communism against democratic capitalism. But because the latter scarcely existed in the region, the primary foes of communist movements were right-leaning militaries, traditional monarchists, and neo-imperial foreign forces. US-USSR superpower rivalry, expressed most clearly in the Vietnam War, was also affected by the 1960 Sino-Soviet split over global communist supremacy. Ever in search of international patrons, Southeast Asian communists exploited this split to suit their largely nationalist purposes.

The meddling of three external Cold War powers in the region exacerbated existing conflicts and created new tensions. The most tragic conflict resulted in the rise of the genocidal Khmer Rouge, who, before the illegal US bombing of Cambodia, had demonstrated insufficient capacity to seize Cambodian state power. China, which had supported Vietnamese revolutionaries against both the French and the Americans, turned on its former communist ally in the mid-1970s. In an attempt to outmaneuver the Soviets, who maintained support for Vietnam, the Chinese backed the Khmer Rouge in Cambodia. China's communist leaders count among the very few diplomatic supporters of Cambodia's Pol Pot clique, which is responsible for the deaths of 1.7 million Cambodians during its three-year reign of terror.

Superpower rivalry insidiously politicized ethnic relations throughout Southeast Asia as well. During the Cold War, both communist and noncommunist governments engaged in shocking anti-Chinese violence and brutality over suspicions that ethnic Chinese harbored political loyalties to Beijing. Other ethnic minorities became the mercenaries and puppets of external powers and local opportunists, especially in the mountainous upland areas of Vietnam and Laos. In Southeast Asia's so-called Golden Triangle—the lawless tri-border region where Burma, Thailand, and Laos meet the Mekong River and its tributaries—powerless upland minorities were recruited and coerced to do the bidding of warlords, revolutionaries, arms dealers, opium traffickers, superpower governments, and CIA operatives. Treated as pawns in the strategic calculations of more powerful actors, their true allegiances ever questioned, Southeast Asia's minorities suffered greatly during the Cold War.

The Cold War also produced new alliances and interstate conflicts between Southeast Asian states. Nonalignment, attempted by some, became an impossible position to maintain over time. Thailand and the Philippines, both noncommunist states, joined the Southeast Asia Treaty Organization (SEATO) under the tutelage of the United States. In the 1960s and '70s, both countries provided troops and territory to the United States for staging military action in Vietnam. After the Vietnam War, and the reduction of US commitments to the region, noncommunist states turned to the Association of Southeast Asian Nations, an organization originally created in 1967 as a bulwark against growing communism in the region.

Indonesia, led initially by the charismatic Sukarno, originally claimed Cold War neutrality only to invite an internal battle between left and right forces within the country. Sukarno's failed balancing act led to the rise of the anticommunist Suharto regime, which took power after a murky 1965 coup and countercoup. Ten years later, General Suharto's Indonesian troops forcibly occupied East Timor in a bloody campaign without US objection. The invasion occurred only nine days after a left-leaning organization had declared East Timor independent from Portugal. Formerly neutral and nonaligned, Indonesia under Suharto contributed to American objectives in the region.

Cambodia, which once claimed Cold War neutrality under King Sihanouk, found itself under the influence of all three major powers during the Cold War. In the wake of its secret bombing campaign, the United States supported Lon Nol's coup over Sihanouk in 1971 only to provoke the Chinese-backed Khmer Rouge and fuel their rise to power in 1975. Later, in January 1979, Soviet-backed Vietnam forcibly occupied Cambodia, putting it under Moscow's ultimate control. Six weeks after Vietnamese troops took control of Phnom Penh and pushed Pol Pot and his followers to jungle redoubts near the Thai border,

China launched a brutal attack against Vietnam. Disastrously, both sides lost thousands of troops in the month-long conflict, in which Vietnam's battle-tested military stripped Chinese troops of seized territory. China's leaders claimed victory, but Vietnamese troops stayed in Cambodia throughout the 1980s until the United Nations brokered their withdrawal.

During the 1980s, the final decade of the Cold War, the US military presence in Southeast Asia included only a few bases in the Philippines. Focused on new reform efforts at home, China and the Soviet Union also began to disengage from the region. As the soldiers, operatives, and advisers of the superpowers departed, a rather unexpected but transformative force became established in the region: Japanese businessmen. Despite the fact that Japan had attacked and occupied all of Southeast Asia in World War II, and that lingering resentment and fear persisted, Japan's meteoric postwar economic success brought Southeast Asia into its economic orbit. Singapore was among the first to benefit. As Japan's export-oriented economy grew, so too did its need for raw materials, petroleum, and other imports. Tiny Singapore did not produce many of these resources but it benefited from increasing oceangoing traffic to and from Japan because of the geographical positions of its port facilities. Singapore joined South Korea, Taiwan, and Hong Kong as models of third-world economic success, known collectively as the "Asian economic dragons."[5]

In the mid-1980s, Japan's growing investments in Southeast Asia expanded rapidly as a result of the appreciating value of the Japanese yen. Escaping the high yen, Japanese industrialists moved production to a number of Southeast Asian countries where cheap labor and favorable currency exchange rates made the region a prime export platform. All of this was timed with policy shifts in many Southeast Asian countries designed to emulate the successful export-oriented industrialization strategies of the Asian dragons and their move away from import substitution industrialization. Southeast Asian governments aggressively courted ties with Japan, causing trade volume to expand. Thailand, Malaysia, Indonesia, and to a lesser extent the Philippines each moved toward a development model of activist state guidance of private sector–driven export growth. Malaysia's prime minister appropriately dubbed the new development approach the "Look East Policy."

As economies grew and middle classes began to coalesce, new interest in democracy and political reform began to surface across the region. In 1986, Philippine president Ferdinand Marcos, a US Cold War ally who had suspended democracy and manipulated law to extend his own rule, was ousted in a massive popular movement known as "People Power." Thailand also moved closer to democracy by electing its first civilian prime minister since a failed period of democracy in the mid-1970s. Even economically autarkic Burma faced new pro-democracy forces. In 1988, demonstrators forced the country's ruling military junta to schedule elections for a representative parliament. In 1990, after officially changing the country's name in English to Myanmar a year earlier, elections were held but the losing generals did not honor the results. However, with the democratic genie now out of the bottle, popular aspirations for representative government in Burma persisted, often provoking brutal suppression.

Elsewhere in the region, authoritarian leaders repressed growing aspirations for democracy even as the Cold War showed signs of thawing in Europe. On the communist left, Vietnamese leaders opened the country's economy but not its political system. On the nationalistic right, long-standing governments in Indonesia, Malaysia, and Singapore viewed greater democracy as a threat to budding economic success. Following the Cold War, public pressure for political reform emerged as a new force that Southeast Asian governments would constantly face.

SHARED SOCIAL PATTERNS

In addition to the religious influences, colonial history, nationalist movements, and Cold War experiences that have shaped this otherwise diverse region, some observable social patterns also add definition to a Southeast Asian political economy. These generalized patterns are not universal, but they are widely shared across the region and contain elements of both "continuity and change"—a phrase commonly used among Southeast Asian specialists who are forever attempting to characterize the enduring and dynamic patterns of socioeconomic behavior in the region.

Southeast Asian nations are characterized by an agricultural base that traditionally has been the heart of everyday life. Historically, the agricultural village served as the major unit of identity for the rural population, acting as its cultural, religious, political, economic, and social center. Although urban growth expanded as trade increased over time—accompanied by Indian, Chinese, Arab, and European influences on the royal and colonial centers of power—the basic economic unit for most Southeast Asians, until recent decades, has been the peasant-style family-operated farm. Generally, the family farm was part of a village economy characterized by subsistence production, with most of the farm products being consumed by the family or within the village. Experiences differed, but feudal-type arrangements across the region fed the development of landed elites, aristocrats, and royals who exploited the labor of rural populations for imperial projects—a pattern repeated later by European colonists (absent any local cultural foundations that historically ameliorated popular resentment of royal power).

Some areas of Southeast Asia today remain characterized by traditional village arrangements and subsistence agriculture, but the socioeconomic picture has grown increasingly complex. The arrival of green revolution technologies, commercial agribusiness, and rising expectations of educational opportunity and material gain defines agrarian change today. "Farmers" are replacing "peasants," and life inside most villages is now fully interdependent with life outside the village due to a host of transformative factors: rural-to-urban migration, expanding nonfarm work, globalized labor markets, remittance economies, new communication technologies, and rising consumerism. Over the past fifty years, the agricultural sector's economic importance has continued to decline relative to industry and services, although employment in the sector remains considerable.

In spite of these changes, the hierarchical structure traditional to the village still finds expression in the region's political life. Southeast Asian societies, generally speaking, remain fundamentally organized into networks of superior-subordinate (patron-client) ties. These networks form the basis of political structures and affect values and the allocation of resources.

In their positive expressions, patron-client relations form "moral economies" where uneven but reciprocal relations bring mutual benefit to participants in a context of cultural appropriateness and meaning. Where there are marked inequalities in wealth, status, and control, and where resources are insufficient, those with limited access can seek alliances with individuals at a higher socioeconomic level or with better access to state resources. The relationship is reciprocal in the sense that the patron expects support, protection, labor, or some other service in return for dispensing benefits to the subordinate.[6] In their pejorative interpretation, patron-client systems prop up authoritarian forms of government with vast networks designed for patrimony. The strongest networks are capable of manipulating rivals or depoliticizing opponents through co-optation and participation.[7] Such relational asymmetry fosters exploitation and risks producing endless power struggles between elites who vie for each other's client networks.

Representative forms of democratic government in Southeast Asia both benefit and suffer from these patron-client systems. Such networks can potentially link those who wield state power with ordinary citizens and voting constituencies with public-spirited elected officials. Unchecked, however, patron-client partiality can threaten the legitimacy of democracy through favoritism, nepotism, corruption, and abuse of official power. Throughout Southeast Asia, rising demands by individuals and groups for increased governmental accountability, transparency, and recognition of civil and political rights clash with the deep-seated impulses of power elites to defend traditional forms of patronage. Citing cultural appropriateness, Southeast Asian elites often fashion regimes that are, in the name of social order, structurally designed to institutionalize state patronage.

Socioeconomically, a common pattern throughout Southeast Asia is the presence of an influential overseas Chinese business community. In most Southeast Asian urban centers a deeply rooted overseas Chinese community discernibly, and disproportionately, influences commercial life. The experiences of such communities differ from country to country, and degrees of assimilation, hybridization, and communalization differ markedly. During the

Cold War, tensions between China and Taiwan, and communists and Kuomintang nationalists, often reproduced themselves in cities such as Jakarta, Kuala Lumpur, and Bangkok. Communist movements in the region often had a real or perceived Chinese tilt to them—a reality often proving fatal to overseas Chinese when anticommunist nationalists turned violent, as they did in Indonesia in 1965.

Having established themselves economically over time, Southeast Asia's Chinese communities were well positioned when trade and business expanded in the 1980s as a result of export-oriented policies across the region and market openness in the People's Republic of China. Overseas Chinese networks also linked Southeast Asian countries to the flourishing economies of Hong Kong and Taiwan. By the time the new international era dawned in the 1990s, many Southeast Asian Chinese were now visibly expressing their Chinese roots and identities—what was once considered a social liability emerged as a new personal economic asset.

The influences, experiences, and social patterns common to Southeast Asia described above compose only a partial set of factors able to explain the various events and trends associated with politics in the region. The country chapters that follow illustrate this fact by employing much greater sensitivity to the particular conditions, events, individuals, groups, and institutions that make up political life. Moreover, in addition to historical influences and shared social patterns, profound changes to the international system following the end of the Cold War now influence political economy across the region in new and unprecedented ways.

THE NEW INTERNATIONAL ERA

An extraordinary sweep of international change occurred as a result of the end of the Cold War. The extent of these changes, which occurred rapidly, stunned the world and irrevocably recast international relations. The major catalyst responsible for causing a break with the past was Soviet president Mikhail Gorbachev, whose policies in the 1980s put in motion the end of the bipolar conflict that had structured world relations since World War II. In addition to economic and political reforms at home, Gorbachev pursued a foreign policy of reconciliation and imperial disengagement. Even before the Berlin Wall collapsed in 1989, dramatic changes in geopolitics reverberated across the globe.

In Asia, Gorbachev's policies meant the withdrawal of Russian troops from Afghanistan, demilitarizing the Sino-Russian border, and cutting ties with leftist insurgencies in the region. It also meant ceasing aid to Vietnam and abandoning military bases at Cam Ranh Bay and Da Nang. Responding to Gorbachev's changes, Vietnam moved to restructure its own economy. Pursing a new strategy called *doi moi* (renovation), Vietnam's communist leadership began to permit free-market activity and foreign investment. These moves were in line with changes already sweeping communist China under Deng Xiaoping. Since 1978,

Deng had encouraged international trade and foreign investment in China by establishing ties with Western multinationals, East Asian businessmen, and overseas Chinese in Southeast Asia. By the 1990s, the People's Republic of China, a once-feared Cold War power in Southeast Asia, enjoyed a new economic role as a regional economic partner and a formidable export competitor.

In the new international era, the bipolar world of communists and noncommunists rapidly transformed itself into a more multipolar world where states, regions, international organizations, and nonstate actors exhibited new forms of power and influence. Although the United States stood alone as the dominant global power, it soon learned that relative power is far from absolute power. Asia's own rising economic influence and Europe's deepening integration with the former communist states of the old Soviet bloc created new poles of economic and political power in a globalizing world.

The new era also became defined by increasingly assertive international bodies such as the World Trade Organization (WTO), the International Monetary Fund (IMF), and the World Bank. These organizations established and enforced the rules of economic globalization, and Southeast Asian countries sought their involvement and perceived benefits. Nongovernmental organizations (NGOs) also proliferated across the world in the 1990s, promoting humanitarianism, development, and human rights. As for the United Nations, its increasingly visible blue-helmeted peacekeepers became symbols of a new activist (but often impotent) international community. Added to all of these new forces were powerful stateless actors tied to nefarious networks of international terrorists, drug lords, and human traffickers that operated even as Southeast Asian economies benefited from the post–Cold War peace dividend.

The region's boom economy from the mid-1980s to the mid-1990s resulted in large part from increased trade and investment between East and Southeast Asia and domestic entrepreneurship. Joint ventures and foreign-financed enterprises expanded quickly and deliberately into textiles, footwear, electronics, automobile parts, cosmetics, agribusiness, petroleum refining, and other diverse industries and manufactures. Local entrepreneurs cut deals with each other and with investors arriving daily from Japan, Hong Kong, Taiwan, and South Korea. Double-digit economic growth and trade balance surpluses soon characterized the Southeast Asian "tiger economies," as they came to be known. Singapore, Malaysia, Thailand, and Indonesia drew the greatest attention and fueled the region's rapid economic growth. The passing of Cold War tensions unleashed a phase of rapid economic liberalization and forward-looking optimism.

Encouraged by Western governments, the IMF, and globalization advocates, Southeast Asian governments also liberalized their financial markets, putting an end to many restrictions (and safeguards) that formerly regulated the flow of capital into and out of their countries. As a result, portfolio investment from Europe and America quickly found its way to the region's fast and furious "emerging markets." Hot money from New York, London, and Tokyo poured into the region.

The phenomenal economic growth rates the tigers experienced in the new international era—as high as 10 percent per year during this period—fundamentally changed the Southeast Asian landscape. The most obvious change was the increase in per capita gross national product (GNP). Per capita GNP in Thailand in 1977, for example, was $300; by 1997 it had climbed to $2,970. Similar growth in per capita GNP occurred in the other countries over the same period: Malaysia, $660 to $3,531; Indonesia, $150 to $692; the Philippines, $310 to $1,049. Singapore's per capita GNP rose most dramatically, from $2,120 to $24,664, hence its "dragon" status. Corresponding figures for reforming but populous Vietnam and for economically stagnant Burma, Cambodia, and Laos indicated less improvement, by contrast. By 1997, per capita GNP in these countries had improved but still averaged less than $500.

By the mid-1990s, so confident were Southeast Asians in their path to success that regional leaders began to engage the world in a debate that pitted "Asian values" against "Western values." The chief spokesmen in this debate were politicians from Singapore and Malaysia. Their contention was that because Asian culture valued social order over political freedom, it allowed economic markets to thrive even as societies remained orderly. Centuries of pent-up resentment against Western superiority unleashed itself in trans-Pacific rhetorical punches. The West's high crime rates, divorce rates, declining educational standards, and sedentary lifestyles were cited repeatedly as evidence of American inferiority. "You Americans have this mantra about your high standard of living," argued a senior Asian diplomat, "but if standard of living means not being afraid to go outside after dark, or not worrying about what filth your children will see on all those TV channels, then our Asian societies have the higher standard."[8] The message was unambiguous: the world would be a better place if countries began to learn from Asia rather than the West. Journalists writing from New York and London countered by listing human rights injustices and corruption tied to Asian governments.

The Asian values debate symbolized the sweeping changes that had come to the region in the new international era. Political ideology, interstate war, and superpower meddling were no longer central concerns for the modern states of Southeast Asia. Instead, the key issues became economics, development, integrated markets, and stable political development. Southeast Asian societies also became more concerned with the negative effects of rapid growth, such as deforestation, pollution, traffic, corruption, and (contrary to the rhetoric of some Asian politicians) increased drug use, criminal activity, and alienation among Southeast Asian youth. Still, in the bigger picture, Southeast Asian governments and their societies benefited by no longer building walls around their countries and isolating their economies.

The exception was Burma, which, after reneging on promised political reform and refusing to recognize the 1990 election results, persisted in its strategy of socialist economic autarky. Burma's dreadful standard of living only reinforced the dominant view in the region that interaction, not isolation, was necessary for a country to flourish. Indeed, every Southeast Asian country that tested the open market proposition experienced unprecedented economic dynamism. The results of openness included a phenomenal rise in average standard of living, but success was accompanied by widening gaps between the rich and poor, not to mention unprecedented policy challenges in infrastructure, public health, and education.

The new international era also saw Southeast Asian societies transformed by new forms of communication. Television, mobile phones, Internet cafés, satellite communications, and the entire digital revolution changed the way information was spread from person to person in this new era. No longer could governments fully control information flow among the populace. In the new era, the challenge for governments became balancing the effects of technological change, foreign investment, and international trade against political demands for greater openness and governmental transparency. Another challenge that emerged was, alas, the threat and reality of financial crisis—something that would affect all the booming countries of Southeast Asia.

A classic lesson of international political economy is that economic interdependence creates greater sensitivity and vulnerability to global markets.[9] The globalization of Southeast Asian economies had made the region's countries increasingly sensitive and vulnerable to external forces and the volatility of international markets. The vulnerabilities proved to be all too real when the region suffered financial disaster in 1997.

In the early 1990s, China's government, already advantaged by the country's seemingly endless supply of cheap labor, devalued its currency, making its exports even more competitive than those coming from Southeast Asia. With their currencies pegged to the US dollar, many Southeast Asian countries' exports became more expensive than China's in international markets. Subsequently, China also began to attract foreign investment more rapidly than Southeast Asia. Export revenue in the tiger economies began to level off after a decade of breakneck expansion.

By the mid-1990s, the current account surpluses enjoyed by Southeast Asian tiger economies turned into current account deficits. With more buying power for imports, foreign products and luxury goods entered local markets, causing imbalances to grow. Many remained unworried by the imbalances and moved investment into new sectors. With export opportunities slowing, Southeast Asians increasingly engaged in real estate speculation and invested in lavish projects (such as five-star hotels and condominiums). Local stock markets continued their climb.

Capital inflows and easy credit also expanded in the mid-1990s, made possible by the earlier deregulation of financial and capital markets. Because local currencies were pegged to the US dollar, local borrowers often denominated their loans in US dollars to take advantage of lower interest rates. Over a few short years, debt obligations mounted across the Southeast Asian business community. Slowing revenues from declining exports and an oversupply of new housing and high-rise office space caused the real estate bubble to burst. Debtors then began to default. Stress on financial institutions grew and the financial mismanagement of banks and investment firms began to make headlines. Corruption in both the public and private sectors drew greater attention, and government scandals invited fierce public criticism, especially in Thailand and the Philippines, where democratization had expanded a free media. In Indonesia, Suharto's thirty-year regime, built on performance legitimization, faced unprecedented signs of weakness.

By June 1997, international investor confidence in Southeast Asia's tigers began to slip. Global currency traders, recognizing the shakiness of the region's economies, bet against the Southeast Asian currencies, undermining their worth even more. Government efforts to support the currency pegs proved futile. The result was a cascade of overnight currency devaluations from country to country. In herd-like fashion, investors instigated a massive outflow of capital from all the tiger economies. The sudden devaluation of local currencies, combined with rapid economic contraction, left local Southeast Asian investors saddled with massive loads of debt. Many local investors faced the impossible task of meeting inflated repayment obligations in the face of declining revenues. Banks became insolvent. Southeast Asia found itself in a full-fledged financial crisis.

Leaders in Southeast Asia responded ineffectively to the crisis, allowing the downturn to spread throughout all of Asia and eventually across the globe. Southeast Asia's politicians seemed incapable of making the difficult decisions necessary to resolve the crisis. Instead, they hunkered down, blamed Westerners, and continued to protect cronies while undermining public-spirited technocrats. The public, more educated and savvy than ever, knew better and realized that whatever the sins of international investors, their own government and business leaders also shared the blame. The region's shell-shocked leaders eventually turned to the IMF, the world's lender of last resort, to help them finance their way out of the crisis. Seeing itself as the economic doctor of the new international era, the IMF announced its readiness to administer the treatments countries needed for financial recovery. It offered multibillion-dollar loans on the strict conditions that recipient governments would raise interest rates, increase tax rates, adopt strict budget austerity, and completely restructure their ailing financial sectors. It was the wrong medicine.

The IMF's ill-conceived rescue packages proved damaging to already suffering economies. The cash liquidity the IMF provided to the stressed tiger economies largely went to pay off foreign creditors and financial institutions; it did little to spur economic growth. Government budget austerity measures exacerbated existing economic contraction, and local investment plummeted. Higher interest rates and tax burdens further inhibited local investment at a time when Keynesian stimulus was most desperately needed. Rather than stimulate their economies with greater public spending, governments were bound by IMF conditionality only to starve their economies further.

Social and political disruption followed. Rampant unemployment, rapid inflation, and economic hardship turned into antigovernment protests and disorder. The once-famed emerging markets and their proud political leaders collapsed in succession. All but a few governments changed in the wake of the crisis and effects of the IMF rescue packages.

The 1997 Asian economic crisis shook Southeast Asia's confidence. Asian leaders stopped talking about Asian values. In fact, the crisis set Southeast Asian countries on disparate courses that continue to the present day. Recovery patterns have differed markedly from one case to the next. Indonesia, which suffered the most severe setback, sunk into deep political crisis, ending thirty years of rule under General Suharto. The collapse of his regime led not only to greater democracy in Indonesia but also to the birth of East Timor, which had been under Indonesian occupation since 1975. Thailand, after cycling through rotations of parliamentary coalitions, eventually elected a new party (the Thai Rak Thai, or Thais Love Thais, Party) whose billionaire leader turned to populist policies that ignited new political crisis and two military coups. Philippine voters turned to an action-movie hero to manage their recovery only to throw him out of office for corruption a few years later. Vietnam slowed its pace of reform and increased surveillance of the regime's political opponents. Then, in the wake of the Asian economic crisis and the political changes it spawned, the new international era grew even more complex as a result of terrorist attacks half a world away.

Southeast Asia's newly installed leaders faced a new, more complicated foreign policy matrix following the September 11, 2001, attacks in the United States. Already worried about their sluggish economies, Southeast Asian officials now had to concern themselves with US president George W. Bush's declarations of an international "axis of evil" that tied rogue states to stateless terrorist groups. His announcement that the countries of the world were either "with us or against us" put unwanted pressure on the region's new governments. Predictions by the Bush administration that Southeast Asia would become the "second front in the War on Terror" caused even wider reverberations of concern and anxiety in the region.[10]

Aside from the Philippines, which had long battled Muslim separatists in the country's south, none of the ASEAN governments enthusiastically embraced Bush's view of a post-9/11 world. Thailand proved to be a reluctant partner and Singapore turned to the United States only pragmatically, especially after Islamist groups bombed hotels and embassies in neighboring Indonesia. Wars in Afghanistan and Iraq turned many of Southeast Asia's large Muslim populations against the United States. Over time, events (or more precisely nonevents) proved American predictions that Southeast Asia would be "the second front" of international terrorism erroneous. Internationally sponsored terrorism in the region was sporadic at most. Since 9/11, five internationally linked bombings, all in Indonesia, have led to over two hundred deaths and hundreds of injuries. While no doubt a matter for local and international concern, the frequency and intensity of terrorism in the region is on par with that experienced by Europe. Compared to terrorist violence hotspots in the Middle East and South Asia, Southeast Asia has remained relatively calm.

As government officials adjusted to a post-9/11 world and pursued policy packages with hopes of returning to the high growth rates of the previous decade, another global concern caught their attention: rising China. Southeast Asian countries continued to be outperformed economically by China throughout the first decade of the 2000s. In a matter of two decades, China had become Asia's new economic power. Because of its strict currency regime and regulated foreign capital markets, China's economic competitiveness was less affected by the Asian economic crisis. China's direct and indirect influence in Southeast Asia came through new free trade deals, tariff reductions, business connections, and even increased cultural influence. By the time Southeast Asians watched Beijing's impressive pageantry and execution of the 2008 Olympiad, ASEAN's combined economies ranked as China's fourth-largest trading partner. By 2015, ASEAN's combined economies had surpassed both Japan and South Korea in terms of total trade volume with China.

Since recovering from the 1997 economic crisis, only modest economic growth has returned to the tiger economies. Although incomes have recovered and general progress in overall development is visible, aggregate comparisons of basic indicators now illustrate the vast economic disparities that characterize the region. In terms of economic power, performance, and poverty, Southeast Asia's economic dynamism has created a region of remarkable disparity. Tables 1.1 and 1.2 highlight select economic and development indicators for the region.

When adjusted for purchasing power parity, microstates Singapore ($82,763) and Brunei ($75,700) lead the region in terms of gross domestic product (GDP) per capita (2014 figures). Malaysia ($24,715) follows at a distant third, with Thailand ($14,600) and Indonesia ($10,585) further behind. The Philippines ($6,916), Vietnam ($5,629), and Laos ($5,162) come next followed by those in the lowest tier in terms of per capita production: Myanmar ($4,800), Cambodia ($3,242), and Timor-Leste ($2,277). Even with the most optimistic forecasts, it will take many decades for Southeast Asia's poorest to reach the average living standards that the region's richest countries enjoy today.

By combining 2015 World Bank income classifications with broader development indicators that consider poverty rates, education, health, access to water,

TABLE 1.1 Country Comparisons: Select Economic Figures

	2015 Total Population (millions)	2014 Total Estimated GDP (nominal; $US billion)	2014 GNI per Capita (Atlas method; US dollars)	2014 GDP per Capita (PPP; US dollars)	2014 Total Estimated Exports ($US billion)	2012–2014 Estimated Poverty Rate (percentage below national poverty line)	2010–2014 Estimated GINI (higher values equal higher income inequality)
Brunei	0.4	$17.3	$39,778	$75,700	$11.4	—	—
Cambodia	15.7	$16.7	$1,010	$3,242	$7.6	19%	36.0
Indonesia	256.9	$888.5	$3,650	$10,585	$175.3	11%	38.1
Laos	6.9	$11.8	$1,600	$5,162	$2.8	23%	36.7
Malaysia	30.5	$326.9	$10,660	$24,715	$231.3	1.7%	46.2
Myanmar	56.3	$64.3	$1,270	$4,800	$10.3	26%	38.0
Philippines	101.9	$284.6	$3,440	$6,916	$47.8	25%	43.0
Singapore	5.7	$307.9	$55,150	$82,763	$409.5	—	43.2
Thailand	67.9	$373.8	$5,410	$14,660	$224.8	13%	40.0
Timor-Leste	1.2	$1.6	$3,210	$2,277	$0.15	41%	31.9
Vietnam	93.4	$186.2	$1,890	$5,629	$147.0	9%	35.6

Sources: World Bank, UNDP, ADB, OECD, and CIA World Factbook.

and levels of corruption, the countries of Southeast Asia can be divided into four general groups:

High income/high development   Brunei, Singapore
Upper-middle income/medium development   Malaysia, Thailand
Low-middle income/medium development   Indonesia, Philippines, Vietnam
Low income/low development   Cambodia, Laos, Myanmar, Timor-Leste

In total, the dynamic economic forces of the new international era have bolstered and expanded the economic power of Southeast Asia and its tremendous economic diversity. ASEAN's combined 2014 GDP of $2.4 trillion is already larger than India's and is predicted to overtake Japan's by 2028.[11] Yet, generalizing the region's progress in economic production and human development as a whole is increasingly challenging (and increasingly meaningless). In spite of the integration of the region's disparate economies through the ASEAN Free

TABLE 1.2 Country Comparisons: Select Development Figures

	Percentage of Rural Population 1975 → 2014	2014 HDI Value (0.0–1.0)	2014 HDI Ranking (out of 179 countries)	2010–2013 Estimated Percentage of Births Attended by a Skilled Professional	2012 Estimated Percentage of Rural Population with Access to Improved Water	2014 Corruption Ranking (out of 175 countries, where #1 equals least corrupt)	2015 Freedom Rating (political and civil liberties)
Brunei	38 → 23	0.852	#30	100%	—	#38	not free
Cambodia	90 → 79	0.548	#137	74%	66%	#156	not free
Indonesia	81 → 47	0.684	#108	83%	76%	#107	partly free
Lao PDR	89 → 62	0.569	#139	42%	65%	#145	not free
Malaysia	62 → 26	0.773	#62	99%	99%	#50	partly free
Myanmar	76 → 66	0.524	#150	71%	81%	#156	not free
Philippines	64 → 56	0.660	#118	73%	91%	#85	partly free
Singapore	0 → 0	0.901	#12	100%	—	#7	partly free
Thailand	76 → 51	0.722	#89	100%	95%	#85	not free
Timor-Leste	85 → 68	0.620	#129	29%	61%	#133	partly free
Vietnam	81 → 67	0.638	#121	93%	94%	#119	not free

Sources: UNDP, World Bank, Transparency International, and Freedom House.

Trade Area, the development trajectories of Southeast Asian countries seem to grow more disparate with each passing year. A similar trend of divergent paths characterizes the political regimes of the region.

COMPARING POLITICAL REGIMES

Because of the great diversity among Southeast Asian states, as well as the many influences and changes they experience over time, categorizing Southeast Asian political regimes is an imprecise process and must be complemented by analyzing the unique attributes of each country's experience. The country chapters that follow are written precisely because the analysis in the remainder of this chapter is demonstrably inadequate—an exercise captive to the discursive and analytical limits of overgeneralization and categorization. Therefore, the following discussion should be read with these limitations in mind.

If one is primarily interested in identifying the regime types of Southeast Asia's countries, a standard approach would be to use accepted regime classifications and to analyze which countries fit those definitions. By employing Larry Diamond's sixfold typology and the widely used Freedom House ratings (*free*, *partly free*, and *not free*), such a general analysis is possible and fairly straight-forward.[12] Diamond's typology distinguishes two types of democratic regimes (*liberal* and *electoral*); three types of authoritarian regimes (*competitive, hegemonic electoral,* and *politically closed*); and *ambiguous regimes*, a residual category for systems too difficult to classify due to changing conditions or ongoing instability.

With respect to countries that label their own systems "democratic," Diamond encourages a useful distinction between regimes in transition that aspire to liberal democracy from those that are *pseudodemocracies*; that is, systems where elections exist but institutional arrangements are deliberately designed to inhibit party competition, pluralism, or civil liberties.

From the perspective of Diamond's typology, only Indonesia and the Philippines currently fall within the general category of democracy. Each of these systems, however, is an *electoral democracy* and falls short of meeting the criteria to be classified as an established *liberal democracy* (where political and civil liberties exist and endure, and where changing sets of elected leaders are chosen by and accountable to an electorate through fair elections that are repeatedly held).[13]

Indonesia, one of two Southeast Asian *electoral democracies*, was rated *free* by Freedom House as recently as 2012. It has since slid and is once again rated *partly free* due to newly imposed restrictions on civil society that require organizations to pledge allegiance to a state ideology that itself inhibits freedom. Indonesia's young democratic system, developed only after Suharto's departure in 1998, also remains deficient in some aspects of electoral fairness and durability.

The Philippines, accurately classified as *partly free* by Freedom House in 2015, is also closer to an *electoral democracy* than a *liberal democracy*. This fact is discouraging given Filipino aspirations for liberal democratic rule and the country's long experience with democratic constitutions, dating to the 1940s. Democratic institutions in the Philippines are in fact semidysfunctional in that they often serve as a veneer for oligarchic rule. Corruption, lawlessness, intimidation, and violence permeate politics and competitive elections for public office. The Philippines' *electoral democracy* serves elite interests over those of the broader public.

Only a few years ago, Thailand had a pluralistic system that was approaching the definition of *liberal democracy*. In fact, Thailand was classified by Freedom House as *free* for seven consecutive years (1998–2005). Once a democratic beacon in the region, Thailand has since suffered from multiple electoral-driven political crises, two military coups, constitutional instability, politicized judicial interventions, and episodic clashes between civilian demonstrators and government security forces. In flux from one year to the next, Thailand saw its freedom rating swing over four consecutive years (2005–2008) from *free* to *partly free* to *not free*, and then back to *partly free*. Since the May 2014 military coup and subsequent dictatorial control, Thailand's classification has depressingly returned to *not free*. Classified as a *free, electoral democracy* as recently as 2008, Thailand tragically ranks among Southeast Asia's least democratic systems as a *politically closed regime*.

Under Diamond's typology, Malaysia is best classified as a *competitive authoritarian regime*, where a significant parliamentary opposition exists but a dominant party coalition has been able to retain governmental power for decades at a time. The country is often cited as an example of an illiberal democracy. Recent developments indicate that the authoritarian features of the country's system are weakening and party dominance is under stress. The Malaysian political regime—under the weight of more intense parliamentary contestation and changing public attitudes favoring liberal democracy—may eventually improve its current regime label.

In contrast is Singapore, where the ruling People's Action Party has perpetually inhibited the development of a significant parliamentary opposition by restricting oppositional speech, harassing government opponents, and manipulating a politicized judiciary. Singapore is a pseudodemocracy or, more precisely using Diamond's terms, a *hegemonic electoral authoritarian regime*.

Somewhat similarly, the Cambodian People's Party, under the tight grip of strongman Hun Sen, has used extra-electoral mechanisms to intimidate opposition parties, politicians, and activists to ensure ongoing rule. Rated *not free* in 2015 by Freedom House, Cambodia is also classified as a *hegemonic electoral authoritarian regime*.

Due to the lack of competitive elections and serious restrictions of political and civil liberties, Vietnam and Laos share classification as *politically closed authoritarian regimes*. Each is governed as a communist party-state and has annually maintained *not free* ratings by Freedom House throughout the new international era. Tiny Brunei, a rigid absolute monarchy, also meets the criteria of these same general classifications.

Myanmar, until recently an oppressive military regime, underwent dramatic political reforms between 2010 and 2015. At the time of writing, the country is the most difficult political regime to classify in the region. In late 2015, the National League for Democracy (NLD), led by Aung San Suu Kyi, defeated the country's primarily military-backed party in the first free and open general election in decades. The NLD assumed control of Parliament in early 2016. Because of these events, Myanmar's history will forever be divided between the era before and the era after 2016. Myanmar has been a *politically closed authoritarian regime* for the previous five decades; now, its partially elected Parliament will enjoy the majority powers held by the NLD but will be checked by constitutional limits and, ominously, by the military, which retains a formal political role. It is too early to predict how this situation may develop. Myanmar's future may be brighter than it once was, but it is anything but certain. Thus, Myanmar, for the time being, is best classified as an *ambiguous regime*.

Timor-Leste, an infant state still dependent on international support, is also best classified as an *ambiguous regime*. Although the practice of parliamentary politics evolves and it may aspire to liberal democracy, the country's most pressing problems remain political uncertainty and weak state capacity. Democracy enjoys general legitimacy among Timorese but electoral instability, political violence, and growing regionalism on the island undermine state development and the rule of law. With more time and experience, Timor-Leste may evolve into an electoral democracy, but it is not one at the moment.

Taken together, one observes that political freedom and democracy in Southeast Asia barely exist. It is distressing to note that in 2015, Southeast Asia remains less democratic than Latin America, sub-Saharan Africa, Oceania, South Asia, and East Asia, not to mention Europe and North America. By 2015, no Southeast Asian countries enjoyed a rating of *free* from Freedom House. In fact, more countries in Southeast Asia rate as *not free* than *partly free*. At a regional level, only the autocratic regimes of the Middle East and North Africa surpass Southeast Asia in their suppression of political freedoms and civil liberties. A joint study by Harvard and the University of Sydney examining recent elections in 107 countries across multiple regions revealed that Southeast Asia ranks dead last among all other regions in electoral integrity.[14] After decades of struggle, effort, and reform to develop it, democracy in Southeast Asia seems as elusive as ever.

Such broad generalizations are useful to a point. But, again, it is critical to emphasize that regime classification is useful only because it is a general comparison. As an analytical tool, regime classification does not adequately portray Southeast Asian nations and their complexities over time. Without supplementary analysis, regime labels are simply insensitive to the particular political structures, events, and behaviors that animate the political life of particular countries. Countries may share classifications but political life and individual opportunities may in fact be quite disparate. Singapore and Cambodia share the same general classification but are worlds apart in every other way. Dynamic polities such as Myanmar, Thailand, and Malaysia, as well as young Timor-Leste, virtually defy the rigid criteria demanded by categorization.

Because of the difficulties and limitations of regime analysis and classification, only case-by-case examinations sensitive to the unique experiences and attributes of individual countries are capable of generating for readers a nuanced understanding of political and economic life in Southeast Asia. The chapters that follow are structured in an effort to meet this objective.

The country chapters begin with Thailand, Myanmar (Burma), Vietnam, Cambodia, and Laos—the countries of *Peninsular Southeast Asia* (sometimes referred to as "Mainland Southeast Asia"). The book then completes the regional survey with chapters on the Philippines, Indonesia, Timor-Leste, Malaysia, Singapore, and Brunei—the countries of *Insular Southeast Asia* (sometimes referred to as "Maritime Southeast Asia").[15]

NOTES

1. The phrase to describe Southeast Asia's transformation "from a battlefield to a marketplace" was famously coined by Thai prime minister Chatichai Choonhavan at a speech to the National Press Club in Washington, DC, June 16, 1990.

2. The conventional forms of country names are generally used throughout this book. On June 18, 1989, Burma's military rulers announced that the country's official name (in English) would be, henceforth, Myanmar. From 1989 until around 2010 this name change was not recognized by those who rejected the legitimacy of Burma's military rulers. The name Myanmar was officially used in the United Nations and some official international circles but was significantly rejected by opposition politician and longtime political prisoner Aung San Suu Kyi. Earlier editions of this book used the name Burma exclusively. In 2010, a new set of leaders in the country launched a process toward greater democratization and released Aung San Suu Kyi from house arrest. Following Suu Kyi's subsequent practice of using both "Myanmar" and "Burma" interchangeably, revised editions of this book adopted the use of both names. Since 2010, many governments have also reestablished relations and adopted the use of "Myanmar" without hesitation. This book also uses "East Timor" and "Timor-Leste" interchangeably.

3. Because this book focuses on contemporary politics it unfortunately devotes little attention to precolonial and colonial history. Readers will need to search elsewhere for a better understanding of historical trends and cultural foundations of the region and particular countries. A common place to begin such a study is with the classic text edited by David Joel Steinberg, *In Search of Southeast Asia* (Honolulu: University of Hawaii Press, 1987); D. R. Sardesai's *Southeast Asia: Past and Present* (Boulder: Westview Press, 2009); and *The Emergence of Modern Southeast Asia: A New History* (Honolulu: University of Hawaii Press, 2005), edited by Norman G. Owen.

4. See Thongchai Winichakul's *Siam Mapped: A History of the Geo-Body of a Nation* (Honolulu: University of Hawaii Press, 1994); James C. Scott, *The Art of Not Being Governed: An Anarchist History of Upland Southeast Asia* (New Haven, CT: Yale University Press, 2009).

5. Also called "Asian economic tigers."

6. James C. Scott, *The Moral Economy of the Peasant: Rebellion and Subsistence in Southeast Asia* (New Haven, CT: Yale University Press, 1976).

7. David G. Timberman, *A Changeless Land: Continuity and Change in Philippine Politics* (New York: M. E. Sharpe, 1991).

8. Quoted by Kishore Mahbubani, a Singaporean scholar and diplomat, from T. R. Reid, *Confucius Lives Next Door: What Living in the East Teaches Us about Living in the West* (New York: Random House, 1999), 62.

9. See Robert O. Keohane and Joseph S. Nye, *Power and Interdependence*, 4th ed. (Boston: Longman, 2012).

10. George W. Bush, "Address Before a Joint Session of Congress on the State of the Union Address," January 29, 2002; John Gershman, "Is Southeast Asia the Second Front?" *Foreign Affairs* 81, no. 4 (July/August 2002): 60–74.

11. This prediction was made by the reputable economic forecasting firm HIS Global Insight in 2012. See Michael Richardson, "Region Could Drive Global Economic Revival," *Japan Times Online*, August 22, 2012, www.japantimes.co.jp/text /eo20120822mr.html.

12. Larry Diamond is the founder and editor of the *Journal of Democracy* and is a noted regime classification expert. The typology here is taken from his article "Thinking about Hybrid Regimes," *Journal of Democracy* 13, no. 2 (2002): 21–35. Freedom House bases its

ratings on a system that assigns values to indicators of "political freedoms" and "civil liberties." Visit www.freedomhouse.org.

13. Fair elections are defined as being administered in a transparent manner by neutral authorities and characterized by ballot secrecy, the impartial treatment of candidates and parties, impartial procedures for resolving complaints and disputes, and minimal political violence.

14. Max Gromping, "Southeast Asian Elections Worst in the World," *New Mandala*, February 19, 2015, http://asiapacific.anu.edu.au/newmandala/2015/02/19/southeast-asian -elections-worst-in-the-world.

15. Although part of Malaysia is located on the Thai-Malay peninsula, and is geographically connected to mainland Southeast Asia, the Federation of Malaysia (which includes both peninsular and insular territories) is conventionally grouped with the countries of Insular Southeast Asia due to generally-accepted historical and cultural similarities.

2

THAILAND

Thailand's promise of evolving into a modern society with a prosperous economy and functional democracy dates to 1932, when Siam (as it was formerly called) transitioned from absolute to constitutional monarchy. Since that time, the country's people have demonstrated a remarkable capacity to generate economic growth and improve their quality of life. Ranked among Southeast Asia's "tiger economies," Thailand trailed the rise of Asia's miracle economies by a decade or so. Although it has yet to reach the economic heights of South Korea, Taiwan, Hong Kong, or Singapore, its complex modern economy participates fully in today's global supply chains, financial markets, and digital-savvy consumer culture. Compared to its immediate Southeast Asian neighbors, Thailand's economic progress over the past fifty years is wholly measurable in quantitative and qualitative terms. Its 68 million people enjoy the highest level of overall development in mainland Southeast Asia.[1]

Contrasting with its demonstrable capacity to make progress in the economic realm, Thai society has proven incapable of developing politically, at least with respect to its own democratic aspirations. Since the events of 1932, Thai aspirations for democracy have steadily evolved, finding articulation in the country's intellectual and political discourse, multiple revisions to its constitution, and a vibrant participatory politics. Thais relegitimize their democratic aspirations each time they vote at polling stations, demonstrate en masse at Bangkok's Democracy Monument, or debate the meaning of *prachatipatai* (democracy). Thais are no strangers to idealizing political freedom: the word "Thai" itself means "to be free." And for long periods of time, even years at a time, political order in the "Kingdom of Thailand" has been derived from democratic institutions: representative government, free elections, political parties, parliamentary law, and recognized civil liberties. The most recent democratic regime lasted over six years. Marred by turmoil and disorder, it persisted nonetheless from late 2007 until May 22, 2014, the day the constitutional order was overthrown by a military coup d'état, Thailand's twelfth such coup since 1932.

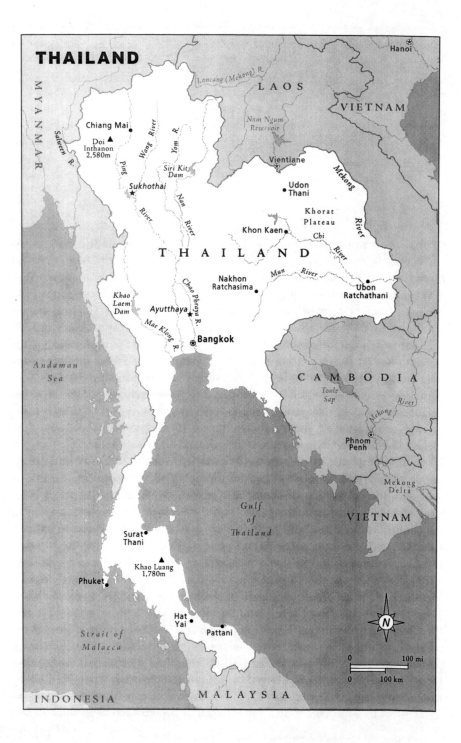

THAILAND

MYANMAR

LAOS

VIETNAM

Hanoi

Lancang (Mekong) R.

Salween R.

Chiang Mai

Doi
Inthanon ▲
2,580m

Wang River

Ping River

Yom R.

Siri Kit
Dam

Nan River

Sukhothai ★

*Nam Ngum
Reservoir*

Vientiane

Udon
Thani

Khorat
Plateau

Khon Kaen

Chi

Mekong River

T H A I L A N D

Nakhon
Ratchasima

Mun River

River

Ubon
Ratchathani

Khao
Laem
Dam

Ayutthaya ★

Chao Phraya R.

Mae Klong R.

Bangkok

*Andaman
Sea*

CAMBODIA

*Tonle
Sap*

Mekong River

Phnom
Penh

VIETNAM

*Mekong
Delta*

*Gulf
of
Thailand*

Surat
Thani

Khao Luang ▲
1,780m

Phuket

Hat
Yai

Pattani

*Strait of
Malacca*

N

0   100 mi

0   100 km

INDONESIA   MALAYSIA

Given the country's discernable economic progress, its experience with elected government, and societal aspirations for democratic order, it is all the more curious that Thailand has failed to develop politically. Plagued by political crises and recurrent institutional breakdowns, Thailand suffers from a vicious cycle of political dysfunction: an endless succession of military coups, constitutional rewriting, irregular elections, corrupt governments, institutional failure, and repeated monarchical intervention.[2] Although the country generally slogs on through the fog of all this instability—to the point where episodic political chaos has become ritualized into a sad type of normalcy—Thailand's political dysfunction sank to new depths over the past decade. Indeed, since about 2005, Thailand has been, categorically speaking—in the most precise academic jargon available—a miserable political mess.

Although recent political instability derives, no doubt, from various proximate causes, Thailand's general political dysfunction stems in great measure from its long-standing struggle to build a modern nation-state amid the powerful forces of Thai history and cultural sensibilities about rightful authority. With origins dating to the kingdoms of Siam, an ongoing evolutionary battle of ideals, wills, and beliefs has contributed to the maldevelopment of Thailand's modern political life and left aspirations for democratic governance unmet.

In Siam, unlike other areas of Southeast Asia, the historical clashes between East and West did not result in colonization—the Thais were never colonized by Europeans. The initial Siamese response to outside influences was to make use of foreigners for trade, labor, and knowledge and to selectively embrace cosmopolitanism even while defending Buddhist values and absolute monarchism. This strategy reached its end in 1932. The more enduring response of successive generations of Thai elites has been to construct hegemonic notions of "Thainess" in an attempt to shape peoples, cultures, and territory into a single ideational "geo-body."[3] By actively contrasting "Thai" with "non-Thai" (or Western), elites have framed the process of accommodating modern political values through self-justifying definitions of cultural appropriateness.

Thai notions of political authority find deep roots in the Ayutthaya era, which persisted from the fourteenth to the eighteenth centuries.[4] Reports from early European explorers described Siam as a striking Buddhist kingdom characterized by opulence, officialdom, a refined ceremonial court culture, and a merciless social hierarchy. The influences upon Siam during these centuries came from multiple sources.

The Thais adapted much from the Hindu-influenced Khmers, who previously dominated the region from the ninth through the fourteenth centuries. In particular, Ayutthaya's kings were considered *deva-raja*, or god-kings, with the attributes of a Brahmanic deity. Theravada Buddhism, astrology, and numerology had also spread to Siam during the fifth to thirteenth centuries from Indic and Mon settlements to the West, as well as from Sri Lanka. A royally patronized Buddhist monastic order reciprocated loyalty to the king by promoting a religious cosmology that placed the king at the center of universal harmony.[5] Thais also shared many linguistic forms, animist beliefs, and social practices familiar in other ethnically "Tai" peoples and kingdoms to the north (e.g., Sukhothai, Lanna, Lan Xang, Tai Shan, and Sipsongpanna).[6] Eventually, the Europeans arrived, beginning in the sixteenth century. Ayutthaya's kings, for some time, made use of what these new arrivals offered as long as authority structures were generally respected.

As Siam absorbed these various influences, political institutions were established at Ayutthaya with a lingering impact on Thai political culture. The feudal-like *sakdina* (field power) system produced such an effect. Virtually all persons in the Ayutthaya kingdom were given official rankings or designated status according to the amount of land or people they controlled or their status as *corvée* conscripts or hereditary slaves. The ranking determined the salary of officials, the deference due them, and the labor obligations others had to the state. Although the quantifiable character of the *sakdina* system ended by 1932, the hierarchical nature of its social system has endured as an element of Thai society.

Classical Siamese-Thai government was autocratic in form and spirit. Power was the privilege of a small elite as well as of absolute monarchs who were not accountable to the people but derived authority from an aura of divinity. Those who ruled were believed to possess superior ability and "moral goodness" (*khuna*).[7] Thai perceptions of kingly virtue and elite privilege remain today, as demonstrated by the veneration shown to the king by his subjects and by elite preferences for the appointment of "good people" over the popular choices of the electorate.

The destruction of Ayutthaya's capital by invading Burmese in 1767 was a traumatic event in Thai history. The political-social system was torn asunder. Despite the near-total destruction of the kingdom, the Thais displayed remarkable recuperative powers and in a short time resumed life under a new, centralized government in Bangkok led by the Chakri Dynasty. Some of the Chakri kings were reform oriented—systematizing administrative structures, freeing slaves, bringing in highly educated technocrats, and negotiating away border territory for Siam's continued independence. From 1851 through 1910, two legendary Chakri monarchs, King Mongkut (Rama IV) and his son King Chulalongkorn (Rama V), advanced significant reforms to modernize Siam.[8] The present king, Bhumibol Adulyadej, is the ninth monarch of the Chakri Dynasty, or Rama IX.

Following the 1932 revolt and establishment of a constitutional monarchy, politics remained in the hands of a small elite group of civilian bureaucrats and military generals with little competition or balance from forces outside the bureaucratic arena. The military, which emerged as the country's dominant institution, has since controlled political power in Thailand for over fifty of the past eighty years. From 1932 to 1973, Thailand's political system was a classic bureaucratic polity. The basis of political power was highly personalized and sub-ject to informal political manipulations and loyalties. It was also very unstable. During this period a repetitive cycle emerged of military control followed by weak parliamentary government, constitutional crisis, and coup d'état.

During World War II, Thailand acquiesced to Japanese occupation and suf-fered only modest war damage. Toward the end of the war, its government changed and joined the Allies, avoiding any postwar punishment as a belliger-ent. Having avoided the debilitating struggles for independence that its neigh-bors suffered, Thailand emerged from World War II relatively secure and stable. Initially, it seemed headed toward a constitutional system of parliamen-tary democracy, but the army soon took power.

The most influential of the early postwar leaders was Marshal Sarit Thanarat, the army commander in chief who became prime minister in 1957, declared martial law, and ruled dictatorially for six years. Sarit was the first prime minis-ter to make economic development the cornerstone of his rule. He also culti-vated the popularity of the monarchy for his political advantage.

Sarit's successor, Marshal Thanom Kittikachorn, followed in his predeces-sor's footsteps by keeping the military in firm control of every aspect of govern-ment and by pursuing economic development. During both administrations, the legislature was impotent, political parties were constrained or forbidden, and corruption was rampant. These leaders also cooperated with the United States during the Vietnam War, providing logistical support, Thai troops, naval bases, and airfields that were used throughout the Cold War campaign against communists in the region.

In response to the low level of political accountability and the high level of corruption, the "Great Tragedy" of October 14, 1973, occurred when the citi-zenry rose against the military government. Thanom ordered the massacre of hundreds of unarmed protesters at Democracy Monument in Bangkok, a bloody event that resonates in Thai society to this day. At the behest of King Bhumibol, Thanom and his ruling partners were subsequently forced into exile. The king followed their expulsion by appointing the first civilian government since the immediate postwar period. Thailand's next experience with democ-racy thus began as a result of courageous student protests and the ouster of military rulers.

The 1973 student revolt raised the expectations of many Thais that funda-mental economic reforms would be carried out. The succeeding three years, however, coincided with a worldwide recession and period of market instability that temporarily ended the country's improving economy. The hopes of many Thais that democracy would improve their lives were tragically dashed. Aside from establishing a minimum wage and some new funds for rural develop-ment, little was accomplished by the civilian government during this period—a government that faced an international and regional situation over which it had little control.

The change to communist governments in Vietnam, Laos, and Cambodia in 1975, and the rise of insurgency throughout the Thai countryside, shocked many Thais. Because Thailand's traditional security ally, the United States, was withdrawing from Southeast Asia, the civilian government renewed ties with China in hopes of counterbalancing a rising Soviet-backed Vietnam. This destabilizing state of affairs led some Thais to conclude that only an authoritarian, military-dominated government could deal effectively with potential threats. Thai society became polarized between left and right.

Democratic civilian rule lasted only until October 1976, when the military overthrew the government, proclaimed martial law, and abrogated the constitution. The takeover followed a series of events, including another massacre in which scores of unarmed students were brutally executed in a crackdown at Thammasat University in Bangkok. The students had been fervently protesting the high-profile return of the exiled dictator, Thanom. Dramatically clothed in saffron robes, Thanom nevertheless returned to Thailand and promptly took up residence as a Buddhist monk at Wat Boworniwet, the king's favored temple. During the protests, King Bhumibol and Queen Sirikit paid a visit to Thanom, and only days later, the military, aided by border police and right-wing paramilitary forces, launched a violent crackdown on student demonstrators. Scores died and thousands were arrested. The king's moves this time suggested support for the military rather than the protesting students.

Having seized power, the new military leaders predictably adopted a strong anticommunist agenda. They suspended all political activities and civil liberties and went after any person or group perceived as a threat. Many of their targets were leftist students or the civilian politicians of the previous government. Fearful of the military, thousands fled into the countryside, joining peasant insurgents. The leftist coalition of intellectual urbanites and rural revolutionaries, however, never materialized into a massive insurgency capable of usurping state power. The ongoing presence of the covert Communist Party of Thailand and its associated insurgency, however, allowed for successive Thai governments, generals, and bureaucrats to justify strict national security policies and to harass opponents in the name of anticommunism—a practice that continued until the end of the Cold War and beyond.

The military remained the dominant government institution until 1988. Under General Prem Tinsulanond's prime ministership, from 1980 until 1988, the country began to liberalize politically into a type of semidemocracy. Prem included civilian technocrats in his cabinet and relied on the freely elected legislature for support of his programs. Despite two coup attempts against him, he remained in power with the king as a close ally. After elections in 1988, he voluntarily stepped down in favor of Chatichai Choonhavan, the first elected member of Parliament to become prime minister since the 1973–1976 period. The smooth transition from Prem to Chatichai reflected new optimism about Thailand's potential to evolve toward stable democracy.

As a former ranking military officer and minister in Prem's cabinet, Chatichai held a reputation as a big-business playboy. As executive, he initiated a number of highly popular policies, such as raising the salaries of government officials, increasing the minimum wage for laborers, banning the indiscriminate cutting of trees, and standing up to the United States on trade. He also became famous for promoting an idea to transform Southeast Asia from a "battleground into a marketplace," a policy especially popular with the business community. It was not empty rhetoric.

Under Chatichai, Thailand led the region into a period of phenomenal economic growth fueled by East Asian investors and local entrepreneurship. Large amounts of capital came into the Thai economy. These new resources became the targets of public officials who sought them for private gain. Huge telecommunications projects, massive road and elevated commuter railway ventures, cable television contracts, and new oil refineries became well-known examples of multibillion-dollar contracts arranged by Chatichai government ministers who used the deals to perpetuate their own power base and personal wealth. Thai newspapers, unencumbered by censorship, began to publish reports on the rampant corruption among top-level cabinet members. For the many Thais stuck in the informal economy, the new wealth at the top was trickling down, but just barely.

On February 23, 1991, hopes that Thailand was beginning to institutionalize democratic-civilian processes were once again dashed when a military coup d'état ousted Chatichai's government. For justification, coup leaders charged government politicians with having become "unusually wealthy." They claimed that a "parliamentary dictatorship" had formed that was built on rampant vote buying during elections. A more direct cause for the coup, however, was a pattern of slights carried out by Chatichai and perceived by military leaders as threats to their traditional prerogatives.

Initially, the people greeted the 1991 coup with acquiescence, though not enthusiasm, and there were no public protests or demonstrations. The usual pattern followed. Led by army commander Suchinda Kraprayoon, coup leaders abrogated the constitution, dismissed the elected government, and set up a temporary National Peace Keeping Council (NPKC). The NPKC then established an interim charter and named Anand Panyarachun, a distinguished civilian businessman, as prime minister. Political parties were retained and a national legislative assembly was established to approve the new constitution and authorize a general election, scheduled for March 1992.

During the interim, the junta gave Anand wide leeway in running the government, but asserted its own views forcefully regarding the promulgation of the new constitution. The final document returned Thailand's legislative body to its former system, in which the appointed upper house of Parliament was given equal power with the elected lower house in matters of policymaking. Anand's administration set forth policy measures supporting privatization, trade liberalization, deregulation of the economy, a value-added tax, infrastructure projects, and constraints on labor unions.

For the March 1992 polls, military-backed parties formed a joint campaign scheme to minimize competition and elect pro-military candidates. On the other side were parties opposed to continued military dominance in Thai politics. A chief leader of this latter group was Bangkok governor Chamlong Srimuang, who had given up his gubernatorial position to lead a new party, Palang Dharma (Moral Force). Chamlong, a former military officer, enjoyed a reputation for being incorruptible. He campaigned wearing an indigo farmer's shirt and cultivated an austere image as a faithful devotee of Santi Asoke, a new Buddhist sect that rejected superstitious practices and demanded a strict lifestyle of celibacy, vegetarianism, and material sacrifice.

Following a campaign featuring party jumping and allegations of vote buying, the March 1992 elections resulted in a narrow victory for parties aligned with the NPKC. Ironically, the coalition government produced by the victory included many "unusually wealthy" politicians of the ousted Chatichai government. After the coalition's first nominee for prime minister was withdrawn (the nominee, said the US embassy, ran drug-trafficking operations in the infamous Golden Triangle), pro-military parties then nominated coup leader General Suchinda, who had previously promised that he would never seek the prime ministership. In what many Thais referred to as "the second coup," General Suchinda blithely accepted the nomination and, in the process, reversed the steps Thailand had taken toward democracy. To express dismay, some 50,000 protesters flooded Bangkok's streets in demonstration against Suchinda's ruling coalition.

The anti-Suchinda demonstrations grew larger in the days that followed, bringing well over 100,000 Thais onto the streets of Bangkok in May 1992. Led by Chamlong and opposition leaders, mobile phone–carrying urbanites, members of the middle class, and white-collar professionals all demanded that Suchinda step down. Many began a hunger strike around Democracy Monument, the site of the 1973 mass demonstrations. Anachronistically, Suchinda claimed (three years after the Cold War) that the demonstrators were the pawns of "communist elements" and thus anti-monarchists. Tensions increased, and the size and intensity of the protests grew.

In an episode eerily reminiscent of 1973 and 1976, Thai soldiers then filed into Bangkok upon Suchinda's orders and began indiscriminately shooting into the defenseless crowds. Troops took control of the country's media and communications networks, but demonstrators with cameras and handheld video equipment recorded the violence and broadcast the images outside of Bangkok via fax machines and videotape. The unprecedented and effective method of spreading uncensored information undermined the military's standard practice of propagandizing coup events to manipulate Thai and global opinion. Although the full count is not known, hundreds of people died from soldier-fired weapons in the crackdown of "Black May 1992," a tragic product of Suchinda's hubris and miscalculations.

After the violence, Prime Minister Suchinda was driven from office, his legacy a disastrous forty-eight-day reign. His welcome removal came after a globally televised rebuke by King Bhumibol, who made both Suchinda and Chamlong kneel before him as he sat regally on his throne. Suchinda was reprimanded for bringing death and shame to the country. Chamlong was scolded for forcing headstrong protests that put civilians at risk. The king dismissed Suchinda, declared amnesty for all persons involved in the demonstrations, and supported constitutional amendments designed to reduce the military's dominance in politics.

In a second extraordinary royal intervention related to the May 1992 crisis, the king approved the return of Anand Panyarachun as prime minister. With the king's appointment legitimizing his authority, Anand demoted top military leaders responsible for the violence, removed important state enterprises from military control, and scheduled a new round of parliamentary elections, announcing that he would remain in office for only four months, a promise he kept.

The September 1992 elections featured sixteen parties. Few of the candidates were newcomers, and many simply jumped to new parties. Some parties changed their names and distanced themselves from the tainted "devil" parties affiliated with the military. The "angel" parties won the poll and formed a government under the leadership of civilian politician Chuan Leekpai, a soft-spoken leader of the Democrat Party from Trang Province in the south. From his offices in Government House, the country's executive center, he led a shaky 207-seat coalition in the 360-member House of Representatives.

Chuan's immediate challenge was to find a balance between democratic rule and sensitivity to the traditional prerogatives of the military. He also faced the challenge of keeping together his fragile administration, which included leaders of the coalition parties who themselves coveted the prime ministership. Opposition leaders pointed to Chuan's lack of charisma and ill-defined policy initiatives to address the growing list of problems facing the country: traffic congestion, pollution, environmental degradation, child labor, HIV/AIDS, centralized decision-making, water shortages, and ubiquitous corruption. In May 1995, his parliamentary coalition fell apart owing to a land reform scandal in the south (a Democrat stronghold) and conflicting demands among the ruling coalition of political parties. New elections were called.

In the July 1995 election, about 40 million people voted. Predictably, campaign issues were vague, because political parties in Thailand at the time did not articulate clear platforms or represent particular ideologies. Party hopping ensued again, with competitive candidates being offered up to 5 million baht ($200,000) to switch parties. Voters were offered 100 to 300 baht ($4 to $12) if they promised to vote for a particular candidate. The election resulted in yet another weak coalition government, led by Banharn Silpa-archa, a wealthy rural businessman and longtime government minister. Nicknamed "Khun Ae-Thi-Am" (Mr. ATM), Banharn bore a reputation for managing huge networks of patronage, particularly in the realm of public infrastructure. His administration turned out to be a disaster. It collapsed after fifteen months under the weight of economic scandal and inept policymaking.

New elections in November 1996 brought retired general Chavalit Yong-chaiyudh to the prime ministership. Little had changed. Unpopular among Bangkok's elites and leading newspapers, Chavalit, like Banharn, drew support from upcountry provincial voters. As prime minister, Chavalit faced two tremendous challenges: the passage of a new constitution, and the 1997 Asian economic crisis. Following an inclusive drafting process that began long before Chavalit took office, the new constitution was complete. It had brought many segments of Thai society into its creation in a democratic manner. The "People's Constitution," as it was dubbed, was designed to be the country's last constitution. It was considered to be the most legitimate constitution in Thai history, and it received overwhelming approval by Parliament on September 27, 1997.

Chavalit's support for the passage of the new constitution bought him some time amid crisis conditions owing to the collapse of the Thai baht months earlier in June 1997. Under his watch, the baht had lost half its value against the dollar, the stock market had fallen precipitously, and the International Monetary Fund was asked to bail out the country with a loan of some $17 billion. Most Thais blamed the political system for the economic crisis, believing that politicians were more concerned about perpetuating their own power and adding to the profits of their business associates than about enhancing the public good. After just eleven months, the embattled Chavalit announced his resignation. Chuan Leekpai, of the opposition Democrat Party, subsequently managed to forge a coalition majority; he was appointed interim prime minister until elections could be held under the country's new constitutional provisions. Chuan instituted reform measures to rescue the economy and mandated transparency, but the crisis continued to hurt the bulk of the population financially. IMF guidance and austerity policies proved unable to resuscitate the economy.

A new election in 2001 led to the rise of Dr. Thaksin Shinawatra, a telecommunications mogul and founder of the Thai Rak Thai (Thais Love Thais, or TRT) political party. Thaksin was among Thailand's richest businessmen, having made his fortune selling computers to Thai government agencies, and had extensive holdings in the communications sector involving mobile phones, broadcast television, and satellite communications. His business empire spanned most of Southeast Asia's rapidly growing markets and his name appeared on *Fortune*'s list of the world's richest people. However, Thaksin was not a member of the traditional Bangkok bureaucratic or intellectual elite. His early career was in criminal justice, a field that had brought him to the United States for graduate degrees and then back to Thailand, where he worked in the

Metropolitan Police Department. Of Sino-Thai origin and a proud son of silk traders in provincial Chiang Mai, Thaksin was ranked among the country's un-refined nouveaux riche in the eyes of Bangkok's urbane aristocrats.

Because of his business savvy and meteoric success, and his former political associations with Chamlong's Moral Force Party, Thaksin seemed to embody the two qualities many common Thai voters believed were needed in an eman-cipator capable of freeing them from the economic crisis and dreaded IMF loan conditions: competence and trustworthiness. What voters did not fully appre-ciate at the time was Thaksin's unmatchable political acumen and limitless po-litical ambition. Indeed, his political genius enabled him to methodically create an unprecedented party machine with die-hard loyalists: the Thai Rak Thai Party.

Thaksin's TRT election victory in 2001 came principally from public dissat-isfaction with the slow pace and uneven distribution of Thailand's economic recovery. Chuan Leekpai's Democrats had held power for much of the 1990s, and Thais criticized their recovery policies for catering to international inves-tors first. Many Thais believed it was time for a change. Thaksin, adopting a populist platform, promised to solve the economic problems, provide funds to villages, and grant debt relief to farmers. Critical of the Democrats' embrace of IMF austerity programs and the market fundamentalism of the Washington Consensus, Thaksin offered a more Keynesian approach, where the govern-ment would stimulate the economy with its own spending programs.

While most new Thai parties eschewed specific policy platforms, centering instead on individual politicians or single-issue concerns such as clean govern-ment or national security, Thaksin's TRT embraced a multi-issue party plat-form that seemed to offer something for everyone. Because the new constitution mandated that some seats in the Parliament be filled through a party-list ballot, TRT was able to pull in many new loyalists. The TRT party aggressively wooed established party bosses, provincial politicians, and members of erstwhile party factions who sought to attach themselves to Thailand's newest rising star. Even many in the ever-expanding nongovernmental organization (NGO) commu-nity caught Thaksin's attention. He promised to support rural development and pledged to maintain a ban on the commercial use of genetically modified agricultural products.

TRT thus built itself as a broad coalition tied to a wide array of promises. It projected an image of self-confidence, deliberateness, and dynamism—a party suited to lead a "new Thailand" in the emerging international era of economic dangers. At its ideological core, however, Thaksin's TRT was a walking para-dox: it was fiercely nationalist, but not isolationist; it was populist, but also fa-vored the business elite; it was hedged with military allies, but it was not pro-military. TRT was a classic patronage-based party network, but it offered a fresh message unwedded to staid notions of bureaucratism, moderation, or nostalgic "Thainess."

Thaksin went on to become the longest-serving civilian prime minister in Thai parliamentary history. Playing in his favor was the reformed 1997 constitution, which was purposefully designed to inhibit party jumping, foster more stable party competition, and strengthen prime ministerial authority—all in the hopes of ending the revolving doors of leadership that had plagued the Parliament and Government House in the 1990s.

As prime minister, Thaksin won unprecedented support from upcountry provinces with his policies. His popular programs provided inexpensive medical care, gave loans and grants to villages, canceled and postponed debts owed by farmers, and established an asset management agency to reduce corporate debt. He also developed programs to support small and medium enterprises, and he encouraged every district in the country to develop at least one exportable product or handicraft. In the world of agriculture, he championed a policy to turn Thailand into "the kitchen of the world" as a top-five food exporter. His strategy to do so ranged from funding research and development in agricultural biotechnology to promoting authentic Thai ingredients and Thai restaurants abroad.

Using weekly radio addresses and ensuring favorable media coverage, Thaksin worked relentlessly to propagandize TRT's efforts to the public. By the end of his four-year term, Thaksin could boast of having engineered Thailand's economic recovery, reviving exports, and completing loan payments to the IMF ahead of schedule. Nevertheless, TRT's massive government spending drove concerns about the sustainability of so-called Thaksinomics. Many feared that Thaksin's spending strategy was hollow and lacked investment potential, portending a false recovery. Critics labeled the approach incoherent. Public cynicism grew, especially in Bangkok.

Observers also took note that Thaksin's business networks were benefiting from the village loans and redistributionist schemes in rural areas. Unprecedented sales of pickup trucks, motorcycles, and mobile phones were accompanied by allegations of ties to TRT corruption and local-level scheming. Programs such as the "million cows project," designed to give "one farmer, one cow," were disparaged by opposition politicians as mere vote-buying schemes veiled as antipoverty programs. Heavy criticism also came from human rights groups and the international community for Thaksin's brutal 2003 antidrug war, which included over 2,000 extrajudicial killings. Militarily, Thaksin also proved unable to keep his promise to end the ongoing separatist insurgency in Thailand's Muslim south, which bordered Malaysia.

Having been sidelined by TRT's dominance, Bangkok's elites, middle-class urbanites, bureaucrats, academics, and Santi Asoke Buddhists formed a wrathful oppositional bloc and began to demand Thaksin's removal. Thaksin responded to criticism by trying to muzzle the free media, further angering his accusers, who then charged him with dismantling democracy. In fact, some of Thaksin's most vocal critics were disillusioned TRT supporters who had turned on the party and its populist direction. Thaksin had become Thailand's most polarizing figure in decades.

In spite of mounting pressures, Thaksin Shinawatra was able to stay in power until his government's four-year term expired. With the economy back on track and rural constituents satisfied, TRT found itself in solid command for the scheduled 2005 general election. The small chance that opposition Democrats had to unseat TRT became even smaller after the 2004 Indian Ocean tsunami hit southern Thailand—a Democrat stronghold—weeks before the election. Thaksin's actions during the disaster won him praise from both Thais and members of the international community.

In the February 2005 general election, TRT won big—bigger than any party in the history of Thai democracy—securing 375 of 500 seats. The opposition Democrats won only 96 of the 125 remaining seats, which were filled by only three parties (a record low). TRT thus secured an unprecedented majority in the Parliament. Standard allegations of vote buying were drowned out by the obvious support rural voters expressed for TRT policies. Thaksin's party support and political machine appeared invincible. Bangkok's city voters and southern Democrats could not foresee an election scenario in which Thaksin and TRT would lose power.

Anti-Thaksin demonstrations began on the streets of Bangkok in late 2005, centering on allegations of official corruption. A few months later, in a gift to Thaksin's critics, a major scandal broke, with Thaksin unambiguously caught in the middle. Having used laws crafted by his own government, Thaksin had benefited from a transaction where his family sold its $1.9 billion communications empire to a Singaporean entity, tax-free. The news was more than his critics could bear. Street demonstrations mounted, with slogans that Thaksin had not only benefited from the sale, but that his family had put the nation at risk by permitting foreign control of Thailand's vast communications network. Thaksin, facing serious pressure, dissolved Parliament and called a snap election in an attempt to reestablish his legitimacy. Knowing that without upcountry support they would lose the election, Democrats and other opposition parties boycotted the election, publicly citing TRT vote-buying strategies and alleging that Thaksin held dictatorial ambitions.

Predictably, TRT won the April 2006 polls but was unable to establish a functioning Parliament due to the boycott and cries of illegitimate results. A deadlock ensued. With demonstrations for his ouster expanding, and a court ruling that annulled election results, Thaksin was forced to take audience with King Bhumibol. Visibly shaken from the event, Thaksin agreed to step down. He arranged, however, to continue on as a caretaker prime minister, at least until new polls could be held. To his critics it was a false resignation; to his supporters it was a shrewd political victory.

His dissenters, organized under the People's Alliance for Democracy, or PAD, became enraged when they realized Thaksin would still run the country as a caretaker prime minister. Earlier contempt for Thaksin transformed into sheer hatred. Standing at the head of the anti-Thaksin movement were two PAD leaders: Sondhi Limthongkul, a media mogul himself, and Chamlong Sri-muang, the resurrected leader of the "angel" forces of Black May 1992, a Santi Asoke adherent, and founder of the defunct Palang Dharma Party, of which Thaksin was once a part. To distinguish their movement, they co-opted the royally significant color yellow and identified themselves with yellow protest signs, hats, bandannas, and T-shirts.

Added to the growing list of Thaksin's alleged sins was the most serious ac-cusation of them all—that Thaksin sought to eclipse the *baramee* (cultural cha-risma) of the king himself and even coveted republicanism. For evidence, the PAD pointed to Thaksin's increasing ceremonial activities, which depicted him as a head of state rather than as the head of government. Rumors of the royal family's disdain for the prime minister circulated. The color yellow, regularly donned by the PAD faithful, took on heightened symbolism: no longer did wearing yellow simply celebrate monarchy, as it had previously—it now im-plied anti-Thaksin support.

Thaksin had tried earlier during his tenure to form alliances within the royal camp, but his meddling was viewed as calculating and disingenuous. King Bhu-mibol's most trusted adviser, Privy Councilor Prem Tinsulanond, emanated contempt for Thaksin.[9] The charge of republican ambition was political dyna-mite, upping the stakes of politics to a new level.

Thaksin's greatest ally amid the rising controversy was the democratic prin-ciple of majority rule. In 2001 and 2005, Thai voters had overwhelmingly sup-ported him, which was a point he cited often. The decision of opposition parties to boycott the April 2006 snap election was proof that Thaksin's opponents also recognized this fact. They knew that for all their charges in labeling rural voters as uneducated, stupid, and foolish, little could be done to change electoral real-ities. They calculated that Thaksin's grip on power would hold as long as major-itarian elections were in the picture.

The military denied coup rumors, but with another election pending in late 2006, and yet another TRT victory virtually assured, military coup d'état did indeed return to Thailand in the early morning hours of September 19, 2006. The event was quick, bloodless, and thoroughly welcomed by members of the country's anti-Thaksin minority who had given up on a constitutional means to remove the popular leader. King Bhumibol offered no disapproval of the junta leaders' actions. While seizing power, the military muzzled the media and streamed images of the monarch on television throughout the day of the take-over. Thaksin, in New York to deliver a speech at the United Nations, was un-able to return to Thailand. TRT ministers inside the country were ordered to report to other coup leaders for temporary detainment.

The country was put under martial law for months. No groups of more than five people, including political parties, were allowed to gather and discuss politics. Media restrictions were put in place. Armed troops were sent to Thaksin's home province of Chiang Mai as well as to other provinces, inhibiting any opportunity for backlash by pro-Thaksin forces. The reasons cited for the coup included corruption, the need to restore political order, and Thaksin's failed security policies over the country's restive south. The coup group announced itself as the Council for Democratic Reform under the Constitutional Monarchy, a title that was shortened later to the Council on National Security, or CNS.

Though it was never revealed officially, Thailand's public and its outside observers knew that the hands of Prem Tinsulanond had engineered the coup. As a longtime privy councilor, he emanated royal authority more than any other figure. The coup leaders garnered legitimacy shortly after the event's execution through personal visits to Prem's Bangkok home. Broadcast images of top brass shaking hands with the smiling Prem on his home driveway delivered the desired message: the events had full royal sanction.

An appointed government was soon authorized. Its legitimacy rested on royal approval, Prem's backing, and support from the country's Bangkok-based, anti-Thaksin political minority. The majority voters who backed Thaksin privately expressed anger and disillusionment with Thai politics. Martial law prevented organized dissent. Political scientists inside and outside the country shook their heads in dismay, with one writing, "What had seemed like a firm march toward democratic consolidation from May 1992 onward had suddenly fizzled and relapsed into military-authoritarian rule."[10]

In the fifteen months of military rule between September 2006 and December 2007, new initiatives enacted by coup leaders attempted to roll back Thaksinomics and set Thailand on a course of political reform. Nevertheless, the CNS (paradoxically) combined new fiscal austerity policies with its own quasi-populist policies in an attempt to win affection from provincial Thais and even outdo Thaksin himself. It announced totally free health care and offered extended village loan schemes. Then, in a move alarming to international investors, the CNS announced that all government decisions, including those from economic ministries, would be based on the principles of Sufficiency Economy, the royal-inspired economic theory advocating Buddhist moderation, reduced consumption, and small-scale family farming. It was a clear signal away from Thaksin's pro-growth policies.

In its most substantial act, the junta abrogated the 1997 People's Constitution, which was viewed as culpable in fostering Thaksin's rise. A new one was hastily drafted later by a select group of appointees and put up for approval by national referendum in 2007. The junta-crafted constitution barely passed, with a weak 58 percent of the national vote; a majority of voters in the pro-Thaksin northeast voted against it.

Ironically, new elections in December 2007 proved that the coup had resolved nothing from the perspective of anti-Thaksin forces. Although Thaksin was in exile, his party lived on, and so did its majority support from Thai voters.

Even a ruling by a constitutional court that forcibly dissolved Thai Rak Thai for past election violations could not prevent it from re-forming under a different name: the People's Power Party (PPP).

The PPP won the December 2007 general election and, in coalition with like-minded parties, formed a new government under Samak Sundaravej. Samak, at seventy-two years old flirting with political retirement, was a surprising choice. He was a veteran politician with an independent, *nakleng* (tough-guy) image that had long been tainted by allegations of involvement in the 1976 Thammasat University massacre. During the Thaksin years, Thais viewed him as a loudmouthed TV gadfly, and he was known for hosting a popular cooking show called *Chim Pai, Bon Pai (Tasting and Complaining)*. With his appointment, however, the independent Samak appeared to have sold out to serve as Thaksin's puppet. In the meantime, Thaksin took up residence in the United Kingdom and purchased the Manchester City Premier League football team.

By May 2008, PAD forces were back on the streets demanding Samak's resignation and the dissolution of Parliament. Numbers of yellow-clad protesters grew by the thousands. Amid the protests the PAD introduced its proposal for "New Politics," which called for reform of the country's Parliament to become 70 percent appointed and only 30 percent elected. The proposal also encouraged the full embrace of the king's idealized Sufficiency Economy. The New Politics proposal, which sought nothing less than the overthrow of majoritarian democracy, was considered a slap in the face to upcountry voters who would find themselves disenfranchised under the plan.

By August, PAD protesters had audaciously seized Government House, forcing the prime minister to govern from a military base for a time. Demonstrations continued for weeks on end. The anti-government protests of the People's Alliance for Democracy disrupted parliamentary business, clogged Bangkok streets, and created a tense atmosphere in the city. Prime Minister Samak refused to resign but chose not to remove the protesters by force, claiming prudence and restraint. A state of emergency was nevertheless declared after bloody clashes between pro-government groups and PAD protesters left scores wounded and one dead. Coup rumors swirled. Just as events began to crescendo, a court ruling forced Samak to step down from his post. The charge: paid appearances on a TV cooking show while serving as prime minister.

Samak's departure resolved little. To the astonishment of the anti-Thaksin movement, the PPP rallied around a new choice for prime minister: Somchai Wongsawat, Thaksin's brother-in-law. This move infuriated PAD supporters. It also proved to be a miscalculation on the part of the PPP. Somchai was unskilled and weak as the PPP's leader. Among other failures, he bungled a tense standoff with Cambodia over a long-disputed Angkor-era temple near the Thai-Cambodian border. Pro-Thaksin forces began to lose ground.

The PAD, relentless in its efforts to force TRT remnants out of power, then occupied Parliament itself, trapping elected officials inside. Prime Minister

Somchai was forced to jump over the back fence of the assembly compound to escape the siege. The PAD's risky actions pushed Somchai to the edge. He dispatched police, who then engaged protesters in a serious clash that led to the death of one female protester. Queen Sirikit attended the protester's funeral, an act that emboldened the PAD faithful.

By late 2008, the PAD announced its "final battle" to remove the pro-Thaksin PPP government from power. Thousands of "Yellow Army" protesters moved first to occupy a government-run television station and then both of Bangkok's airports, including Thailand's new Suvarnabhumi International Airport, which was a Thaksin project showcase. The PAD's seizure became front-page news in Asia, Europe, and North America. Thailand's main artery of transportation with the world was shut off. Thousands of business travelers, tourists, Haj pilgrims, and others found themselves unable to get into or out of Bangkok. Airport authorities scrambled to accommodate the trapped travelers, sending some to a military transport center on the eastern seaboard. Days passed without any serious attempt to remove the protesters. Surreal images were broadcast globally of PAD protesters in yellow T-shirts setting up food stalls, playing badminton, and waving plastic hand clappers at speech rallies inside Suvarnabhumi's space-age stainless steel terminal.

Prime Minister Somchai, forced to govern from Chiang Mai, refused to step down and issued calls for the PAD to withdraw before force would be employed. Subsequent orders for the police and military to remove the protesters were largely ignored. Thailand's crisis reached an impasse. Pro-Thaksin "Red Shirt" supporters of the sitting government, organized as the United Front of Democracy against Dictatorship (UDD), began to stage counter-rallies around the city. Fears of confrontation grew. Expectations of a military coup to end the standoff rose with each passing day.

The siege finally ended in its eighth day, just prior to the annual birthday celebration for the monarch. As with Samak's expulsion, it was the courts that proved consequential. In an expedited case, a constitutional court ruled that the People's Power Party had violated election law during the 2007 elections, and the party was ordered dissolved. Dissolution meant that Somchai was disqualified for office and would be banned from politics for five years. The remaining PPP members reorganized themselves into a third incarnation of Thaksin's TRT, the Pheu Thai Party (For Thais Party), but it was unable to form a coalition government.

After the "final battle" of airport seizures, Sondhi and Chamlong declared victory and PAD protesters returned home. It was the end of what was essentially a three-year protest, which had begun with an unsuccessful effort to force Thaksin's resignation in September 2005. Since that time and in the name of "democracy," the anti-Thaksin movement had (ignominiously) encouraged the boycott of a democratic election; a military coup d'état; the sacking of the 1997 People's Constitution; a proposal to disenfranchise the majority of the electorate; the unlawful seizure of Government House, Parliament, and the country's airports; the politicization of Thai courts to force dissolution of the country's largest political party (twice); and the removal of three prime ministers who had enjoyed the confidence of elected parliamentary majorities.

The intensity of the events left many members of Parliament weary. Party defections spurred talks of a new government coalition led by Democrat leader Abhisit Vejjajiva, an Oxford-educated, forty-four-year-old protégé of Democrat veteran Chuan Leekpai. On December 15, 2008, Abhisit won enough votes in Parliament to become Thailand's new prime minister. Ironically, the possibility of a Democrat-led coalition surfaced only when a faction of pro-Thaksin members of Parliament (MPs) opted to switch sides, denying the opportunity for the newly formed Pheu Thai Party to form a successor government. Some called the Democrats' capture of power a "silent coup." The pro-Thaksin UDD began to organize with the goal of removing Abhisit's government from office.

Bangkok's urban poor and red-shirted UDD demonstrators from upcountry provinces launched protests in the capital that lasted over three months, in part at Thaksin's urging from abroad. With his visa revoked by the United Kingdom months earlier, Thaksin now operated from countries that lacked extradition treaties with Thailand. In a series of dramatic events, the UDD protesters successfully disrupted the 2009 ASEAN summit hosted by the Thai government in the resort town of Pattaya. The UDD's actions forced Prime Minister Abhisit to embarrassingly request that his fellow Asian leaders return home. Crestfallen, Abhisit then declared a state of emergency and ordered the military to disperse the protesters, who had grown in number to over 100,000. After a handful of deaths on both sides, the UDD's leaders called off the protests but pledged to continue their fight to restore Thaksin to power. Months later, both sides actively called for new demonstrations against each other. More fractured than at any time since the polarized 1973–1976 period, Thai society teetered on the brink of major civil conflict.

Throughout 2009, Red Shirt protesters relentlessly challenged the "silent coup" and the legitimacy of Abhisit's Democrat-led coalition. In April, during the festive week of Thai New Year and the Songkran Water Festival, the UDD staged massive rallies, and tensions rose to a fevered pitch. At a bridge in Bangkok's historic government district, over 120,000 Red Shirt protesters gathered, camped, and harassed the Democrat-controlled Parliament until security forces broke up the demonstrations in an event recalling the crackdowns of 1976 and 1992. More than 800 were wounded and over 25 killed in the standoff.

Undeterred, the Red Shirts fearlessly reorganized a year later at Ratchaprasong intersection, a square in the center of Bangkok's commercial district. Encamped for weeks on end—complete with loudspeaker systems, platform stages, and even live feeds of Thaksin speaking from abroad—UDD protesters disrupted downtown traffic, business, and tourism for leverage in negotiations with the Abhisit government. The 2010 Red Shirt occupation of Ratchaprasong mirrored the PAD's "final battle" and impudent occupation of Suvarnabhumi International Airport in 2008.

The UDD's primary demand was for the dissolution of Parliament within thirty days and for new general elections to be called. The situation grew volatile. Red Shirt demonstrators erected barriers to demarcate a protest zone and, for a six-week period, engaged in skirmishes with pro-government demonstrators and police. Infighting among UDD–Red Shirt leaders left the movement with a poorly organized negotiating strategy. It was unclear the extent to which Thaksin (from abroad) was in control. On May 13, while giving a sidewalk interview to *New York Times* reporter Thomas Fuller, a rogue Thai army general who was a favorite leader of hardline Red Shirts was fatally shot in the head by a gunman on a motorbike. Soon after, top UDD leaders first agreed to, and then rejected, Abhisit's offer to call elections in six months. The prime minister then issued an ultimatum: leave the protest site or face security forces. Although some evacuated, many stayed. Authorities cut off all water and electricity to the area in an attempt to force the protesters out. A splinter group of hardline Red Shirts calling themselves "Black Shirts" pledged to stay indefinitely and wage "civil war" if needed, though their arsenal included little more than rocks, slingshots, pipe bombs, and a small collection of assault rifles.

For the next few days, the protests transformed into a fervent but feeble armed rebellion. Pockets of young men wearing red and black hunkered down behind makeshift barricades and daringly faced off against well-armed Thai troops and riot police. Sporadic clashes erupted throughout the commercial district and other parts of the city. Graphic videos of some of the violence went worldwide, with much of it posted on YouTube. Government officials claimed the armed soldiers were merely firing rounds into the air, but eyewitness reports, video footage, and forensic evidence indisputably proved otherwise. Subsequent investigations confirmed that many government soldiers exceeded rules of engagement and "frequently fired into crowds of unarmed protesters," and that snipers shot demonstrators "who were unarmed or posed no imminent threat of death or serious injury to the soldiers or others."[11]

With Bangkok's glitzy shopping malls and hotels as a backdrop, disturbing images of intense street battles, soldier-on-civilian violence, and bloodied protesters gripped the global news cycle. UN secretary-general Ban Ki-moon and other world leaders urged a peaceful resolution to no avail. Violence also spread to Chiang Mai and other cities where Red Shirt supporters erupted in anger by rioting and setting fire to government buildings. Over one-third of Thailand's seventy-seven provinces fell under emergency decrees. Talk of civil war mushroomed, but realistic assessments predicted that such a war was unlikely to ensue, given the overwhelming mismatch in force capability.

The standoff ended on May 19 after a final push by Thai army forces into the heart of the protest site. Red Shirt leaders surrendered and were brought under immediate arrest. Defeated, angered, and hopeless, a number of cowardly Red

Shirt arsonists set fire to nearby shopping malls, government buildings, and the Thai stock exchange, causing billions of dollars in damage. When it was over, central Bangkok looked like a war zone, and the country's collective soul was shattered, shell-shocked, and traumatized.

Ultimately, 91 people died and more than 1,800 were injured in the confrontation. Both sides share blame, and both can be criticized for employing illegal, imprudent, and immoral methods that resulted in needless injuries and tragic deaths. Arguably, the violence and chaos could have been avoided had Abhisit and UDD leaders not given up on negotiations. As is often the case in Thai politics, however, neither side could tolerate the appearance of defeat; hubris clouded judgment.

Less than a year later, on May 6, 2011, following months of recriminations, investigations, and further political difficulties—including PAD leaders turning against the Democrat-led government—embattled Prime Minister Abhisit Vejjajiva dissolved Parliament and called for new elections six months ahead of schedule. Thus, only eleven months after the army had been ordered to forcibly disperse protesters, the key demand of the Red Shirts for new elections was effectively realized. The 2011 general elections were the country's ninth in nineteen years. In Thailand, where general elections are even more frequent than military coups, the impatience of the body politic to demand that events, rather than constitutional rules, dictate political change once again proved extremely costly.

The new election date, June 3, 2011, opened the door for the Red Shirt camp to enlist its most powerful weapon: the ballot box. Although Thaksin's family was stripped of half their wealth by Thai courts in 2010, they proved more than capable of remaining key players in the Thai political game. Yingluck Shinawatra, the younger sister of the exiled Thaksin, was selected by Pheu Thai to be its candidate for prime minister. With a background in business and a young, fashionable image, the forty-four-year-old Yingluck took the Red Shirt electorate by storm. As with the four previous elections following its creation, Thaksin's party machine won another resounding victory. With a 75 percent national turnout, Yingluck became Thailand's first female prime minister. Pheu Thai had secured 253 of 500 seats and control over 53 percent of the lower house. Abhisit's Democrats came in a distant second, winning 159 seats, which was just less than one-third of the Parliament.

A political novice, Yingluck struggled after her election, but the strength of Pheu Thai and its five coalition partners gave her adequate political space. Then, only months into her tenure, Thailand experienced its worst spate of seasonal flooding in fifty years. Ravaging 80 percent of Thailand's provincial districts and engulfing Bangkok's suburban outskirts and industrial parks for weeks, the floods caused over 700 deaths; many other areas remained under water for weeks on end. Most estimates put the damage near $45 billion. Thailand's growth rate for 2011 dropped to 0.1 percent as a result.

For sitting governments, the difficulties involved in managing large-scale natural disasters typically produce corresponding political damage. Despite some serious missteps by the new government, economic recovery slowly returned. By mid-year 2012, the hard-hit industrial sector had recovered from the floods more quickly than expected. Still, pointing to ineffective policies in the restive south and Yingluck's populist (and fiscally dubious) rice-purchasing scheme, the Democrat-led opposition pushed for a vote of no confidence in spite of her high approval ratings among Thais. Yingluck predictably survived the vote. For a brief time, it seemed that Thailand's deep-seated political cleavages were once again being channeled through the country's historically beleaguered institutions of parliamentary democracy.

In the aftermath of the 2010 political violence, Red Shirt supporters wanted Abhisit's government to be held accountable for killing protesters. Yellow Shirt supporters wanted UDD protest leaders to be brought to justice for the protests that turned destructive. Prime Minister Yingluck, fearing political consequences, initially approached national reconciliation with only vague pledges and promises. She seemed reluctant to use her powers to hold her Democrat Party predecessors accountable or to engineer a process to bring her brother Thaksin home from abroad.

Her reluctance disappeared by 2013. That year, with Yingluck's blessing, the Pheu Thai–dominated legislature pursued two explosive bills. The first sought to amend the military's post-coup constitution by restoring the direct elections of senators (a feature of the once-popular 1997 People's Constitution). After the bill passed over Democrat Party objections, Thailand's Constitutional Court—politically aligned with the Yellow Shirt camp—overturned the amendment. The country's constitutional guardians ruled that restoring a fully elected Senate to Thailand would "repeat the flaws" of the past and be a "backward move" for the country.[12]

The other consequential legislation was a blanket amnesty bill aimed at fostering national reconciliation. To the contrary, the bill enraged people on all sides. Intense public outcry caused Yingluck to reverse course and rapidly pull the bill. Many Red Shirts could not abide the impunity the bill would grant Abhisit and those responsible for deaths during the 2010 crackdown. Even more infuriated were the Yellow Shirts, who believed the bill had exposed Yingluck's true motives—to return Thaksin home.

Although the amnesty bill was pulled, new street protests erupted led by Democrat Party veteran Suthep Thaungsuban, a southerner with a long track record of corruption. Setting aside the PAD's typical canary yellow, the reorganized protesters under Suthep opted for the Thai flag's red, white, and blue for their anti-Yingluck protest colors. Calling themselves the People's Democratic Reform Committee (PDRC), they took to the streets to "shut down Bangkok." For weeks and then months they actively blocked roads and key intersections; they set up rally stages, raised money, and held raucous anti-government events featuring firebrand nationalists, pop culture celebrities, and members of Bangkok's elite *hi-so* (high society). Some protesters donned Guy Fawkes masks, imitating the international hacker group Anonymous, clearly unaware that Guy Fawkes had been an anti-monarchist who had plotted to assassinate his own king.

Suthep's PDRC basically repeated three demands: that Prime Minister Yingluck and her government resign; that Parliament be dismissed so an unelected "people's council" could be authorized to guide the country; and that no new election occur until after complete "political reform." Their fundamental goal of reform sought to replace a majority-rule parliamentary system with an authoritarian version run by "good people" (as determined by Buddhist values and royalist institutions). More narrowly, they wanted to ensure that, going forward, the majority electorate could never again return a pro-Thaksin government to power. Embedded in their cause was the long-running narrative of promoting "Thainess" over the adoption of Western democratic values. To PDRC supporters, any Thai opposed to such elite-managed "Thai democracy" was considered to be "stupid," if not anti-monarchy, "republican," or un-Thai.

In a survey of 315 pro- and anti-government demonstrators, the Asia Foundation found that only 5 percent of PDRC street demonstrators related "democracy" to elections or majority rule; over 60 percent responded that their primary motive in joining anti-government protests was to end "Shinawatra family rule" or "protect the monarchy." By contrast, 77 percent of UDD protesters cited "protecting democracy" or "protecting the elected government" as their motivation for demonstrating (only 4 percent cited protection for the Shinawatra family or Thaksin's return). The same survey also found that 68 percent of PDRC protesters held bachelor's or graduate degrees and enjoyed monthly incomes far higher than pro-government Red Shirt supporters, of whom only 27 percent held university degrees.[13] Suthep's camp was composed of well-heeled Bangkok elites and Democrat Party supporters from the south.

In December 2013, amid ongoing protests, 150 Democrat Party MPs resigned their seats en masse, claiming the House of Representatives was "no longer justified." A day later, Yingluck dissolved Parliament and called for another election, scheduled for February 2, 2014. Red Shirt supporters started a pro-democracy campaign around the slogan "Respect my vote." Knowing their own party had no chance to win the poll, the Democrats declared another election boycott. In southern provinces, Democrat Party supporters also blocked Pheu Thai candidates from even registering their candidacy. As before, the Democrat Party chose the "strategy of sabotaging parliamentary democracy and then complaining democracy was not working."[14] Sporadic acts of violence occurred, with each side trading blame. Rumors of a coup or royal intervention predictably surfaced.

When the election took place, the effects of the boycott and fears of violence inhibited participation. Although close to 50 percent of the electorate voted

(20.1 million people), the turnout was much lower than in previous elections. There was, in fact, minimal violence, but PDRC protesters did physically blockade polling stations in Bangkok and elsewhere to prevent voters from casting ballots. After much controversy, polling opened in many of these districts a few days later. A Pheu Thai victory assured, the Democrat Party formally challenged the results of the election that the party itself had not contested. Thailand's Constitutional Court eventually nullified the election results on the technical point that all the polling did not occur on the same day—in other words, the Court granted victory to those who had actively disrupted the polls.

The ruling put the country's executive institution in limbo. Yingluck, absent a sitting legislature, functioned as a powerless caretaker prime minister for a few weeks until she was forcibly removed by separate judicial order on the specious charge that she had abused her powers as prime minister by removing an appointed official in 2011.

Days after her removal, on May 22, 2014, the final act took place: Thailand's twelfth coup d'état since 1932 (and its second removing elected governments led by pro-Thaksin parties). During a meeting with the Pheu Thai acting prime minister—a meeting supposedly set up to negotiate a political settlement, as the planning of a coup in Thailand is illegal—the Royal Thai Army commander General Prayuth Chan-ocha, a known ally of the queen, abruptly declared sovereign control. Using ostensibly unplanned words, General Prayuth told everyone mid-meeting to "sit still" and declared: "We are taking over powers. Please do not panic." The elected officials at the meeting were then immediately detained, and government ministers were summoned to report to the military. Although no shots were fired, the military's monopoly on state weaponry, and its ability to threaten violence against any who resisted their commands, guaranteed their success.

PDRC forces cheered. They had won. Suthep called it "victory day for the Thai people." In fact, it was only a victory for opponents of democratic constitutionalism and the rule of law. The PDRC and the military had effectively "conspired to make Thailand ungovernable, and then used the chaos and discord they themselves had sown as a pretext for seizing power and denying Thai voters their democratic rights."[15] The vicious cycle had turned again—another karma-esque rebirth where weapons, not words, would again dictate the national political order.

As head of the self-appointed National Council for Peace and Order (NCPO), General Prayuth imposed martial law and appointed a rubber-stamp legislative assembly—this body, in turn, selected him as prime minister, an act endorsed by King Bhumibol. Then, over the following months, Prayuth imperiously crafted an oppressive dictatorial order unknown in Thailand for generations.

Unlike previous coups, where military leaders had delivered post-coup promises to swiftly restore civilian rule, Prayuth pledged to stay in power as long as necessary, until "political reform" was complete. Although he mouthed vague rhetoric about restoring democracy, everyone knew his actual design. Because the 2006 coup did not remove all "Thaksin influence" from the political system, this coup had to. From the perspective of Prayuth and coup supporters, majoritarian democracy had been responsible for Thaksin and Yingluck, so it had to therefore be dismantled. What followed over the next months and years, nevertheless, surprised even some in the anti-Thaksin camp.

As Thailand's ruler, Prayuth stripped the Thai people of all political and civil liberties in the name of loyalty to the monarch. No open opposition to the coup or to the NCPO was tolerated. Political gatherings were banned, including all political party activity. Thailand's relatively free media and press were harassed, threatened, and bullied into submission. Dissenting officials, professors, and students were forcibly detained for "attitude adjustment," like Orwellian thought-criminals. Prayuth encouraged heightened lèse-majesté enforcement, and the junta began to closely monitor print and social media—Big Brother was indeed watching. Regime opponents were labeled as traitors, disloyal, or "mentally ill." In fact, students reading George Orwell's *1984* in public were arrested on live TV. *The Hunger Games*, the globally popular dystopian book and film series, was banned, and Prayuth criminalized the iconic three-fingered salute from the story (Thai dissenters had adopted the gesture as a nonverbal protest against the coup). In post-coup Thailand, political life began imitating political art.

Entrenched in the career culture of the military hierarchy, Prayuth seemed to believe that Thailand's deep political divide could be transcended by the force of his authoritative command and by his orders for societal "unity" and "happiness." He dispatched military and bureaucratic underlings to organize a campaign to "restore national happiness." At the same time as he forcibly repressed all opponents with detentions, arrests, and attitude-adjustment sessions, Prayuth launched "Happiness for Thailand" events for the people. On stages across the country, officials delivered celebratory post-coup speeches while military brass bands played patriotic songs alongside dancing girls in camouflage short-shorts. Offstage, people enjoyed complimentary health check-ups, food, and free haircuts provided by the military. The junta also ordered theaters to give moviegoers free tickets to a feature film about a legendary Ayutthaya-era king, and it directed TV channels to broadcast 2014 World Cup soccer matches free of charge. To publicly communicate his dictates and policies, Prayuth began to deliver weekly addresses each Friday night, broadcast by mandate during prime time to interrupt TV soap operas.

Prayuth's public style was off-the-cuff, prone to outlandish rants and shocking statements, and accompanied by egomaniacal pomposity and fabrication. Shortly after the coup he caustically pledged that he "would not violate human rights too much." At a press conference he quipped he would "probably just execute" journalists who did not "report the truth." Regarding university professors critical of restrictions on academic freedom, he said, "If someone finds a gun and shoots them, or throws a grenade at them, well, they have to live with that."[16]

Out of "love for the nation," Prayuth also wrote two songs. The first, "Returning Happiness to the People," was produced by the junta as a music video featuring cameo montages of sympathetic Thai celebrities singing each line in turn. The second, "Because You Are Thailand," he wrote as a 2016 New Year's gift to the Thai people; it featured lyrics such as, "We are asking for a little more time," in reference to unrealized political reforms. Eighteen months after the coup, Prayuth bragged to the world about a government poll indicating that "99 percent" of Thailand's people were "happy" with the government's performance. Internationally, among his diplomatic equivalents and international investors, Thailand's new chief executive cultivated no confidence. To all but his dearest supporters, Prayuth was an embarrassment to the Thai nation.

In terms of foreign relations, Prayuth and his supporters ridiculed Western governments who called on Thailand to restore civil liberties, elections, and inclusive politics. It "saddens me," said Prayuth, that "the United States does not understand the way we work."[17] He moved Thailand toward China, a country he openly admired. Prayuth was unable to extradite Thaksin, who remained abroad. As for Yingluck, still at home, he leveled court charges of official negligence over her ill-fated rice-pledging scheme. If convicted, the former prime minister could face a ten-year prison sentence.

Regarding actual political reform, Prayuth produced few results. He champions "absolute democracy," a vague term that somehow reconciles monarchy and "Thainess" with various nouns of liberal democracy. His first attempt to rewrite the constitution for "absolute democracy" failed when the junta openly disagreed with its own appointed charter drafters over how to define "citizen."[18] The failed draft included language to establish an unelected "National Morality Assembly" that would monitor all elected officials. Ultimately, the delay over the charter proved convenient to Prayuth, who showed little enthusiasm to deliver on his coup-day promise to restore elections. Moreover, with the ailing King Bhumibol approaching his ninetieth birthday, Prayuth's grand design from the beginning was likely to stay in power long enough to manage the next monarchical succession.

INSTITUTIONS AND SOCIAL GROUPS

Monarchy

Theoretically and legally apolitical, the Thai monarch is the national symbol, the supreme patron who reigns over all, and the leader of the Buddhist religion. The monarchy's prestige and veneration grew following the coronation of the current king, Bhumibol Adulyadej, the kingdom's longest-reigning monarch. During the early decades of his reign, the king cultivated a role as patron of rural development. He intervened publicly in politics on rare occasions, such as in 1973. In the 1980s, King Bhumibol supported the government of Prime

Minister Prem Tinsulanond during two military coup attempts. In 1991, he chose not to publicly intervene to stop a successful coup against Chatichai Choonhavan. Operating outside of constitutional authority, monarchical interventions followed mass protests in 1992 and 2005, altering political outcomes each time. More recently, royal antipathy for Thaksin has allowed coup leaders in 2006 and 2014 to operate with the monarch's blessing.

As a political actor, the king's influence is best understood through what is described as "network monarchy"—a "parapolitical institution" or "subsystem" in Thai politics inclusive of privy councilors and royalist allies who advocate illiberal values over democratic principles, and the leadership of "good men" over elected politicians.[19] The network monarchy enjoys significant institutional autonomy. During periods of political normalcy or instability, the king's proxies (such as Prem) can involve themselves directly in national problem-solving. They operate with tremendous latitude and no vertical accountability.

Although the king does not stand "above politics" in actuality, this idea is publicly cultivated every year on December 5, which is the king's birthday and a major national holiday. Each year, near Bangkok's Grand Palace, before celebratory crowds of up to 100,000 people or more, the king delivers a hopeful, fatherly speech advocating Buddhist values, identifying national priorities, and chiding bickering politicians. In his famous 1997 speech, for example—made during the gut-wrenching Asian economic crisis—the king declared that the nation had lost its way trying to achieve "tiger economy" status. He offered a new vision of "Sufficiency Economy," a political-economic philosophy of moderation that he had developed with his advisers. At other times he has reproved elected officials, blaming them for the country's failing politics.

The monarch, though not above politics, is beyond public accountability. Long-standing lèse-majesté laws shield the king and royal family from public criticism. Thai intellectuals and common citizens who comment critically about the king or royal family members have faced charges and detention for offending the dignity of the monarch. A London-style royal paparazzi does not exist in Thailand. Discretion, self-censorship, and self-imposed exile made lèse-majesté court cases fairly rare until recently.

Increasingly, lèse-majesté has been abused as a political tool. While only one case of lèse-majesté went to prosecution in 2000, hundreds are now filed each year. In 2011, Thailand's government announced campaign rules that forbade any mention of the monarchy during elections. It later issued a warning that anyone who "likes" or "shares" a Facebook comment insulting the Thai monarchy could face prosecution—and foreigners are not exempt from the law and may face prosecution if they go to Thailand. The announcement governing social media came just days after a sixty-one-year-old former truck driver from Bangkok was convicted of insulting the queen via text message.[20] He died of cancer a year later while still in prison.

Squaring the practice of lèse-majesté with liberal notions of free speech remains a sensitive subject in Thailand. Many Thais see no contradiction; others openly favor it over democratic values. Local critics and international human rights groups condemn the practice as draconian and wholly incompatible with free speech. Some argue that Thailand's "defamation regime" is a potent form of discursive power used by the state to shape how Thai society understands "Thainess."[21]

The Thais' veneration of their monarch raises concerns about a looming succession crisis. Crown Prince Vajiralongkorn, who has been groomed to assume the throne, has long been criticized for his lack of commitment and discipline. Thrice married, he has been the subject of hush-hush conversations and rumors among Thais. The king has elevated his daughter, Princess Sirindhorn, to the rank of *maha chakri* (crown princess), a move that could qualify her to serve as queen or regent. That Prince Vajiralongkorn is believed to enjoy confidence with Thaksin adds a layer of complexity to the inevitable event of succession.[22]

Constitutions

Thailand suffers from endless constitutional change and claims of constitutional illegitimacy. Nothing at the present time indicates that its troubled history with constitutional change will be resolved soon. Almost all of the major incidents in modern Thai political history (e.g., political crises, coups, mass protests) have included some dimension of constitutional crisis. While there is a value placed on the rule-of-law concept, enduring agreement on basic law has yet to be realized. Moreover, the impulse to resort to extraconstitutional means to resolve political crises (namely, military coup and royal intervention) undermines the consolidation of democratic constitutionalism and the rule of law in Thailand.

Since 1932, Thailand has been governed under twenty constitutions, of which fewer than half were democratic and based on a parliamentary model with an accountable executive. In the 1990s a public consensus emerged for a constitution that allowed for a strong executive who was still accountable to an elected Parliament. In 1996 and 1997, a "People's Committee" that included experts, academics, and members of civil society drafted the 1997 constitution. The result was a document perceived to be the most legitimate, inclusive, and potentially sustainable democratic constitution ever promulgated in Thailand's long constitutional history. Nevertheless, because Thaksin's TRT was believed to have benefited from the 1997 People's Constitution, which favored larger parties and stronger central authority, the 2006 coup group abrogated the constitution as one of its first acts upon taking power. The 2007 constitution, which was itself written by military-appointed elites, was similarly scrapped by the military following the 2014 coup. The hastily drafted 2014 interim constitution gave boundless power to Prayuth under its Article 44, rendering him unaccountable to even military courts.

Thailand's coup supporters who have placed their hopes in Prayuth's government believe that constitutional reform is the key to engineering some lasting system of Thai-styled semi-democracy. Given that a majority of the electorate desires to remain enfranchised with the right to choose the country's leaders through democratic elections, one would be foolish to wager that a Prayuth-era constitution will be Thailand's last. Going forward, political conflict in Thailand will likely include elements of constitutional disagreement over claims of illegitimate provisions, promulgation, or abrogation. At the core of the country's political instability lies the fundamental inability of basic law to endure or institutionalize. "Constitutionalism," after all, is Thailand's "political disease."[23] Until it is cured, the practice of resorting to extraconstitutional measures to resolve constitutionally driven political crises is likely to continue for the foreseeable future.

Military

Since the overthrow of the absolute monarchy, the Thai military has played the dominant role in Thai politics. Of the fifty-plus cabinets organized since 1932, more than half can be classified as military or military-dominated governments. The reasons for military dominance include the weakness of civilian governments and the fact that the military is the most highly organized institution in the kingdom. They also have weapons of war to force compliance.

Because of perceived external and internal threats to Thai security, the military has proclaimed itself the only institution capable of protecting Thai sovereignty. Moreover, the hierarchical nature of the military is congruent with the tendencies of Thai political culture. Because Bangkok, as Thailand's primary city, dominates every aspect of the country's political and economic life, the military has needed to control only this one city in order to control the entire kingdom.

Civilian governments, especially those coalesced around provincial parties, have traditionally faced difficulties maintaining good relations with top generals. Because the military is factionalized itself, forging alliances with one set of generals can pose trouble later. Owing to their own previous military experiences, Chatichai, Chavalit, Chamlong, and Thaksin all bore ties with particular military factions that proved consequential later, altering the course of events during the political crises they each faced. Standing above all the military, of course, is the venerable privy councilor Prem Tinsulanond, the retired general with unparalleled approbation from the crown and singular influence over the direction of Thai political development.

After Black May 1992, it appeared for a time that the Thai public had lost all tolerance for military intervention. However, the 2006 coup d'état restored the military's domestic political power. Following coups, the military and its supporters engage in international propaganda campaigns in the attempt to gain international legitimacy for a power seizure. Invariably, as they did in 2006 (and later in 2014), they claim the coup was needed to "protect" or "restore democracy."[24]

Eighty years after it toppled the country's absolute monarchy, Thailand's military remains the country's most formidable and secure state institution. Highly politicized and forever royalist, its influence casts a long praetorian shadow on the country's political future.

Bureaucracy

For most of the contemporary era, Thailand has been a bureaucratic polity with the arena of politics remaining within the bureaucracy itself. The bureaucracy has been the bedrock of stability in a political system where top leadership positions have changed unpredictably. Although elections and coups may bring new factions into power, the bureaucracy continues its conservative policy role with little change in direction. Thai bureaucrats remain major actors in the country's political life, as demonstrated by their sizable support for the anti-Thaksin movement, because of the continuity they provide to a system with frequent changes of leadership at the top.

The bureaucracy's formerly exclusive role has been widened in recent years by the new role of technocrats, who have attained important positions and brought a more rational style to policymaking. These highly trained technocrats lost some of their luster in 1997 when the Thai economy collapsed, at least partly because they did not adequately interpret the warning signs of the coming disaster. Higher salaries in Thailand's growing private sector have increasingly depleted the talent pool in the bureaucracy that formerly boasted Thailand's best and brightest.

Parliament and Political Parties

Over time, Thailand's bicameral Parliament evolved from a rubber-stamp body for a ruling party or strongman to an arena of genuine political debate and legislative activity. It became less peripheral to governmental decision-making during the democratic period in the 1970s as well as in the 1980s under Prime Minister Prem, who allowed the Parliament to act more independently, particularly on economic matters. Although characterized by frequent changes in its structure and membership, Thailand's national assembly has more actively engaged in public debate about important issues than other legislatures in the region.

One of the reasons that Thai political life is so lively and contentious is because parliamentary power matters. Establishing a parliamentary majority, and the corresponding right of that majority to choose a prime minister and cabinet, rank among the high-stakes events in the Thai political system. Because governments change so frequently, coalition forming can be more politically significant than actual lawmaking functions, which, though consequential, are not prone to wide shifts in ideology following elections. Access to government coffers is crucial. Crafty veteran politician Banharn Silpa-archa once let slip that, "for a politician, being in the opposition is like starving yourself to death."[25] Though the Parliament was formerly dominated by bureaucrats, military figures, and local elites, in recent decades its membership has diversified, with greater representation from the business community, provincial political families, women, and (owing to party-list ballots) technocrats, academics, and other public figures.

With few exceptions it has not been particularly useful to visualize Thai political parties as falling along a neat left-right political spectrum, because many parties fall into the moderate or nonideological middle. Until the recent emergence of Thaksin-oriented parties, ideological platforms have not been paramount in Thai campaigns, because voters tended to favor candidates who served their district or regional interests first. Thai Rak Thai differed in this respect in that its populist message appealed across districts and regions. It conceived its patronage system as national rather than local or regional. A key distinguishing feature of TRT was not ideology, but its desire to expand patronage in wider dimensions than previously successful parties had. Another key distinction of TRT was its new "professional party" approach to electoral politics: that is, it prioritized savvy marketing of the party as a media product over rigid commitments to ideals, platforms, or maintaining cumbersome membership rolls.[26] Thai political parties today argue more about the rules of the game than about ideologically driven policies.

The Democrat Party is the longest-surviving party in Thailand, with over sixty years behind it. Its base was and remains in urban Bangkok and the country's southern provinces. Having institutionalized as a party, it weathers changes in leadership and can withstand long periods in the opposition. It tends to be a party that is either leading the government or leading the opposition. When it does lead the government, its policies tend to satisfy bureaucrats, the military, traditional elites, and international investors. The party enjoys strong relations with royal institutions, and its members often boast degrees from top institutions at home and abroad. Although it is the most institutionalized party in Thailand, the Democrats have never enjoyed a parliamentary majority. In fact, their last plurality victory occurred over twenty years ago, in 1992.

Today the Democrats occupy one pole of the country's now bifurcated party system. The July 2011 general elections reflected the increasing polarization of Thai politics and affirmed that the weak party coalitions of the 1980s and 1990s were a feature of the past. Of the available 500 seats in the national assembly, 424 (85 percent) went to only two parties: Pheu Thai (265 seats) and the Democrat Party (159 seats). The remaining seats went to nine other parties, seven of which combined to occupy a meager 23 seats.

Thaksin's party machine (TRT, PPP, and Pheu Thai in succession) won more seats than any party in five straight elections (2001, 2005, 2006, 2007, and 2011). Election victories for Thaksin's camp continued through 2011 with no end in sight, in spite of attempts by opponents to reverse its dominance via military coup, constitutional revision, judicial activism, protests, plots, and the intimidation of its supporters by armed forces—not to mention legitimate party competition. Whether or not Pheu Thai supporters will abide a post-2014 coup constitution written to constrain majority rule remains to be seen.

Absent an elected Parliament, and because of severe restrictions on political party activity, Thailand today functions with a fully appointed National Legislative Assembly (NLA). The NLA is compliant with Prayuth's objectives; the rubber-stamp Parliament has returned.

STATE-SOCIETY RELATIONS AND DEMOCRACY

Until the 1980s, scholars referred to Thai politics as a "bureaucratic polity," a polity in which politics took place within the bureaucracy and where extrabureaucratic institutions were negligible. External institutions, such as the Parliament and political parties, were deemed to have little influence over the state's policy decisions. The bureaucratic polity included the military, as many of the generals held important government posts (including the position of prime minister). The state, then, was considered strong and autonomous, and independent of such societal organizations as political parties, business associations, farmers' groups, and labor unions. The enduring pillars of the Thai state— "nation, religion, and king"—provided the ideological troika upon which state supremacy was based. When extrabureaucratic groups began to emerge, they were initially co-opted, manipulated, or oppressed by the bureaucracy, which used the military as its controlling force. By integrating the military into the political process, the government established a broad-based regime. Utilizing both collaborative and coercive forces, the state increased its stability and capacity.

Since the student-led revolt against the military in 1973, however, Thai political institutions have increased in number and have broadened their bases considerably, strengthening the roles of the legislature, political parties, and business associations while reducing direct military domination. As societal groups have come to play a more important role in Thai politics, the state has lost some of its autonomy and consequently become weaker.

The expectation many Thai elites have for state autonomy stems at least partially from the past success of Thai authorities in preserving the state's independence and sovereignty—that having averted colonial rule, established a generally peaceful country, and met the basic needs of the majority of the citizenry, the Thai state had proven its effectiveness. Nevertheless, if autonomy is a key variable for assessing strength, the Thai state is weak in the sense that officials

who make authoritative decisions are not insulated from the state-based patronage networks upon which they depend. Thailand's state officials are integrated into some of the country's most established networks of patron-client
exchange. These relationships act as links between bureaucrats and traditional
networks in old business, agriculture, labor, the aristocracy, and the intelligentsia. Quasi-state enterprises, including public utilities and their organized employees, are also tied into long-standing networks of patronage that emanate
from the state. The loss of these networks threatens the erosion of associated
state institutions and, thus, state strength.

Thai authorities thus expect autonomy from societal actors, especially rural
citizens who have been historically more politically passive than radical. Because rural citizens constitute a majority of the population and have made relatively few demands on the central authorities, this notion of passivity has been
central to the argument that the Thai state can (and should) act autonomously.
Many state elites began to hold the rural electorate in contempt for their increasing assertiveness in the political system in the 1990s, particularly through
their participation in party politics, vote buying, and organized protests against
state projects, such as rural dams. Among traditional elites, the development of
a Thai version of the agrarian myth creates a static view of rural Thailand—a
view that *chao naa* (farmer peasants), *baan* (village community), *phophiang*
(sufficiency), and historically based rural contentedness are (and always will be)
the essence of "Thainess." This view contrasts with Thaksin's populist assump-
tions that rural producers desire a modern lifestyle commensurate with that
experienced by urbanites, not a return to some bucolic past measured simply
by a sufficient supply of "fish in the water, and rice in the fields."[27]

Thaksin Shinawatra's TRT network of patronage worked to displace many
of the traditional channels of bureaucratic and state patronage. Much of the
resentment that state elites held toward Thaksin was due to his disruption of
the business-as-usual operations of a state-society patronage apparatus that
had weathered so many changes in political leadership before. Thaksin's efforts
to reprioritize state goals and create new state agencies caused antipathy and
confusion among traditional bureaucrats. His bold attempts provoked a forceful response. As predicted by one Thai scholar well before Thaksin's rise, the
conservative alliance of the military, technocrats, and old-style business elites,
when threatened, may turn to "General Prem's influence to put pressure on any
government which they deemed unpopular or unresponsive to their demands."[28] Thaksin, the most skilled and powerful political figure to challenge
this conservative alliance, now lives in exile, a fugitive from the Thai justice
system.

A state's legitimacy is a potent factor accounting for the strength of the
state. Through socialization and the deliberate exploitation of the king's popularity by whichever regime is in power, the Thai state has become identified
with the king and Buddhism, resulting in an extraordinarily high level of accep-

tance.[29] Questions about the strength of the monarchy (as an institution) in contrast to the strength of King Bhumibol (as an individual figure) will face Thai society in the future. Absent the aura of the king to bask in, state authorities could find challenges from elected governments far more difficult to repel in the future.

Constitutionalism is a possible alternative anchor of state strength in the absence or loss of royal aura due to succession. However, until common agreement on actual constitutional arrangements is achieved, implemented, and able to endure political crises, much of the strength of the Thai state will depend on the monarchy and on the royal approbation of state institutions and practices.

With respect to democracy, Thailand's traditional culture, with its emphasis on deference to authority and hierarchical social relations, has not proven conducive to stable democratic rule. A considerable degree of skepticism exists among state elites about the "cultural appropriateness" of majoritarian democracy. In the past, the Thais' democratic orientations have been formalistic in the sense that they have had little depth. Other values—such as security, development, deference, personalism, and economic stability—have often taken precedence over values more directly related to citizen participation in governmental affairs.

Even as traditional notions of deference and hierarchy have given way to modern notions of political equality, the outcome in Thailand has been less a Western-style "civic culture" centered on rights and laws than a "political society" where special interests and voting blocs seek to control the state's resources. In such a state-society arrangement, "benefits flow primarily from connections, manipulation, calculation, and expediency," rather than from "civic virtue" or claim to "universal rights."[30] Thus, conditioned by the influence of Thai political culture, attempts to democratize Thailand have produced, at best, a competitive-oriented, patronage-driven electocracy; at worst, they have created a bifurcated polity with ever-hardening cleavages between traditional elites who are accustomed to state power and populist newcomers desperate to access and allocate the state's resources so long denied to them.

In spite of repeated coups, most Thais have always desired democracy. Results from opinion polls taken in 2002 and 2006 (four months before the 2006 coup) revealed that eight in ten Thais were generally satisfied with democracy and believed it was "suitable" for Thailand.[31] It is meaningful that Thais often justify the country's frequent military coups to foreign audiences as necessary to "save democracy"; that mass protests are viewed as rightful democratic expressions to advance "democratic political reform"; and that constitutions are tinkered with to "enhance democracy" or to "make democracy more stable."

The sources of Thailand's inability to consolidate democracy are many. One source fueling Thailand's democratic instability may be the unrealistic expectations Thai society places on democratic governance. As successful democracies have learned, the utility of democracy is its ability to manage conflict, to demand government accountability, and to peacefully transfer power from one set of rulers to another. Democratic practice outside of Thailand has not escaped the hazards of abuse of power, corruption, and official mismanagement; nor does it necessarily produce democratic outcomes of equitable resource allocation. The difference between Thailand and established democracies is that the latter tend to resolve political crises without turning to extraconstitutional methods. Unrealistic expectations that democracy should be orderly, produce completely fair outcomes, and be devoid of political crisis produce disappointment and lead to justification of extraconstitutional means to solve political gridlock.

Another possible source of Thailand's democratic instability may be too little respect for the principle of the rule of law. Evidence for this source comes from the verbal justifications used to dismiss existing law by those who find its presence an obstacle to political goals (e.g., Thaksin's extrajudicial killings during his 2003 drug war, or elite support of military or royal intervention to resolve political crises). Such justifications can stem from a cultural milieu where power often justifies itself (through karmic beliefs of rebirth and fate), producing in turn a societal tolerance for rule by law, rather than the unyielding defense of the rule of law.

A final source of democratic instability may come from endless debate over constitutional arrangements. All sides in these debates tend to interpret their preferred arrangement as democratic. What the protagonists fight over are the precise institutional arrangements believed necessary to produce some magical, durable democratic order. The false assumption underneath this volatile debate is that institutional arrangements matter more than realistic expectations of democracy. It is possible that an enduring democratic order will escape Thailand as long as societal norms respecting the limits of democracy are overridden by unrealistic expectations that some perfect institutional formula for constitutional democracy actually exists. An enduring democratic order will exist in Thailand only when political losers transcend their impulse to turn to extraconstitutional military intervention, royal trump cards, or politicization of the judiciary *and* when political winners transcend the impulse to abrogate or reengineer democratic constitutions or disregard constitutional limits on executive power.

ECONOMY AND DEVELOPMENT

In the postwar period, Thailand's economic performance was unimpressive until a 1957 military coup ushered in a new set of economic policies under the authoritarian leadership of General Sarit Thanarat. During much of the Cold War, Thailand's neighbors were embroiled in conflict and suffering economically. In this context, it can be said that Thailand "won" the Vietnam War. While the war left Vietnam, Cambodia, and Laos economically devastated, and left the United States a weaker global power, Thailand emerged with improved economic infrastructure, roads, and airports, and also with transferred technology—a result of over a decade of US military aid, development projects, and circulated cash.

During the 1970s and 1980s, Thailand sustained a 7 percent rate of annual economic growth, a pace equaled by only a few other developing nations. More remarkably, the kingdom's economic growth between 1987 and 1996 averaged close to 10 percent, higher than in any other country during that period. During these boom years, inflation also stayed under 5 percent. The 1997 Asian economic crisis, which began in Thailand, brought this rapid growth to a halt. Recovery under Thaksin returned Thailand to a pattern of growth, but a sluggish economy has been the consequence of political instability since the 2006 military coup.

Coincident with these high growth rates in the boom years was an increase in the export sector, which in the late 1980s grew by almost 25 percent each year. Foreign investment grew rapidly, with Japan, Taiwan, the United States, Hong Kong, and South Korea as the leading investors. Manufacturing also replaced agriculture during this period in terms of share of the country's gross domestic product.

Although over 60 percent of the Thai people are involved in the agricultural sphere of the economy, the number of those in rice farming is decreasing. Thai farmers have diversified into crops such as various vegetables, fruits, maize, tapioca, coffee, flowers, sugar, and rubber, as well as livestock. The rise of agribusiness processing and related industry has also pulled ruralites out of the fields. Although farming areas have not developed as rapidly as urban areas, the standard of living in the countryside has improved noticeably since the 1970s. A peasant class of rural producers no longer meaningfully exists.[32] Nevertheless, the urban bias of Thai economic development is clear from both the emphasis on manufacturing and the higher percentage of budget allocations centered on Bangkok.

The factors responsible for the kingdom's economic successes have included a commitment to market-oriented, export-driven policies carried out by highly trained and generally conservative technocrats as well as general policy continuity. For the most part, officials were not as steeped in personalistic, clientelist politics as were their peers in neighboring countries. Where corruption did exist, officials and politicians earning kickbacks or skimming from contracts generally plowed their ill-gained wealth back into the booming Thai economy. Moreover, although coups have been a standard mechanism for changing governments, they have rarely undermined the continuity of macroeconomic policy controlled by senior technocrats.

The vital involvement of Thailand's Chinese minority cannot be overstated as a factor explaining the vibrancy of the economy. This dynamic minority has provided leadership in banking, export-import manufacturing, industrialization, monetary policy, foreign investment, and diversification. The autonomy granted the Chinese has resulted in an entrepreneurial minority that reinvests its profits into the kingdom, with comparatively little capital leaving the country. As investments in Asia have grown, the Chinese have used filial and cultural ties to China to expand Thai investments abroad. For much of the 1990s, the single largest foreign investor in China was a Thai agribusiness company, Charoen Pokphand, founded by overseas Chinese in Bangkok.

Population control is another factor influencing economic success. In just one generation, Thailand managed to lower its population growth rate from 3.0 percent to 0.5 percent. The decrease resulted from a massive government-sponsored education program that has changed attitudes about the optimum family size and made birth-control products available throughout the kingdom. The lack of population pressure has resulted in a higher standard of living for families, higher educational attainment and literacy, and lower poverty rates. According to the United Nations Development Program (UNDP), the percentage of Thai people living in poverty between 1990 and 2004 was 14 percent, compared to 27 percent in Indonesia, 29 percent in Vietnam, and 43 percent in the Philippines over the same period.

During the economic boom, rules favoring the expansion of foreign investment made possible a capital influx from industrial nations. Thailand became further integrated into the world capitalist system and gained access to foreign credit and technical assistance, in addition to enjoying flourishing trade relations throughout the world. Thailand has been a favorite site for production plants owned by Japanese, South Korean, and Taiwanese firms. Under pressure from foreign governments and international financial institutions, Thailand liberalized its capital markets too far, however, sowing the seeds of loose credit, bad loans, and shaky investments that contributed to the 1997 economic crisis.

The nearly three decades of sustained economic development came to an abrupt halt in mid-1997 after the Chavalit administration stopped propping up the Thai baht. Having futilely spent billions of baht from foreign reserves on a lost cause, on July 2, 1997, the government unpegged the baht from the US dollar and allowed it to float. Within weeks, the currency had lost 40 percent of its value. Simultaneously, the stock market suffered a precipitous decline, losing 70 percent of its value. To strengthen the economy, the Thai government accepted a $17 billion bailout from the IMF along with strict conditionality to adhere to market fundamentalism.

Many reasons for the debacle were debated in government, business, and academic circles. The long list of culprits included poor political leadership, the refusal of recent governments to make hard decisions about fiscal responsibility, pervasive corruption that blocked important infrastructure projects and educational reform, and the undisciplined opening of the economy to foreign capital. During the boom, offshore debt had also grown steadily as Thais borrowed dollars at cheaper rates than they could borrow baht. Borrowed money was often spent on real estate and a wide range of investments that offered meager returns, such as convention centers, hotels, condominiums, and private hospitals. Bad loans flourished at the end of the boom. The baht became over-valued when the dollar gained value against the yen, making Thai labor and exports more expensive and therefore less competitive. Currency speculators then bet on the devaluation of the baht, borrowing baht at one price and selling the currency back at a devalued rate, thereby making tremendous profits.

The Thai government's hope was that the devaluation would boost exports, curb imports, and cut the current account deficit. To keep the budget balanced, the Chavalit government raised the value-added tax from 7 percent to 10 percent. Interest rates were also raised to guard against a surge in inflation. These policies were in keeping with the conditionality set by the IMF. Recovery did not return. Chavalit was ousted, and Democrats, led by Chuan, were given the opportunity to steady Thailand's sinking economic ship. Democrat leaders also followed the general IMF prescriptions of implementing budget austerity and restoring inflows of foreign capital. It was not until the election of Thaksin Shinawatra in 2001 that the Thai government noticeably changed its response to the economic crisis.

Once elected, Thaksin moved to set up a national asset management company to buy most of the financial system's remaining nonperforming debt, estimated to be about $30 billion. He moved to restructure the agricultural sector by providing debt relief for farmers and funds to villages to promote income-producing activities. The debt restructuring featured a three-year suspension on debts owed by poor farmers to the state-owned Bank for Agriculture. Grants to villages amounted to about 1 million baht ($23,000) to each of the nation's 70,000 villages. The Keynesian stimulus policies worked. Inflation was generally kept in check, exports expanded, and the rural economy experienced an unprecedented flow of government money.

Following the 2006 coup, the rate of the Thai economy's recovery slowed into the 4 percent range in 2007 and 2008. Concerns over the coup group's aggressive promotion of Sufficiency Economy waned, however, as the policies associated with its promotion proved to be vague goals rather than concrete measures. The global financial crisis caused Thailand's economy to contract by over 2 percent in 2009. The economy recovered in 2010 with 7.8 percent growth, only to be stalled again by the massive floods of 2011. Under the post-coup Prayuth government, economic growth has fallen to an anemic 1 percent. Through it all, Thailand's poverty rate has declined, but overall economic inequality remains among the highest in the developing world. When adjusted for income inequality, Thailand's Human Development Index (HDI) figure of 0.72 (the highest in mainland Southeast Asia) drops to 0.58 (on par with Brazil, Mexico, and the Philippines).[33]

Observers also worry that Thailand may be destined for a "middle-income trap." All of the recent governments in Thailand—the Thaksin-linked governments, Abhisit's Democrat-led coalition, and both post-coup governments—have shown a commitment to populist policies. Allowing Thailand's have-nots greater access to state benefits is a logical short-term political strategy, but neglecting long-overdue public investments in education and worker productivity, failing to reform the country's regressive tax system, and doing little about endemic corruption is a formula for economic stagnation in the long run.[34]

FOREIGN RELATIONS

Following the Cold War, Thailand's foreign policy perceptions shifted regarding regional or great-power threats to Thai security and the decline of the US security role in Southeast Asia. Thailand's sustained economic development and the rise of nonbureaucratic interests in the political sphere have unambiguously pushed foreign policy into the economic realm. For most of the 1990s and 2000s, the military reduced its role in foreign policy in favor of the Ministry of Foreign Affairs, cabinet ministers, and political party leaders. The increased profile of some of Thailand's top economic diplomats also brought the country international esteem. One such diplomat served as head of the WTO for three years and led the United Nations Conference on Trade and Development (UNCTAD) for eight. In the past twenty years, foreign affairs in Thailand have been dominated by trade liberalization negotiations with the United States, the European Union, China, Japan, and ASEAN.

Thailand increasingly relates to the United States as an equal rather than as a client. As the Cold War ended, Thai foreign policy lessened security dependence on the United States, asserted equidistance in its relations with allies and adversaries, and launched a dramatically new Indochina policy without seeking US support. In economic relations with the United States, Thailand became more assertive in bilateral negotiations over trade, intellectual property rights enforcement, and general economic policy independence (the exception being the IMF rescue package for Thailand during the 1997 economic crisis, which US officials strongly encouraged).

Major aspects of Thai-US relations also include joint military exercises; cooperation on suppressing narcotics trafficking, international crime, and terrorism; coordination on refugee matters involving Burmese activists and Hmong groups fleeing Laos; and ongoing support for educational exchange and the Peace Corps. Thailand provided some logistical support to the United States' war on terror but never became a major military partner. Cooperation in tracking suspected terrorists proved worthwhile, however, when Hambali, a top al-Qaeda-linked bomb plotter, was discovered hiding in Ayutthaya and arrested in 2003.

The single most important issue in recent Thai-US relations, however, has been negotiations over a United States–Thailand free trade agreement. Initiated by Thaksin and George W. Bush at an Asia-Pacific Economic Cooperation (APEC) meeting in 2003, the agreement showed some early progress. Business communities on both sides actively promoted it, countered by an equally active resistance from Thai and international NGOs. Political instability after 2006 stalled the agreement. More recently, Thailand chose not to be party to agreements establishing the Trans-Pacific Partnership (TPP) finalized in 2015, although it has recently indicated interest in joining. It has been more enthusiastic in its support of regional integration, such as in the new ASEAN Economic Community (AEC), launched on December 31, 2015.

Military coups, such as those in 2006 and 2014, put US diplomats in an awkward position. They denounced coups as undemocratic and harmful, yet at the same time trod carefully so as not to become the defenders, patrons, or saviors of the embattled pro-Thaksin parties. Thaksin's murky status that tied him to corruption, undemocratic practices, and alienation by Thailand's power elite weighed heavily on the US position regarding the coup. The common refrain from Washington and the US embassy in Bangkok was a call for the coup leaders to "return the country to democracy as soon as possible." Stronger US criticisms of the 2014 coup landed two American ambassadors in hot water with the Thai public. In late 2015, Thailand's government launched a lèse-majesté probe into comments made by US ambassador Glyn Davies to journalists in Bangkok.

Even when elected governments are in power, Thailand's ongoing political crisis complicates Thai relations with Washington. Snubbing Thailand in favor of a visit to democratic Indonesia, Secretary of State Hillary Clinton's first diplomatic trip to Southeast Asia left Thailand—and Abhisit Vejjajiva's fledgling government—off the itinerary. Barack Obama later visited Indonesia as part of the 2011 East Asian Summit in Bali, where he met with Yingluck. Months later, the United States granted Thaksin a visa, prompting an online firestorm by Yellow Shirt supporters in Thailand.

Since the passing of the Cold War, abrupt changes have come to Thailand's relations with its mainland Southeast Asian neighbors as well. Chatichai's initial efforts toward normalizing relations with Vietnam, Laos, and Cambodia were followed by support for the three countries' membership in ASEAN—a feat accomplished before the 1990s concluded. Lingering border disputes with Laos were also resolved as Cold War tensions dissipated. The completion of an Australian-funded bridge across the Mekong River, which forms much of the border between the two countries, became a symbol of improving relations between the two countries. It was the first of three such bridges, all of far greater economic significance to landlocked Laos than to Thailand.

Thailand's relations with Cambodia also deepened during the 1990s. Foreign investment from Thailand brought Cambodia needed foreign exchange. Thai-driven investment in textiles, mobile phones, satellite communications, and other industries contributed to Cambodia's gradual economic recovery. Other industries driven by Thai investment—border casinos, brothels, and logging operations—proved less encouraging. The degree of rising Thai foreign investment in Cambodia was demonstrated in 2003 when a popular Thai actress claimed that Cambodia's famed Angkor Wat temple complex actually belonged to Thailand. The comment sparked unruly anti-Thai riots in Phnom Penh. Images of Cambodian youths vandalizing Thai-owned businesses and interests spread anger across Thailand.

Mutual anger also erupted in 2008 through 2011 over Preah Vihear, an Angkor-era temple set on a cliff near the Cambodian-Thai border. Troops on both sides mobilized after Thailand objected to Phnom Penh's application to have the temple designated a World Heritage Site by the United Nations Educational, Scientific, and Cultural Organization (UNESCO). Multiple skirmishes over a three-year period resulted in nationalist rhetoric, firefights, and multiple deaths on both sides. The legality of ownership of Preah Vihear had long been settled in Cambodia's favor in the 1960s by the International Court of Justice (ICJ). Much of the dispute related to conflicting claims over border demarcations in the temple area. Phnom Penh's application was approved by UNESCO in 2011, and the ICJ once again intervened by ordering each side to remove troops beyond a newly designated demilitarized zone.

In the new international era, Thailand also supported Burma's application to ASEAN as part of its "constructive engagement" strategy with the Burmese regime. The purpose of this approach, which countered the policies of most of the world's nations, was to reduce tensions between the two countries and to gain access to Burmese resources. The latter objective transcended any particular government that has controlled Thailand. Thaksin enjoyed strong relations with Burma's ruling junta, and Burma was the first country the 2006 coup leaders visited following Thaksin's ouster. After political reforms began in 2010 in Myanmar, the released and newly elected parliamentarian Aung San Suu Kyi traveled to Thailand in an event that irritated Myanmar's top brass. After meeting with Prime Minister Yingluck, the Nobel laureate visited cheering Burmese refugees stuck in camps near the Thailand-Burma border. Thai relations with Myanmar have centered largely on mutual economic interests. How Prayuth will respond to a democratically elected government led by Aung San Suu Kyi remains an open question.

In regional affairs, Thailand strongly supported the post–Cold War initiative to create the ASEAN Free Trade Area (AFTA). A response to the European Union and the creation of the North American Free Trade Agreement (NAFTA), AFTA was viewed as a move to reduce economic dependence on Japan and East Asia. With a market of 320 million people in a rapidly growing region, AFTA sought to expand trade by lowering trade tariffs. AFTA's economic significance to individual countries, however, remained minimal, because the partners shared similar economic and export profiles, and the volume of bilateral trade each enjoyed with Japan, the United States, the European Union, and China far exceeded levels of intra-AFTA trade. Thailand's role as a leader within ASEAN has suffered as a result of the country's ongoing political turmoil. Increasingly, a more democratic and confident Indonesia has emerged as a regional leader. Indonesia is the only G-20 member in ASEAN.

Of all the changes in the new era, China's rise as a power is arguably the most consequential international development for Thailand. Concerns about the Asian giant, however, are almost exclusively in the realm of trade competitiveness and economic relations, not direct security interests. Thailand's relationship with China improved markedly after the Vietnam War, but even more so following the Cold War. In particular, the new environment expanded people-to-people contacts between Sino-Thais and Chinese business interests. Once a liability in Thai cultural circles, the Chinese heritage of prominent business families in Bangkok became a cause for celebration and resulted in visits to ancestral villages in China's coastal provinces. Cultural goodwill translated into good business.

As part of the ASEAN Plus Three process that launched the ASEAN-China Free Trade Agreement (ACFTA), Thailand enjoyed "early harvest" provisions of free trade with China in agriculture and other sectors by 2003, seven years before the agreement went into effect.[35] As a consequence, an increased flow of fruits and vegetables has transformed Thailand's agriculture markets, but it has also put stress on its environment. In northern Thailand, for example, small-scale tangerine producers have been pushed out by large, plantation-size tangerine exporters who employ low-paid Burmese migrants. Cheap produce from China also affects Thai producers.

The new international era has also witnessed Thai troops participating as UN peacekeeping forces in East Timor. Thailand also won praise from the United Nations for efficient handling of the 2004 Indian Ocean tsunami. Following the disaster, Thaksin Shinawatra led the international push to create an Indian Ocean tsunami warning system. In 2008, when Burma's military rulers initially refused foreign aid following Cyclone Nargis, Thailand helped to convince the regime to allow it to act as an intermediary to funnel aid to the country. Thai relations with Muslim states, on the other hand, are often strained due to perceptions of harsh, ineffective, and unfair policies toward Thailand's Muslim population in the deep south.

CONCLUSION

Thailand today is fundamentally different from what it was decades ago, when a military-dominated bureaucracy fully controlled society. Although the military has returned to power twice since 2006, the challenges facing traditional political elites to retain control of the system have only increased. Economic development, evolving expectations for democracy, and extended periods of parliamentary governance have brought new groups into the political system. Conservative state elites still wield sufficient power to alter events, but unless societal norms for representative government, accountable leadership, and civil liberties completely disappear among the majority of Thais, the country's bureaucrats, generals, and royals will find constant frustration in trying to undermine societal attempts to establish democratic institutions.

Thailand's future is nothing if not daunting. The ailing health of King Bhumibol and the events that his inevitable passing could put into motion may lead to even greater unpredictability and instability. Reveals one Thai political scientist in the *Journal of Democracy*: "All Thais fear but do not dare say in public, that Thailand's future is up for grabs. What happens after the current king leaves the scene could be the most wrenching crisis yet."[36] Another confirms that "the monarchy's future looks precarious indeed."[37] Over their modern history, the people of Thailand have improved their economic condition even as they escaped foreign occupation, revolution, violent tyranny, and interstate war. What they cannot seem to escape is cyclical political crisis, perpetual constitutional change, and the uncomfortable sense that 1932's promise of democracy seems as distant as ever.

NOTES

1. Based on 2014 Human Development Index (HDI) figures. See Tables 1.1 and 1.2 in chapter 1.

2. Thai political scientist Chai-Anan Samudavanija is famously credited with first describing this pattern.

3. Thongchai Winichakul, *Siam Mapped: The History of the Geo-Body of a Nation* (Honolulu: University of Hawaii Press, 1994).

4. Siam is the Portuguese name for Ayutthaya; likely converted from Xian, the Chinese name for the region. See Chris Baker and Pasuk Phongpaichit, *A History of Thailand*, 3rd ed. (Sydney: Cambridge, 2014), 8.

5. Donald Swearer, *The Buddhist World of Southeast Asia* (Albany: State University of New York, 1995), 64.

6. Within Thailand, the dominant linear narrative of Thai history places the thirteenth century kingdom of Sukhothai at the origins of the modern Thai polity. However, evidence suggests it was merely one of many ethnically "Tai" *mueang*, or city-states, that were disrupted by an expanding Ayutthaya that benefited new firearms arriving from China, Arabia, and Europe. This linear history of a legendary Sukhothai kingdom emerged during the later Bangkok period as Chakri kings cultivated a narrative of Thainess. See Baker and Pasuk, *A History of Thailand* (Port Melbourne: Cambridge University Press, 2005), 7.

7. Niels Mulder, *Inside Thai Society: An Interpretation of Everyday Life* (Bangkok: D. K. Book House, 1994), 20.

8. These reforms later became the backdrop of the popular twentieth-century stage musical *The King and I*, based on the largely apocryphal tales of English tutor Anna Leonowens. All print, stage, and film versions of her stories are officially banned in Thailand for offending the dignity of the Thai monarchy.

9. Paul Handley, *The King Never Smiles: A Biography of Thailand's King Bhumibol Adulyadej* (New Haven, CT: Yale University Press, 2006), 425–426.

10. Thitinan Pongsudhirak, "Thailand Since the Coup," *Journal of Democracy* 19, no. 4 (October 2008): 143.

11. Human Rights Watch, *Descent into Chaos: Thailand's 2010 Red Shirt Protests and Government Crackdown* (New York: Human Rights Watch, 2011), 82–83, www.hrw.org /sites/default/files/reports/thailand0511webwcover_0.pdf. Many details in this section are drawn from this documented report.

12. Warangkana Chomchuen, "Thai Court Rules Against Constitutional Amendment," *Wall Street Journal*, November 20, 2013, www.wsj.com/articles/SB10001424052702303653 004579209584204486364.

13. "Profile of the Protestors: A Survey of Pro and Anti-Government Demonstrators in Bangkok," *The Asia Foundation*, December 2013, https://asiafoundation.org/resources /pdfs/FinalSurveyReportDecember20.pdf.

14. Andrew MacGregor Marshall, *A Kingdom in Crisis: Thailand's Struggle for Democracy in the Twenty-First Century* (London: Zed Books, 2014), 203.

15. Marshall, *A Kingdom in Crisis*, 206.

16. Teeranai Charuvastra, "Prayuth Can't Guarantee Safety of Academics Who Criticize Him," *Khaosod English*, November 25, 2015, accessed February 14, 2016, www .khaosodenglish.com/detail.php?newsid=1448441773.

17. Amy Sawitta Lefever, "Thailand Warns US to Mind Its Own Business," Reuters, January 28, 2015, www.reuters.com/article/us-thailand-politics-idUSKBN0L10LZ20150128.

18. Duncan McCargo, "Peopling Thailand's 2015 Draft Constitution," *Contemporary Southeast Asia* 37, no. 3 (2015): 329–354.

19. Duncan McCargo, "Network Monarchy and the Legitimacy Crises in Thailand," *The Pacific Review* 18, no. 4 (December 2005): 499–519.

20. "Thai Facebook Users Warned Not to 'Like' Anti-Monarchy Groups," *The Guardian*, November 25, 2011, www.theguardian.com/world/2011/nov/25/thai-facebookers -warned-like-button.

21. David Streckfuss, *Truth on Trial in Thailand: Defamation, Treason, and Lèse-Majesté* (New York: Routledge, 2011).

22. Marshall, *A Kingdom in Crisis*, chapter 10.

23. McCargo, "Peopling Thailand's 2015 Draft Constitution," 331.

24. James Ockey, "Thailand in 2006: Retreat to Military Rule," *Asian Survey* 47, no. 1 (January/February 2007): 139.

25. Quoted in Kevin Hewison, *Political Change in Thailand: Democracy and Participation* (London: Routledge, 1997), 31.

26. Duncan McCargo and Ukrist Pathmanand, *The Thaksinization of Thailand* (Copenhagen: NAIS Press, 2005), 77–79.

27. Robert Dayley, "Thailand's Agrarian Myth and Its Proponents," *Journal of Asian and African Studies* 46, no. 4 (August 2011): 342–360; Robert Dayley and Attachak Sattayanurak, "Thailand's Last Peasant," *Journal of Southeast Asian Studies* 47, no. 1 (February 2016): 42–65.

28. Chai-Anan Samudavanija, "Old Soldiers Never Die, They Are Just Bypassed: The Military, Bureaucracy, and Globalisation," in Hewison, *Political Change in Thailand*, 56.

29. Joel S. Migdal, *Strong Societies and Weak States: State-Society Relations and State Capabilities in the Third World* (Princeton, NJ: Princeton University Press, 1988).

30. Andrew Walker, *Thailand's Political Peasants: Power in the Modern Rural Economy* (Madison: University of Wisconsin Press, 2012), 22–23.

31. Robert Albritton and Thawilwadee Bureekul, "The State of Democracy in Thailand," paper presented at the Conference on the Asian Barometer, Taipei, Taiwan, July 2008, 4–5.

32. Dayley and Attachak, "Thailand's Last Peasant."

33. *Thailand: Human Development Reports*, UNDP 2015, http://hdr.undp.org/en /countries/profiles/THA.

34. Peter War, "A Nation Caught in the Middle-Income Trap," *East Asia Forum Quarterly* 3, no. 4 (October/December 2011): 4–6.

35. Robert G. Sutter, *Chinese Foreign Relations: Power and Policy since the Cold War* (Lanham, MD: Rowman & Littlefield, 2008), 269.

36. Thitinan, "Thailand Since the Coup," 149.

37. Patrick Jory, "The Crisis of Thai Monarchy," *East Asia Forum Quarterly* 3, no. 4 (October/December 2011): 13–14.

3

MYANMAR (BURMA)

On June 18, 1989, the martial law government of Burma declared that the country's official name (in English) would henceforth be Myanmar. Officially, the move attempted to separate the country from its colonial past and to internationalize a locally used name ostensibly more inclusive of the country's non-Burmese minorities. Critics viewed the name change as little more than a ploy by the military junta to legitimize its repressive rule. Respecting the wishes of persecuted opposition groups within the country, many foreign governments, news organizations, and international scholars rejected the name change and continued to refer to the country as Burma. Many international organizations and non-Western governments adopted the country's new name, but the usage of either carried with it political overtones.[1]

Burma's two names—and all that they imply domestically and internationally—symbolize the country's challenge of ethnic diversity as well as Burma's story of promise, disappointment, tragedy, and potential. One of its greatest political tragedies occurred in 1990, when ruling generals refused to recognize election results that would have ousted them from power. In the aftermath, Burma found itself an international pariah. Dictatorial, repressive, and economically isolated, the country with two names persisted along an autarkic path for over two decades, inviting unwanted (and sometimes overdrawn) comparisons with North Korea.

Around 2010, however, Burma's ruling generals surprisingly began to reform the state's governing institutions and opened political space for opposition parties to once again participate in the country's politics. The military partially stepped aside a year later by appointing a civilian government to run the country. A commensurate relaxation of long-standing economic sanctions by Western governments followed. Optimism filled the air. On November 8, 2015, the freest general elections in twenty-five years resulted in a landslide victory for the opposition National League for Democracy (NLD), the same party

denied its rightful victory in 1990. Military leaders agreed to honor the election results.

At the time of writing, the country's new parliamentary majority is scheduled to assume legislative seats and organize a government in February 2016.[2] Its de facto leader, Nobel Peace Prize laureate Aung San Suu Kyi, still openly refers to her country as Burma, although she interchangeably uses Myanmar in public speeches. Whichever name is used, the Republic of the Union of Myanmar, as it is formally titled, is no longer viewed as an international pariah. It remains far from fully democratic but few would deny the future holds promise and potential. The extent to which democratic change fully institutionalizes in a country with long-standing ethnic, social, and political challenges, however, remains an open question.

Burma, like other Southeast Asian countries, is diverse, but uniquely so. About a dozen major ethnic groups and scores of smaller minorities make up more than one-third of the total population of 56 million. For the Chin, Kachin, Shan, Karen, Wa, Rohingya, and other minority groups, there has long been ethnic sensitivity to the dominant position of Burmans, or Bamar, the country's largest ethnic group at 65 percent. Moreover, although 89 percent of the population is Theravada Buddhist, indigenous belief systems, as well as Christianity and Islam, are widespread among ethnic minorities. Geographically, most ethnic minority groups live in the frontier terrains along the country's mountainous perimeter, and most Bamar populate the country's grain-producing center, which is fed by the massive Irrawaddy River. More than any other feature, Burma's geodemography—its large core majority group surrounded by a mosaic of divergent minority groups—influences and shapes the country's politics.

In January 1948, the Burmese won their independence after several years of demonstrations and often violent opposition to over sixty years of British rule. The independence struggle was led by the Thakin movement, a Burman group of anti-British nationalists headed by Aung San, the father of modern Burma and a fiery nationalist who received his training in Japan during World War II after the Japanese had occupied Burma. Subsequently, the movement turned against the Japanese as their occupation became increasingly repressive. Aung San, who was expected to be Burma's first head of state, was assassinated in 1947 and thus became the nation's martyred hero.

The Thakin movement became the core of the Anti-Fascist People's Freedom League (AFPFL), a united front group opposed to the Japanese. AFPFL forces cooperated with the British to oust the Japanese and then turned against the British in the struggle for independence. The AFPFL negotiated independence and formed the country's first parliamentary government in 1948 under the leadership of forty-one-year-old U Nu.

A devoted Buddhist, U Nu's goal for Burma was to achieve *pyidawtha*—the ideal peaceful, pleasant, and prosperous society. He commissioned the drafting of a state plan with ambitious goals in agriculture and industry alongside the immediate delivery of welfare state–quality social services. In spite of the country's rich resource base, U Nu's elaborate plan failed miserably. One problem revolved around ethnic-based antigovernment sentiment. The period from 1948 to 1958 became known as the "Time of Troubles." Well-organized minority ethnic groups actively opposed the government's move toward a national state and instead supported establishing autonomous states for each group. The Shans, Karens, and other groups rose against the central authorities, precipitating a struggle that evolved into multiple ongoing civil wars.

The second major postindependence problem concerned the poorly trained civil service, which was not able to carry out government programs effectively. U Nu's socialist policies required a high degree of centralized administration, but the Burmese bureaucracy floundered, causing severe political and economic disturbances. U Thant, one of U Nu's closest advisers, was unavailable to fully assist in postindependence rebuilding, being tied up in New York as the third UN secretary-general. Absent independence martyr Aung San and the pragmatic U Thant, the charismatic U Nu struggled to guide Burma's Parliament and bureaucracy. Poor governance added fuel to ethnic resentments and a fledgling communist movement.

By 1958, Burma's political condition was so chaotic that U Nu turned the functioning of the government over to the Tatmadaw (the military), led by General Ne Win, who was also a leader of the Thakin independence movement and a compatriot of Aung San. Following this "constitutional coup," Ne Win reorganized the bureaucracy to make it more efficient and restored a semblance of law and order. Corruption within the bureaucracy was also uncovered, and violent crime and gangsterism were rooted out in the countryside.

Despite the success of the Tatmadaw's caretaker government in a number of areas, in 1960 the electorate chose to return to U Nu for leadership. Again, however, he was not able to control the economy. U Nu's leadership was based on his charismatic religious qualities and reputation for impeccable honesty, but he was a poor day-to-day administrator. The nation was reeling from multiple rebellions among minority groups, and therefore a large share of the central budget was allocated to internal security, but U Nu concentrated on establishing Buddhism as the state religion. U Nu believed Buddhism was the best defense against rising sympathy for communism within Burma. His efforts to conceptualize an idealistic vision of a Burmese welfare state based on Buddha's teachings were not matched by a parallel plan for implementation and administration.

The military, which perceived that the civilian government was weak and dependent upon Western-style political institutions that were incompatible with Burmese culture, carried out a coup on March 2, 1962, led by Ne Win. This seizure of power, which was rapid, nonviolent, and without major challenge, began an era of military rule that continued for fifty years. Ne Win disbanded the Western-style Parliament, banned political parties, and restricted civil liberties. Hundreds of thousands of ethnic Indians living in Burma, a legacy of British rule, were forced back to India and East Pakistan. He then devised a program of radical economic and political policies called the "Burmese Way to Socialism," which included nationalizing major industries, schools, rice mills, small and large businesses, and financial institutions. Although Ne Win was not communist, his economic approach resembled Marxism, with an emphasis on cultivating nationalism, neutralism, and economic autarky.

To mobilize support for the socialist program, Ne Win established the Burmese Socialist Program Party (BSPP), organized to reach down to the village level along hierarchical lines but with all power remaining firmly at the party's military-dominated top echelon. The party's main function was to legitimize army rule. To keep Western "bourgeois decadent" ideas from infiltrating Burma, Ne Win arrested those who opposed his policies, restricted travel to Burma by foreigners, and ended academic freedom at the universities. His move toward a neutralist foreign policy took the form of isolationism.

In January 1974, Burma became the Socialist Republic of the Union of Burma after the electorate had passed the new socialist constitution. Although Ne Win discarded his military uniform in 1971 and became the "civilian" president of the new government, the military continued to be the dominant political force. Ne Win nominally stepped down as president in 1981 but retained his more powerful position as head of the BSPP. In that position, he was able to continue his dominance over political and economic policymaking. Influencing Ne Win's decisions were his beliefs in astrology and numerology. The policies emanating from the military junta became increasingly erratic.

In the summer of 1988, hundreds of thousands of farmers, urban workers, students, monks, and civil servants took to the streets of Burma's major cities to demonstrate against their government leaders. This revolt was the culmination of years of frustration and disgust at the failures of the military government to bring development to Burma. Although rich in natural resources, Burma had been humiliated by the UN decision in 1987 to declare it one of the world's least-developed nations. The revolt was also a response to the pervasive suppression of the people's political rights since 1962, when the military had assumed all political power.

A more immediate cause of the revolt was the 1987 decision of Ne Win's administration to declare valueless some 80 percent of the Burmese money in circulation. Any kyat note over $1.60 in value became instantly worthless. As part of the policy, the junta unexpectedly ordered that old notes be removed from circulation to be replaced by ones denominated on a base ninety—because nine was Ne Win's lucky number. To the public's astonishment, new notes of fifteen, forty-five, and ninety were issued by the government. Sudden demonetization, justified as a measure to undermine black-marketeers and control inflation, adversely affected the entire population, rich and poor. The bulk of the working economy was sustained by the black market (the government's socialistic economy having collapsed), so the demise of this unofficial market was seen as a catastrophe. Moreover, no recompense was given to holders of kyat notes above the maximum allowed; in effect, then, the savings of the entire population were wiped out. The price of food skyrocketed, and even government supporters began to grow uncomfortable with the country's direction.

The incident that sparked the 1988 revolt occurred in a tea shop when students and other patrons squabbled over the choice of music tapes being played. When the police arrived, a student was killed. Thousands of his schoolmates later returned to avenge their colleague's death, but they were met by weapons and security police. In a particularly dreadful incident, forty-one students were herded into a police van, where they suffocated in the intense heat. More demonstrations and security clashes occurred during the ensuing weeks. Unofficial estimates of student deaths from beatings, bayonet stabbings, and suffocation were in the hundreds, but the government blandly announced a total of only two student deaths.[3]

In the midst of the unrest, General Ne Win gathered with leaders in a special session of the BSPP Central Committee. In an alarming speech, he took responsibility for the student deaths and resigned his post as party chairman in favor of General Sein Lwin. Most astonishingly, Ne Win called for a popular referendum and a return to multiparty democracy. He also warned, ominously, that future mob disturbances would invite the use of military force. The party rejected the idea of the referendum but agreed to accept his resignation and the appointment of Sein Lwin, known as "the Butcher" for his 1974 decision to violently quell demonstrations by grief-stricken students honoring U Thant's death.

Ne Win's moves sparked more demonstrations and more killings by security police. Students, distrustful that Sein Lwin could ever lead reform, began to mobilize, joined by dockworkers, laborers, and members of the general population. Sporadic protests erupted in Rangoon and other major cities. Then, on August 8, 1988 (i.e., 8/8/88), the army followed through on Ne Win's warning. Sein Lwin ordered the use of lethal force against the demonstrators. Dozens were killed on the initial night of the crackdown, but the violence hardened the protesters' resolve. Mass demonstrations continued for five consecutive days, as did the lethal violence. In yet another shameful incident, government soldiers shot and killed a group of exhausted doctors and nurses in front of Rangoon General Hospital.[4]

International outcry followed the junta's crackdown on the "8888 Uprising," as it became known. The US government was one of the first to issue a protest and became a visible symbol of democratic government; thus, the grounds of the US embassy in Rangoon became an important site for antigovernment demonstrations. Other governments condemned the crackdown as well. Demonstrations in Rangoon and in Mandalay grew to more than a million people.

Facing mounting protests, Sein Lwin abruptly resigned, and the army began to withdraw from Rangoon five days after its slaughter had begun. Maung Maung, a civilian academic and Ne Win's personal biographer, was appointed president. For a brief time, a sense of victory swept the population and suggested that regime change was possible. Opposition politicians emerged after years of suppression and began to discuss plans for action. Aung San's daughter, Aung San Suu Kyi, visiting Burma from her home in London, began to offer public speeches encouraging reform. Top diplomats signed an open letter calling for an end to Burma's isolationism.

Then, just as systemic change seemed within reach, a series of cascading events redirected Burma's historical course. The civil administration collapsed, and the police went on strike. Prisoners were released, and a sense of insecurity developed among the public. Revolutionary-style protests grew in size and audacity, and a number of government offices were stormed by unruly crowds. An attitude of recrimination surfaced. In a few cases, "suspected government agents were gruesomely beheaded or hacked to death in front of cheering crowds."[5] Burma faced the prospect of a bloody social revolution.

With the knowledge that the military's dominance was in jeopardy, army commander in chief General Saw Maung, ostensibly on orders from Ne Win, crushed the revolt and restored the military to power on September 18, 1988. The military's coup was not against an opposition government, as none existed, but was against the civilian facade government under Maung Maung that the army itself created. The violent coup was followed by the arrest of demonstrators, the censorship of all forms of communication, and the flight of tens of thousands of students to the nation's borders to escape the military and organize for a future rebellion. Altogether, some 3,000 Burmese lost their lives in their attempt to end military rule.

Saw Maung, taking his orders from Ne Win, established the State Law and Order Restoration Council (SLORC) to endure "until anarchy and demonstrations could be brought under control." SLORC, consisting of generals who were loyal to Ne Win, was given responsibility for administering the state. Ruling by martial law, SLORC brutally suppressed regime opponents even as it announced plans for a new election to be held in May 1990. SLORC argued, incredibly, that its harsh policies were necessary because of an alleged collusion between the Burmese Communist Party and the US Central Intelligence Agency, which was the cause of demonstrations and antigovernment dissidence. Aung San Suu Kyi, who formed the National League for Democracy (NLD) in the days following the uprising, was placed under house arrest for having been "manipulated" by communists and foreign intelligence agencies. SLORC also argued that a highly centralized, military-oriented administration was necessary to ensure the country's continued unity in the face of potential rebellion by minority ethnic groups. None of these explanations were accepted by the vast majority of Burmese, who were extremely angry that their people's revolt had been crushed. The Tatmadaw, once a symbol of stability in Burma, became a hated organization.

Following the crackdown, SLORC ramped up its methods of oppression by silencing writers, banning assemblies, and forcefully moving some half a million people from their homes with the aim of breaking up pro-democracy neighborhoods and areas favorable to opposition leader Aung San Suu Kyi. The relocation of urban residents in late 1989 from cities to satellite towns was particularly egregious; it was justified by SLORC as a "beautification measure."

Despite these human rights violations, SLORC organized the May 27, 1990, election to choose legislators in the Pyithu Hluttaw (House of Representatives), which was the sole organ of legislative authority. Under the election law, each constituency was to elect one representative. Some 492 constituencies, determined by population size, were to choose representatives; seven constituencies of ethnic minorities, however, were not allowed to vote because of "security" threats in their regions. SLORC believed the election could be controlled to ensure that pro-government forces would prevail. In fact, the government was given the power to censor the speeches and publications of parties and candidates. Television time was limited to one ten-minute period per party during the entire campaign, and statements had to be submitted for approval seven days in advance. Candidates who gave speeches that had not been scrutinized and approved by the authorities were imprisoned.

Popular opposition leaders were harassed and kept from participating in the election. Aung San Suu Kyi, for example, was disqualified, as were former prime minister U Nu and another prominent opposition leader, former general U Tin Oo. All of these leaders were placed under house arrest. Pro-government candidates who joined the successor party of the BSPP, the National Unity Party (NUP), received government funds for campaigning, but funds were not available to opposition leaders. The authorities banned outdoor assemblies and relocated citizens from their voting constituencies to ensure a pro-government vote.

Despite these measures, and in an extraordinary display of independence, Aung San Suu Kyi's National League for Democracy (NLD) won more than 80 percent of the seats (396 of 485) in the Pyithu Hluttaw. The NUP won only 10 seats, losing even in areas dominated by the army. Such a sharp rebuke of the martial law government was unexpected by junta leaders. The military then refused to turn the government over to the newly elected legislators, even though the latter were ready to install a new constitution based largely on the country's last democratic constitution of 1947. Although the Burmese had expressed their anger toward the military government and their support for democratic rule through their vote, the regime in power was unwilling to act in compliance with the people's will.

Although world reaction to SLORC's oppression was strongly critical, the military continued to jail opposition leaders, dominate every facet of society, and isolate the regime from global currents. When in December 1991 Aung San Suu Kyi received, in absentia, the Nobel Peace Prize for standing up to the military junta, many believed that SLORC could not withstand the negative worldwide publicity. However, despite global condemnation and economic sanctions, SLORC dug in even deeper, claiming that freeing the Nobel laureate would threaten the nation's peace and tranquility.

In 1992, General Saw Maung stepped down as chairman of SLORC and was replaced by General Than Shwe, who was the nation's military commander and minister of defense. The new leader released some five hundred political prisoners, although the principal NLD leaders were not freed. Colleges and universities were reopened, and a constitutional convention was called. The latter was viewed as a sham by both the Burmese people and foreign observers, who pointed out that the convention was dominated by the military and that opposition leaders were still in jail. The convention met in January 1993 but did nothing to undermine military rule. Indeed, the conference specifically approved a leading political role for the army in the country's future governance.

During the postelection period, Than Shwe persisted in denying elected parliamentarians their rightful seats. In response, 250 would-be delegates formed a "parallel government" outside of the country in December 1990: the National Coalition Government of the Union of Burma. It called for the release of Aung San Suu Kyi and all other political prisoners, the transfer of power to those properly elected, and a halt to the civil war. But the military rulers ignored their requests.

Sometime in 1994 the generals realized that SLORC's policy of isolation had brought devastation to Burma. They allowed small openings in the economy, but the lack of capital, the country's poor infrastructure, and general disdain for the regime by much of the world made change difficult. Nevertheless, in the mid-1990s Burma's economic growth rate improved, ending the total stagnation of previous decades. Asian entrepreneurs began setting up investments and a "Visit Myanmar Year" promotional campaign was launched. New hotel projects soon changed the face of Rangoon. The opening did almost nothing to improve the standard of living of the people, among the world's poorest, most of whom lived at a subsistence level. Corruption, an inflated bureaucracy, political mismanagement, and the continued imprisonment of the democracy leaders were all reasons for the ongoing economic problems.

In July 1995, Aung San Suu Kyi was "released" from house arrest. In reality, she was guarded closely to ensure that she and her followers would not jeopardize SLORC's control over the nation. The government felt compelled to release her because of growing foreign pressure and Myanmar's desire to join ASEAN.

Although thousands of Burmese citizens came to hear her speak following her release, Aung San Suu Kyi was effectively silenced. Her talks were not allowed to be broadcasted or printed in the government-controlled press. Indeed, the official press attacked her daily. In 1997, when her British husband, Michael Aris, was near death from prostate cancer in Great Britain, Burma analysts believed the junta would show compassion by allowing him to spend his last days with his wife. However, he was denied a visa, and she was reluctant to leave Burma, fearing she would not be allowed to return. Aris died in Britain in 1999 after Aung San Suu Kyi had been returned to full house arrest.

Throughout the 1990s, SLORC continued to rule in a despotic manner. Political opponents were jailed or executed. Military officers replaced civilians at all levels of the bureaucracy. Opposition political parties remained banned. E-mail and Internet communication were permitted in the country but only under tight control by censors. The military junta fashioned a few cease-fire agreements with a number of long-standing ethnic rebel groups, but for those still engaged in civil war, such as the Karens, the military stepped up its suppression, forcing hundreds of thousands to flee to Thailand, where they languished as refugees in terrible living conditions.

In an attempt to improve its international image, SLORC officials renamed the ruling council the "State Peace and Development Council" (SPDC) in 1997. Subsequently, SPDC policies remained virtually the same as those of SLORC. Although the SPDC liberalized trade and investment further, most new foreign investment permitted into Burma explicitly benefited state officials who doubled as businessmen.

In 2000, a special UN envoy attempted to bring about talks between the government and the democracy leader Aung San Suu Kyi, still under house arrest for the second time. Talks broke down but about a year later, Aung San Suu Kyi was released from house arrest and allowed to travel within Burma. In 2003, while she was touring Depayin, a provincial town in upper Burma, a violent clash erupted between NLD sympathizers and the government. Opposition leaders claimed the confrontation led to seventy deaths, whereas the government reported only four. Pro-democracy groups accused the government of orchestrating the Depayin massacre. Soon afterward, NLD leaders were arrested and Aung San Suu Kyi's third detention began.[6]

Intrigue within the military has also punctuated Burmese politics. Following an alleged coup attempt by Ne Win's son-in-law in March 2002, Ne Win was placed under house arrest by Than Shwe. Months later, at age ninety-one, Ne Win died at his home on Inya Lake. The military junta refused to recognize Ne Win's passing with a state funeral or official salute of honor.

Around this time, the newly appointed prime minister Khin Nyunt, a former head of the military's intelligence service and Ne Win protégé, outlined a seven-point road map for a transition to multiparty democracy. Reviving the moribund National Convention, the new leader aimed to redraft the constitution. The move drew some interest and Khin Nyunt began to broker discussions with Aung San Suu Kyi. Burmese diplomats paraded the reforms at the United Nations. Still, very few inside or outside Burma viewed the process as legitimate. A year later, Senior General Than Shwe forcibly removed Khin Nyunt from office, placed him under detention, and purged officials tied to him from their posts.

In 2006, the SPDC announced a surprise relocation of the country's capital to an undeveloped rural area four hundred kilometers north of Rangoon. The decision is believed to have derived from consultations with the junta's favored astrologists. Naypyidaw, the new capital, required a massive construction effort and the relocation of government offices and residences. By literally distancing ministers and administrators from the population, the paranoid Tatmadaw resurrected the age-old court practice of isolating officials.

If intended to decrease the likelihood of antigovernment activism in Rangoon, relocating the capital to Naypyidaw failed. In August 2007, the government imposed a drastic 500 percent hike in fuel prices. Protests followed, led by saffron-robed Buddhist monks and veteran leaders from the 8888 Uprising. The government reacted violently, using plainclothes goons at first and then uniformed soldiers later. Protesters, including monks, were brutally beaten and arrested. The Buddhist clergy demanded an apology from the government, which never came. What followed became Burma's most significant mass protests since 1988, similarly drawing global attention.

On September 28, 2007, throughout the country thousands of monks went to the streets under the banner of the All Burma Monks Alliance, a hitherto-unknown group. As ordinary Burmese joined the monks, demonstrations grew massive in many parts of the country. In Rangoon, some protesters headed for the famous Shwedagon Pagoda; others flocked to Aung San Suu Kyi's residence near Inya Lake. Still under house arrest, the Nobel laureate appeared at her gate, engaging with monks and others. The blessing of the movement by Burma's leading dissident served as yet another catalyst. Within a few days, over 100,000 monks and their followers paralyzed the country's major cities. Predictably, the Tatmadaw stepped up its brutality in return. At least thirty-one protesters were killed and many others were wounded. Pictures and video sent from digital cameras and cell phones flooded newswires worldwide; images of unarmed, shaven-headed monks and students lying dead and bloodied on Rangoon streets produced shock and dismay. Despite an international outcry from Western governments, human rights groups, and sympathetic international celebrities, the thuggish junta retained the upper hand.

By October, the "Saffron Revolution" had been fully suppressed. Buddhist temples were raided by security forces and many monks were detained; others simply disappeared never to be found. To reduce tensions, a UN envoy arrived in an attempt to meet with junta leaders and Aung San Suu Kyi. The protests affirmed widespread discontent among Burma's population, but they also exposed the weakened state of Burma's opposition to effect political change.

Undeterred by unrest, the SPDC announced plans for a May 2008 referendum on a new constitution, a document drafted exclusively by regime insiders to ensure the military's continued dominance. In opposition to the draft constitution, National League for Democracy leaders organized a massive "No!" campaign that distributed leaflets throughout the country.

On May 2, 2008, eight days before the scheduled referendum, Cyclone Nargis hit Burma's densely populated delta region with devastating consequences; it was the worst natural disaster in the country's history. With massive force, Nargis caused over 138,000 deaths and left 2.4 million survivors stranded and desperate, according to UN figures. Most disturbing was Than Shwe's initial reluctance to allow foreign aid and disaster relief to the cyclone's victims. Injured, homeless, and hungry, millions of Burmese suffered unnecessarily in the days and weeks that followed. Foreign journalists, restricted by the regime, produced underground reports offering the world a glimpse of the disaster's massive scale.[7]

While Myanmar's leaders allowed millions to suffer by denying visas to aid workers and entry to supply ships, the SPDC audaciously went forward with its constitutional referendum, postponing voting in affected areas. State-controlled media announced weeks later that voters had approved the new charter with a 92.4 percent vote. International condemnation for mishandling the disaster and staging a farcical referendum on constitutional reform was nearly universal.

Then, ten days after Nargis, a new event in Asia gripped the world's attention: a 7.9 earthquake in southwest China that killed 90,000 people and left 5 million homeless. For their quick action, Chinese officials won praise from their own public and from UN secretary-general Ban Ki-moon. China welcomed international aid from any source. As the world watched the contrasting relief efforts in China and Burma, the true incompetence and paranoia of Myanmar's military junta was laid bare. Than Shwe became the object of anger and bewilderment from inside and outside Burma. French diplomats even called for the military junta to be charged with crimes against humanity and raised the prospect of the UN Security Council authorizing humanitarian intervention under the emerging principle of "R2P," or Responsibility to Protect. Only following a face-to-face meeting with the UN secretary-general did Than Shwe relax entry restrictions on aid workers, although United States Aid for International Development (USAID) workers were never allowed in. Burma's worst natural disaster was thus exacerbated by a tragic man-made catastrophe.

In 2008, ASEAN leaders took the opportunity to chide Myanmar's leaders, a rare event due to the regional body's commitment to noninterference. In a report at its ministerial meeting, it was announced that $1 billion would be needed for reconstruction. The cyclone had destroyed 450,000 homes, damaged 350,000 others, flooded 600,000 hectares of farmland, and severely damaged or destroyed 75 percent of hospitals and clinics in the region. For their part, Myanmar's leaders played down the document's conclusions. They also claimed that critical reports by survivors had been faked and falsely portrayed government aid efforts. Gradually, the junta allowed more and more aid to trickle in to the worst-hit areas.

In the aftermath of Cyclone Nargis, government repression of political opponents continued. In late 2008, sixty-five-year prison sentences were handed down to fourteen pro-democracy activists, including veterans of the 8888 Uprising. Months later Aung San Suu Kyi's house arrest was extended after the Tatmadaw discovered she had briefly sheltered a fifty-three-year-old American civilian who, in a bizarre nighttime rescue attempt, surreptitiously swam to her home on Inya Lake, believing he could miraculously free her single-handedly. John Yettaw, the Vietnam War veteran and PTSD sufferer at the center of the incident, was later deported after intervention by US senator Jim Webb, a fellow veteran and longtime critic of the effectiveness of Western sanctions.

As 2009 closed, Burma remained in political and economic misery, seemingly stuck on an endless path of repression, poverty, and failed governance. Because of its trajectory, few observers predicted that 2010 would inaugurate a new era of political reform at the behest of the regime itself. The reform program—deliberate, democracy-oriented, and very incomplete—has since transformed the regime in an arguably irreversible fashion. Following decades of tragic and failed military rule, the promise of democracy has emerged once again in Burma. Remarkably, its instigation did not come through a revolutionary change of regime, but from reformist change within the regime.

Under the authority of the new 2008 constitution, Myanmar's leaders began a series of surprising reforms that pivoted around scheduled elections in November 2010. At the beginning of that year, regime leaders released a number of political prisoners, including prominent NLD leader U Tin Oo. Tatmadaw representatives then started formal conversations with Aung San Suu Kyi, who remained under house arrest. In preparation for the elections, Prime Minister Thein Sein and a group of moderate SPDC leaders resigned from their military posts and formed the Union Solidarity and Development Party (USDP) out of an existing pro-government social organization, similarly called the Union Solidarity and Development Association (USDA). Most analysts saw the USDP as a proxy party for the military.

Then, in another unexpected move weeks before the elections, military leaders unilaterally announced changes to the country's flag, its national anthem, and its official name (from the Union of Myanmar to the Republic of the Union of Myanmar). Skeptical critics, understandably, viewed all of these preelection changes as cosmetic; in hindsight, the SPDC's moves demonstrated its intention to recreate Myanmar's governing institutions after the election was complete.

The 2010 election, boycotted by the NLD because Aung San Suu Kyi remained under house arrest, was predictably won by the USDP and internationally condemned for being fraudulent. Another reason the NLD boycotted the
election was that its participation would have meant an end to its long-standing
claims to rightful power stemming from the overturned 1990 elections. Shortly
after the election, the SPDC announced the formation of a civilian government
and the end of military rule. In an event formalizing this action, strongman
Than Shwe officially dissolved the SPDC and announced his retirement. The
USDP's Thein Sein, the majority party leader in Parliament, was installed as
president of Myanmar as a civilian. Myanmar's generals, ostensibly, had just
handed the reins of power to a civilian government. What followed was even
more astonishing.

President Thein Sein, under the concept of "discipline-flourishing democracy," furthered reforms. He reorganized the government's cabinet, installed
pro-reform ministers, and retired hard-liners. He also began to release political
prisoners by the hundreds. From 2010 on, Thein Sein removed hundreds of
blacklisted names from Tatmadaw records and invited exiled Burmese to return with amnesty. In 2011, the government shockingly ended all prepublica-
tion censorship and allowed formerly verboten images of Aung San Suu Kyi to
appear in public. Thein Sein also announced that unions could freely organize.
He then sought new deals with restive minorities and allowed for constitutionally mandated elections of local assemblies.

In the economic sphere, Thein Sein sold off over 300 state-owned enterprises (without public auction), reformed the country's exchange rate regime,
liberalized foreign investment rules, and imprudently announced a goal of tri-
pling Myanmar's GDP per capita by 2016 (a feat the Asian Development Bank
forecasted as possible by 2030 at the earliest).[8] He also pushed through Parliament a law establishing central bank autonomy. In the social realm, the new
government relaxed cultural controls as well, symbolized by permitting movie
theaters to screen once-forbidden Western films. In August 2012, *Titanic 3D*
became the first Hollywood film to be legally viewed by Burmese audiences in a
generation.

Diplomatically, Thein Sein was also active. He eagerly held meetings with
ambassadors and foreign guests to tout his reform program, including high-
profile face-to-face meetings with US secretary of state Hillary Clinton and
British prime minister David Cameron. Engaging regional leaders, he sought to
secure Myanmar's chairmanship of ASEAN, scheduled for 2014—which was
once a controversial prospect. At each event, President Thein Sein appeared in
public donning civilian clothing rather than the military garb that defined the
Myanmar led by his predecessors. In a matter of months, Thein Sein adeptly
changed the international image of Myanmar's government. A sense that the
country was finally embracing the new international era permeated the global
community. Western governments, which once isolated Myanmar as a pariah

state, began to ease sanctions. Beijing, however, proved less enthusiastic about Burma's new tack, especially after Thein Sein suspended construction of a Chinese-funded dam in Kachin State after fierce local protest.

Most dramatically, one week after the 2010 election, Aung San Suu Kyi was suddenly released from house arrest. She soon held direct meetings with Thein Sein and made public statements extending confidence that his government's reform program was genuine. After she was freed, the NLD reregistered as a political party and named Aung San Suu Kyi as a candidate for the Pyithu Hluttaw, Myanmar's lower house.

In by-elections held in April 2012, the NLD won all but one of the forty-four seats it contested. Daw (Aunt) Aung San Suu Kyi—whose party was denied power in 1990 after winning 81 percent of the national vote; the international human rights icon and Nobel Laureate; the daughter of the country's slain independence hero; the admiring subject of countless news articles, books, documentaries, films, and a critically acclaimed rock anthem; the graceful woman known as "The Lady" who keeps flowers in her hair and who suffered fifteen total years under house arrest as a prisoner of conscience—finally, at last, took her rightful seat in Burma's Parliament on May 2, 2012.

In her new parliamentary role, the intrepid Aung San Suu Kyi remained cautiously cooperative in her dealings with the regime. Agreeing to stay within constitutional bounds, she pushed Thein Sein's government for greater reform but avoided overt attempts to delegitimize his authority. Western governments followed her lead. In July 2012, only months before Aung San Suu Kyi visited Washington, DC, where she was awarded a Congressional Gold Medal, the United States reestablished diplomatic relations with Myanmar to the full ambassadorial level. An exchange of visits then followed over the next two years between Thein Sein and Barack Obama—the first US president to publicly refer to the country by its official name, Myanmar. In spite of some setbacks, confidence in Myanmar's reforms continued to grow inside and outside the country.

Undermining confidence in Myanmar's reforms, however, was Thein Sein's xenophobic response to horrific sectarian violence between Rohingya Muslims and Buddhists—a festering conflict that erupted in 2012 and fully metastasized in 2015. Initially, in Rakhine State, where both groups live, vigilante gangs of Buddhist nationalists began to roam the streets and torch homes and mosques. These attacks led desperate Rohingya to seek refuge and flee by sea on fishing boats, first to neighboring Bangladesh and then later to Malaysia and Indonesia. Upwards of 100,000 Rohingya "boat people" eventually became the subject of international humanitarian focus. Over the duration, Thein Sein's government fueled the conflict with implicit (and explicit) support of fascist Buddhist monks and Burmese nationalists who publicly encouraged the pogrom.

Having become a regional crisis, neighboring governments, following the ASEAN Way of noninterference, were slow to condemn Myanmar or assist the refugees, at least until Muslim groups in Malaysia and Indonesia pressured their own governments to act. Internationally, human rights groups, organizations, and foreign governments stepped in to partially fill the gap, although most Rohingya remain displaced in Myanmar as of this writing. The NLD, oddly quiet over the matter, seemed worried about the bigger electoral picture, fearing overt support for the Muslim Rohingya might alienate them from majority Buddhist voters. Even Aung San Suu Kyi, having now assumed her new role as a calculating pragmatist, failed to speak out strongly on the issue.

The Rohingya crisis aside, cautious optimism emerged about the prospects of the November 2015 general elections. In the run-up to the elections, Thein Sein, with the backing of Tatmadaw generals, pledged to honor the election outcomes, whatever the results. For its part, the USDP ran a straightforward campaign even as rifts between it and its military allies surfaced. The NLD pursued an aggressive strategy, including a door-knocking campaign and rallies that paraded NLD party founder, former general U Tin Oo (then ninety years old), as one who could build bridges between the NLD and military. One troubling reality for the NLD was the fact that new constitutional rules mandated 25 percent of all legislative seats be reserved for Tatmadaw appointees. Another concern was a carefully crafted rule that disqualified anyone with foreign family ties from officially assuming the presidency.

Myanmar's fifty-year dictatorial period of military-backed leadership effectively ended on November 8, 2015. On that day, Aung San Suu Kyi's National League for Democracy won 53 percent of the national vote and secured nearly 80 percent of contested seats. Serving principally as a "referendum on authoritarian rule," the historic election was open, lively, and widely engaged by everyday Burmese.[9] Although the Tatmadaw retains a constitutionally mandated legislative role, including the power to block proposed constitutional amendments and control key security ministries, the new NLD-dominated parliament can form a government, select a president, and oversee lawmaking for at least the next five years. As the most powerful figure in the country, Aung San Suu Kyi will begin to lead Burma as its de facto president on February 1, 2016.

INSTITUTIONS AND SOCIAL GROUPS

The Military

Since independence, the Burmese military has played the central role in governmental affairs. No other institutions or social classes have even been allowed to legitimately compete with the military. This reality is highlighted even today by the fact that the military wrote the country's current constitution, a charter that ensures the military's control over all security-related ministries, one-quarter of all legislative seats, and the power to block any attempt by elected leaders to amend the constitution.

Initially, the Tatmadaw, a popular pro-independence force under Aung San, was the only credibly unified force in the country during its early years of self-governance. This fact is a major reason why U Nu asked the army to step in and restore political order in 1958. Such a view also underpinned Ne Win's 1962 full takeover as guardian of state power from elected political parties. In 1988, facing a social revolution, the military reasserted itself again by shuffling top leaders and engaging in a brutal crackdown on protesters. Another major episode of military suppression occurred in 2007 that targeted monks, students, and ordinary citizens engaged in antigovernment protests. Throughout these events, very little was known about how decisions were made among the ruling generals. Whether controlled by Ne Win, SLORC generals, or Than Shwe's SPDC, meetings remained subject to secrecy among the dozen-plus generals who composed the junta.

The Tatmadaw grew rapidly from a force of 190,000 in the early 1990s to an estimated 375,000 by 2011, a military second in size only to Vietnam's in Southeast Asia. The joint US-UK invasions of Afghanistan and Iraq confirmed the junta's belief that outside powers can and will team up to invade weak countries. Forever obsessed with security concerns, Than Shwe subsequently expanded the country's armed forces, doubled the size of its naval fleet, and sought new arms purchases in deals with countries such as China, India, and Israel.

Arms trade with North Korea during Than Shwe's tenure even raised concerns over the possible exchange of nuclear technology and of a nuclearized Myanmar. In 2012, reformist president Thein Sein publicly vowed to end all arms trade with North Korea and to limit any dealings with Kim Jong Un's regime within the framework of Security Council resolutions. In the process, comparisons of Myanmar's generals with the martial state xenophobes who rule North Korea began to disappear.

Going forward, the extent to which the Tatmadaw remains a praetorian king-maker or develops a new role as a professionalized military remains an open question. Constitutional arrangements assure it a role in politics, and unresolved ethnic unrest throughout the country ensures an ongoing role in domestic security and nation building.

Aung San Suu Kyi

Known affectionately by supporters as "Daw Suu" (Aunt Suu) or "The Lady," Aung San Suu Kyi remains unparalleled as a popular political figure in modern Burma. With a Mandela-esque aura, she remains wildly beloved at home and abroad, a figure of immense significance in the history of Southeast Asia.

Aung San Suu Kyi was schooled in Burma, where she spent her first fifteen years. A member of a prominent family, she was then sent to India, where her mother was ambassador, and then to England to study politics, philosophy, and economics at Oxford University. She later published books on Burmese history and literature. Prior to 1988, she had no direct political experience and was known primarily as the daughter of Aung San.

Shortly before the 8888 Uprising, she returned to Burma from England to care for her ailing mother. She joined the opposition and, because of her name and superb oratorical ability, began to draw large crowds to her speeches. Burmese women imitated her hair and clothing style. She was cheered for her straightforward attacks against the government and against Ne Win. Her military adversaries, frightened by her mounting popularity, suggested that she was manipulated by communists. On July 20, 1989, the military placed her under house arrest and cut off all communications between her followers and the outside world.

While still under arrest, she was awarded (in absentia) the Nobel Peace Prize in December 1991 for her courageous struggle against the military dictatorship.[10] As a political prisoner, she suffered three detentions for a total of fifteen years following her return to her homeland. Her last detention followed the 2003 clash at Depayin, where she and her supporters were brutally attacked by over 1,000 plainclothes thugs, who held ties with the USDA. Her 2010 release came shortly after Myanmar's first legislative elections in over twenty years. In 2012 by-elections, in which she was permitted to run, she won 55,902 votes of 65,471 votes cast in her Rangoon township, or 85 percent of the vote. Constitutionally barred from the presidency because she married a foreigner, Aung San Suu Kyi leads the NLD from her constituency seat, which gives her standing in the legislature.

Legislature

Prior to 2010, Burma's legislature experienced only two periods of extended life: as a multiparty bicameral body during the contentious U Nu era (1951–1962), and as a rubber-stamp unicameral body during the Ne Win–controlled BSPP era (1974–1988). After the 1990 elections were overturned, military leaders under SLORC and the SPDC removed all vestiges of legislative power and ruled as a military dictatorship. Constitutional reform revived the legislature in 2010.

As a means to outmaneuver the NLD, and annul any claims to the electoral results of the 1990 election, the SPDC began to engage in constitutional reform in 2003. The new charter, approved by voters during the immediate aftermath of Cyclone Nargis in 2008, established a new bicameral Parliament, the *Pyid-aungsu Hluttaw* (Assembly of the Union). Currently, the lower house, the Pyithu Hluttaw (House of Representatives), seats 440 representatives: 330 elected from constituencies and 110 appointed military delegates. The upper chamber, the *Amytha Hluttaw* (House of Nationalities), seats 224 representatives: 168 elected and equally divided between Myanmar's regions and states, and 56 appointed military delegates. Thus, by constitutional mandate, 25 percent of both houses are designated for the Tatmadaw, a convenient number since any constitutional amendment requires over 75 percent approval in both houses.

After reforms permitted the inclusion of genuine opposition parties since the 2012 by-elections, the Pyidaungsu Hluttaw began to develop the feel of a more authentic legislature. Aung San Suu Kyi and opposition colleagues filled a needed role speaking out on issues without recrimination. With majority control following the 2015 elections, the NLD legislative leadership will be put to the test. It remains to be seen how the military bloc will respond to this leadership. Beginning in February 2016, the opportunity for Burma's reformed Parliament to become a truly legitimate, democratic, lawmaking institution begins.

Political Parties

The most important party in Myanmar is the National League for Democracy. The party was founded in the wake of the 8888 Uprising by Aung Gyi, U Thura, U Tin Oo, and Aung San Suu Kyi. Both Aung Gyi and U Tin Oo were dissident generals forcibly removed from the Tatmadaw for turning on the regime. Aung Gyi later turned on the NLD itself, resigning after accusing it of being infiltrated by communists. U Tin Oo, after a falling out with Ne Win in 1976, spent years in prison and endured long stints under house arrest, much like Aung San Suu Kyi. After a decade of continuous detention, he was released in 2009 and remains party chairman of the NLD at the spry age of ninety.

That the NLD has survived in spite of being denied power in 1990 by military fiat and suffering subsequent persecution from anti-democracy SLORC and SPDC governments stands as a remarkable testament to its strength and durability. Its victorious reemergence in the 2012 by-elections (winning 43 of 44 contested seats) and its landslide victory in 2015 (winning nearly 80 percent of all contested seats) indicates its current popularity. The extent to which it can maintain this level of support is perhaps doubtful, given that it has never governed. It currently controls 369, or 55 percent, of the Pyidaungsu Hluttaw's total 664 seats (of which 166 are designated for the military and only 498 are contestable).

The party of former president Thein Sein, the Union Solidarity and Development Party (USDP), grew out of a 1993 organization founded by Than Shwe, the Union Solidarity and Development Association (USDA). Set up as a "social welfare organization," the USDA served as an arm of the SPDC but was not a political party. With branches in major cities and towns throughout Burma, its grassroots presence rose rapidly. Due to privileged access to state resources, it fronted the regime's cooperative efforts with nascent civil society groups. Its followers appeared in public wearing white long-sleeved shirts and dark green sarongs. Pro-democracy advocates accused the USDA of deploying paramilitary thugs at the Depayin massacre and the crackdown on the 2007 Saffron Revolution.

Prior to the 2010 elections, the USDA formalized itself as a political party and called itself the Union Solidarity and Development Party (USDP). Echoing the strategies of Golkar, which was Suharto's pro–New Order quasi-party that forcibly co-opted Indonesian bureaucrats and interest groups for three decades, the USDP once stood as the largest pro-junta organization in the country.[11] The USDP's potential to serve as a public counterweight to the NLD proved negligible in the 2015 elections. Where it once held 259 seats in the lower house, it now holds only 28, a staggering net loss of 231 seats resulting from free elections.

Myanmar's party system is characterized by two types of parties: national parties and ethnic minority parties. National parties, which run candidates across districts throughout the country, include the NLD and the USDP. Ethnic minority parties coalesce around the regional aspirations of larger minority groups such as the Rakhine (formerly known as Arkanese), Chin, Shan, Mon, and Wa. Some ethnic groups have yet to embrace party politics or are too small to organize their own. In the immediate aftermath of the 2015 elections, some ethnic parties grew anxious that NLD promises to include ethnic parties in a government would not mean any appointed positions. Before the NLD had officially taken its seats in Parliament, it was already feeling the pressure of Myanmar's complicated ethnic politics.

Monks

Burma's 400,000 Buddhist monks number the same as today's military. Monks are highly respected as teachers and religious leaders, and in the past their predecessors have toppled kings. Burma's Buddhist *sangha*, or monastic order, has been more politically active than the *sangha* in neighboring Thailand. Keeping the monks from rebellion was a key goal of SPDC policy. The SPDC even tried to infiltrate the monkhood with its own agents, who reported to the junta any dissident activity.[12]

The power of the monks to put political pressure on the junta was demonstrated in 2007. Led by the All Burma Monks Alliance and other groups, the monks brought a moral legitimacy to the demonstrations greater than that of Aung San Suu Kyi. At her gate, monks blessed Suu Kyi. In 2007, they also engaged in the rare practice of *thabeik hmauk*, or overturning of the offering bowls, by denying opportunity to immoral leaders to make spiritual merit. When Than Shwe and the military refused to apologize for mistreatment at protests, leading monks led several hundred monks on marches around Rangoon's Shwedagon Pagoda with offering bowls turned symbolically upside-down, a nonviolent affront to regime leaders.

Buddhist monks also are not immune to sectarian politics. In 2012, many marched in support of Thein Sein's proposal to deport the country's 800,000 Muslim Rohingya minorities to other countries. In 2012, an ultranationalist Buddhist group dubbed the "969 Movement," led violent attacks against Rohingya communities at the behest of its chief agitator, monk U Wirathu. The 969 Movement was later superseded by an organization titled the Patriotic Association of Myanmar, known as Ma Ba Tha in Burmese. This association rapidly organized in a matter of months, developing branches throughout Myanmar using broadcast and social media. It defines itself as a pro-nationalist, pro-Buddhist movement but critics labeled it fascist, citing as evidence its harsh anti-Muslim rhetoric and push for new restrictions on Muslims under the guise of population control laws.

Ethnic Minority Groups

During the postindependence period, Burma's ethnic minority groups have continued to view themselves primarily in terms of ethnic nationalism. The Karens, Karenni, Shans, Kachins, and other groups that fought for state autonomy do not trust the government. In their struggle for minority rights, these groups joined the National Democratic Front (NDF) in revolt. The NDF assumed that the peoples of Burma were members of ethnic-linguistic communities who voluntarily came together in 1947 to form the Union of Burma.[13] In this union, equality of communities was to be reflected in their organization as political units, each having power to govern itself, claim to a reasonable share of the nation's resources, an equal right to develop its land and society, and equal representation in the national government.[14] The states were to be strong and the central government weak. In reality, however, and despite promises to state leaders at the time of independence, the central government became strong and the separate states became weak.

To achieve their goals, the minority ethnic groups organized armed insurgencies to protect their territories and pressure the central government to accept a federated Burma, with ethnic states having autonomy under a federal umbrella government. The most infamous such ethnic warlord was the opium-trading Khun Sa, a Shan figure of Golden Triangle lore who eluded Burmese troops, Thai rangers, and US drug enforcement authorities for over two decades.

Opium itself has a long history in Burma and Southeast Asia. The British, of course, profited from the opium trade and introduced opium poppies for production in upland minority areas. Later, ethnic insurgents such as Khun Sa, as well as the Burmese Communist Party, relied on opium profits to finance their guerrilla activities. At its height, Khun Sa's Shan United Army commanded 20,000 men. The United States set a $2 million bounty for his capture and estimated that he was responsible for 45 percent of the global heroin trade and sourced 80 percent of heroin trafficked on New York City streets. Ethnic Chinese brokers and Thai traffickers also became players in a drug-dependent civil war. In the late 1980s and 1990s, Burma's generals got into the action through cease-fire deals where, in exchange for loyalty, they granted rebels autonomy and basic freedom to pursue narcotics. After US agents thoroughly disrupted his network, Khun Sa finally surrendered to Burmese authorities in exchange for immunity from extradition to the United States. After idling away in Rangoon with four wives and making sundry ruby deals, he died in 2007.[15]

Deals between ethnic groups and Myanmar's government, combined with rising Thai demand for methamphetamines, put Burma's legendary opium production in decline and into the hands of smaller criminal elements. To service Thailand's insatiable sex industry, criminal syndicates also engage in human trafficking of Burmese women, many of whom are poor minorities. Ever vulnerable to power, guns, and the mechanisms of exploitation, many of Burma's ethnic minorities, with long-held goals of state autonomy in a federalized system, await a full conclusion to the world's longest ongoing civil wars.

In 2001, the NDF and the United Nationalities League for Democracy–Liberated Areas (UNLD-LA) cofounded the Ethnic Nationalities Council (ENC). Moving the fight from armed insurgency to political diplomacy, the ENC's mandate has been to engage in a "tripartite dialogue" between Burma's ethnic minorities, the SPDC, and the NLD. Under Thein Sein, armed conflict gave way to negotiation, with some exceptions. New firefights between Burmese soldiers and the Kachin Independence Army erupted in 2011, in spite of a long-standing truce, and have continued ever since. Various Shan and Wa groups also remain outside any negotiated settlements.

Months prior to the November 2015 elections, the country's senior general, Min Aung Hlaing, pledged that the military would continue to oversee political life in Myanmar "until ceasefires and peace deals have been concluded with all of Myanmar's many ethnic armed groups."[16] The elections themselves were marred by the effective disenfranchisement of many ethnic minorities and the disqualification of ethnic candidates, especially in Muslim areas. It remains to be seen if Aung San Suu Kyi's government will change course or continue the past approach of insisting that minorities accept central government definitions of "unity" over any federalized arrangement of ethnic autonomy. Only eight of the country's fifteen armed groups were willing to sign a nationwide cease-fire agreement before elections that the NLD was sure to win, which suggests that many ethnic minority groups are taking a wait and see approach.

STATE-SOCIETY RELATIONS AND DEMOCRACY

For most of its modern history, the Burmese state has been dominated by a small number of rulers and institutions. Absolute monarchs, British administrators, and Burmese military generals have, in turn, borne responsibility for the authoritative decisions affecting Burma's citizenry. From Ne Win's 1962 coup until political reforms began in 2010, Burma functioned essentially as a dictatorial state where sovereign authority was concentrated in the hands of a despotic military elite.

As reforms gradually opened political space, and opposition parties began to share power in Parliament, Burma's state began to transform. The 2015 election marked the definitive end to Burma's long-standing dictatorial state. The authority of Myanmar's rulers is now legitimate—the moral right to rule derives from direct popular election. Nevertheless, given current constitutional constraints that ensure a formal military role in politics and governance, it remains unclear how changes to Burma's state may evolve under the bounded authority of Aung San Suu Kyi and the National League for Democracy.

Because of its long history of dictatorship, Burma has poorly developed state institutions outside the military. With the possible exception of the Buddhist *sangha* (monastic order), Burma's dictatorial state has been autonomous—independent of societal organizations. External institutions such as Parliament, independent political parties, interest groups, and a free press were forcefully kept at bay, exerting no real influence on state policy. Despite attempts, the Tatmadaw failed to institutionalize pro-regime support through subsidiary social and political organizations such as the BSPP, NUP, USDA, and USDP.

As the Cold War faded in favor of a new international era, Burma's dictatorial state demonstrated little desire or capacity to adjust to a world of globalization, open markets, and greater democratization. As punctuated by the 1988 protests and the aborted election victory of the NLD in 1990, this failure to adapt undermined the popular legitimacy the Tatmadaw had enjoyed during independence. By the time genuine reform began in 2010, the Burmese people had grown suspicious, skeptical, and cynical about the military, state elites, and an erratic reform process. Society came to view military leaders as crass opportunists rather than as the respected unifiers of the nation. Burma's dictatorial state had evolved into a patronage operation with low capacity and legitimacy levels. Even under Thein Sein's civilian leadership, the state retained close management of economic reforms for self-serving ends. New policies and measures promoted oligopolistic control by a select few rather than encouraging societal innovation or entrepreneurship.

During Burma's dictatorial period, Tatmadaw generals forever justified centralized authority on the grounds of national unity (threatened by ethnic separatism) and national sovereignty (threatened by foreign meddling and intervention). Civil society groups were viewed with suspicion. Travel outside the country was tightly controlled. Myanmar's rulers were also reluctant to invite technocrats, politicians, intellectuals, or socioeconomic elites to participate in state affairs. The few outsiders brought into the polity had no autonomous political base or constituency.

Burma's only historical experience with democracy was a brief period under the 1947 constitution after independence, when U Nu supported representative institutions, free elections, and civil liberties. The ineffectiveness of U Nu's rule was used to rationalize the military takeover of the government in both 1958 and 1962. The military leaders viewed democratic institutions and behavior as foreign to the traditions of the Burmese and a rejected legacy of Western imperialism. In dictatorial Myanmar, democracy was embraced only when qualified. Than Shwe's road map to democracy bore the much-touted and oxymoronic label "discipline-flourishing democracy," a term the reformist Thein Sein used until he lost power in the 2015 election.

It is difficult to determine if Myanmar is experiencing a genuine democratic transition or trending toward something else. Although profound changes in state-society relations are observable, and progress toward electoral democracy is evident, many questions remain about the country's institutional development and democratic path. The unleashing of pent-up societal forces, combined with unresolved ethnic conflict, high expectations from an emboldened electorate, and the policy inexperience of the country's new decision-makers suggest the road ahead may range from bumpy to treacherous. As has been observed globally, the introduction of democracy is too often a risky venture that mercilessly exposes the health of a society rather than serving as its elixir.[17]

ECONOMY AND DEVELOPMENT

The historical similarities between Burma and Thailand are striking. Both nations have had histories of absolute monarchy; both have citizens who have practiced Theravada Buddhism; and both have comparable natural resources and fertile soils for agriculture. In the 1950s, Burma and Thailand also shared a similar size of GNP. In view of these similarities, why has Thailand achieved greater economic success while Burma has failed?

One answer stems from the most obvious difference between the two nations: The Burmese were colonized by the British, whereas the Thais have been independent throughout their history. More so than the Thais, the Burmese have consciously eschewed Western ways, including the materialism and commercialism of Western culture, which the Burmese generals believe have ruined Thai society.

Another answer is that the postindependence governments of Burma chose to isolate their nation from the global economic system, relying instead on government-controlled socialistic economics and autarky. Thailand, on the other hand, opened its economy through a policy of greater market freedom and export-driven growth. The results are dramatic: Thailand's per capita GDP rose from $100 in the 1950s to almost $5,192 in 2011, whereas in the same period Burma's rose from $100 to less than $900. Even after Thein Sein's reforms, when calculated in terms of purchasing power parity, Burma's per capita income in 2014 was a nearly $10,000 less than Thailand's ($4,800 and $14,660, respectively).

The "Burmese Way to Socialism," a nationalist ideology that sought the marriage of Marxism and Buddhism, proved to be an economic failure; it led to neither socialism nor development. In addition to weaknesses inherent to state-controlled production, policies associated with the ideology repressed the Chinese and Indian minorities who served as the core of business and entrepreneurship in other Southeast Asian countries. It also led to a dual economy with a large unofficial black market. Black market prices in Burma were regularly higher than official prices, creating participation incentives for those with access to state resources or imported goods. On the other hand, sellers in the black market ironically benefitted by increasing their incomes and expanding supply, thus reducing consumer frustration. Combined with weak educational and rural development programs, isolation kept Burma poor.

Burma's economy reached its economic nadir in 1987 when the United Nations granted the once prosperous nation the ignoble status of least-developed country, placing Burma in the same category as Chad, Ethiopia, and Haiti. Whereas Burma once controlled 28 percent of the world's rice trade, it then controlled only 2 percent.[18] Moreover, the brutal suppression of demonstrators in 1988 ended the few ongoing Western development projects, reducing the external capital that had previously been available to the government.

To counter this cessation of aid, Than Shwe opened border trade in the 1990s with Thailand and China and promulgated more liberal foreign investment laws. Foreign investors were permitted to form either wholly owned enterprises or joint ventures in which the foreign partner was required to hold a minimum 35 percent stake. However, little investment was induced by the government's policy because of the country's political instability. What did arrive left quickly. Multinational firms such as PepsiCo, Wal-Mart, Levi Strauss & Co., Tommy Hilfiger, and Liz Claiborne all pulled out after short stints. Unfavorable business conditions, pressure from human rights activists, and a 1998 US government ban on new American investment in Burma further inhibited Western investment. In 2004, even more restrictive US laws targeted Burmese imports and prohibited any payments into the country. China, Japan, and ASEAN governments, however, increased economic dealings with junta leaders through policies of "constructive engagement." Burma joined ASEAN in 1997 and then gradually integrated with the ASEAN Free Trade Area (AFTA).

Unable to compete with Southeast Asia's newly industrialized countries and China in textiles, manufacturing, and foreign direct investment, Burma's leaders in the 1990s shifted attention to natural resources. Extractive industries and the energy sector, they realized, were in high demand, and sector revenues often went directly to the state. Burma began to export natural gas and has sold offshore exploration rights to Asian and Western partners. China, for its part, became Burma's most interdependent trading partner under the SPDC. Seeking to change the route of its Middle East oil shipments to bypass the Malacca Strait, China financed a 1500-mile pipeline from Burma's western coast to Yunnan, in China's southwest. Burmese leaders also expanded biodiesel production, coercing some farmers to plant biofuel-friendly physic nut trees. One program, with a goal to convert 8 million acres of farmland to physic nut production, resulted in forced land allocation and production quotas nationwide.[19]

It is difficult to be precise about economic growth in Burma because government figures are unreliable. Even so, confidence in the overall picture is possible. In the early 1990s, Burma's annual economic growth rate hovered around 1 percent to 2 percent, and the overall standard of living, especially among rural people dependent on agriculture, had fallen. Only the presence of a black market made the economy tolerable. In the mid-1990s, economic growth rates improved to the 4 percent to 6 percent level, as foreign firms flirted with in-country investments. Following its shift in focus to the energy sector and natural gas exports, state revenues rose and civil servants received large pay raises. The country's trade surplus also grew. Since 2000, Burmese government officials commonly report double-digit growth rates, though many analysts estimate actual rates in the 5 percent to 6 percent range. Growth rates dropped below 4 percent during the 2008 global financial crisis, recovering to 8 percent by 2014.

Whatever claims state officials make regarding growth, Burma's overall socioeconomic picture remains bleak. Ordinary citizens struggle mightily through a chaotic maze of dual prices, inflation, shortages, bribery, and uncertainty. Periods of high inflation, caused in part by sundry salary increases for state employees, have plagued the economy. To finance its chronic budget deficit, the dictatorial regime often resorted to printing money to cover imports of military matériel and luxury goods. At the street level, Burma's informal sector continues to rival its formal economy in size, and black markets persist in certain controlled areas of the economy, such as banking and currency. The country's basic infrastructure is poor or nonexistent, especially in the countryside. Wasteful construction projects, such as rebuilding the country's administrative capital, imposed unnecessary opportunity costs on public funds. Corruption at all levels has been rampant. In its 2014 rankings of 175 countries, Transparency International ranked Myanmar 156. In all of East and Southeast Asia, only North Korea ranks worse.

Years of economic autarky and isolation have left Burma's people worse off than almost all of their Southeast Asian neighbors. The 2014 Human Development Index, which measures income, life expectancy, and education, now ranks Burma the lowest of all countries in Southeast Asia. Even the neophyte nation-state of Timor-Leste ranks higher. If economic growth picks up in Myanmar as a result of extended NLD leadership, it may still take decades before the country develops the required administrative experience to manage market-based growth on par with Southeast Asia's economic tigers.

FOREIGN RELATIONS

There are many good reasons why the Burmese have emphasized the importance of national security. Their colonial heritage and the Japanese occupation are reminders that Burma has been a victim of both imperialism and aggression. Burma is surrounded by nations with far greater populations and military strength, sharing an 800-mile border with India and greater than 1,000-mile borders with China and Thailand. At times, Burma's ethnic minorities have been supported by outsiders, linked with the drug trade, and associated with elements of the Burmese Communist Party. Moreover, the nation's Indian and Chinese minorities have an influence in the Burmese economy disproportionate to their numbers. Finally, military governments have viewed Westernization as a threat to Burmese traditional culture.

The government's response to this insecurity has been a policy of nonalignment. Earlier, Burma attempted to maintain an isolationist foreign policy by refusing to participate in the Indochina conflict, eschewing aid from various nations, and, until the late 1990s, forgoing membership in ASEAN. However, isolationism did not foster economic growth and, under the SPDC, Burma moved to a policy of modified isolationism. Under Thein Sein, modified isolation gave way to a new strategy to open the country. For the first time since 1962, Burmese leaders have begun to prioritize economic imperatives over security concerns and paranoia.

Relations with Thailand have often been tense because of the history of conflict between the two nations. However, relations improved following the 8888 Uprising when Burma, after renaming itself Myanmar, desperately agreed to Thai requests to exploit its teak forests in exchange for needed foreign capital. Burmese concessions to Thai companies, which were prohibited from logging in Thailand due to new environmental laws, permitted the extraction of 1.2 million tons of logs annually.[20] Thai politicians and military leaders later visited Myanmar to coordinate trade, drug eradication, and offshore oil exploration. Unsurprisingly, Thailand was the first country Burmese generals permitted (belatedly) to offer relief aid for cyclone victims in 2008. After her 2010 release, Aung San Suu Kyi's first visit was to Thailand and to Burmese refugees on the Thai-Burma border. In 2012, President Thein Sein and Prime Minister Yingluck signed a Memorandum of Understanding to jointly establish Myanmar's first economic zone: the Dawei Deep Seaport and Special Economic Zone.

As a result of economic reform, relations with Myanmar's other major neighbors, India and China, warmed up as well. After the 8888 Uprising, the Indian government expressed support for the Burmese people's resolve to achieve democracy. The two countries now trade in arms and share interests in Myanmar's offshore gas and oil. China, even more aggressively than India, cultivated relations with Myanmar during the SPDC period of modified isolationism. Border trade, energy interests, the prospect of a trans-Burma oil pipeline to Yunnan, and common interpretations of state sovereignty brought the two countries closer together; however, concern over ongoing minority unrest along the China-Myanmar border, and Kachin refugees fleeing into China, did not. Moreover, leery of President Barack Obama's strategic "pivot" to Asia, China has been less sanguine about improved US-Myanmar relations. China's fears were assuaged somewhat as a result of a week-long party-to-party visit to China by NLD leader Aung San Suu Kyi months prior to the 2015 general election.

In 1990, the United States downgraded its representation in Burma from an ambassador to a chargé d'affaires but did not fully sever relations following antigovernment protests. To the extent that any cooperation between the two governments followed, it was primarily to address narcotics trafficking in the region. Otherwise, after abrogating 1990 election results, Burma faced one tough US sanction measure followed by another. The Clinton and Bush administrations repeatedly condemned Burma's oppressive system, imposed various trade restrictions, and limited the international financial activity of regime leaders. In a rare foreign policy venture, First Lady Laura Bush publicly chided junta leaders following Cyclone Nargis in a speech to an international audience.

On her first trip to Asia as President Obama's secretary of state, Hillary Clinton announced that the US policy on Burma was under review in hopes of encouraging "more effective" political and economic reform to "help the Burmese people." In November 2011, Thein Sein's reform program received official American endorsement when Secretary Clinton paid a visit to Naypyidaw, as well as to the Rangoon home of the recently released Aung San Suu Kyi. A year later Thein Sein was granted a visa to the United States, something that was unthinkable for junta leaders just a few years earlier. While in the United States, he addressed the United Nations General Assembly in New York and pledged that he would not backtrack on reforms, drawing comparisons to Soviet reformer Mikhail Gorbachev. A full restoration of diplomatic relations between the two countries occurred in 2012.

ASEAN, a body committed to noninterference, struggled with the junta's ongoing repression since it admitted Burma into the organization. In the body's history, no single member has put ASEAN's aversion to political interference to the test as much as has Myanmar. Following the violent events of 2007, one caucus of ASEAN state parliamentarians even proposed Myanmar's expulsion from the body. In general, however, ASEAN leaders had long argued that international sanctions only deepened Myanmar's isolation and instead pursued constructive engagement, which they believed was more likely to produce democratic reform.[21] By 2015, Myanmar's trajectory toward political democracy, ironically, appeared as robust or more robust than most of its ASEAN partners, many of whom were rapidly backsliding into illiberalism and authoritarianism.

Nonetheless, no sooner had Western countries restored ties, eased sanctions, and begun to claim policy success with respect to Myanmar's democratic progress than the Rohingya crisis erupted and dampened international optimism. Widely broadcasted images and headline stories of desperate Rohingya families fleeing Myanmar's sectarian violence gripped the international community for much of 2015. Thein Sein's initial indifference to the matter was eventually called out by observers as tacit complicity with Burma's ultranationalist Buddhists. Due to his failures, as well as ASEAN's reluctance to lead, the United Nations ultimately stepped in to organize an international response that helped ameliorate the crisis.

As world leaders welcomed the 2015 elections and sent formal congratulations to NLD leaders, few were able to do so publicly without also referencing the Rohingya humanitarian crisis. Given the decades of principled support for her human rights cause, many in the international community struggled to simply dismiss Aung San Suu Kyi's noticeable silence on the Rohingya matter as excusable pre-election posturing. It was a reminder to foreign governments that, going forward, Myanmar's foreign policy is likely to be driven by domestic pressures, regardless of who may be in power. Like elsewhere, it is possible that Myanmar's new NLD government will respond to foreign pressure, defer to international law, and conduct its foreign policy on democratic principles when it is most politically expedient to do so.

CONCLUSION

However condemned by the NLD and international critics, the 2008 post–Cyclone Nargis constitutional referendum was, to Myanmar's ruling generals, the beginning of a new era of political and economic reform. Starting in 2010, through a series of unexpected but welcome moves, Myanmar's ruling generals began to irreversibly transform their own regime.

The political changes under way in Myanmar today are the most promising political developments the Burmese have experienced in decades. Cautious optimism that they will be successful is shared by Aung San Suu Kyi and the international community as well as the United Kingdom (Burma's former colonizer) and the United States (the major force behind long-standing sanctions against its leaders). Arguably, Burmese society is now poised to enjoy some of the political, economic, and social opportunities common elsewhere in the region. If current trends persist, overall human development in Myanmar, currently the lowest in Southeast Asia, is likely to improve going forward.

Because the consequences of democratic reversal at this point would be so severe politically and economically, it is difficult to imagine yet another 1990-style about-face by the Tatmadaw. Undeniably, the country has experienced political disappointment and tragedy before, such as with the 1947 assassination of Aung San and the 1990 nullification of election results by the military. In these cases, the promise of visionary leadership was unexpectedly ripped from the Burmese people. One must not rule out the possibility that the Tatmadaw leadership, or some faction within it, may engineer yet another political reversal, but that scenario seems increasingly unlikely.

Only hours after the 2015 poll, Daw Suu, "The Lady," revealed her party's plans that she alone would stand "above the president"; "I'll make all the decisions," she declared to the world.[22] However justified in victory she was to make such a pronouncement, it is fair to wonder if Aung San Suu Kyi may one day regret those words. Given the country's long-standing ethnic and developmental challenges, taking responsibility for "all of the decisions" that will affect 56 million people who have yet to coalesce into a stable nation stands as a daunting task.

The track record of democratic development elsewhere in Southeast Asia suggests a rocky road lies ahead for Myanmar. The country's fundamental ethnic tensions persist, and questions over regional autonomy and federalism remain unresolved. Indeed, the biggest challenge for any Burmese government—whether liberal, illiberal, or authoritarian—lies in crafting the yet-to-be-discovered formula of federalism that keeps ethnic tensions at bay while allowing for the equitable allocation of both the powers of the state and the benefits of the market across Burma's disparate populations. Myanmar's restless borderlands, its pervasive poverty, and rising sectarian tensions between Buddhists and Muslims ominously remind both Burmese and outsiders alike that the twin ideals of republicanism and union—which now share a place alongside "Myanmar" in the country's official name—currently remain more aspirational than real.

NOTES

1. The r in Burma is not pronounced but serves to lengthen the "ah" sound. The word is pronounced approximately as "Bamar" with the "b" and "m" sounds fairly indistinct. This chapter uses the names Burma and Myanmar interchangeably, with some preference for using Burma for historical, cultural, and social contexts and for continuity with previous editions. Written prior to recent political reforms, the first five editions of this book used only Burma. Most governments, scholars, and media outlets have now adopted the use of Myanmar, although Burma is still widely acceptable.

2. December 2015.

3. Burma Watcher, "Burma in 1988," Asian Survey 29, no. 2 (February 1989): 174.

4. Thant Myint U, The River of Lost Footsteps: A Personal History of Burma (New York: Farrar, Straus and Giroux, 2006), 32–34.

5. Ibid., 35.

6. Kyaw Yin Hlaing, "Myanmar in 2003: Frustration or Despair?" Asian Survey 44, no. 1 (January/February 2004): 88.

7. For an excellent account of Cyclone Nargis, see Emma Larkin, No Bad News for the King: The True Story of Cyclone Nargis and Its Aftermath in Burma (New York: Penguin, 2010).

8. David Steinberg, "Myanmar in 2010: The Elections Year and Beyond," in Southeast Asian Affairs 2011, ed. Daljit Singh (Singapore: Institute of Southeast Asian Studies, 2011), 173–189; Michael Schuman, "Will Burma Become Asia's Next Economic Tiger?" Time, August 22, 2012, http://business.time.com/2012/08/22/will-burma-become-asias-next-economic-tiger.

9. Chaw Chaw Sein and Nicholas Farrelly, "The Meaning of Myanmar's 2015 Election: Summary Paper," 2016, ANU Myanmar Research Center.

10. Aung San Suu Kyi later accepted her award in person in a second ceremony in 2012.

11. See chapter 8 of this book for a full account of Indonesia's Golkar party under Suharto.

12. Larkin, No Bad News for the King, 138.

13. Josef Silverstein, "National Unity in Burma: Is It Possible?" in Durable Stability in Southeast Asia, ed. Kusuma Snitwongse and Sukhumbhand Paribatra (Singapore: Institute of Southeast Asian Studies, 1987), 80.

14. Ibid., 80–81.

15. "Obituary: Khun Sa," The Economist, November 8, 2007, www.economist.com /node/10097596.

16. Jonah Fisher, "Myanmar's Strongman Gives Rare BBC Interview," BBC.com, July 20, 2015, www.bbc.com/news/world-asia-33587800.

17. Robert Kaplan, "Was Democracy Just a Moment?" *The Atlantic Monthly*, December 1997.

18. Maureen Aung-Thwin, "Burmese Days," *Foreign Affairs* 68, no. 2 (February 1989): 150.

19. Ardeth Maung Thawnghmung and Maung Aung Myoe, "Myanmar in 2006: Another Year of Housekeeping?" *Asian Survey* 47, no. 1 (January/February 2007): 197.

20. James F. Guyot and John Badgley, "Myanmar in 1989," *Asian Survey* 30, no. 2 (February 1990): 191.

21. For an excellent treatment of ASEAN and the dilemmas that shape the organization, see Donald K. Emmerson, "Introduction," in *Hard Choices: Security, Democracy, and Regionalism in Southeast Asia* (Stanford: The Walter H. Shorenstein Asia-Pacific Research Center, 2008), 3–56.

22. Claire Phipps and Matthew Weaver, "Aung San Suu Kyi Vows to Make All the Decisions—As It Happened," *The Guardian*, November 10, 2015, www.theguardian.com /world/live/2015/nov/10/myanmar-election-aung-san-suu-kyi-nld-historic-win-live.

4

VIETNAM

Stretching some 1,200 miles from its border with China to its southernmost point in the South China Sea, Vietnam is shaped like two rice baskets at either end of a pole. The bulk of the population lives in the two baskets: the Red River Delta in the north and the Mekong River Delta in the south. The pole is the mountainous stretch of territory in the central, sparsely populated part of the country.

Vietnam, with more people than France, Germany, or Egypt, is the world's thirteenth-most-populous country. The majority of Vietnam's 93 million people work in agriculture. Formerly, most Vietnamese practiced Mahayana Buddhism, but Vietnamese society has been secularized since independence and now most residents do not actively practice or pursue religious beliefs. Among those who do, Buddhism still predominates, although about 7 percent are Roman Catholics, a religion brought to Vietnam during the French colonial period. Confucianist principles from the nation's Chinese heritage remain widespread across society and stress centralized political authority, duty, and subordination to superiors: ruled to ruler, son to father, and pupil to teacher. Many minority religions also exist in Vietnam, including the indigenous Cao Dai and Hoa Hao sects, with over 1 million adherents each.[1]

Nationalism has been the key concept for understanding Vietnamese politics. Indeed, Vietnam's search for a national identity received its greatest impetus during the thousand-year Chinese domination (111 BCE–939 CE). The ability of the Vietnamese to emerge from that period with many of their traditions intact is a clear indication of the nationalist urge that has pervaded the country's history. Similarly, the struggle against French colonialism, Japanese occupation, and US intervention reflects the importance of that nationalism.

Vietnam has not always been united. During the era of French colonialism, the country was divided into three areas: Tonkin in the north, with Hanoi as the capital; Annam in the middle, with Hue as the capital; and in the south, Cochin China, whose capital was Saigon. Traditionally, the northerners have

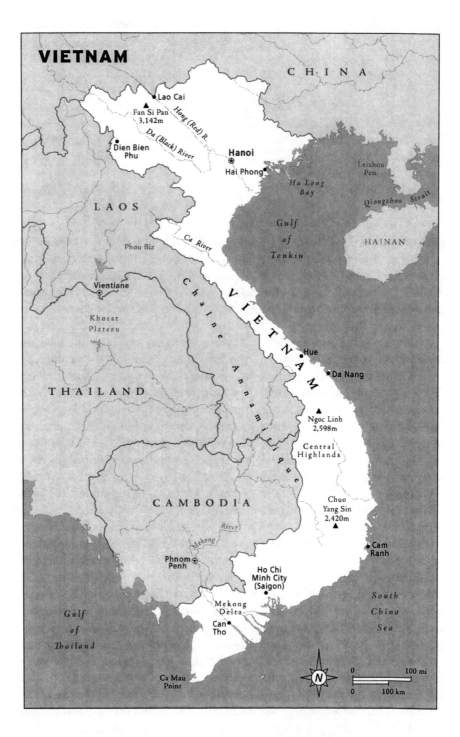

VIETNAM

CHINA

Lao Cai

▲ Fan Si Pan
3,142m

Hong (Red) R.

Da (Black) River

Dien Bien
Phu

Hanoi
⊗
Hai Phong●

Leizhou
Pen.

*Ha Long
Bay*

Qiongzhou Strait

LAOS

Ca River

*Gulf
of
Tonkin*

HAINAN

Phou Bia

Vientiane
⊗

Chaine Annamitique

V
I
E
T
N
A
M

Khorat
Plateau

Hue●

●Da Nang

▲
Ngoc Linh
2,598m

THAILAND

*Central
Highlands*

CAMBODIA

Chuo
Yang Sin
2,420m
▲

River

Mekong

●Cam
Ranh

Phnom
Penh
⊗

Ho Chi
Minh City
(Saigon)

*South
China
Sea*

*Gulf
of
Thailand*

Mekong
Delta

Can●
Tho

Ca Mau
Point

Ⓝ

0   100 mi

0   100 km

seen themselves as modern, progressive, and efficient, and they have viewed the southerners as lazy. The Annamese have seen themselves as highly cultured, the northerners as grasping, and the southerners as rustic. Southerners have regarded themselves as pacifistic and their northern neighbors as aggressive and violent.

In addition to these differing regional perceptions, national unification had to overcome the cultural and political dichotomy between the rural areas and the cities. Interactions consisted largely of the exploitation of the peasantry by the country's mandarin class of officials. Moreover, Vietnam is populated by minority groups that have traditionally been treated with disdain by the Vietnamese majority. Many of these fifty-four official minority groups, which compose about 14 percent of the total population, are upland dwellers in the central and northern mountains.

Despite the divisiveness that has characterized much of Vietnamese history, a nationalist continuity has remained in the form of anticolonialism and antineoimperialism. Following the Japanese defeat in 1945, Ho Chi Minh—the leader of the League for the Independence of Vietnam, known as the Vietminh—proclaimed the country's independence and set up a provisional government that he headed. The first lines of Ho's historic speech on Vietnamese freedom were lifted directly from the US Declaration of Independence. The French and representatives of the newly established Democratic Republic of Vietnam, led by Ho, initially agreed that a new independent state existed and that the French would not move to reclaim their former colony. However, the agreement broke down, and a series of clashes ignited the First Indochina War, which lasted eight years and became an object of US Cold War interests.

The military defeat of the French led to the Geneva Conference of 1954, which sought to separate the rival French and Vietminh forces by setting up a temporary military demarcation line at the seventeenth parallel. This line was not intended to be a political or territorial boundary. In addition, the Geneva agreements called for eventual national elections to establish a single administration throughout the country. During the Geneva Conference, an anti-Vietminh administration emerged below the seventeenth parallel, led initially by the former Annamese emperor Bao Dai and subsequently by the strongly anticommunist Catholic mandarin Ngo Dinh Diem. On October 26, 1955, Diem proclaimed the Republic of Vietnam, better known as South Vietnam, with its capital in Saigon and himself as the first president; he had the support of the United States. He repudiated the Geneva agreements, specifically the provision for national elections.

Ho Chi Minh had agreed to the Geneva agreements at least partly because he believed that national elections would ensure reunification under communist Vietminh leadership. Ho, who was both a nationalist and a communist, saw the two ideologies as inseparable. His goal of a united Vietnam was scuttled when it became clear that Diem had no intention of merging with the north.

During Diem's increasingly repressive rule in the late 1950s, South Vietnam became the site of a guerrilla insurgency against his government. The political arm of the guerrilla activity was the National Liberation Front (NLF), which was initially an autonomous, southern-based movement. The military arm was known as the Viet Cong (Vietnamese Communist). A large number of northerners who had moved to the south following the Geneva Conference joined these guerrillas. In the early 1960s, the North Vietnamese provided increasing military support to the NLF. The People's Revolutionary Party—South Vietnam's communist party, which was controlled by the north—gradually came to dominate the NLF until ultimately the two organizations were indistinguishable.

To counteract the insurgency, Diem relied on US advisers, weaponry, money, and soldiers. US support began in 1954 with 1,000 advisers, which increased to 12,000 by 1962. Despite this support, Diem's own position deteriorated until US president John Kennedy acquiesced to a coup d'état against Diem by South Vietnamese generals. The coup, which took place in October 1963, and Diem's concurrent death, paved the way for a dozen ineffective and unstable military governments, which were less interested in economic or social reforms than in a military victory over the Viet Cong and the North Vietnamese.

US involvement continued to escalate. In February 1965, the United States began massive bombing of the north to interdict North Vietnamese supply lines, erode morale, and provide time for the south to strengthen its forces. None of these purposes were achieved. By 1968, half a million US military personnel were in Vietnam, but the Tet Offensive by the north, which involved coordinated attacks on all major cities and towns in the south, demonstrated the ineffectiveness of the US bombing policy, demoralized American troops, and fully revealed the communists' unyielding will to suffer mass casualties for their cause. Opposition to the war in the United States intensified, and President Lyndon Johnson announced he would not seek reelection.

Ho Chi Minh's death in 1969, meanwhile, hardened his followers' resolve to realize the vision of a unified country. A collective leadership arose in Ho's absence with Le Duan the first among equals. No one could replace Ho, for his stature was too vast to be inherited by a single person. The leadership transition proceeded smoothly, without major shifts in war strategy or destabilizing factional purges. The Soviet Union, China, and other countries of the communist bloc continued to give the north material support. The guerrilla warfare tactics of General Vo Nguyen Giap thoroughly frustrated US troops and commanders. US losses mounted from month to month.

South Vietnam had increasingly become a client state of the United States. To reduce this dependency and to blunt rising US protests against the war, in the early 1970s President Richard Nixon began a policy of "Vietnamization"—the gradual withdrawal of US troops from Vietnam—while escalating the bombing against the north. In May 1970, US and South Vietnamese troops invaded Cambodia, ostensibly to halt Viet Cong use of Cambodian sanctuaries. The result, however, was a massive escalation of the war to all of Indochina, unparalleled demonstrations in the United States against the war, and the unification of insurgent forces in Cambodia known as the Khmer Rouge.

Following Nixon's historic 1972 visit to China and the Christmas bombing of Hanoi later that same year (in which 40,000 tons of bombs were dropped), the Paris Peace Accords were signed by the contending powers in January 1973. North Vietnam agreed to a cease-fire, while the United States agreed not only to a cessation of bombing in the north but also to withdrawal of its troops. The Paris Peace Accords were essentially a victory for the north because North Vietnamese troops were able to stay in place. Without US bombing support and financial aid (the United States had spent over $112 billion in Vietnam since the 1950s), South Vietnam could not withstand the pressure from the North.

The rationale for US intervention in Vietnam had several foundations. The first concern was the perceived national interest of the United States itself. Most US policymakers saw the fall of Vietnam to communism as one more stage in the growth of a cancer that could eventually spread to America itself. Thus, South Vietnam became a testing ground for communist wars of national liberation. It was believed that anything less than a committed stand against communist aggression would be tantamount to an invitation for further aggression in other parts of the world. American policymakers also cited the commitment of five presidents, the terms of the Southeast Asia Treaty Organization (SEATO), and agreements with South Vietnam as justification for US involvement; they believed that American credibility as a world power was at stake.

Finally, decisions regarding Vietnam were also a function of internal pressure. Each president feared a political backlash if he were seen as soft on communism or responsible for the defeat of South Vietnam. Therefore, Vietnam became the test of presidential strength, especially for Johnson and Nixon, both of whom articulated the need for total victory.

The US rationale for intervention was also a function of the ignorance and arrogance of American policymakers at the time. A lack of appreciation for Vietnamese history, society, and culture, combined with a blind belief in faulty theories of democracy and mistaken assessments of US power, doomed US policymakers from the start. US policy in Vietnam was the unfortunate result of several small steps, gradual escalatory moves that by themselves seemed to strategists to be restrained but that in sum committed American blood and treasure to an unwinnable war. Policy decisions resulted in a war in which over 2 million American soldiers fought and 58,000 died.

In April 1975, North Vietnamese troops moved swiftly through the south, conquering province after province and eventually capturing Saigon. A war for Vietnamese independence that had endured for three decades came to a swift close. The cost of victory was over 2 million Vietnamese dead, with millions more injured and displaced. Cities, towns, and rural villages were left devastated from years of conflict. More bombs were dropped during "the American War"—as the Vietnamese refer to it—than were dropped in all past wars combined. About 4 million Vietnamese (as well as thousands of US veterans) would also become long-term sufferers of the crippling effects of Agent Orange, a toxic defoliant dropped from US planes to clear forests for war.

The immediate causes of the communist victory included the corruption of the South Vietnamese army and the end of its US support. Longer-term reasons for the communist success included the artificiality of South Vietnam's political system. The South Vietnamese government, which did not meet the needs of the people, was viewed by northerners as well as many southerners as a lackey of the United States. Also, the war was never fully understood by US policymakers, who underestimated the importance of nationalism and the tenacity of the Vietnamese people to withstand great pressure. Moreover, the war never received the wholehearted support of the American public or of even a large element of the government. As the war continued, more and more Americans became convinced that the means used by the US government were disproportionate to the stated goals.

The North Vietnamese moved swiftly to consolidate their power. Not since the 1860s, when the French began appropriating Vietnamese territory, had Vietnam been fully unified and absent foreign occupation. The newly united nation was named the Socialist Republic of Vietnam. Ho Chi Minh's goal of a united Vietnam under communist rule was reached, and in his honor Saigon was renamed Ho Chi Minh City. Hanoi became the nation's capital. Plans were carried out to transform the south's economy from capitalism to socialism, and "reeducation camps" were established to indoctrinate former partisans of the South Vietnamese government with socialist values. An estimated 2.5 million Vietnamese were sent to these camps, which lasted into the mid-1990s.

The southerners did not take well to the economic programs of their new rulers, and many fled the country in a first wave of refugees. They resisted efforts to collectivize and redistribute the land. Moreover, the Vietnamese economy deteriorated, worsened by drought and the diversion of resources to its military in Cambodia and along the Chinese border. Poor management and planning by the central authorities were also responsible for the economic catastrophe the new revolutionary government faced.

As the Vietnamese government ended the traditional free-market system in the south, the indigenous Chinese, long the mainstay of entrepreneurship in Saigon (now Ho Chi Minh City), fled the country. The government's reform of the monetary system had wiped out the savings of these shop owners. The result was a second wave of refugees, this time ethnic Chinese who fled by sea and thus became known as "boat people." During 1978 and 1979, 75,000 refugees per month fled Vietnam, arriving on the shores of Thailand, Malaysia, Singapore, Indonesia, the Philippines, and Hong Kong, overwhelming those countries' humanitarian resources.[2] Nearly 2 million Vietnamese, representing all ethnic backgrounds, left the country in the years following the communist takeover.

On December 25, 1978, with the concurrence of the Soviet Union, Vietnamese troops invaded Cambodia and within a month captured Phnom Penh. They then established a new government led by an unknown Vietnamese-trained Cambodian named Heng Samrin. The Vietnamese claimed that they launched their invasion to restore order and security in border areas by punishing Cambodia for a long series of border incursions and for intransigence in negotiations. The Vietnamese also insisted that they were liberating Cambodians from the genocide and repression of the Pol Pot regime. The invasion acted as an impetus for the subsequent Chinese invasion of Vietnam in February 1979. The Chinese hoped their own offensive would force Vietnam to withdraw its occupation force of 200,000 troops from Cambodia. China desired to "teach Vietnam a lesson," to convince the Vietnamese that China was not a paper tiger, to punish the country for its harsh treatment of overseas Chinese, and to send a signal to the Soviet Union that China would not acquiesce to growing Soviet influence in Southeast Asia. Although neither country was able to claim clear-cut victory, Vietnamese forces remained in Cambodia.

Vietnamese expectations that independence from foreign exploitation for the first time in over a hundred years would bring them a better life were dashed by the continued deterioration of the economy. In the 1980s, a decade after their defeat of the United States—the world's mightiest and most technologically sophisticated nation—the Vietnamese people's standard of living was worse than before the war. Indeed, the economy had advanced little since the French colonization of Vietnam in the late nineteenth century.[3]

The Sixth Congress of the Communist Party of Vietnam (CPV) realized the seriousness of the economic malaise and met in December 1986 to implement a plan to remedy the problems. Nguyen Van Linh, a prominent reformer, was named CPV general secretary. His appointment and the retirement of such old-guard communist revolutionary leaders as President Truong Chinh, Premier Pham Van Dong, and Foreign Minister Le Duc Tho signaled a significant turn in Vietnamese politics. The leadership shift to the more pragmatic, economically oriented, reform-minded younger officials from the ideologically conservative, security-minded party leaders was the first major break in leadership patterns since Ho Chi Minh came to power after World War II.

At the December 1986 party congress, Linh set forth a policy of *doi moi* (renovation), a plan publicly approved by the CPV leaders, all of whom agreed that the policies of the previous eleven years—since the end of the war—should not be continued. *Doi moi* called for major economic and political changes with the proviso that the party-led dictatorship of the proletariat remain sacrosanct. The move was timed, not coincidentally, with Mikhail Gorbachev's decision that the Soviet Union would reduce support for client states and move domestically toward perestroika, or economic restructuring.

Nevertheless, despite past failures, reform was difficult because a strong coalition of conservative party leaders felt threatened by the changes. CPV leaders feared that the party's dominance would be lost, and military leaders—who played an important role in the Politburo—believed that *doi moi* threatened national security because it diminished the importance of military strength in favor of economic development.[4]

The changes included rapid movement away from the centrally planned economy and development of a more market-oriented model. The shift built upon the economic reforms that had begun in the late 1970s when a contract system was introduced and decentralization of various sectors of the economy was carried out. The contract system had allowed peasants to sell a small portion of their crops after meeting their obligations to the government. That system had stagnated when peasants refused to cooperate because their profits were so small that they had no incentive to produce more. The new plan provided greater incentives, including the leasing (and later purchasing) of land formerly nationalized by the government.

Renovation also called for more public debate and more power for the National Assembly, the main legislative branch of the government. Many political prisoners were released and corrupt officials ousted from their positions. The press was allowed to criticize government policies more aggressively, at least until the Seventh Party Congress in 1991. The destabilizing protests in Burma (1988) and China (1989) that preceded the CPV's five-year congress, and the collapse of the Soviet Union that followed, cemented party resolve: *doi moi* would go forward but open political expression would not.

Although popular, renovation met with sharp criticism when new policies initially failed to improve the economy. In 1988, for example, famine was barely averted in the northern provinces, and inflation increased to almost 1,000 percent. Vietnam's reformers increasingly found themselves on the defensive.

As Vietnam entered the 1990s, the government was in transition from the old-guard revolutionary forces, who had held power in the north since independence, to younger (although still elderly) reform-minded communists, who were more willing to try new means to achieve their aims. Dramatic and far-reaching changes occurred in Vietnam in 1995, when the country normalized diplomatic relations with Washington and became a member of ASEAN, an alliance originally formed to oppose "Vietnamese intervention." Vietnam's Southeast Asian neighbors, eyeing Vietnam's large market, had accepted Vietnam's economic rebirth.

Economic ties were also the impetus for reconciliation with the United States. Conservative American politicians and business leaders, having seen the advantages to American business from the 1994 lifting of the US embargo against Vietnam, threw support behind plans to form new ties. There was virtually no negative reaction by Americans to the new policy, except for minor complaints against President Bill Clinton himself for not having participated in the war thirty years earlier. The first US ambassador to the Socialist Republic of Vietnam, Douglas "Pete" Peterson, had spent six years in Hanoi as a prisoner of war. Reconciliation, not recrimination, became the new standard in US-Vietnam relations.

Doi moi has created new challenges for the CPV, but from the mid-1980s to the present, the effects of new policies, on balance, have been positive for the Vietnamese. A major challenge has been the disproportional benefits of reform. Vietnam's northern and southern regions, once divided and at war, soon found themselves competing under *doi moi* policies for foreign investment, largesse from the state, and political influence. Whereas the north had followed communist economic policies since the 1950s, the south had experienced communist planning for only ten years, from 1975 to 1986. These differences meant many southerners were better equipped with entrepreneurial skills and business acumen when *doi moi* began. Foreign investors, sensitive to business climate and government meddling, also preferred the expansive Ho Chi Minh City and its more hands-off investment zones to smaller and more bureaucratic Hanoi. By 2004, Ho Chi Minh City, with 5 percent of the country's total population, was producing over 20 percent of Vietnam's GDP. The party's top positions increasingly began to favor southerners with track records of reform success.

After a decade of fits and starts and many frustrations on the part of foreign investors, Vietnam's policy shift began to produce dramatic results. Following the south's lead, the Red River Delta region in the north, including many rural provinces, also began to experience rapid economic growth. Remarkably, between 1993 and 2004, overall poverty rates in Vietnam fell from 59 percent to 20 percent.[5] Political life remained circumscribed, but individual freedoms were expanded. Socially, a new youth culture emerged, symbolized by rock music, fast motorbikes, and high levels of material consumption. The country's first generation raised in a unified, postwar Vietnam found common ground not in "Uncle Ho's" vision of simple living but in pop culture, music videos, and designer logos.[6]

Beyond strong economic growth, ASEAN membership, and normal relations with the United States, Vietnam's final mark of *doi moi* success came in 2007 when it achieved membership in the WTO. At the CPV's Tenth Party Congress, held in the year prior to WTO ascension, party business was confined largely to reshuffling leadership positions and staid pledges to enhance government efficiency. Nevertheless, indicating a measured shift toward greater rule of law, the party allowed unprecedented preconference openness and increased transparency of party business.[7] Vietnam's party of reform-minded communists was now more concerned with growth-related official corruption than with corrupt policies unable to produce growth. Vietnam's track record of economic success and poverty alleviation was in fact drawing praise from the international community.

On April 8, 2006, 118 signatories led by a bank official and former army officer published the *Manifesto for Freedom and Democracy* two weeks before the Tenth Party Congress. It called for "a separation of powers" and a "pluralistic and multiparty system." Some members of the group, known as Bloc 8406 (the date of the manifesto's release), subsequently attempted to form opposition political parties, introduce new publications, and form workers' associations. A swift state crackdown followed, and Bloc 8406's leaders were imprisoned. Other members were harassed and their organizations were forcibly dismantled.[8] The group generated only 2,000 open members and proved unable to replicate mass movements such as those witnessed in Eastern Europe in 1989. The episode also affirmed the party's intolerance for oppositional politics.

Post-1986 economic growth in Vietnam has produced inequality, but at lower levels than in Thailand, Indonesia, and China. Although 70 percent of Vietnamese still reside in rural areas, it is not uncommon for particular provinces to report double-digit economic growth, driven by food production and agriculture exports. Changes to budgeting procedures have also permitted local authorities more autonomy to allocate expenditures to suit local needs.[9] Improvements in rural development are also credited to Vietnam's collaborative programs with the World Bank and United Nations agencies. Vietnam, unlike many of its globalizing neighbors, has not achieved economic growth by abandoning its rural majority.

Unfortunately, Vietnamese leaders have not heeded all the lessons of their neighbors' experiences with boom and bust capital markets. Vietnam's young stock markets in Ho Chi Minh City and Hanoi reached new heights only to collapse precipitously. Between January and June 2008, Vietnamese stocks lost 60 percent of their value. Ho Chi Minh City's market, catering to foreign money, dropped every day it traded in May of that year. Inflation soared over 25 percent, and angry consumers reacted by hoarding goods and abandoning the Vietnamese currency. The experience began to raise new questions about the sustainability of *doi moi*–driven growth and CPV governance of the economy.

A series of macroeconomic policy adjustments gradually improved the economic situation by 2013, but regained economic confidence has not engendered additional trust in the CPV. Foreign investors from Asia are particularly drawn to opportunities in Vietnam, but others remain more cautious over worries about large debts held by Vietnam's many state-owned enterprises. Vietnam stands to benefit greatly from the Trans-Pacific Partnership (TPP) trade initiative, which its leadership enthusiastically supports. Among the TPP's twelve founding members, Vietnam enters with the lowest level of development, expecting to gain greatly from new trade, investment, and job growth.

The greatest challenges the country faces remain in the political realm, where government crackdowns on both political speech and activity range from general restrictions on the internet and social media to particular attacks targeting prominent dissidents. As the old independence generation begins to fade from the scene, younger CPV elites find themselves confronting a less pliable society that has fewer memories tying communism to war victories.

Overall, however, the picture remains positive. In the thirty years since reforms began, Vietnam's economic achievements remain noteworthy. Vietnam today is a different country than it was in the decade following "the American War." Before *doi moi*, 60 percent of Vietnamese lived in poverty, forced to suffer in a hopeless economy and with a government unable to provide basic services. Today, less than 10 percent of Vietnam's large population lives below the poverty line, and almost everyone has access to basic education, health care, decent employment, and economic opportunity. In comparative terms, over 80 percent of Vietnamese enjoy a standard of living currently unknown to a third of all Burmese, Cambodians, Filipinos, Laotians, and East Timorese. Vietnam today is a Southeast Asian success story—one qualified nonetheless by the cost that single-party rule imposes on civil liberties, political freedom, and official justice.

INSTITUTIONS AND SOCIAL GROUPS

Ho Chi Minh

As the founding father of independent, communist Vietnam; the victorious leader over the Japanese, French, and Americans; and the founder of the CPV, Ho is the most important Vietnamese of contemporary times and perhaps the most important leader in recent Southeast Asian history. He was and remains a central institution—the symbol of united, nationalist, communist Vietnam. Pictures of "Uncle Ho" are ubiquitous in Vietnam, statues and busts of the leader adorn public places, and millions of people have viewed his embalmed body in the Soviet-built mausoleum in Hanoi.

Ho's father was a Confucian scholar who was active in anticolonial activities; his mother died when he was ten. Throughout his life he used numerous pseudonyms (the name Ho Chi Minh means "he who enlightens"). He spent thirty years abroad, living in and traveling to the Soviet Union, China, New York, London, and Paris. He became a committed communist and founded the forerunner parties of the CPV, including the Indo-Chinese Communist Party in 1930 and the Vietminh in 1941. His tastes were simple, even ascetic, yet he was tenacious and sometimes ruthless in the means he used to achieve his goals.

Ho died six years before the nation was reunited. His last testament requested that at his death there be a one-year moratorium on farm taxes and that his ashes be placed in urns in the three parts of Vietnam: Cochin China, Annam, and Tonkin. However, these requests were not heeded by Ho's successors. Instead, taxes were raised, and his body was embalmed and put on display in a massive building similar to Lenin's mausoleum in Moscow. No Vietnamese leader has subsequently received the adulation Ho received during his life, although every leader has attempted to wrap himself in Ho's mantle. "Ho Chi Minh Thought" is nominally the party's guiding philosophy.

Communist Party of Vietnam

Although the communist party rule in postwar Eastern Europe was imposed from without by Soviet arms, the Communist Party is indigenous to the Vietnamese and was the vehicle for the independence struggle against the French colonialists and, later, the Americans. In modern Vietnamese history, the CPV has had an almost exclusive claim to represent the broader ideals of nationalism and patriotism. For many Vietnamese, the CPV and nationalist struggle are identical.

Party membership numbers around 3 million, more than 3 percent of the population. After stagnating membership in the 1990s, the party quickly expanded membership, raising questions by some about whether quantity has reduced quality. For many youth, party membership is not attractive. A recent decision to allow party members to engage in business—something many were already doing—rankled revolutionary party purists, in particular.

Vietnamese politics as practiced in the Politburo is best understood by an analogy to the great game of *bung-di*, or faction bashing.[10] Party factions, long prevalent in the communist party, form around individuals but traffic in issues. They are enduring but not permanent, and they can divide and re-form to meet changing needs. Despite attempts to contain factionalism, they remain ubiquitous. In the early *doi moi* period, Vietnam's Politburo divided into four major factions: reformers, neoconservatives, bureaucrats, and the military.[11] Today, the divide between reformers and neoconservatives has softened with successful economic growth. Political liberalization, to the extent it is discussed at all, excludes any suggestions of radical reform to multiparty democracy. In Vietnam, no opposition parties are allowed to form and challenge the CPV for state power.

Nationalism remains the glue that binds the CPV's generations, factions, and regional interests together while underpinning the party's ongoing legitimacy to govern. The party's elevation of Ho Chi Minh Thought to official ideology in 1989 was designed to buttress this legitimacy amid policy reforms. At that time the party claimed that its *doi moi* policies were consistent with Ho's views about how socialism could be built in Vietnam—views that, they qualified, had been previously kept from the public. Citing rediscovered "original" documents, the CPV used Ho's "view of socialism" to justify market-oriented *doi moi* and to "delegitimize the policies of the leadership from 1975 to 1986."[12]

Since Ho's death, collective leadership has characterized Communist Party rule in Vietnam. Today, the party Politburo is made up of younger members. These leaders are better educated and concern themselves more with Vietnam's economic productivity and technological improvement than with revolution and ideology. However, younger Vietnamese of the millennial generation seek careers outside of the party-state in the private sector where pay is higher, a development that could affect the talent entering the CPV.

In a system where party and state overlap extensively, top party leaders hold all significant offices of state government. Out of the Eleventh Party Congress in 2011 emerged an all-powerful fourteen-member Politburo, inclusive of Vietnam's current ruling triumvirate: (1) Party Secretary Nguyen Phu Trong, a conservative and former chair of the National Assembly; (2) President Truong Tan Sang, a southerner and pragmatist who functions as head of state; and (3) Prime Minister Nguyen Tan Dung, a southerner known for his anticorruption agenda now serving a second five-year term. Northerner Nguyen Sinh Hung, a former finance minister, is currently chairman of the National Assembly. This position wields less power than the other three but plays an important role in Vietnam's party-controlled rule.

The National Assembly

Formerly insignificant, the National Assembly of the Socialist Republic of Vietnam is beginning to perform functions similar to legislatures elsewhere in Southeast Asia. The CPV revamped the National Assembly's role at its Seventh Party Congress in 2001. Increased attention to the rule of law in the Vietnamese system is requiring the National Assembly to do more than simply rubber-stamp party dictates. Changes have included greater participation in law-based policy formation and new constitutional powers that permit votes of no-confidence in ministers and officials appointed by the assembly.[13] With recent changes, the "role of the National Assembly is not to let the people rule but to widen the range of voices heard in the political mainstream."[14] In 2010, for the first time in its history, the National Assembly blocked a government spending package and all of its related projects.

National Assembly delegates are chosen through national elections. These elections involve more candidates than available seats. Nonparty candidates may run for office, and many do win seats, but all candidates must first be vetted by the Vietnam Fatherland Front (VFF). No parties opposed to the CPV or Ho Chi Minh ideology are free to compete in assembly elections. In 2011, Vietnamese voters elected delegates to the Thirteenth National Assembly. A total of 827 candidates competed for 500 seats; almost 9 percent of delegate winners were nonparty, but VFF-approved, candidates.[15] The Fourteenth National Assembly is scheduled for 2016.

Vietnam Fatherland Front

The Vietnam Fatherland Front is a constitutionally mandated corporatist-style umbrella organization. Under its aegis are all state-sanctioned mass organizations, including all unions (e.g., Women's Union, Farmer's Union, Lawyers' Association), all religious organizations, and all NGOs that are local or internationally based. Civil society in Vietnam is thus thoroughly monitored through the VFF, which acts as gatekeeper, rule-maker, and enforcer of permissible activity. Its stated goal is to unify the country in all "political and spiritual matters." The VFF forcibly co-opts civil society organizations to provide services to society that the state fails to or chooses not to provide. No foreign NGOs legally operate in Vietnam without VFF sanction. Officially, the CPV itself is under the authority of the VFF, but the reality is exactly the opposite.

Military

The Vietnamese army is the CPV's creation, and the leading generals are members of the party leadership. The 4.4 million–member People's Army of Vietnam (PAVN) is the largest in Southeast Asia and includes one of the world's largest reserve forces. After 1975, the PAVN, initially given the mission of re-unifying the nation, was charged with defending Vietnam from external attack, such as when the Chinese crossed Vietnam's northern border in 1979. In contrast to armies elsewhere in Southeast Asia, the Vietnamese army has not threatened a coup against the communist leadership. Its role remains subordinate to that of the party.

STATE-SOCIETY RELATIONS AND DEMOCRACY

According to Article 4 of the Constitution of the Socialist Republic of Vietnam, the Communist Party of Vietnam is "the force assuming leadership of state and society." In its first few decades, the CPV and the Vietnamese state were virtually synonymous, and society remained wholly subordinate. As a single-party dictatorship, all authoritative decisions were made by the party and then disseminated to the populace through a tightly controlled state organization that allowed no dissent. Since reunification, and especially since 1986, a more complex array of forces has emerged within both state and society.

With *doi moi*, the CPV-led state lost dictatorial control over economic and social life. Factions, alliances, and debates within the party grew and increasingly began to mirror those emerging in Vietnam's rapidly changing society. The state remains Leninist, but the scope of political debate has broadened. The distinctions between party, state, and society have blurred as market activity, personal choice, and party-business networks have replaced centralized planning.

The legitimacy of the Vietnamese state is rooted in its communist revolution, which expelled foreign occupiers, unified the country, and established the socialist republic. This legitimacy has not been seriously challenged by the Vietnamese since 1975. Channels through which the people could mount such a challenge have been limited by strict, single-party rule.

As for the party's own legitimacy to govern (distinct from the legitimacy of the socialist republic itself), disastrous economic results of the 1975–1986 period resulted in a growing domestic legitimacy crisis. *Doi moi* policies breathed new life into the party. Today, the CPV leans on performance legitimization, combined with official interpretations of Ho Chi Minh Thought, as the bulwark against a possible domestic challenge to its legitimacy. It is important to note that the party has never delegitimized its authority through any traumatic, Tiananmen-style crackdowns where the military turns on its own people.[16]

The party formerly ruled through dictates generated by its own governmental apparatus. Today, Vietnam is home to a more complex state apparatus attempting to institutionalize procedures, processes, and laws for a mixed economy. Many demands on the state today are more technical than political; others remain purely political. External demands to comply with UN programs, World Bank projects, and WTO membership, for example, differentiate the technical nature of the state's role today from its prereform past. Even with these changes, Vietnam remains closer to "rule by law" than to the "rule of law."

In the economic domain, where performance legitimacy is largely established, democratic ideals such as decentralization and accountability are accepted as necessary for an effective economy. Economic principles such as "the market" and "competition," once viewed as decadent bourgeois concepts, have become the centerpieces of renovation. The same cannot be said for political democracy more generally.

Somewhat ironically, *doi moi* has in many ways expanded the state's role vis-à-vis society. A form of "state capitalism" has replaced a Soviet-style planning system. Vietnam's unprofitable state-owned enterprises (SOEs), for example, are gradually being divested, but many with potential remain under state ownership. The biggest SOEs, known as "General Corporations," monopolize major sectors (e.g., the cement, coal, rubber, and shipbuilding industries), engage international markets, and often own their finance companies. The risks of these South Korean chaebol-style arrangements lie in the obvious hazards of self-financing and unethical or criminal behavior by corporate and party elites.[17]

The Vietnamese state, after transferring over 100 military-owned enterprises to civilian rule, has also created a sovereign wealth fund, the State Capital Investment Company, along the lines of Singapore's Temasek and Malaysia's Khazanah Nasional. The party uses the fund to influence strategic investments in key Vietnamese industries and to ensure that new wealth generated in the private sector comes back to the state. The state bailed out businesses and banks in the wake of the 2008–2009 global financial crisis, provided massive funds for economic stimulus, and created a national asset-management company to deal with spiraling bad debts. Of course, none of these recent initiatives, which expand the state's market role, have been subject to public accountability through elected representative institutions.

Vietnam has no history of democracy. State-society relations have been Confucianist, stressing hierarchy and order, and more recently, communist, emphasizing the party's unquestioned supremacy. The movement of the Eastern

European communist governments toward democracy has not impelled the Vietnamese leadership or the Vietnamese people to initiate a similar transformation of their own government. Indeed, in 1989, the central committee of the CPV, alarmed by developments in Eastern Europe, Burma, and China, rejected appeals for political pluralism in Vietnam. President Nguyen Van Linh stated that the party rejected calls for "bourgeois liberalization, pluralism, political plurality, and multi-opposition parties aimed at denying Marxism-Leninism, socialism, and the party's leadership."[18] Since that time, sporadic attempts inside and outside the state to test the party's commitment to these principles have resulted in failure. In spite of expanding economic and social freedom, the party "seems absolutely determined to maintain its political monopoly."[19]

Compared to elected leaders in open, pluralistic democracies, Vietnam's governors have fewer constituencies to satisfy. Bureaucratic loyalties lie primarily with the state rather than with autonomous religious, ethnic, or class interests. Intellectuals and academics have largely been depoliticized, co-opted, or otherwise silenced, as typified by the treatment of dissidents associated with Bloc 8406. In Vietnam, the highest government leaders are generally one and the same as top party leaders. Intertwined networks of party leaders and business entrepreneurs dominate the state and private sectors. Entanglements between private and public, state and market run thick.

With respect to progress in civil liberties, the government's record is mixed at best. Conflict over religious freedom occurs, for example, between dissident Buddhist monks and communist government officials. Many Buddhists wish to establish the Unified Buddhist Church in place of the Vietnam Buddhist Church, long under the dominance of the CPV. The exiled Vietnamese monk Thich Nhat Hanh (once nominated for a Nobel Peace Prize by Martin Luther King Jr.) has been permitted to return for visits to Vietnam in recent years, but tensions between CPV leaders and Vietnam's Buddhist community remain. On the other hand, Vietnamese Catholics, initially persecuted by communists, practice with less fear than in the past. Unlike in China, where allegiance to the pope in Rome is disallowed, Catholics in Vietnam are permitted to engage with the Roman Catholic Church.

Labor rights, a major target of the international rights community, are slowly improving. In the early 2000s, the government entered into programs with the International Labour Organization to reform labor laws and practices. New laws have made it easier for migrant workers from rural areas to obtain benefits that were once denied to them.[20] Collaboration has yet to produce labor protection in line with global standards—union organizing, for example, is still limited by party approval. Recent economic troubles have produced greater labor discontent, challenging the regime. According to Vietnam's Labor Ministry, nearly 1,000 labor strikes erupted in 2011—twice as many as in 2010 and four times as many as in 1997.[21]

Freedom of the press does not fully exist in Vietnam, but the Internet functions more freely than in neighboring China. Even so, bloggers who turn into reporters or activists can face difficulty with the authorities. Facebook has nearly 4 million users in the country, and bad news travels faster than ever outside of state control. This activity creates a dilemma for party officials who fear the demonstrable capability of social networking to coalesce public opinion against them. In 2011, Vietnamese bloggers organized large protests in the wake of Chinese provocations in the Spratly Islands, located in the South China Sea (see the discussion below). The protesters, angry at China, also expressed derision of their own government's "weak response."[22] Press accounts exposing government corruption are increasingly permitted, but such stories also permit top leaders to showcase "anticorruption" campaigns.

ECONOMY AND DEVELOPMENT

After the end of the war in 1975, the Vietnamese economy declined for a full fifteen years. Inflation rates were astronomical, and unemployment hovered at about 20 percent. Infrastructure essentials such as ports, roads, and electricity were primitive, and housing was abysmal. Vietnam's banking system was barely viable, partly because there was so little managerial expertise. Annual per capita income was estimated to be $200, making Vietnam one of the poorest nations in the world. Famine, which threatened the northern provinces in the 1980s, affecting 10 million farmers, forced Vietnam—a country once self-sufficient in rice—to appeal for international food aid. Ho Chi Minh's favorite aphorism, emblazoned on red banners strung across streets throughout Vietnam— "Nothing is more precious than independence and freedom"—was interpreted in an ironic and sardonic sense. In unguarded moments, Vietnamese stated that "nothing" was exactly what they had.

Given Vietnam's superb natural resources, the country's poverty was all the more shocking and embarrassing to Vietnamese leaders. However, there were important reasons why the country was unable to develop in parallel fashion to the neighboring ASEAN countries. A major reason was the extensive war damage, which required tremendous resources to repair. In the south alone, the war produced 20,000 bomb craters, 10 million refugees, 362,000 invalids, 1 million widows, 880,000 orphans, 250,000 drug addicts, 300,000 prostitutes, and 3 million unemployed. Two-thirds of the villages and 5 million hectares of forests were destroyed.[23]

The US involvement in South Vietnam created a dependent economy, and the billions of dollars spent on the war brought a surfeit of capital that disappeared abruptly when the United States disengaged. Hanoi had expected to receive some $3 billion in reparations aid, which had been promised by US secretary of state Henry Kissinger but was later refused when the United States maintained that North Vietnam had not carried out the terms of the Paris

Peace Accords. Soviet aid did not make up for the loss of Western aid and trade resulting from the US-sponsored trade embargo. Moreover, the Soviet Union's technological aid was insufficient in many ways.

Adding to Vietnam's woes was mismanagement by its leadership. Alternating between reform and orthodoxy, Vietnam's leaders "displayed a paranoid world view, a low adaptability level, perfidy consistently perceived in the motives of others and perpetuation of a cult-type leadership capable of believing the illogical, the irrational, even the absurd."[24] Nationalization and collectivization, thrust upon the south after reunification, failed miserably because southerners would not adhere to socialist policies. Peasants refused to meet their obligations to the state when the state's prices for their crops did not cover even the costs of production.

To overcome the crisis, the CPV's Sixth Congress, in December 1986, proposed major reforms under *doi moi*. Rice output in 1986 was far below 1942 levels, and northern farmers, as members of state-organized cooperatives, produced 52 percent less than farmers from the south who resisted collectivization. To alleviate this situation, land laws were modified to guarantee farmers a ten- to fifteen-year tenure on land they cultivated, although the expectation was that land could henceforth be owned in perpetuity and be inherited. This policy change signaled the end of efforts to collectivize agriculture in the south.

The 1986 reforms gave farmers the legal right to sell their produce on the free market after each paid a tax based on his or her output. Approximately 10 percent to 20 percent of the tax went to the state for the farmers' use of cooperatively owned machinery and for fertilizer and other necessities. Under the new system, farmers could keep a far larger percentage of their output than under the former contract system. Although it took several years for the policy to have a positive impact, Vietnam reemerged in 1989 as a major rice exporter for the first time since the 1950s. It became one of the world's three largest rice exporters, along with Thailand and the United States; today, most of its rice is exported to West Africa, the Philippines, India, Sri Lanka, and China.

Vietnam's foreign investment code was also revised to attract more foreign investors. To draw joint ventures, the government liberalized tax policies and extended guarantees that investment capital would not be expropriated or joint ventures nationalized.[25] The 1987 investment law offered a two-year tax moratorium for joint ventures and established export processing zones in which foreign companies could import materials, use low-cost local labor for assembly, and export final products. A large proportion of the new investors were overseas Vietnamese.[26] The new code increased trade with Japan, Singapore, Hong Kong, France, Indonesia, and India, but did not bring in the amount of capital hoped for because of the continuing US trade embargo. More and more countries, however, broke the embargo to take advantage of the liberalized trade and investment opportunities, especially regarding offshore oil exploration.

The reforms made a dramatic difference in Vietnam's everyday economy. Construction of homes, office buildings, bridges, roads, and schools, for example, burgeoned throughout the country, even in the north, where the economy had been stagnant for many decades. Privately run restaurants and shops opened and flourished. Inflation dropped to more manageable levels as a result of the devaluation of Vietnam's currency, the dong, to the free-market rate, and as government austerity measures—recommended by the IMF, with which Vietnam hoped to restore relations—were adopted to attract investment, credit, and technology from the West. Vietnam also reformed its meager, Russian-based tourist industry by investing in new hotels and encouraging more air traffic from Western countries.

Vietnam remained impoverished, but for the first time since the end of the war there was economic development. In a sense, however, the country remained divided because development occurred more rapidly in the south than in the north (partly as a result of the millions of dollars sent back to relatives from the 2 million southern Vietnamese living abroad). Unemployment remained high, especially among those considered "unreliable" because of their involvement with the former Saigon regime.

In the 1990s, Vietnam's leaders remained committed to *doi moi* and their goal to become the next Asian tiger. GNP growth hit highs nearing 10 percent and Ho Chi Minh City's economy grew by an astonishing 15 percent. The ending of constraints on the IMF's assistance to Vietnam in 1993 and the lifting of the American embargo in 1994 contributed to large increases in foreign direct investment. The new free-market system inexorably affected every sector of the economy, including a rise in tourism. Vietnam was increasingly viewed as Asia's new economic frontier because of its disciplined workforce, cheap labor and materials, and zeal to join the global capitalist system.

In the wake of the regional economic crisis in 1997, however, the economic boom hit a plateau and growth rates declined. Confidence in reform dropped. During the regional crisis, foreign entrepreneurs, citing additional frustration with Vietnam's byzantine bureaucracy, reduced their investment. Many multinational corporations (MNCs) shut down their factories in the absence of legal contracts and protested under-the-table payments demanded by both private business elites and public officials. Added to these problems were underdeveloped economic institutions and government corruption, a primitive banking system, an overvalued dong, and low-quality exports. The slowdown continued through 2002, but GDP rates never dropped below 5 percent. Relative to some of the established economic tigers, Vietnam fared rather well. By the early 2000s, Vietnam's growth returned to rank among the strongest in the world.

Part of Vietnam's recovery was due to a US-Vietnam bilateral trade agreement signed in 2000 that enhanced manufactured exports and invited new investment. Growth rates pushed upward to nearly 7.5 percent by 2003, and export growth again reached double digits. Observers noted, however, that much of this new growth was taking place in the state sector, driven by "low quality" state investments tainted by official corruption.[27] Questions also persisted about how Vietnam could again handle continued rapid growth without quickly upgrading the country's infrastructure and educational system. Low-quality investments and structural limits notwithstanding, Vietnam's GDP climbed higher still, into the 8 percent range, by 2005.

WTO membership starting in 2007 further accelerated Vietnamese exports to the United States, Japan, South Korea, and Singapore. Investment growth improved as well. Intel Corporation, for example, selected Vietnam for its new $300 million chip-testing facility. Vietnam's economic performance seemed to be moving from strength to strength. "Securities fever," as it was called, hit local and foreign investors. For a couple of years, Vietnam's stock market was among the world's most promising. Ordinary Vietnamese, many for the first time in their lives, began to float money on new exchanges in Ho Chi Minh City and Hanoi. However, poor government regulation made the fledgling Asian bourses vulnerable to manipulation, misinformation, and fraud. The government, with many state enterprises listed on the Hanoi exchange, grew increasingly nervous and hastily passed securities laws it had little capacity to actually enforce.

By 2007, the two-decade-old reform movement produced one of the country's highest GDP growth rates under *doi moi*: 8.5 percent. Crude oil, textiles, seafood, coffee, rubber, and rice were pouring out of the country. The United States became Vietnam's largest export trading partner. Vietnam's economic winners looked for places to both spend and multiply their new earnings. Consumption of import luxuries ballooned due to lower import taxes. Vietnam's insatiable class of super-rich gobbled up European luxury cars, designer cosmetics, and high-priced mobile phones. Winners also poured money into land. Commercial real estate in Hanoi and Ho Chi Minh City soared, fetching higher prices per square meter than in New York, Singapore, and Tokyo. By the end of 2007, the economy was racing. Vietnam's two stock exchanges reached a combined value of $29 billion, about $28 billion more than just three years earlier.

This peak of investor exuberance was followed, as many predicted, by a spectacular collapse of Vietnam's stock markets in 2008. Vietnam's rapid growth had generated a growing trade imbalance and rising inflation. In a matter of weeks, the world's hottest stock markets became the world's worst performing. Consumers, many with memories of hyperinflation in the past, began to hoard commodities and buy gold, exacerbating inflationary pressures. Vietnam's currency also fell under pressure. Ominously, observers pointed to parallels with Thailand and Indonesia in 1997.

Vietnam's shell-shocked government, facing its first real capital market crisis, tightened the reins on the economy. Officials moved quickly to raise interest rates and announce a temporary ban on the importation of gold. Import taxes on luxury goods also were adjusted upward. Also, hoping to ward off black-marketeers and currency speculators, officials quietly devalued the dong by 2 percent against the dollar. International investors took the devaluation as a bad sign—as the beginning of much larger devaluations accompanied by a serious economic crisis. State and foreign enterprises faced new uncertainties. Vietnam's twenty-year, *doi moi*–driven ride of rapid growth began shifting into lower gear.

Since 2008, Vietnamese officials have battled inflation and twice devalued Vietnam's currency while trying not to cripple growth or incite social unrest. Hovering near 15,600 dong per US dollar in early 2008, devaluations left the currency two years later at rates above 20,800 dong per US dollar. GDP growth in 2009 dropped to 5.3 percent and has averaged just over 6 percent since. With one of the world's weakest currencies, and rising trade and fiscal deficits, Vietnam's economy came to a near standstill in 2011. In response, Vietnam cut its growing debt and rebuilt foreign reserves, leading to stronger economic growth in 2014. Vietnam celebrated continued growth through 2015 along with two other key achievements: the signing of the TPP and global recognition for meeting its major UN Millennium Development Goals, a feat accomplished by few developing nations.

FOREIGN RELATIONS

In the post-1975 period, Vietnamese foreign policy was framed by fundamental Marxist-Leninist principles. The nation's reliance on socialist solidarity versus the interventionist, exploitative capitalist world narrowed its options and reduced the flexibility that the conduct of foreign relations requires in a world of rapid change. Foreign policy was carried out in *dau tranh* (struggle) terms, in which diplomacy was treated strategically—like protracted military conflicts—over an extended period of time.[28] This approach made negotiations with allies and adversaries difficult because Vietnam's arguments were presented as statements of superior virtue, not as expressions of national interest.

Before 1986, the major goal of Vietnamese foreign policy had been to secure the sovereignty of the country against all aggressors. To meet this goal, Vietnamese foreign policy sought to ensure a cooperative, nonthreatening Indochina firmly allied with Vietnam; prevent an anticommunist front from threatening Vietnamese interests; limit the role of the United States, China, and the Soviet Union in Vietnam's sphere of influence; and establish working relations with neighboring ASEAN countries. These latter, more specific goals were met with varying degrees of success. Vietnam's ongoing occupation of Cambodia, which began in 1979, complicated its relations with major powers and regional neighbors.

After 1986, ideological fundamentalism decreased, and policymakers stressed the need for Vietnam to play a greater role in the global economic system. Vietnam's leaders saw that communist governments were failing around the world, that Vietnam was economically isolated, and that the nation had become too dependent on the Soviet Union; thus, they moved in fundamentally new directions in foreign policy.

Politburo liberals argued that keeping Cambodia as a friendly neighbor was important but not to the point of threatening Vietnam's economic collapse. These reformers argued that a withdrawal from Cambodia would end Vietnam's international isolation by leading to the normalization of ties with the United States, halting the multilateral trade embargo against Vietnam, and inviting Western aid.[29] Adding to pressure to withdraw was the restiveness of Vietnam's armed forces, demoralized by the military stalemate in Cambodia that had cost some 55,000 Vietnamese lives.

However, withdrawal from Cambodia, begun in September 1989, did not bring the expected international gratitude. Instead, ASEAN and the United States faulted the troop withdrawal for not being part of a comprehensive peace plan for Cambodia and for not allowing monitoring by an international control mechanism. Without such a plan, US officials made no moves toward normalizing relations, and the trade embargo continued.

For the United States, Vietnam had been a low foreign policy priority since the end of the war. The American foreign policy establishment was no longer concerned about Vietnam or its fate. The noncommunist countries of Southeast Asia, for their part, were flourishing in the 1980s and no longer viewed themselves as potential victims of Vietnamese aggression. Many agreed with the sentiment of a Thai prime minister that the time had arrived to turn Southeast Asia "from a battlefield to a marketplace."

In this environment, Vietnam moved to improve relations with Asian and Western nations interested in developing economic ties. Hundreds of trade and investment delegations from Japan, Taiwan, South Korea, Thailand, and various European countries arrived to set up business ventures. Relations with China also improved, partly because of the vast border trade between the two nations.

Meanwhile, Soviet aid to Vietnam had decreased, and Soviet president Gorbachev confirmed his country's intention to give up its military bases in Vietnam. Russians were not liked in Vietnam, and a surprising feeling of warmth for Americans in both the northern and southern areas developed.

Vietnam was still very poor, and normalization with the United States could open doors to international aid from the West. Vietnam soon became more cooperative on the issue of unaccounted-for American prisoners of war. Hanoi accepted a standing US offer to conduct US-funded joint searches in provincial areas where the remains of those listed as missing in action were thought to be located. The prospects for normalizing relations between the United States and Vietnam began to improve.

From a Vietnamese perspective, normalization was desirable. Leaders believed *doi moi* reforms would benefit from greater investment from the United States. On the US side, Vietnam had become more enticing to business ventures because of its inexpensive labor and disciplined workforce. It was also believed that closer economic relations with the Vietnamese (the so-called engagement thesis) would help spur political liberalization and even democracy in Vietnam. Military arguments for normalization stressed US strategic interests. The need to deepen US ties in the region seemed timely, given the uncertain status of bases in the Philippines, the USSR withdrawal, and China's rise.

Arguments against normalization stressed that diplomatic relations with Vietnam would legitimize a repressive government. Indeed, many Vietnamese refugees in the United States opposed normalization for that reason. In their view, the North Vietnamese had brutally and illegally taken control of the south, and they should not be rewarded for that action. Many US veterans' groups were also embittered by talks of normalization, emphasizing the unresolved POW/MIA issue.

Because Vietnam had withdrawn its troops from Cambodia, supported the Cambodian peace process, and begun to cooperate on POW/MIA issues, George H. W. Bush began the process of normalization but did not complete it before leaving office. Bush softened the terms of the embargo by allowing telephone links with Vietnam to resume, a welcome event for the 1.5 million Viet Kieu (overseas Vietnamese) living in the United States. He also permitted US firms to sign contracts, which could quickly be executed once the trade embargo was lifted.

Early in his presidency, Bill Clinton announced that diplomatic relations would not be restored until "every MIA and POW is accounted for." This impossible condition discouraged supporters of improved ties between the two nations. Meanwhile, virtually every other Western nation was involved in various economic relationships with the Vietnamese. It was not until 1994 and 1995 that the Clinton administration lifted the embargo and diplomatic relations were established.

The demise of the world's socialist nations undercut Vietnamese foreign policy, which was based on solidarity with the Soviet Union and its allies. This dramatic change made improving Vietnam's ties with the Western capitalist world the best means of future economic aid and trade. At the same time, Vietnam mended fences with its traditional adversary, China; leaders of the two nations attended a summit and restored many crucial ties. Although these improved relations were damaged by Chinese claims of sovereignty in the South China Sea (see below), the positive aspects largely outweighed the negative ones. The two communist neighbors, once enemies battling over the fate of Cambodia, normalized relations in 1991. Cooperation and noninterference increasingly defined their relationship in the 1990s. By the early 2000s, a mature stage of normalcy came to characterize Sino-Vietnamese trade relations, symbolized most importantly by Vietnam's lucrative exports of crude oil to China. Although the relationship is asymmetrical, Vietnam has been merely deferential, not subordinate, to rising China.[30]

Since 1995, Vietnam has also basked in its status as an ASEAN member. The country's foreign policy has demonstrated how the development of regional economic ties and cordial relations outweighs the CPV's previous suspicions and worries over the country's security. Symbolic of this transformation was a major diplomatic event in 2006 when twenty heads of state gathered in Hanoi for the Asia-Pacific Economic Cooperation (APEC) meeting. Following that meeting, Vietnam, once a war-torn pariah state to Western countries, achieved a string of diplomatic successes and firmly established itself as a cooperative partner in the community of nations. First, it was permitted to join the WTO as a full member in 2007. Then, one year later, Vietnam's member peers in the United Nations elected it (on a vote of 190 to 183) to a two-year spot on the UN Security Council. In rotation, Vietnam served two successful stints as president of the world's most powerful body, leading it through debates over sanctions on North Korea and Iran, among other matters.

Subsequently, Vietnam has chaired ASEAN and served as country host for annual meetings of ASEAN, ASEAN+3, the Asian Regional Forum, and the East Asian Summit. It also partnered with trade officials from the United States in pushing forward TPP negotiations, completed in 2015. Vietnam's rising credibility as a solid diplomatic partner has enhanced its global image as a stable, forward-looking nation that is supportive of multilateralism and the broad objectives of the international community, a rarity among similarly politically closed regimes.

The Spratly Islands Dispute

Without question, the most important security issues for Vietnam involve disputes over the Spratly Islands. The island group, located in the South China Sea (called the "East Sea" by Vietnamese), is believed to hold vast untapped oil and natural gas resources. The Spratlys are variously claimed by six countries: Vietnam, China, Taiwan, the Philippines, Malaysia, and Brunei. No native inhabitants reside on the islands, but all claimants, except Brunei, have military outposts and often station ships in the archipelago. When added together, the exposed land of the islands and the atolls, reefs, and outcroppings in the disputed area equals about 5 square miles. Nonetheless, potential underwater oil and natural gas resources, as well as mineral extraction and fishing rights, have become the high-stakes prizes for competing claimants. More broadly, the South China Sea is a vital strategic waterway linking the Persian Gulf with Japan, Taiwan, and South Korea, all of which rely on free passage for their oil imports. It is a sea-lane of immense importance to every Asian country, to Middle East oil exporters, and to the United States.

With respect to claimants, both China and Vietnam make competing "historical" claims over the Spratlys, as well as the nearby Paracel Islands. In the 1970s and 1980s, China and Vietnam came to blows over the islands, and a 1974 clash left the Paracels in Chinese hands. Forty years of skirmishes and conflicts between the two rivals have cost over 100 Vietnamese lives. The Philippines, another major claimant, argues its own history, its own geographic proximity to the Spratlys, and the provisions of the 1982 United Nations Convention on the Law of the Sea (UNCLOS) justify its legal claims to the territory (see chapters 7 and 13).

Malaysia, also citing UNCLOS, makes a claim on a small number of islands. Brunei makes no claims of territory but seeks to protect its UNCLOS rights of economically controlling waters that are within 200 nautical miles of its shoreline. Taiwan, or the Republic of China, makes the same claims over the area as the People's Republic of China. Though it is active in the area and controls a landing strip on the largest island in the Spratlys, Taiwan's ambiguous diplomatic status inhibits its ability to maneuver on the issue, and it does not coordinate with Beijing on the matter whatsoever.

A diplomatic solution to competing claims remains elusive. Even the language used to describe the islands is disputed. Many islets, outcroppings, and reefs share three or four names: in Vietnamese, Tagalog, Chinese, or often in English, Spanish, or Portuguese. In 2002, at annual ASEAN meetings, a major agreement was struck between interested parties to lessen tensions. All countries agreed to a code of diplomatic conduct stating that no party would use force or the threat of force in resolving the matter. In 2004, state-supported oil companies from China, the Philippines, and Vietnam agreed to seismic exploration of the area. Over time, however, cooperation has broken down and new tensions and skirmishes have erupted, including a widely broadcasted showdown between a Vietnamese ship and a Chinese patrol boat in 2011 that fully reignited the row.

China, which has a "talk and take" reputation—talk peace, but take islands forcibly—openly prefers bilateral talks as a means to resolve the dispute. Other claimants prefer regional talks and a multilateral resolution. Honoring boundaries demarcated by UNCLOS is unacceptable to China unless all parties recognize Beijing's territorial claims (all of the islands). UNCLOS, designed to demarcate territorial waters based on sovereign land boundaries, is ill-equipped to solve rival claims of above-ground territory. In effect, UNCLOS causes claimants to use their own maps to justify their interpretation of international boundaries. The result is overlapping claims of sovereignty that each party bases on international law. Exacerbating the issue is the fact that the United States—which actually views the convention as the best viable avenue for conflict resolution—has yet to ratify UNCLOS itself. Without credibility as a full signatory, the US push for a multilateral, UNCLOS-based agreement smacks of hypocrisy, particularly as viewed by China.

Domestically, the issue makes great political hay for leaders eager to cultivate nationalist sentiment and to win local support, including in Vietnam. Diplomatic and military posturing, including live-fire exercises or the dispatching of "combat ready" patrols, can lead to favorable op-eds in home papers and spark street protests in opposing capitals. In recent years, Spratly-related anti-Chinese protests have become more frequent in both Hanoi and Manila. Vietnam has loudly accused the Chinese of cutting and damaging its cables in the area and recently sent Buddhist monks to renovate and reside in old temples found on some of the islands. The issue has even inspired low-grade cyber-attacks: In 2011, Vietnamese nationalists accessed Chinese government web portals and defaced them with Vietnamese symbols and content. Chinese hackers reciprocated.

Beyond the passions generated by public protests, cyber-violence, and sea-lane stare-downs, it is the changing structural forces at work that prove just how volatile the Spratly dispute could become for Vietnam and the region. Strategic activities by both China and the United States, and inter-ASEAN disagreements, have produced new geopolitical dynamics and dangers. After conciliatory talks in the early 2000s, Beijing has since delivered multiple policy statements warning governments in the region against pursuing any oil exploration or mineral surveys of the disputed areas. Chinese "law enforcement" ships have regularly patrolled waters in intimidating fashion. Accusations of sovereign interference have been volleyed back and forth publicly between claimants.

Perhaps most significantly, a new strategic context developed around the Spratly Islands dispute when US president Barack Obama announced in 2011 a "strategic pivot" to rebalance diplomatic attention and US forces from the Middle East to Asia. A year later, ASEAN held its annual meeting in Phnom Penh with China and the United States present. The United States, represented by Secretary of State Hillary Clinton, pushed for multilateral progress on a Spratly Islands agreement beyond the 2002 code of conduct, but the conference ended without an agreement on the matter. Vietnam and the Philippines welcomed the US effort, but Cambodia, siding with China, refused to address the issue. The meeting regrettably produced only vague statements affirming that ASEAN members will continue to respect UNCLOS and the 1976 Treaty of Amity and Cooperation of Southeast Asia.

One of the reasons an agreement failed to emerge at the 2012 ASEAN summit was an emphatic declaration by Vietnam just weeks prior to the conference. After a year of repeated statements by Prime Minister Nguyen Tan Dung that Vietnam had "indisputable sovereignty" over the Paracels and Spratly territories, the National Assembly codified the claim by passing the Vietnamese Maritime Law. China responded with "resolute and vehement opposition" to the law and emphatically restated its own sovereign claims.[31]

A bilateral crisis erupted in 2014 over Chinese exploratory drilling near the Paracel archipelago. Vietnam's denunciations of the act continued for about six weeks until China withdrew, saying its operation was "complete." The incident produced massive public outcry in Vietnam that included an online petition launched by members of the CPV. They denounced China's bullying and provocatively labeled socialism "a mistaken path," while arguing for greater democratization in Vietnam. The following year, a 2015 meeting of ASEAN defense ministers failed to produce a joint communiqué after China, attending as a non-member invitee, pressured ASEAN's delegates to exclude any mention of the South China Sea dispute from the communiqué. These acrimonious events suggest that the dispute is further from resolution than ever.

CONCLUSION

Hanoi's hosting of the 2006 APEC meetings served as a symbolic benchmark of Vietnam's progress. At the event, as is customary at annual APEC meetings, visiting state leaders took time for a photo dressed in the traditional local attire of the host country. For the Vietnamese people—recent survivors of European colonialism, Japanese occupation, a US-USSR proxy war, and a dreadful border war with another former occupier, China—the image of George W. Bush, Vladimir Putin, Shinzo Abe, and Hu Jintao adorned in colorful, silk-woven *ao dai* tunics and standing side by side with Vietnamese president Nguyen Minh Triet, symbolized more than cordial relations. The image stood as evidence of the sovereignty and respect the Vietnamese had finally won from decades of struggle. As "Uncle Ho" had promised, nothing would be more precious than to realize freedom and independence from foreign control.

Although its communist government undermined Vietnam's advantages with oppressive policies and mismanagement before 1986, the regime's economic reforms have since produced impressive developmental gains. With rich natural resources, a large and disciplined workforce, and a long tradition of entrepreneurial activity, Vietnam has become one of Asia's newest economic frontiers. Vietnamese today enjoy a blend of opportunity, wealth, and personal freedom that their ancestors never knew. In spite of the CPV's monopoly on political life, constraints on civil society, and endemic corruption among its elites, the balance sheet for Vietnam today is solidly positive, especially in comparison to its poorer Indochinese neighbors.

Vietnam's future is linked to the ability of the Vietnamese Communist Party to balance economic reform with strict one-party rule. Whether official corruption and greater demands for political liberalization by future generations will eventually destabilize the country is an open question. For the foreseeable future, Vietnam's Leninist party structure seems poised to remain one of the lone survivors of the collapse of global communism.

NOTES

1. The Cao Dai religion, founded in the 1920s and located in South Vietnam, eclectically blends Buddhism, Taoism, Confucianism, Christianity, and other beliefs into a

single, monotheistic religious system. Hoa Hao, founded in the 1930s and also located in the Mekong Delta region, is a variant of Buddhism that deemphasizes monastic temple worship in favor of lay practice.

2. Frederick Z. Brown, *Second Chance: The United States and Indochina in the 1990s* (New York: Council on Foreign Relations, 1989), 39.

3. David G. Marr and Christine P. White, eds., *Postwar Vietnam: Dilemmas in Socialist Development* (Ithaca, NY: Southeast Asia Program, Cornell University, 1988), 2.

4. Ronald J. Cima, "Vietnam's Economic Reform," *Asian Survey* 29, no. 8 (August 1989): 789.

5. *Vietnam Country Brief*, World Bank, February 2007, www.worldbank.org.

6. For an excellent account of social change related to Vietnam's youth in the 1990s, see Robert Templer, *Shadows and Wind: A View of Modern Vietnam* (New York: Penguin Books, 1998).

7. Vo X. Han, "Vietnam in 2007," *Asian Survey* 48, no. 1 (January/February 2008): 33–34.

8. For an excellent account that reviews the dissident activity of Bloc 8406, see Bill Hayton, *Vietnam: Rising Dragon* (New Haven, CT: Yale University Press, 2010).

9. *Vietnam Development Report 2005: Governance*, Joint Donor Report to the Vietnam Consultative Group Meeting, December 2004 (Hanoi: Vietnam Development Information Center, 2004), i.

10. Douglas Pike, "Political Institutionalization in Vietnam," in *Asian Political Institutionalization*, ed. Robert A. Scalapino, Seizaburo Sato, and Jusuf Wanandi (Berkeley: Institute of East Asian Studies, University of California, 1986), 49–51.

11. Douglas Pike, "Change and Continuity in Vietnam," *Current History* 89, no. 545 (March 1990): 118.

12. Thaveeporn Vasavakul, "Vietnam: The Changing Models of Legitimation," in *Political Legitimacy in Southeast Asia: The Quest for Moral Authority*, ed. Muthiah Alagappa (Stanford, CA: Stanford University Press, 1995), 277.

13. *Vietnam Development Report 2005: Governance*, i.

14. Hayton, *Vietnam: Rising Dragon*, 96.

15. Vo, "Vietnam in 2007," 34.

16. "Vietnam: Country Report," Transformation Index BTI 2012, www.bti-project.org /countryreports/aso/vnm.

17. Ibid., 18–19.

18. *Asia Yearbook, 1990* (Hong Kong: Far Eastern Economic Review, 1990), 241.

19. Hayton, *Vietnam: Rising Dragon*, 114–115.

20. Hy V. Luong, "Vietnam in 2006," *Asian Survey* 47, no. 1 (January/February 2008): 170.

21. David Brown, "Vietnam's Not-So-Rare Protests," *Asia Sentinel*, July 30, 2012, www .asiasentinel.com.

22. Ibid.

23. Marr and White, *Postwar Vietnam*, 3.

24. Pike, "Political Institutionalization in Vietnam," 43.

25. Ronald J. Cima, "Vietnam in 1988: The Brink of Renewal," *Asian Survey* 29, no. 1 (January 1989): 67.

26. Cima, "Vietnam's Economic Reform," 797.

27. Adam Forde, "Vietnam in 2003: The Road to Ungovernability," *Asian Survey* 44, no. 1 (January/February 2004): 124.

28. Douglas Pike, "Vietnam and Its Neighbors: Internal Influences on External Relations," in *ASEAN in Regional and Global Context*, ed. Karl D. Jackson, Sukhumbhand Paribatra, and J. Soedjati Djiwandono (Berkeley: Institute of East Asian Studies, University of California, 1986), 240.

29. Ronald J. Cima, "Vietnam in 1989: Initiating the Post-Cambodia Period," *Asian Survey* 30, no. 10 (January 1990): 89.

30. Brantley Womack, *China and Vietnam: The Politics of Asymmetry* (Cambridge, UK: Cambridge University Press, 2006), 29.

31. Jane Perlez, "Vietnam Law on Contested Islands Draws China's Ire," *New York Times*, June 21, 2012, A8.

5

CAMBODIA

The many names under which Cambodia has lived in the past few decades reflect the turmoil its people have experienced. Cambodia was once known as the Kingdom of Cambodia, but the country became the Khmer Republic when the military came to power in 1970. From 1975 to 1979, the period of tyrannical Khmer Rouge leadership, the country's name was changed to Democratic Kampuchea, followed by the People's Republic of Kampuchea when the Khmer Rouge was replaced by a Vietnamese-backed government. In 1989, the country became the State of Cambodia only to return to its former name, the Kingdom of Cambodia, when the country restored royal institutions under a constitutional monarchy in 1993.

Cambodians trace their heritage to the great Khmer civilization, which culminated in the twelfth century when the Khmers ruled over most of modern-day Cambodia, Laos, Thailand, and the Mekong Delta in Vietnam. This magnificent civilization, symbolized by the great temples at Angkor, lasted over five hundred years and reached a level of military, technological, political, and philosophical achievement that was unmatched in Southeast Asian history. The "hydraulic city" of Angkor was sustained by an impressive system of earthen *baray* (massive rectangular reservoirs), moats, ponds, and irrigation canals. Over the centuries, Hinduism (following Vishnu and Shiva) and Buddhism (for the most part Mahayana but eventually Theravada) guided *deva-raja* (god-king) rulers and the estimated 1 million people who lived in the world's largest pre-industrial settlement. The excessive demands created by uneconomic activities such as monument building and war, decades-long drought, and hydroclimate variability contributed to Angkor's fall in the fifteenth century to Ayutthaya.[1] Subsequent kingdoms suffered from instability and external pressure until 1864, when the French took over a weak Cambodia as a protectorate.

The great Khmer civilization has now become the Kingdom of Cambodia, with 14.3 million residents. Most Cambodians are rural farmers who live in poverty. At 79 percent, the country retains the highest percentage of rural

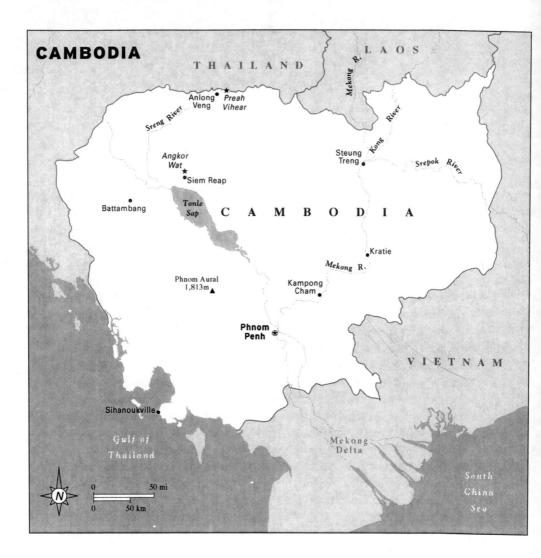

CAMBODIA

population in the entire region. Religiously, Theravada Buddhism predominates among the populace. As a nation, Cambodia personifies tragedy, its people having suffered unspeakable horrors during the Khmer Rouge era, from 1975 to the beginning of 1979. Indeed, neither the people nor the nation has fully recovered from these horrors. Signs of improvement are emerging, but progress remains inhibited by corrupt leadership, a plundering of the country's natural resources, and dependence on foreign assistance.

Cambodia's search for identity and nationhood, once the country was freed from French colonialism, was dominated by Prince Norodom Sihanouk, whom the French had placed on the throne in 1941. In 1955, one year after Cambodia's independence was granted, King Sihanouk abdicated, named his father as king, and entered politics directly as Prince Sihanouk. His unrivaled dominance of Cambodian life from the end of World War II to 1970 was due to the way he had achieved leadership, which was by plebiscite, and to the unsurpassed loyalty of rural Cambodians. He was revered as a *deva-raja* in the tradition of the Angkor kings, and his authority rested on charismatic, traditional, repressive, and legal foundations.

Sihanouk, who controlled all important policymaking institutions, exhibited a remarkable capacity to keep each major sector of society in check, thereby maintaining political stability. His overthrow, on March 18, 1970, was therefore a surprise to most analysts of Cambodian politics. On that date, while Sihanouk was in the Soviet Union, the Cambodian National Assembly—charging Sihanouk with abuses of office—unanimously condemned him to death for treason and corruption. His position was assumed by General Lon Nol, the premier in Sihanouk's government.

Sihanouk's downfall stemmed from the presence of North Vietnamese and Viet Cong forces in so-called Cambodian sanctuaries. Against his army's wishes, Sihanouk had allowed the Vietnamese to use this territory, although his trip to Moscow was to request Soviet aid in ousting the Vietnamese. The Vietnamese had become so entrenched in Cambodia that by mid-1969 they had built a base of support in a region that encompassed nearly one-fourth of Cambodia's total area. Sihanouk had also allowed shipments of Chinese arms across the country from the Cambodian port of Sihanoukville.

Sihanouk's relations with the United States during this time were both acrimonious and supportive. He opposed US involvement in Vietnam, although as the North Vietnamese established themselves in Cambodian territory, he reversed policy and argued the need for an American force in Asia to provide a balance of power to the communist nations. From the US perspective, Sihanouk was mercurial and untrustworthy; thus, his ouster was welcome. Although it remains the subject of much speculation, no definitive evidence has yet proven that Sihanouk's overthrow was supported by covert US government assistance.

From Sihanouk's perspective, his frequently changing policies were consistent with his overall objective of keeping his country neutral and sovereign. His vacillation, nevertheless, cost him the loyalty of elite groups in Cambodia. The army united around General Lon Nol, sharing the view that Sihanouk was not moving strongly enough to remove the Vietnamese from Cambodian territory. Bureaucrats resented Sihanouk's total control over policymaking and personnel decisions; intellectuals opposed his policies of press and speech censorship; and young graduates were frustrated by the lack of job opportunities. Although Sihanouk retained the loyalty of the rural masses through his charisma, that group wielded little influence in Cambodian politics. His total dominance of Cambodian political life, consequently, undermined the country's major institutions.

After taking power, the army became the dominant institution in Cambodian politics. For a short time Lon Nol had the support of many Cambodians, but within months it became clear that the new government was not only inefficient but corrupt. At the end of April 1970, US president Richard Nixon, without first informing Lon Nol's government, announced an American invasion of Cambodia to protect the lives of US soldiers, to ensure the success of his "Vietnamization" program, and to gain a decent interval for US withdrawal from Vietnam. He announced that the intervention would clear Cambodia of all major enemy sanctuaries, including the headquarters of the communist military operation in South Vietnam.

In fact, the Nixon administration had been secretly bombing Cambodia since 1969, without the knowledge or authorization of the US Congress. US forces dropped an estimated 550,000 tons of bombs on Cambodia, about twenty-five times the explosive force of the atomic bomb that devastated Hiroshima, Japan, and three and a half times as many bombs as were dropped on Japan during World War II. Nearly half the population was uprooted, and Cambodians became refugees in their own country.[2] The bombing had no substantive effect on the protection of South Vietnam, serving only to create chaos and panic in the Cambodian countryside.

Five years of total war on Cambodian soil followed. The US-backed Lon Nol government proved incapable of coping with either international or domestic crises. The regime was corrupt, food shortages occurred, inflation was out of control, and hundreds of thousands of Cambodians were displaced—the population of Phnom Penh, Cambodia's capital and largest city, swelled from 600,000 to 2 million. One out of ten Cambodians was killed in the war—most from US bombings and suicide missions sent by Lon Nol to repel the Vietnamese. From his exile in Beijing, Prince Sihanouk announced his support for the radical rebels, the Khmer Rouge, who opposed the Lon Nol regime. The country fell into a civil war that did not end until April 1975, when the Khmer Rouge took control of the countryside and forced Phnom Penh into submission.

The massive US bombings, the social dislocation, and the corruption of the Lon Nol government attracted support to the formerly weak Khmer Rouge, which many believed was made up of nationalist "peasant reformers."[3] That myth was quickly dispelled when the Khmer Rouge ordered the complete evacuation of Phnom Penh within hours of the takeover.

Pol Pot, the leader of one of several Khmer Rouge factions who eventually became the dominant individual in the new government, headed a tightly disciplined party vanguard called Angka (the organization), which ruthlessly ran the country. Angka represented itself as the leader of oppressed workers, farmers, and peasants against the "feudal, imperialistic, capitalist, reactionary, and oppressor classes" of the former regimes. The name Cambodia was changed to Democratic Kampuchea, and Prince Sihanouk was brought back as the nominal head of state but in reality lived day-to-day under house arrest.

The faceless Angka used draconian measures to silence even potential voices of opposition and to reduce to impotency every person believed to be allied with the former ruling groups. The means to this end included strict discipline, total control, terror, and isolation from "impure" societies. The new regime's first undertaking, carried out immediately after the fall of Phnom Penh, was the evacuation of every person from Cambodia's major cities to the countryside. At first it was believed the evacuation was to last for only three days because the new government feared mass starvation in Phnom Penh and other cities, which had very limited supplies of rice. Khmer Rouge soldiers also motivated the city's evacuees to flee by deceptively claiming that a US attack on the capital was imminent. The evacuation, in fact, was meant to be permanent, to "purify" Cambodian society of decadent urban ways and to ensure internal security by ridding the country of "spies, imperialists, and enemies." The evacuations led to thousands of deaths and the separations of countless families.

Angka also purged persons who were in any way connected to the Lon Nol regime or were believed to harbor the slightest "bourgeois" values. Former residents of Phnom Penh were treated especially harshly by the regime. Cambodians with Chinese or Vietnamese ethnicity, considered impure and untrustworthy, were imprisoned and killed. Temples were closed, and Buddhist monks were forcibly disrobed or murdered. The country's entire intelligentsia was executed, often in hideous ways. Those who wore eyeglasses or had soft hands fell under suspicion. In places where displaced people were resettled, high death rates resulted from starvation, illness, and forced labor. An estimated 1.7 million people were executed or worked to death between 1975 and 1979, an act of genocide that has few parallels in history.

Further "enhancing" the Khmer Rouge's rule was the policy of forced labor through collectivization and the total restructuring of the economy. All Cambodian entrepreneurs lost their money when the regime halted the use of currency and nationalized private businesses. The family unit was replaced by collectives of up to a thousand households, which ate and worked together. "New people," so labeled in contrast to the "old people" already living in the countryside, were beaten and humiliated no differently than draft animals, all to serve Angka. Khmer Rouge troops enforced these harsh new policies and made sure that no one resorted to the bourgeois values of privatism, hierarchy, individualism, and the nuclear family. For over three years, agrarian idealism in the form of forced labor defined the sum total of economic production. Unlike communist-led countries elsewhere, the Khmer Rouge made little attempt to develop industry, education, or technology. They sought to create an autarkic agrarian utopia that rejected not only capital and markets but also Soviet-style heavy industrialization.

Survivors reported that Cambodian society was rigidly organized into separate groups of men, women, the elderly, children six to fifteen years of age, and older teenagers. Only small quantities of food were available for communal workers. No schools were open, and no money was in circulation. Buddhist temples were converted into granaries for storing rice, and 80 percent of all books in Cambodia were thrown into rivers. Recalibrating history, the Khmer Rouge declared it "Year Zero"; nothing from the past would be tolerated. Under Pol Pot, Cambodia became one of the most closed societies on earth. During his three-year rule, only a few diplomats and reporters were allowed to enter the country, under tightly controlled conditions for propaganda purposes. The extent of economic hardship and the regime's brutality was foggy to outsiders. Horrific stories retold by traumatized refugees became one of the few windows into Democratic Kampuchea.

The xenophobic ideology that underpinned Khmer Rouge policies included elements of Marxism-Leninism and Maoism, mixed with Khmer nationalism and a romanticized agrarian utopianism. Some of this ideology was informed by 1950s doctoral theses submitted to French universities written by Hou Yuon and Khieu Samphan. These theses argued that the exploitation of Cambodia's peasants was the source of the country's problems; that only by recapturing the peasantry's agrarian potential could the country achieve self-reliance. Hou Yuon, known to be critical of Khmer Rouge methods, died of uncertain causes in the early period of Pol Pot's rule. Khieu Samphan eventually served as state president of Democratic Kampuchea.

The Khmer Rouge's fervent nationalism partly explains their aggression toward fellow communists in Vietnam. In 1977 Pol Pot launched raids into Vietnamese border towns, intending to reclaim the territory of the ancient Khmer Empire, which once included the Mekong Delta—home to a sizable Cambodian minority. An estimated 30,000 Vietnamese civilians were killed during these attacks. Vietnamese-backed Cambodians antagonistic toward Pol Pot launched a civil war against the Khmer Rouge, which only intensified the executions and mass killings of Angka's regime of terror.[4]

On Christmas Day 1978, a Vietnamese-led invasion overthrew Pol Pot's regime and installed Heng Samrin as president. Heng Samrin was an unknown former Khmer Rouge division commander who had sought refuge in Vietnam when his faction was overpowered by Pol Pot. He was later replaced by Foreign Minister Hun Sen, who became the nation's most important leader for the next four decades. Democratic Kampuchea became the People's Republic of Kampuchea (PRK). Vietnamese troops took Phnom Penh after less than two weeks of fighting and forced the Khmer Rouge to flee to the mountains in the western part of the country near the Thai border. Many Cambodians took advantage of the Vietnamese invasion to flee the country. Refugee camps in Thailand became overwhelmed with new arrivals. From these camps, over a million Cambodians would find resettlement in third countries; almost a quarter of a million resettled in the United States.

Vietnam announced that the purpose of its invasion was to end the constant border clashes, which jeopardized Vietnamese citizens, and to expel the hated Pol Pot regime. Vietnam also desired a friendly government, rather than an ally of China, on its doorstep. The Khmer Rouge was Maoist and supportive of China, Vietnam's principal enemy. Because China provided aid to the Khmer Rouge, and the Soviet Union supported Vietnam, the invasion has been interpreted as a Sino-Soviet proxy war.

The new Vietnamese-installed government moved to undo the most onerous policies of the Khmer Rouge, and Phnom Penh was slowly repopulated. The Vietnamese helped to revive piped water and electricity systems but did not impose economic planning or controls. Marriage and family restrictions were ended, forced collectives were abolished, and the practice of Buddhism was again allowed, though monitored. Schools were reopened, and primary school education was reinstituted. After four years of the "killing fields," a semblance of normality appeared in Cambodian society.

Despite reforms, the new government faced severe problems. The Cambodians disliked and distrusted the Vietnamese officials and occupation soldiers (who numbered almost 200,000) but nevertheless realized that the Vietnamese were all that stood between them and the return of the Khmer Rouge. In addition, Pol Pot's annihilation of virtually all skilled and educated Cambodians had caused an administrative vacuum. For example, there were only forty-five doctors in the entire country. Few trained administrators had survived, and the country had no currency, no markets, no financial institutions, and no industry.[5] Due to the remnant mines placed throughout Cambodia during the war years, even routine rice planting became a dangerous activity. Over time, more than 64,000 Cambodians would fall victim to land mines. To this day, Cambodia retains the highest number of amputees per capita in the world.

The new government also faced a famine from 1978 to 1980, in which hundreds of thousands starved to death; to compound the problem, continued fighting between the Heng Samrin and Khmer Rouge forces disrupted the harvest of what little rice had been planted. Farmers were so physically weakened that they could not adequately care for their crops. International agencies were mobilized to provide food, and although thousands of people were saved from starvation, the rescue was only partially successful. As evidence of hoarding, favoritism, and corruption came to light, aid agencies were discouraged, but an even greater problem was the lack of qualified administrative personnel. In general, there was altogether too little food, and it arrived too late.

The international politics of Vietnam's occupation further complicated conditions. Vietnam's 1979 invasion was not welcomed by Asian countries or the international community at large. Although it freed Cambodians from Khmer Rouge rule, Vietnam's aggression was considered a violation of international law. Cold War politics influenced the positions of countries in the region. In 1979, China began a border war with Vietnam as "punishment" for overtaking their Khmer Rouge allies. Thailand's military grew nervous about the presence of Soviet-backed Vietnamese troops along its eastern border and became patrons of remnant Khmer Rouge. The United Nations refused to recognize Heng Samrin's regime and instead gave Cambodia's seat to the Coalition Government of Democratic Kampuchea (CGDK), a government-in-exile formed in 1982.

The CGDK was composed of three disparate factions united solely in their opposition to the Vietnamese-sponsored regime in Phnom Penh. It consisted of Sihanoukists, led by Sihanouk's son Prince Norodom Ranariddh; the Khmer People's National Liberation Front (KPNLF), an anticommunist group led by former prime minister Son Sann; and, remarkably, the ousted Khmer Rouge. Coordinating their work from held territory and camps along the Thai-Cambodian border, the CGDK drew the blessing of the international community as an anti-Vietnamese alliance. Although the Sihanoukists and KPNLF had no affection for the Khmer Rouge, their common goal of ousting the Vietnamese from power produced the uneasy alliance. Prince Sihanouk was named coalition president largely because he was recognized internationally.

Although all factions were supported by different international patrons and held their own militias, only the Khmer Rouge offered a serious military threat to Phnom Penh. Fronted by Khieu Samphan, it drew support from China with infantry weapons, rocket-propelled grenades, and mortars. With 35,000 troops loyal to Pol Pot it was the best-equipped, most capable, and best-organized fighting force in the country. By virtue of the CGDK's recognition by the United Nations, the Khmer Rouge, astonishingly, was represented at the United Nations in New York throughout the 1980s.

Years of infighting, resignations, and scheming among the three factions did not come to an end until Vietnam, facing declining Soviet support in the late 1980s, and focused on *doi moi* reforms at home, announced plans to withdraw its troops from Cambodia. In an effort to resolve the Cambodian situation, the three coalition partners met with Hun Sen's government in 1991 and agreed to a UN-brokered peace plan signed in Paris.

The historic agreement—established with the concurrence of permanent members of the UN Security Council now operating in a post–Cold War world—created a four-party Supreme National Council (SNC) headed by Sihanouk, who would serve as Cambodia's head of state. The agreement also planned for a multinational force of UN peacekeepers and administrators to be stationed in Cambodia: the United Nations Transitional Authority in Cambodia (UNTAC). UNTAC's purpose would be to manage a cease-fire, disarm factions, conduct free elections, begin the repatriation of refugees, and administer the country's foreign affairs, national defense, and finance. The success of the peacekeeping mission thus depended upon the remarkable notion that foreign troops, unable to able to speak Khmer (the Cambodian language) and ignorant of Cambodian culture, could demilitarize all rebel factions, including the Khmer Rouge.

When Prince Sihanouk returned triumphantly to Phnom Penh in November 1991 to become the Cambodian head of state, Cambodians had hopes that the UNTAC experiment could succeed. Shortly thereafter, Khieu Samphan, the Khmer Rouge representative on the SNC, returned as well but was met by a mob that came close to tearing him apart limb from limb. Khieu Samphan was rescued and later returned to participate in the coalition, but the mob action clearly indicated the strong hatred Cambodians still felt toward the Khmer Rouge.

In executing the agreement, UNTAC essentially governed Cambodia from March 1992 to September 1993. About 16,000 blue-helmeted UN peacekeepers blanketed the country, and over 3,300 civilian administrators took control of Phnom Penh. For a time, Cambodia (a sovereign country) was governed by foreign experts: A Japanese served as UNTAC's chief officer, an American ran the finance ministry, a Pole controlled the foreign ministry, and an Australian oversaw all military forces in the country. Famed international diplomat from Brazil, Sergio Vieira de Mello, oversaw the repatriation of 350,000 refugees back to the country. Before the mission was completed, one hundred UN member states had contributed peacekeepers, civil administrators, and election monitors to UNTAC. The bizarre makeup of the UN program indicated the desperate nature of the Cambodian imbroglio after years of civil war, genocidal rule, foreign aggression, and societal chaos.

It soon became clear that the tasks UNTAC had set for itself were too great to be accomplished in only eighteen months. To run a government, repatriate refugees, supervise a cease-fire among factions that distrusted one another, and conduct the first Cambodian election in decades were impossible goals even for an organization provided with $2.8 billion, the most expensive and far-reaching plan of this type in UN history.

UNTAC, alas, proved unable to fully pacify the situation because numerous violations of the cease-fire occurred, mostly by the Khmer Rouge. Disregarding the Paris agreement, the Khmer Rouge sought actively to expand its zones of influence and thereby control as many people as possible before the elections. The Hun Sen administration in Phnom Penh, which had turned over much of its power to UNTAC, engaged in its own violations and corruption, raising the question of whether any of the factions could run the government once elections had been held.

Despite cease-fire violations, popular support for the National Assembly elections was strong. Hun Sen organized the Cambodian People's Party (CPP), while Prince Ranariddh mobilized the United National Front for an Independent, Peaceful, and Cooperative Cambodia (FUNCINPEC). Both the CPP and FUNCINPEC campaigned on anti–Khmer Rouge platforms. The CPP argued that only the Hun Sen administration was strong enough to prevent a return of the Khmer Rouge. Prince Ranariddh's Sihanoukists, on the other hand, campaigned on the claim that the prince was the only Cambodian alive who had sufficient prestige to reconcile the murderous factions. FUNCINPEC candidates reminded voters that Hun Sen had once been a member of the Khmer Rouge and had been installed in power by the Vietnamese, who remained detested by most Cambodians.

Most troubling, the Khmer Rouge refused to disarm or demobilize its area. Weeks before the polls, Khieu Samphan unsurprisingly announced that the Khmer Rouge would boycott the election and, effectively, the entire peace process. The stated reasons for the boycott were accusations that UNTAC was biased in favor of the Hun Sen administration and Vietnamese troops would take over the country after elections. No evidence was presented to substantiate these accusations.

In spite of Khmer Rouge intransigence, elections moved forward. Between May 23 and 27, 1993, 90 percent of the eligible voters cast ballots for members of a legislative assembly with powers to draft a new constitution. Although the Khmer Rouge did not participate in the elections, they did not sabotage them after it became clear that the overwhelming majority of Cambodians had rejected Khmer Rouge pressure. Prince Ranariddh's FUNCINPEC won the largest plurality of the popular vote, 45 percent; Hun Sen's CPP trailed with 39 percent of the vote.

The UNTAC authorities declared the elections free and fair, and the United Nations evacuated its peacekeepers in November 1993, leaving the government entirely in the hands of Cambodians for the first time since 1979. After Hun Sen threatened civil war if left out of the top position, Prince Ranariddh and Hun Sen were, astonishingly, designated co–prime ministers: Prince Ranariddh as first prime minister and Hun Sen as second prime minister. The elderly Norodom Sihanouk was again named king, but he soon left the country for cancer treatment. The Khmer Rouge was kept out of the assembly and the executive branch. A new era of modern Cambodian politics had begun.

By 1994, Cambodia had achieved a semifunctioning government, and life in the rural areas as well as in the cities had returned to some degree of normality. There was hope that the standard of living would improve with increasing foreign investment and political stability. However, underneath this appearance of normality were deep problems that included ubiquitous corruption, crime, and patronage. Factional struggles between the two prime ministers and their respective parties predictably bogged down the government. The Khmer Rouge continued to launch terrorist attacks, placing an immense financial burden on the national budget. The government could not maintain law and order; dissidents were regularly assassinated, and the government was widely blamed for being incapable of stopping the carnage.

The political rivalry between FUNCINPEC and the CPP was ongoing and involved unsuccessful attempts at power sharing at the district levels—a bizarre situation in which all cabinet ministries were run by top officials from both of the rival parties—and disagreements over policy issues such as how to deal with the Khmer Rouge. Moreover, governance suffered due to lingering anger on the part of Ranariddh's contingent over Hun Sen's forced entry into the government leadership. The rivalry culminated in Hun Sen's coup against First Prime Minister Ranariddh on July 6, 1997—a coup inspired by intrigue occurring within Khmer Rouge holdouts in Cambodia's hinterlands.

Hoping to resolve the outstanding problem of the Khmer Rouge presence in the country, both prime ministers attempted to court dissident Khmer Rouge leaders, the most notorious being Ieng Sary and Khieu Samphan. These men, and a few other top Khmer Rouge leaders, sought amnesty and reintegration into Cambodia's new system by announcing they had formed separate political parties. Ieng Sary also pledged to integrate his 3,000 troops (about one-third of the entire remaining Khmer Rouge force) into the national army. Hun Sen feared a Khmer Rouge–FUNCINPEC alliance, which could isolate his CPP and create a formidable force.

The open split among Khmer Rouge factions proved destabilizing. Fighting erupted in Anlong Veng, a Khmer Rouge stronghold along Cambodia's northern border. Rumors swirled about Pol Pot's fate: that he had ordered the killing of one of his longtime cadres, had been captured, was on the run, hiding in exile, or already dead. Determining what was factual proved difficult. Since the Vietnamese invasion in late 1979, Pol Pot had not been seen or photographed at all. Meanwhile, Hun Sen agreed to amnesty for the defector Ieng Sary, hoping to woo him away from the prince's camp. Prince Ranariddh, in a power play against Hun Sen, began to engage Khieu Samphan, hinting that a deal with Khmer Rouge remnants was on the horizon.

In a sense, the relative stability of post-1993 Cambodia had put the Khmer Rouge in a bind. Any real hope they harbored for a return to power had dissipated. Lacking international patrons (due to the end of the Cold War), and unable to hold on to their shrinking territory (due to government troop advances), Khmer Rouge leaders increasingly realized their days were numbered. Hemmed in and desperate, they began to turn on each other. Cambodia's co-prime ministers faced uncertainty as well due to the imminent dissolution of the Khmer Rouge. Neither could agree on terms of amnesty, participation, or criminal prosecution for the scheming Khmer Rouge leaders. Competing for influence, the co–prime ministers turned on each other, and Hun Sen made a bold grab for power.

Prince Ranariddh was out of the country when Hun Sen's coup took place. He charged Ranariddh with a variety of traitorous acts, including unauthorized negotiations with Khmer Rouge hard-liners. King Sihanouk, still ill and out of the country, refused to endorse the new government, but he did nothing to stop the coup and its aftermath. Because Hun Sen promised to arrest him upon re-entry, Ranariddh remained in exile.

The coup reportedly was financed by alleged drug baron Theng Bunma, president of the Cambodian Chamber of Commerce, who publicly stated that he had given Hun Sen $1 million to stabilize the country's political situation. Following the coup, a number of FUNCINPEC supporters were assassinated; others were imprisoned while their homes were ransacked. Although Hun Sen apologized for the breakdown in law and order, the chaos continued for several months; the precarious balance that had emerged through Cambodia's joint leadership had been destroyed.

Twenty days after Hun Sen's coup, Pol Pot was affirmed to be alive and had been brought before a Khmer Rouge "people's tribunal" in Anlong Veng. The trial was held in an open-air, thatched-roof pavilion with dirt floors and bamboo furniture—symbolic of Khmer Rouge achievements. In a stunning turn-around, Pol Pot, the architect and perpetrator of the "killing fields," sat as an anguished old man, accused of murdering a top Khmer Rouge comrade and his family. He was denounced by the crowd, who screamed "Crush! Crush! Crush!" when his prosecutor identified him. Pol Pot was found guilty and placed under house arrest for life by his erstwhile Khmer Rouge captors.

Pictures of Pol Pot and video of his show trial (taken by the intrepid *Far Eastern Economic Review* correspondent Nate Thayer) were broadcast internationally. It was the first time the outside world had seen Pol Pot since his murderous rule.

The world reacted strongly to Pol Pot's one-day trial. Responsible for the torture and death of millions of people, he appeared like an elderly grandfather. His public statements to Nate Thayer were unrepentant; he asserted that he had a clear conscience. Pol Pot talked about his modesty, his lack of interest in leadership, his unobtrusive style of politics. He claimed his opponents had been executed by the Vietnamese and that the skulls of those tortured and killed at Tuol Sleng prison could not have been Cambodian because they were too small. He seemed most eager to talk about his poor health (he was seventy-two in

1997) and his enjoyment of his new wife and twelve-year-old daughter. Pol Pot epitomized the fabled banality of the truly evil person.

Pol Pot's final days were spent under house arrest with government troops closing in on his jungle redoubt. He died of an apparent heart attack on April 15, 1998, supposedly two hours after listening to a Voice of America broadcast announcing his captors had negotiated his handover to international authorities. Some observers suspected suicide, or assisted suicide by his young wife. The truth will remain unclear since his body was immediately cremated in a disgraceful funeral pyre that included automobile tires, old furniture, and debris.

The chaotic departure of the Khmer Rouge from Cambodian politics in the 1990s complicated the country's effort to develop economically and complete its democratic transition. Hun Sen's 1997 coup was followed by elections for the National Assembly in July 1998. The post-coup elections were marred by corruption, intimidation, and candidate assassinations. The CPP received 41 percent of the votes cast, FUNCINPEC 32 percent, and the Sam Rainsy Party (SRP) 14 percent. Minor parties won the rest of the vote but did not receive seats in the 122-seat National Assembly. Hun Sen was renamed prime minister, and Prince Ranariddh was allowed to return from exile to be the president of the National Assembly under a reborn CPP-FUNCINPEC coalition. Supporters of Sam Rainsy refused to be coopted by Hun Sen and became the opposition in the assembly.

As the new millennium began, the hope for cooperation among political parties and politicians was real. For the first time in decades, no major war was being fought and the Khmer Rouge was no longer a threat. Hun Sen's government turned its focus to becoming the gatekeeper to the Cambodian economy. With promising economic growth rates in the early 2000s, new Cambodian tycoons emerged in the country, all of whom were linked to Hun Sen. Foreign investors, primarily from Asia, likewise sought Hun Sen's partnership. Much of the investment centered on forest resources, tourism, and entertainment. Karaoke bars, casinos, and massage parlors also popped up all over Cambodia, especially along the Thai border to the west. Garment manufacturers from abroad discovered Cambodia's eager and inexpensive labor force. Cambodia's economy grew but the country was not put on a path toward genuine development. The majority of Cambodians still living in the countryside remained poor, left to fend for themselves.

Since Hun Sen's power grab, the CPP has functioned as a de facto state party favoring its own administrative networks throughout the kingdom. To keep opposition politicians and parties boxed in, Hun Sen manipulated the electoral system to keep it far from free and fair. His party's electoral success remains rooted in a patronage system that uses government largesse to support local political CPP leaders. By dividing the opposition and coopting rivals when possible, he has kept opposition politicians weak, unstable, or compromised.

Hun Sen's perpetual campaign strategy has been to contrast the CPP's record of stability with the chaos and disorder of the past—a message that resonates with a war-weary society. In three general elections from 1998 to 2008 the government-connected Cambodian People's Party won handily. In Cambodia's 2008 general election, the CPP secured 58 percent of the vote and 90 of the National Assembly's 123 seats.

With each new challenge to the country, Hun Sen's modus operandi has been to grasp the reins of power ever more tightly. To intimidate and silence those criticizing his indifference to growing problems, Hun Sen discharges the bureaucratic, judicial, and security apparatuses at his disposal. He effectively controls all Khmer security forces, Khmer courts, and all of the Khmer-language print and broadcast media. On his cue, the CPP-controlled legislature passes laws that neuter potential threats to his power, such as laws permitting the jailing of peaceful protesters, allowing state prosecution of labor union activists, or leaving villagers defenseless from land developers.[6] In such a legal environment, businesses and corporations with CPP endorsement have freedom to maneuver with general impunity.

Over time, Hun Sen's long-held election strategy of touting stability over chaos has begun to show observable signs of weakening. For many Cambodians, concerns over corruption, privilege, and the growing gap between the haves and the have-nots have become a greater priority than rewarding the CPP for stability. Results from the 2013 National Assembly elections reveal just how far support for Hun Sen and his CPP apparatus has slid. Although the CPP claimed 49 percent of the vote, and a majority 68 of the assembly's 123 seats, Cambodia's new opposition party, the Cambodia National Rescue Party (CNRP), secured 45 percent of the popular vote and stole 26 seats from the CPP's 2008 total. In fact, among the 6.6 million votes reported cast, a mere 145,001 votes cast for the CPP over the CNRP separated the two parties—and it is possible the "official" vote tallies and polling process were compromised by foul play.

Immediately following the announced results, leaders from the CNRP accused the government of fraudulently cheating the opposition out of 8 seats, enough to swing the balance in Hun Sen's favor. Subsequently, the CNRP refused to join the National Assembly in a boycott, organized protests, and unsuccessfully requested a state commission be formed to investigate the fairness of the election. A coalition of Cambodian NGOs that had dispatched over 11,000 volunteer election observers during the election affirmed many allegations of electoral fraud and irregularities in a devastating report.[7] Democratic governments elsewhere, and international watchdog bodies such as Transparency International and Human Rights Watch, expressed deep reservations about the integrity of the election's results.

Regardless, after the government's election commission claimed to have resolved all complaints, Cambodia's king formally endorsed the election outcome. Hun Sen was reappointed as prime minister. Ten months after the election, the CNRP finally agreed to accept their seats following a violent, politically charged melee at a pro-CNRP rally in Phnom Penh's Freedom Park that embarrassed leaders on both sides. A year later, they boycotted again for two months. By 2015, the CPP-led assembly had stripped the CNRP's leader of his lawmaker status and the two sides refused to speak to one another.

Responding to the 2013 electoral declines, Hun Sen later pursued a revitalization strategy for the CPP. He appointed new faces to his cabinet team, softened a few media restrictions, and encouraged his CPP cadres to make greater use of Facebook and social media. Substantively, however, few policy changes were made. Government abuses continued with ongoing harassment of political activists, officially sanctioned land grabbing, and policy initiatives that predictably favored industry over workers.[8] Meanwhile, already preparing for his next electoral fight in 2018, Hun Sen continues to badger and provoke opposition politicians through political knavery and thuggery.

INSTITUTIONS AND SOCIAL GROUPS

Prince Sihanouk and Norodom Sihamoni

After the 1940s, Prince Norodom Sihanouk dominated all aspects of Cambodian society until his overthrow in 1970. Although placed on the throne by the French in 1941 (when he was nineteen) and thought by the French to be pliable, Sihanouk became the symbol of Cambodian independence. With his shrill voice, he rallied his people during an era when Cambodia was known as "an island of tranquility in a sea of chaos." Conversant in ten languages, the author of five books, and a stage and movie actor and director, he was the country's most cosmopolitan citizen. Dogmatic about the value of neutrality, and willing to play any side to survive politically, he was described by observers as temperamental, duplicitous, and inscrutable.

Although Sihanouk ruled autocratically, exercising dominance over the National Assembly, his government was supported by the overwhelming majority of the people, especially in rural areas. After he was overthrown by his own premier in 1970, he allied himself with the Khmer Rouge rebels while in exile and, when the Khmer Rouge took power, returned to Phnom Penh as a ceremonial leader. Subsequently, he cooperated with the Khmer Rouge, even though it had murdered five of his sons and daughters, fourteen of his grandchildren, and more than a million of his former subjects. Sihanouk was an egotist who was willing to prolong the civil war to maximize his own authority.

Sihanouk denounced the Vietnamese-backed Hun Sen administration; he lived in exile in Beijing and Pyongyang for much of this period, receiving medical treatment for his numerous maladies. His movement in and out of Cambodia solidified his reputation as a mercurial figure. Sihanouk lost much popular support by being out of power for over twenty years and allying himself with the Khmer Rouge. Nevertheless, he remained one of the country's major institutions, eventually returning to Cambodia to become king following the UNTAC-sponsored elections in 1993.

While king, Sihanouk held little formal power and showed regret for some of his actions. He said that if he were not a Buddhist he would kill himself, believing his life to be filled with shame, humiliation, and despair over Cambodia's past and future.

In 2004, King Sihanouk abdicated in favor of his son Norodom Sihamoni. A childless bachelor, and a classical dancer by training, Sihamoni lived most of his life in Prague, Pyongyang, and Paris. As a relatively unknown figure to most Cambodians, his appointment came as a welcome move and dampened rumors that Hun Sen planned to abolish the monarchy upon Sihanouk's death. Before his coronation, the apolitical Sihamoni had served as Cambodia's cultural ambassador to the United Nations but otherwise was uninvolved in national life.

King Sihamoni is gradually winning the affection of his subjects but lacks the charisma and political gravitas of his father. Given the short life of the resurrected monarchy, and the lack of a clear heir, it remains to be seen whether the institution will endure. In 2008, Sihanouk, ever erratic, publicly raised the possibility of his son's own abdication only to recant the comments later. Hun Sen's own behavior has taken on more and more regal tones as he increasingly eclipses Sihamoni's formal role as head of state.

At eighty-nine, Norodom Sihanouk died in a Beijing hospital on October 15, 2012. Days later, his body was returned to Cambodia and a procession in his honor drew hundreds of thousands of mourners. After lying in state for three months, the remains of Cambodia's most beloved cultural figure were publicly cremated by Buddhist monks at Cambodia's Royal Palace.

Hun Sen

Prime Minister Hun Sen has been Cambodia's most important leader in the post–Khmer Rouge period. He was born into a peasant family and did not finish high school. Hun Sen was twenty-four when the Khmer Rouge came to power under Pol Pot. The Khmer Rouge evacuated his family from its rural home, killed his eldest son, and imprisoned his wife. Blinded in one eye by a US cluster bomb, Hun Sen joined the Khmer Rouge as a senior commander and may have become party to its genocidal fanaticism. He defected in 1977, as Pol Pot began his systematic executions of dissident Khmer Rouge members, and escaped to Vietnam.

After becoming Cambodia's prime minister and foreign minister in 1985, under the Vietnamese-installed administration at the time, Hun Sen became the most influential figure in the People's Republic of Kampuchea, although Heng Samrin held the highest position as head of state. Hun Sen's regime controlled the cities and most of the countryside with the aid of Vietnamese soldiers and advisers. His attempts to position his government in the 1980s as being independent of Vietnam improved his popularity in Cambodia.

Hun Sen, who prefers to be called *somdech* (prince), is known more to be a Machiavellian pragmatist than a principled ideologue. Global assessments of Hun Sen's aggressive and self-serving nature only deepened when he demanded a share of the prime ministership in 1993 and when he grabbed power via coup in 1997. Fueled by international aid distributions and Cambodia's economic growth, Hun Sen's vast patronage network has won him many loyalists during his thirty-year domination of political life.

Hoping to challenge the cultural appeal of his royalist rivals, Hun Sen has sought to soften his image by building clinics and schools and by providing special funds for families with triplets. (Some Cambodians believe the lost souls of Khmer Rouge victims find their way into already pregnant women for rebirth.)[9] In spite of such attempts, his grip on power results from his tough handling of domestic and foreign policy. Hun Sen craftily engineers Cambodian nationalism to his political advantage, as witnessed in controversies with Thailand over Angkor-era temples. As the country's most powerful leader and one of the world's longest-ruling executives, *somdech* Hun Sen sits atop Cambodia lacking any serious rivals.

Political Parties

The Cambodian People's Party is by far the largest and most broad-based party in Cambodia. With access to government coffers and bureaucratic connections spread through Cambodia's local areas, the CPP is organized as if it were a grassroots structure; functionally, it is anything but a bottom-up people's party. The CPP is a centralized, patronage-based, hegemonic party that persistently blurs the lines between itself and the state.

Hun Sen and his fellow party leaders cultivate the CPP's image as a party of stability. Trumpeting fear, the CPP tells the electorate that it stands as the lone bulwark between social stability and a return to disorder. The party operates in the absence of ideology or a coherent political platform. It prefers to paint its opponents as dangerous to Cambodia's future. The main opposition parties contesting the CPP over time have been FUNCINPEC, the Sam Rainsy Party, and the Cambodia National Rescue Party.

FUNCINPEC,[10] the CPP's main rival in the 1990s, grew out of the Sihanoukists' tripartite opposition to Vietnamese-backed Hun Sen during the 1980s. A royalist party built by Sihanouk and his son Prince Ranariddh, FUNCINPEC rightfully won the 1993 UN-sponsored election but cowed along with UNTAC to Hun Sen's strategy of blackmailing his way into a role as co–prime minister. The party has strategically joined in coalition governments with the CPP to maintain relevance. Since the 2003 elections, FUNCINPEC's share of seats has dropped and it now struggles to find a place in the political milieu.

The Sam Rainsy Party emerged prior to the 1998 election. Sam Rainsy served as a finance minister and a member of FUNCINPEC until he was forced out of his position in 1994. He built the party, which is a later incarnation of the

Khmer National Party, from liberal segments of society in predominantly urban areas. During the 2000s, a disturbing number of the party's candidates and supporters were persecuted, shot at, and anonymously murdered. For his antigovernment statements, Sam Rainsy perpetually faced defamation lawsuits, stints in exile, a royal pardon, and politically costly deals with Hun Sen.

In 2012, the Sam Rainsy Party merged with Kem Sokha's Human Rights Party to form the Cambodia National Rescue Party (CNRP), with Sam Rainsy as party leader. Its success in stealing twenty-six National Assembly seats from the CPP in 2013 may have been the product of changing dynamics in the electorate more than its particular platform, which emphasizes populist initiatives and social justice. With 70 percent of the electorate now too young to remember the Khmer Rouge era, the CNRP's 2013 campaign slogan "Change!" resonated in Phnom Penh and nearby provinces where it experienced its greatest electoral successes. (The CPP lamely responded with its own campaign slogan: "No Change!")[11]

In 2015, only a year after it ended its boycott to join Parliament, the CNRP again boycotted the assembly for a two-month period after pro-government protesters physically assaulted two of its parliamentarians. Later, octogenarian lawmaker Heng Samrin, in his capacity as National Assembly president, gleefully announced that the CPP-controlled body had voted to strip Sam Rainsy of his lawmaker status and parliamentary seat. Already in self-exile (again) to avoid a past conviction and multiple lawsuits from Hun Sen allies, Rainsy's political future remains uncertain. It is possible that Cambodia's growing opposition may fare better in 2018 without Rainsy at the helm because of his questionable political judgment and tendency toward histrionics, including a flair for anti-Vietnamese demagoguery. It remains to be seen whether Hun Sen would ever allow an honest election result to oust him from power.

International Aid Community

The Kingdom of Cambodia, in its most recent incarnation, was born from international assistance. Few countries have such an intimate history with the broad constellation of the global community's official and private foreign aid organizations. Cambodia, the object of much international sympathy, remains relatively open to government and nongovernmental organizations that provide myriad services: resettlement, education, health care, construction of infrastructure, rural development, technical assistance, and even human rights promotion. Thousands of foreigners and local Cambodians are employed in 450-plus NGOs and dozens of UN-affiliated agencies and bilateral aid programs, such as USAID, the Japanese International Cooperation Agency, and the Australian Government Overseas Aid Program.[12]

So pervasive is the NGO community that everyday life for many Cambodians is currently interwoven with the many schools, clinics, and infrastructure projects that mushroomed in recent years due to foreign support. A sudden departure of aid flows and aid workers would have a crippling effect on the economy and on Cambodian society in general. In 2006, fifteen years after UNTAC was established, around 10 percent to 15 percent of GDP was still derived annually from international assistance, leading to worries about "aid addiction." Much of the annual government budget depends on cash flows from Japan and the European Union, creating opportunities for official corruption. Donor countries often express concerns over bureaucratic corruption, but many Cambodians believe the wide salary gaps between foreign aid workers and local employees are just as morally repugnant.

With a few exceptions, individuals in the foreign aid community steer clear of direct involvement in Cambodia's political life. Indirectly, Hun Sen's government benefits from the incremental improvements to Cambodian life made possible by aid workers and their programs. The large flow of official development assistance, channeled through Cambodia's government, serves somewhat as a check on government behavior, keeping open repression fairly rare.[13] This effect matters far less with the increasing bilateral aid coming from China, which targets large-scale projects such roads, dams, and even a new national stadium.

Extraordinary Chambers in the Courts of Cambodia (ECCC)

Although he lived nearly twenty years beyond his ouster, Pol Pot, one of history's tyrannical mass murderers, escaped retribution and legal accountability for his crimes. Attempts by the United Nations to establish an international tribunal for Khmer Rouge leaders faced constant rejection by Hun Sen due to his desire to control Cambodia's historical narrative. After years of uneasy negotiations involving representatives of multiple countries, Hun Sen finally agreed in 2003 to set up a unique hybrid court, the Extraordinary Chambers in the Courts of Cambodia (ECCC), which would involve both domestic and international judges in trying Pol Pot's living colleagues. Prosecution in the tribunal falls under Cambodian law, inclusive of international crimes.

Twenty-seven years after the Khmer Rouge was expelled from power, the first Khmer Rouge leader appeared before the court on July 31, 2007. In a pretrial hearing, Kang Kek Ieu, or "Comrade Duch" (pronounced "Doik"), the onetime director of the notorious S-21 torture center, faced the Cambodian people on the following charges: crimes against humanity, mass killings, forced movements, forced labor, inhumane living conditions, and torture. Months of testimony and evidence were presented against Duch, who had survived the fall of the Khmer Rouge living in refugee camps under a false identity. Touting his conversion to evangelical Christianity, and generally cooperative with the tribunal, he received a shockingly light sentence that was later changed to life imprisonment. In 2014, two other defendants, Khieu Samphan and Noun Chea, both in their eighties, were also found guilty of crimes against humanity and sentenced to life imprisonment.

To most international observers, however, the ECCC's failures overshadow its successes. Its hybrid nature has led to ongoing tensions between appointed Cambodians and foreign judges and prosecutors, some who have resigned alleging corruption and undue interference by Hun Sen. Cases have developed at a snail's pace, outraging many Cambodians who also express disgust that well-fed Khmer Rouge defendants await trial in air-conditioned cells outfitted with mattress beds (all but wealthier Cambodians typically sleep on mats in tropical heat). Because of its soiled reputation, many international donors have backed out, leaving the ECCC's funding (and future) in doubt.

STATE-SOCIETY RELATIONS AND DEMOCRACY

Since its independence, modern Cambodia has proven to be among the world's weakest states. Viewed from the outside, this weakness is indicated by repeated episodes of foreign occupation as well as penetration of the state by domestic elite interests. Invaded by both Vietnamese and US forces, Sihanouk's state was unable to enforce its own policy of neutrality. Civil war and the threat of civil war also impeded state development before, during, and after Khmer Rouge rule. In 1979, foreign occupation turned Cambodia into a Vietnamese puppet state until 1992, when the United Nations literally took over all state functions. Following UNTAC's departure, the fundamental weakness of the Cambodian state has continued due in large part to Hun Sen's expanding network apparatus, which has displaced the development of autonomous state institutions. Even today, Cambodia has few experienced technocrats whose loyalty is primarily to the state; its army is weak and undependable, and its judges and courts are compromised. Virtually all state officials are beholden to Hun Sen's inner circle and largesse.

As viewed from the inside, in the context of Cambodia's own experience, a weak state is nonetheless preferable to a failed state. Cambodia, a failed state in the late 1980s, recovered due to tremendous international support and Cambodians' willingness to demilitarize warring factions and start over. Brought to its knees, and desperate for peace and order, the state allowed foreigners to reoccupy the ministries the colonial French once controlled. Although the state's capacity remains weak and the state is too often fused with CPP rule itself, Cambodia's viability looks somewhat promising. Whether the country can produce (or endure) a shift in power from one set of rulers to another, without succumbing to the impulses of violence and militarism, remains an open question.

Internationally, world leaders and donor countries have shown patience with Hun Sen, allowing him the political space—too much perhaps—to restore a state formerly subject to foreign control. Hun Sen's political legitimacy has been derived from three sources: (1) his experience as a Cambodian leader who initially guided Cambodia through the post–Khmer Rouge period; (2) his leadership of a party elected multiple times to take the reins of government; and

(3) his public popularity, which is far from unanimous but draws support from beneficiaries of the government and Cambodia's widest patronage network: local-level officials. In the words of one prominent scholar of Cambodia, the majority of the population today sees Hun Sen "as a *fait accompli*, rather like a monarch, rather than an elected and responsive leader. Hun Sen presides in a regal manner over everything that happens in Cambodia; like many kings, he has no respect for pluralism, an independent judiciary, or the separation of powers."[14]

Although relative political stability has been established since 1993, Cambodia is not transitioning to democracy. Unfortunately, the Paris Peace Agreement and UNTAC's rapid efforts to secure peace through cease-fire agreements and popular elections set a low baseline for democratic expectations. By using a strategy emphasizing peace building and national elections, the Paris Agreement actually put Cambodia on a course toward electoral autocracy, not institutionalized democracy. In hindsight, the expectations for democratic transition in the 1990s were naively optimistic. Most Cambodians, bewildered by UNTAC's complex mission, were too inexperienced with popular politics to demand much from representative government. Largely poor, rural, and uneducated, the people had a scope of political expectations at the time that ranged little beyond keeping the Khmer Rouge out of power and receiving help with basic needs. Collective action, public opinion, and exercising individual civil liberties were foreign notions to most Cambodians. The 1993 election unintentionally launched a pattern where electioneering came to reinforce patronage-based authoritarianism at the expense of developing interest representation, oppositional politics, and civil liberties.

Ironically, not only are local and foreign business tycoons reinforcing Hun Sen's corrupt rule as they negotiate contracts and kickbacks with Hun Sen's inner circle, but international donors and NGOs are effectively sustaining this system by setting the policy agenda and helping fund the CPP-managed coffers of patronage (i.e., the budgets of government ministries and departmental programs). With so many foreign actors influencing affairs, the domestic interest groups, associations, and mass organizations that should be applying pressure on elected representatives have little opportunity to evolve and shape the agenda. The donor communities, many of whom openly balk at demanding serious political reform to further their own agenda of staying in operation, have become apathetically tolerant of rampant government corruption and ineptitude.[15] With donors providing resources to both state and nonstate actors, the Cambodian people have yet to wrest democracy from a system of top-down resource allocation.[16]

Cambodia's 123-seat National Assembly, an object of tremendous political attention during national elections, also falls well short of its democratic function to represent societal interests. The assembly's very design virtually ensures the CPP's dominance in the body for the foreseeable future. As it functions today, the National Assembly is deliberately designed to support Hun Sen's hegemonic electoral authoritarian regime. The proportional voting system used to elect the Parliament disproportionately rewards larger parties with a greater number of seats. In 1995, Hun Sen also engineered change in the constitutional threshold of assembly seats needed to form a coalition government from 66 percent to a simple majority. When the charter reform went through the Assembly, Hun Sen threatened to imprison opposition leader Sam Rainsy if his party voted against the amendment.[17] Such cajoling and high-pressure coaxing on opposition figures became even more necessary following the 2013 elections when the CPP lost 26 seats and a two-thirds majority, the threshold required to pass constitutional changes.

Lastly, although Cambodia's constitution calls for adherence to human rights, a disturbing degree of lawlessness still characterizes state-society relations. Those who champion civil society and human rights often risk their personal safety to advance their cause. The politically motivated murders of political radio host Chour Chetharith (2003), prominent labor rights activist Chea Vichea (2004), opposition newspaper journalist Khim Sambor (2008), and environmental activist Chut Wutty (2012)—as well as a dozen other activists since the early 1990s—offer chilling reminders of means employed by those in power to silence critics who openly challenge them. Official investigations of political murders distressingly flounder in courts where government judges, using no witnesses, extend guilty verdicts to defendants with no known political ties. Honest judges, seeking truthful verdicts, often find themselves removed from the bench. Hun Sen's Cambodia, with a constitution pledged to principles of liberal democracy and pluralism, holds the dubious distinction as the only country in Southeast Asia with a democratic constitution to be continuously rated "not free" by Freedom House.

ECONOMY AND DEVELOPMENT

When the Vietnamese-sponsored regime took control in 1979, the government restored a currency system, trade, and wage labor but favored a planned economy based on the Vietnamese model. Private enterprise and private property were not officially allowed but informally tolerated. Beginning in the mid-1980s, the PRK regime instituted its own version of Vietnamese-style *doi moi* by liberalizing foreign investment laws, allowing private industries, increasing international trade, returning land to peasant ownership, permitting private transportation enterprises, guaranteeing the end of the nationalization of private enterprises, and legalizing the private sector.[18] This opening of the economy immediately improved the output of the industrial, agricultural, and private sectors. Under the Vietnamese, only certain UN agencies that provided emergency relief, such as UNICEF and the World Food Programme, were allowed to operate inside Cambodia, whereas the UN Development Program, the

World Health Organization, and other development-oriented UN agencies were not.[19]

In Phnom Penh, the economy changed dramatically following UNTAC's departure, with a boom in consumer goods, mostly from Thailand and China; increased car traffic; out-of-control land speculation; and inflation, driven by a huge supply of money, mostly from the high per diem payments made to foreign aid personnel, whose daily income was often equivalent to Cambodians' average *yearly* income. In addition to NGO activity, manufacturing saw increases. Even with the 1997 Asian economic crisis, the number of factories in the country grew to well over 100 by the late 1990s. Most firms focused on clothing and apparel, benefiting from the Multi Fibre Arrangement, a globally negotiated country export quota scheme to assist developing countries. Other major investments for foreign exchange at the time were made in rubber, timber, and various low-quality service industries. Western Cambodia in particular saw a proliferation of casinos, bars, and massage parlors during this period—a "karaoke economy."[20]

Under CPP-FUNCINPEC coalition governments, Cambodia experienced modest to low growth rates in the 1990s. Since 2000, however, Cambodia's economic growth has taken a rapid turn upward. Cambodia averaged 10.9 percent annual GDP growth between 2000 and 2006; over the same period, per capita income increased from $288 to $513, doubling in only six years.[21] Since experiencing anemic growth in 2009, due to the global financial crisis, the country has rebounded, averaging above 7 percent annually. Per capita income rose to $1,010 in 2014, but that figure remains the lowest among all countries in Southeast Asia. Still, from a domestic perspective, some encouragement can be derived from Cambodia's overall growth. Light industry, manufacturing, and tourism are growing rapidly.

The apparel industry plays an important role in Cambodia's new economy. It employs 500,000 workers in more than 500 factories producing for global brands such as Polo, the Gap, and Banana Republic. The industry alone accounts for around 15 percent of Cambodia's GDP and over 70 percent of its total exports.[22] Somewhat surprisingly, Cambodia consented to implementing higher international standards for textile workers and has won praise from the International Labour Organization. For a time, Cambodia enjoyed a positive reputation among socially minded clothing buyers in Paris, New York, and London. The success of the apparel industry continued despite the expiration of the Multi Fibre Arrangement in 2005, which many observers predicted would cripple Cambodia's competitiveness. However, it was a drop in global demand in 2009 that painfully reversed the industry's expansion. Over 130 factories closed or suspended production and, in turn, 60,000 workers saw their jobs terminated or suspended.[23] The industry today faces increased criticism by labor and human rights observers who have documented abusive practices, especially against women.[24]

The magnificent ruins of Angkor, a popular tourist attraction, were unavailable for most of the 1970s and 1980s. By the early 1990s, even as neighboring Thailand attracted millions of foreign visitors, Cambodia struggled to bring in tourists because the Khmer Rouge still controlled areas around Angkor Wat and land mines remained a problem. Poor roads, rail service, and air transport also deterred visitors. That changed rapidly in the late 1990s after the Khmer Rouge threat abated and Angkor Wat's status as a UNESCO World Heritage Site promoted new investment in tourist infrastructure. Direct air service to Siem Reap, the provincial town near the temples, also became available in 1998. As tourism began to grow, academic delegations and adventure travelers were joined by big-ticket travelers on group tours. Siem Reap, a once-small town near Angkor-era temples, suddenly found itself inundated with large resort-style hotels and busloads of wealthy seniors from Europe, North America, and Asia on package tours. The growth of Chinese tourism in particular has contributed substantially to Angkor Wat's 5,000 daily visitors, who generate $59 million in annual receipts.[25] In 2015, Lonely Planet published a 500-page volume ranking the world's top 500 tourist destinations, as selected by tourism industry insiders and experts: Angkor Wat was ranked #1.[26]

The Kingdom of Cambodia's economic future is now linked to its WTO membership, secured in 2004. Cambodia will not improve economically if it does not diversify and improve the quality and value of its export products. In Southeast Asia, only Laos and Timor-Leste export less. Cambodia's economy remains too dependent on foreign aid and NGO activity. Hun Sen has his sights set on untapped oil resources, both on land and in water, valued at over $1.7 billion annually, an amount that would double the regime's current budget revenues.[27] The new frontier in oil exploration could help, but it raises concerns that Cambodia may substitute one form of revenue addiction for another. New oil revenues could simply act to replenish CPP slush funds currently derived from aid, Cambodia's rapid deforestation, and other profitable natural resources.[28]

From a comparative perspective, however, Cambodia's reality is more daunting. Its economy may be growing, but it is so far behind its neighbors that even years of sustained growth will not raise it to regional averages. Nearly one in five Cambodians remains in poverty and one quarter lack access to improved water. About four in five Cambodians still live as poor farmers in rural areas. Deficient irrigation works limit Cambodia's agricultural potential, demonstrated by record surpluses of rice in 2006, a particularly good rain year. Where Thai and Vietnamese farmers lead the world in rice exports, Cambodian farmers are only beginning to produce beyond domestic needs. Cambodia's progress on the UN Millennium Development Goals was mixed, with progress in poverty alleviation, education, and mortality rates, but serious deficiencies in goals tied to gender relations, disease control, and environmental protection.[29] Cambodians share a level of substandard development similar to most people in Myanmar, Laos, and Timor-Leste. According to Transparency International, Cambodia is Asia's most corrupt country after North Korea.

FOREIGN RELATIONS

Throughout its modern history, Cambodia has been the target of aggression by its larger neighbors and by Western and communist imperialists. The French, Americans, Soviets, Chinese, Vietnamese, and Thais have all attempted at various times to control Cambodian affairs. During the Cold War, Cambodia was the victim of direct US and Vietnamese intervention as well as Chinese support for antigovernment rebels. The Vietnamese intervention of December 1978 occurred with significant support from the Soviets, who financed the operation and provided much of the weaponry.

After the Vietnamese invasion, the United Nations continued to recognize the Pol Pot regime despite the fact that the Khmer Rouge controlled only about 2 percent of the population and that Pol Pot had been branded as one of history's worst violators of human rights. The United States, playing Cold War politics under Jimmy Carter, simplistically viewed the PRK as a puppet of Vietnam and, thus, a surrogate of the Soviet Union.

The end of the Cold War brought new opportunities for a comprehensive peace settlement after a decade of factional conflict. Warmer relations between the United States and the Soviet Union influenced a new US policy toward Cambodia. For many years, US goals in Cambodia included the withdrawal of Vietnamese military forces; the repudiation of the Khmer Rouge; a political settlement that would permit Cambodians to choose their form of government; and an independent, neutral, and nonaligned Cambodia, protected from outside interference by international guarantees.[30] After the October 1991 peace accords were signed, the United States normalized relations with Cambodia and ended its economic embargo.

Because China needed to restore its international reputation following the 1989 Tiananmen Square tragedy, and after China and Vietnam moved to a rapprochement in 1992, China pulled the plug on funding the remaining Khmer Rouge. In addition, UN-imposed sanctions against the Khmer Rouge undermined another important source of their funding: Thai investors who had engaged the border rebels in deals for timber and gems. Lack of external support hastened the Khmer Rouge's decline.

ASEAN was not united on the best means by which to deal with a post–Cold War Cambodia. Whereas Singapore took a hard-line stance against the Hun Sen government, Thailand wished to convert Indochina "from a battlefield to a marketplace," with the Thais themselves taking the leading economic role in mainland Southeast Asia. Gradually the regional environment tilted toward reconciliation. In a matter of a little more than a decade, Cambodia had transformed itself from a Khmer Rouge pariah state, into a Vietnamese puppet state, into an international experiment, and then into a weakling state, dependent on regional and international patrons.

Cambodia's international relations evolved further in 1999 when it became a member of ASEAN, only two years after Hun Sen's power grab via coup d'état. Since that time, relations with Vietnam have been more cordial, but Cambodia has turned actively toward China, the regional power Cambodia now accepts as its main protector, patron, and strategic partner. China has provided military aid to Cambodia and agreed to a "comprehensive cooperative partnership," with Beijing's consultation on "issues of regional peace, stability, and development" as well as economic matters.[31] The ASEAN-China Free Trade Agreement, signed in Phnom Penh in 2002, included a zero tariff classification on certain imports from Cambodia.[32] Cambodian trade with China is expected to climb to $5 billion by 2020.

In terms of foreign assistance, China provided over $1 billion annually in loans and aid to Cambodia in 2010 and 2011, more than any other bilateral or multilateral donor. In 2011, at a ceremonial opening with Hun Sen presiding, the Chinese state-run company Sinohydro activated China's largest hydroelectric dam in Kampot Province. In 2015, four more Chinese-built dams, worth some $1.6 billion, went online through build-operate-transfer schemes to provide a total 915 megawatts for Cambodia's electricity grid.[33] Unlike foreign assistance from Western sources, Chinese aid does not come with any requirements for democratic performance, rule of law, environmental impact, or property compensation. While China has its eye on Cambodia's oil and gas resources, its massive aid packages have also bought China a needed ASEAN ally in the Spratlys dispute. In 2012, when Cambodia hosted annual ASEAN meetings with China and the United States present, progress on a regional solution failed largely due to Cambodian objections.

Cambodia's biggest foreign relations concerns in recent years have been with its Thai neighbors to the west. In 2003, after a Thai actress supposedly commented that she would not perform in Cambodia until Angkor Wat was returned to Thailand, anti-Thai riots erupted on Phnom Penh streets. Rioters attacked several Thai-owned businesses, causing $50 million worth of damages. No Thais were injured or killed, but the incident troubled relations between the two countries, partly because of Hun Sen's poor handling of the situation. Tensions over the matter reverberated for a time, but eventually economic interests triumphed again and the two governments found themselves signing border trade deals and cooperating on oil exploration in the years that followed.[34]

Relations with Thailand subsequently deteriorated in 2007 when Cambodia submitted a celebrated border temple for UNESCO World Heritage Site status. Nestled on a cliff overlooking Cambodia's northern plains, the dramatically set Preah Vihear temple was the subject of a 1962 International Court of Justice case that ruled the temple was in Cambodian territory in spite of Thai claims otherwise. Thai authorities unsuccessfully demanded postponement of the

UNESCO proposal. With much chest-pounding by Hun Sen (reciprocated by his Thai counterparts), Cambodian and Thai border troops engaged in deadly skirmishes near the temple in 2008 and again in 2011. The incident drew the attention of the UN Security Council, which feared a full-scale border war. UNESCO later approved the designation, and the dispute festered until another ruling in 2013 by the International Court of Justice affirmed Cambodian sovereignty over the temple and promontory.

Although the Khmer Rouge is no longer an organized force, its legacy, alas, continues to define international perceptions of Cambodia and its people. Globally, Cambodia's biggest foreign policy challenge going forward may be transcending this image—to create for itself a truly post–Khmer Rouge international identity, much in the same way Vietnam has begun to shed its "Vietnam War" image by redefining itself as one of Asia's emerging economies. Sympathetic governments and aid organizations have afforded Hun Sen a generous degree of political space to engineer this feat, but his regime's reputation for corruption, exploitation, and failed democracy is doing little to improve the country's image or standing.

CONCLUSION

Regime instability, indicated by the country's many name changes, has dictated Cambodia's recent past. No other people in Southeast Asia have undergone the magnitude of horrific trauma that Cambodians suffered from the 1960s to the present. War, genocide, famine, and oppression have devastated the society once known as an oasis of tranquility. With virtually its entire educated class decimated at one point, Cambodia is attempting to rebuild. However, it is still buffeted by the world's great powers, by its neighbors, and by internal political despotism. The phenomenal resilience of the Cambodians is the most hopeful sign that the "killing fields" will never return and that Cambodia can develop and remain independent.

For the foreseeable future, Cambodia will continue to suffer weak state institutions, strongman leadership, and the constant threat of internal political conflict. Without better-trained administrators, an improved infrastructure, and continued external aid, the outlook for political development is bleak. Hun Sen, proven capable of employing any means to ensure power, is unlikely to permit electoral politics, or any other process, to remove him from the apex of power. Patronage, corruption, and disregard for civil liberties are likely to characterize the Cambodian political system for many years to come. Champions of democracy face an uphill battle.

NOTES

1. Factors contributing to the decline of Angkor remain a subject of intense study. The role of monument building and war is emphasized, for example, in D. R. Sardesai's *Southeast Asia Past and Present*, 6th ed. (Boulder: Westview Press, 2009). The significant role of

climate change as a factor in the decline of the "hydraulic city" of Angkor is a relatively recent archaeological discovery; see Brenda M. Buckley et al., "Climate as a Contributing Factor in the Demise of Angkor, Cambodia," *Proceedings of the National Academy of Sciences* 107, no. 15, (April 13, 2010): 6,748–6,752.

2. Eva Mysliwiec, *Punishing the Poor: The International Isolation of Kampuchea* (Oxford, UK: Oxfam, 1988), 2.

3. The most comprehensive account of the effect US bombing had in bringing the Khmer Rouge to power is found in William Shawcross, *Sideshow: Kissinger, Nixon, and the Destruction of Cambodia* (New York: Simon and Schuster, 1979).

4. David P. Chandler et al., *In Search of Southeast Asia: A Modern History*, ed. David Joel Steinberg (Honolulu: University of Hawaii Press, 1987), 381–382.

5. Ibid., 11.

6. Steven Heder, "Cambodia in 2010: Hun Sen's Further Consolidation," *Asian Survey* 51, no. 1 (January/February 2011): 211–212.

7. The Committee for Free and Fair Elections in Cambodia (COMFREL), *2013 National Assembly Elections: Final Assessment and Report*, December 2013, www.comfrel .org/eng/components/com_mypublications/files/781389Final_Report_and_Assessment _National_Assembly_Elections_Final_24_12_2013.pdf.

8. Duncan McCargo, "Cambodia in 2014: Confrontation and Compromise," *Asian Survey* 55, no. 1 (January/February 2015): 71–77.

9. Duncan McCargo, "Cambodia: Getting Away with Authoritarianism?" *Journal of Democracy* 16, no. 4 (2005): 103.

10. FUNCINPEC is an acronym for the party's French name, Front Uninational pour un Cambodge Indépendant Neutre, Pacifique, et Coopératif.

11. McCargo, "Cambodia in 2014," 74.

12. Information about Cambodia's vast NGO community can be found at a website maintained by the Cooperation Committee for Cambodia: http://ccc-cambodia.org.

13. McCargo, "Cambodia: Getting Away with Authoritarianism?" 108.

14. David Chandler, "Cambodia in 2009: Plus C'est la Meme Chose," *Asian Survey* 50, no. 1 (January/February 2010): 229.

15. McCargo, "Cambodia: Getting Away with Authoritarianism?" 110.

16. Melanie Beresford, "Cambodia in 2004: An Artificial Democratization Process," *Asian Survey* 45, no. 1 (January/February 2005): 137.

17. Caroline Hughes, "Cambodia in 2007: Development and Dispossession," *Asian Survey* 48, no. 1 (January/February 2008): 74.

18. Robert J. Muscat, *Cambodia: Post-Settlement Reconstruction and Development* (New York: East Asian Institute, Columbia University, 1989), 88–89.

19. Ibid., 2.

20. A label used during a personal communication with David Oldfield, Asian Development Bank analyst, following a 1998 research visit to the area.

21. Figures are from the Royal Government of Cambodia, Ministry of Economy and Finance. UN Development Program figures for 2007 show a gross national income per capita of $540.

22. Gillian Kane, "Cambodia Factsheet," Clean Clothes Campaign, 2014, https://www .cleanclothes.org/resources/publications/factsheets/cambodia-factsheet-february-2015 .pdf.

23. Chandler, "Cambodia in 2009," 230.

24. Nirmal Ghosh, "Women Have It Hardest in Cambodia's Apparel Industry: Report," *New Straits Times*, March 12, 2015, www.straitstimes.com/asia/se-asia/women-have-it-hardest-in-cambodias-apparel-industry-report.

25. Chan Muyhong, "Ticket Sales at Angkor Wat Exceed 2 Million," *Phnom Penh Post*, January 21, 2015, www.phnompenhpost.com/business/ticket-sales-angkor-wat-exceed-2-million.

26. *Lonely Planet's Ultimate Travel: Our List of the 500 Best Places to See . . . Ranked* (London: Lonely Planet, 2015).

27. Khlem Chanreatrey, "Big Questions over Black Gold," *Economics Today*, July 23, 2012, http://etmcambodia.com/viewarticles.php?articlesid=201.

28. Hughes, "Cambodia in 2007," 72–73.

29. See the United Nations Development Programme–Cambodia, www.un.org.kh/undp.

30. Frederick Z. Brown, *Second Chance: The United States and Indochina in the 1990s* (New York: Council on Foreign Relations, 1989), 11.

31. Oskar Weggel, "Cambodia in 2006: Self-Promotion and Self-Deception," *Asian Survey* 47, no. 1 (January/February 2007): 146.

32. Robert Sutter, *Chinese Foreign Relations: Power and Policy since the Cold War* (Lanham, MD: Rowman & Littlefield, 2008), 268.

33. "Cambodia's Largest Hydroelectric Dam Begins Operation," *Xinhua News*, December 7, 2012, http://news.xinhuanet.com/english/world/2011-12/07/c_131293571.htm.

34. Weggel, "Cambodia in 2006," 146.

6

LAOS

L aos might best be described as a quasi nation. It emerged from maps drawn by European colonialists rather than from a sense of territory and nation-hood among a united people. From the first ethnically Tai settlements to today, the peoples who now populate Laos have attempted to develop politically amid the meddling of external powers—mainly those from Thailand, Vietnam, France, the United States, and, most recently, China.

Since it seized power in 1975, the present communist government has faced the one constant in Lao history: the need to protect the nation's sovereignty and its abundant natural resources from neighbors and outside powers. The current regime must also confront ongoing domestic problems such as uniting diverse ethnic groups, promoting development with an overwhelmingly rural population, educating a citizenry with minimal educational institutions, coping with outmigration and returning refugees, and managing an abundance of nat-ural resources trapped by geography.

Laos is landlocked, but uniquely so. Its isolation is exacerbated by the phys-iographic borders it shares with each of its neighbors. Remote mountains lie along Laos' northern borders with China and Vietnam, and the rugged Annam Cordillera defines its long eastern border with Vietnam (inhibiting overland routes to the South China Sea). To its west, the broad and meandering Mekong River separates Laos from Burma and forms much of its border with Thailand.

Culturally, the Mekong supported Lao peoples on both sides of the river, but the first modern bridge appeared only in the mid-1990s. Laos's river access to the Mekong Delta is inhibited by the unnavigable Khone Falls on the coun-try's southern border. Thus, lowland Laos, inclusive of the Plain of Jars,[1] sits as a land island, disadvantaged in the new international era by the lack of high-ways, railways, and port access. Given the relative economic dynamism of its neighbors, Laos's full economic potential as a modern crossroads for trade and transport is yet unmet.

Contemporary Laos has changed little over the decades in aggregate terms. It remains a largely rural, subsistence, agrarian society of some 6.9 million people divided among over forty ethnic groups, with the dominant lowland Lao consisting of just over 4 million people. The population density of Laos is the lowest of all Asian countries. Theravada Buddhism, variably blended with local spirit beliefs, predominates among the Lao and among many upland groups. Most ethnic Lao in the lowlands enjoy livelihoods quite separate from Laos's hundreds of upland ethnic minorities.

The vast majority of Lao are rural poor. Modern farming techniques and equipment have been slow to reach Lao farmers. The typical household economy is based on rice production with water buffalo employed as draft animals— with over 1.2 million head, there was roughly one water buffalo for every five persons in Laos as recently as 2010.[2] Amazingly, less than 5 percent of the country is suitable for agriculture, yet close to 75 percent of Lao still work in the sector. In spite of recent economic gains from economic reforms, Laos's per capita gross national income (GNI) in 2014 reached only $1,600.

Contemporary challenges in Laos originate from centuries-old conflicts, when ancient Lan Xang—"the Kingdom of a Million Elephants"—was a battleground for the expansionism of neighboring states. It was not until the fourteenth century that a semblance of national unity emerged. Dynastic quarrels in the eighteenth century undermined this unity, and the area was divided into the kingdoms of Luang Prabang in the north, Champasak in the south, and Vientiane in the central region.

Vietnam and Thailand periodically plundered Lao kingdoms until the French colonized the area in the late 1880s. In 1899, the French claim of suzerainty consolidated Laos into a single political unit, but French rule did little to modernize or integrate the nation. On the contrary, a small group of elite Lao families was allowed to consolidate its power; thus, the Lao emerged from colonial rule (after World War II) more divided, isolated, and backward than ever.

From 1941 to 1945, the Japanese ruled Laos, although the collaborating Vichy French administered many governmental affairs. At the end of the war, the Gaullist French recaptured Vientiane, the administrative capital, and fought a group called the *Lao-Issara* (Free Lao), which established a government-in-exile in Bangkok. This group became the forerunner and nucleus of the separate pro-communist, anti-French Neo Lao Hak Sat (NLHS)—the Lao Patriotic Front. Lao-Issara was led by Prince Souvanna Phouma and his half-brother, Prince Souphanouvong, who later broke off and joined the NLHS, which was operating in areas held by the Vietminh. By 1953, the NLHS's military force, known as the Pathet Lao (Lao Nation), had seized control of the nation's northeastern provinces.

In 1954, France accorded self-government to Laos at the Geneva Conference, which effectively gave Laos complete independence. The aftermath of the Geneva Conference was a period of disarray for Laos, as the competing sides vied for control of the populace and the countryside. Also in 1954, when the Pathet Lao was making significant military gains in large areas of the countryside, the United States sponsored a coup by anticommunists against Souvanna Phouma, who had become premier of the new nation but was considered too much of a neutralist by the US government. The coup failed, but Souvanna Phouma was given notice that even neutralist policies were considered intolerable by the United States. When a right-wing government appeared in 1955, the United States immediately began a $45 million annual aid program.

In 1957, the neutralists, led by Souvanna—this time with backing from the United States—set up a government emphasizing national unity, with cabinet posts for leftists and rightists. In special elections called for in the Geneva agreements, NLHS candidates won the majority of seats, an outcome deemed intolerable by Souvanna's government and by US diplomats. To overturn the results of the election and reverse the apparent popular trend toward a communist government, the United States—principally through the CIA—extended massive support to right-wing regimes that excluded NLHS representation. There were numerous coups d'état during this period as anticommunist leaders jockeyed for power. However, the major beneficiary of governmental chaos was the NLHS movement, which continued to expand its control as it received increasing amounts of military supplies and support from the Soviet Union.

At the second Geneva Conference, in 1961, neutralist Souvanna, leftist Souphanouvong, and rightist Boun Oum agreed on coalition rule. The United States reversed its policy and supported Souvanna Phouma's appointment as prime minister (after he gave secret permission to the United States to bomb Pathet Lao areas). The coalition collapsed almost immediately, however, as factions maneuvered for power. The NLHS broke from the coalition, and Souvanna Phouma's Royal Lao government, a constitutional monarchy, became a virtual client of the United States.

Escalation of the Vietnam War changed the nature of the struggle between the NLHS and Royal Lao government forces. Hanoi's interest in Laos increased as its need for sanctuaries from US bombing became paramount. Vietnam, in violation of the Geneva agreements, escalated its presence in the northeastern provinces of Laos as the United States, also in violation of the agreements, began secret bombing missions in Laos in 1964. In the following years, the landlocked nation became one of the most heavily bombed countries in history; some 2.1 million tons of bombs were dropped between 1964 and 1972 (about two-thirds of a ton per Lao).[3] Despite this ferocity, the intended strategic effect of the bombing was minimal, prompting the CIA to train and supply Hmong and other upland peoples, introduce military advisers, and use the US Agency for International Development as a front for intelligence and training purposes. Laos became the battleground for a neighboring war fought by surrogate powers.

The Laos Peace Accords came in 1973 as the American withdrawal from Vietnam was completed. The accords called for stopping the bombing, disbanding foreign-supported forces, removing all foreign troops, and instituting the coalition Provisional Government of National Unity (PGNU). The new ministries were divided between the Royalists and the Pathet Lao. At the time of the signing of the accords, the NLHS controlled about three-fourths of all Lao territory and one-half of the population. Both sides were allowed to keep their zones of control until elections could be arranged.

The well-organized Pathet Lao (now called the Lao People's Liberation Army) prevailed over the Royal Lao faction in the coalition government, which lacked discipline, was enervated by family feuds, and was considered a puppet of the United States. The Pathet Lao spoke convincingly to the rural people of Laos, who had seen their agricultural base and villages destroyed, and their population dislocated.[4] No family had been left unscathed by the civil war and the US bombing.

In December 1975, the Pathet Lao dissolved the PGNU, abolished the 622-year-old monarchy, and established the Lao People's Democratic Republic (Lao PDR). The change in government was preceded by communist victories in Vietnam and Cambodia and by pro-communist demonstrations throughout Laos. The rightist ministers fled, and all power was eventually assumed by the communists. Souvanna Phouma resigned, and Kaysone Phomvihane, general secretary of the newly formed Lao People's Revolutionary Party (LPRP), became the new prime minister. A Supreme People's Council was set up with Prince Souphanouvong as president and chief of state, while Kaysone Phomvihane— virtually unknown to all but a handful of communist leaders before 1975— assumed political and administrative control of the country. In contrast to Vietnam and Cambodia, where communists came to power as a result of military victory, the change of government in Laos came about relatively peacefully.

The communist victory changed Lao politics fundamentally. For centuries the region had been dominated by a small group of wealthy families that wielded great political and economic influence. Most of those families fled to Thailand, Europe, or the United States, and those that remained underwent "reeducation" programs to cleanse them of their "bourgeois mentality." An estimated 300,000 persons, many of them the most educated in Laos, fled to Thailand following the change in government. The flight of educated Lao and the systematic expunging of civil servants of the former administration created a leadership vacuum that seriously impaired the government's ability to administer and implement new programs.

The new government moved quickly to eradicate the worst vestiges of what they considered bourgeois society by banning nightclubs, massage parlors, and dance halls. Private enterprise was stifled, and the government attempted, rather feebly, to collectivize farms. Most farmers resisted collectivization and continued subsistence production.[5] The government's reeducation programs, affecting thousands of Lao, made the populace wary of the new regime. Refugees reported arrogant bureaucrats and repressive rules and regulations.

Another major change was the withdrawal of the United States as a principal player in Lao politics. Most Western aid, which had funded over 90 percent of the Royal Lao government budget, ended when the communists took power, although the countryside was still devastated from the war. Although the United States did not break diplomatic relations with Laos after the communist takeover, US involvement became peripheral, and the Soviet Union and Vietnam filled the vacuum. After Vietnamese troops arrived in Laos, China accused Vietnam of trying to create an Indo-Chinese federation and withdrew the aid it had given to Laos for numerous development projects. The Soviet Union, supplying some 2,000 advisers and $50 million in annual aid, was the superpower patron of Laos until the end of the Cold War.

The Lao PDR was ruled from 1975 to 1991 without a constitution. When one was finally adopted, it strengthened the presidency (at that time held by Kaysone), although the LPRP retained its position as the primary institution. Civil liberties were technically allowed as prescribed by law in the document, but it effectively cemented Laos as a party-state.

President Kaysone's death in November 1992 provided an opportunity for Laos to usher in a new generation of leaders more in tune with the international movement away from communism and toward democracy. However, Prime Minister (and former defense minister) Khamtay Siphandone, who was nearly seventy years old, was named leader of the LPRP and an associate nearing eighty was named president. Their hard-line conservatism and provincial outlook frustrated those who wanted Laos to look more toward the West for direction.

In the late 1980s, Laos, like China and Vietnam before it, opened its economy by pursuing a "new thinking," or a market-based approach. Under the "New Economic Mechanism," the government jettisoned failed collectivization policies and centralized economic allocation. By 1995, the twentieth anniversary of LPRP rule in Laos, market economics was in command and party rule was far less doctrinaire. The LPRP also gave new life to Buddhism by restoring temples and encouraging the *sangha*, or Buddhist monastic order, to play a role in development. In what was surely a communist-world first, the 1995 funeral service for the regime's first president, the "Red Prince" Souphanouvong, was an entirely traditional Buddhist ceremony, with no ideological overtones.

The Sixth Congress of the LPRP in 1996 moved Laos toward more comprehensive but slow economic reform. By the new millennium, the Lao government had liberalized parts of the economy but retained its centralized monopoly on political life. Signs of Asian-style economic dynamism have since emerged, mainly in urban areas, but economic reform has yet to modernize or transform the economy to the degree it has in neighboring Vietnam. Laos continues to be both Buddhist and authoritarian, both Marxist and capitalist. To prop up their legitimacy, regime leaders in the party now portray themselves as the protectors of Theravada Buddhism by building monuments to legendary Buddhist monarchs of the fourteenth-century Lan Xang kingdom.

In 2006, Khamtay, at eighty-three years of age, was replaced as state president by Choummaly Sayasone, another old-line conservative. Other political hard-liners from the Politburo remain entrenched in key posts. Among the party's most notable insiders are the sons of Kaysone and Khamtay, suggesting hints of dynastic rule.[6] Buoasone Bouphavanh, a younger official who was named the regime's fifth prime minister, surprisingly resigned in late 2010 after four short years in the position claiming "family problems" as the cause. Observers speculate that Buoasone's attack on corruption within the party resulted in his removal. That he was replaced by Thongsing Thammavong, old-guard loyalist, was unsurprising.[7]

In November 2015, a month before the December 31 launch of the ASEAN Economic Community (AEC), the leaders of Laos's oligarchic party-state took the helm of ASEAN. The timing was symbolic. Integrating Laos into Southeast Asia's economic pathways is a top government priority. Land-locked Laos seeks to refashion itself as a "land-linked" modern crossroads between China and Southeast Asia. In some respects this prospect is promising. New foreign investments in bridge projects and economic zones have been secured. State profits from hydropower energy sales to neighboring countries are on the rise. Plans for a Chinese-backed $7.2 billion railway project connecting Southwest China with Southeast Asia through Vientiane are under way.

But, alas, questions inseparable from Laos's nascent economic dynamism persist. Transportation crossroads by their very nature attract outsiders all too eager to meddle in local affairs. Whether Laos can retain sovereign control of its core interests is an open question. Moreover, skeptical observers remain unconvinced that Laos can meaningfully reduce poverty, spread the benefits of new wealth, and shed its reputation as a "communist kleptocracy." The prospects of broad-based change are dim in the absence of a civil society, free press, or any organized opposition groups to hold those in power accountable.[8]

INSTITUTIONS AND SOCIAL GROUPS

Lao People's Revolutionary Party

Since 1975, the country's dominant institution has been the LPRP, the communist party that emerged from the Pathet Lao leadership. Led by elderly revolutionaries who fought against the French, Japanese, and Americans, the party has practiced democratic centralism, requiring party leaders' unanimous support in all decisions. Policy was formulated and implemented by the party Politburo, led by Kaysone Phomvihane. Kaysone had emerged in December 1975 from the caves of a northern province where he and his Pathet Lao colleagues had hidden to escape US bombing. Outside the inner circle of the Pathet Lao,

few Lao knew him or knew about him, and Kaysone eschewed a cult of personality, living quietly and making himself available to very few visitors except
communist allies. Little was known about his past except for his close association with Vietnam, where he had studied at the University of Hanoi.

Kaysone held the positions of prime minister and then president, as well as
general secretary of the LPRP. Surrounded by colleagues from his revolutionary days in the 1950s, he changed his rule little after 1975. Continuity and stability were the themes of governmental leadership until 1979, when reforms
were instituted that significantly changed the government's hard-line policies.[9]
After that time, and especially after 1986, when the "new thinking" reforms
were instituted, Kaysone visited noncommunist countries, and his activities
were even reported in the press. Nevertheless, he remained one of the world's
least-known leaders up to his death in 1992.

The LPRP, having failed to achieve popular support for its socialist policies,
launched a series of reform policies in 1986 to decentralize economic decision-
making and to liberalize, both economically and politically. In 1989—for the
first time—the LPRP allowed elections for the National Assembly, Laos's nominal legislative body. Only government-approved candidates were permitted
to run in this and subsequent elections. Assembly elections, little more than
Soviet-style plebiscites for preselected LPRP candidates, mean little in a system
where the assembly institution enjoys little independence from the party apparatus. In the 2011 national elections that followed the 9th Party Congress, all but
4 of the now-132 seats in the body are held by members of the party. In spite of
cosmetic changes, the locus of all power in the system remains the 11-member
Politburo, itself the product of a 61-member Party Central Committee.

To a certain degree, mass organizations that assemble youth, women, labor,
or minority groups to follow party directives are more connected to the grass
roots of Lao society than the LPRP itself. The Lao Front for National Construction (LFNC), for example, is charged with the daunting task of unifying Laos'
disparate ethnic groups. Created in 1979, the LFNC's organizational reach extends to every administrative level of government in an effort to co-opt local
leaders into the state apparatus.

The LPRP is corrupt. "Corruption is the ogre in the woodpile of Lao politics," according to one scholar, who adds, "Members of the Politburo and their
families have become excessively rich."[10] Skimming off of concessions in mining, timber, and hydropower projects is standard practice. Even as aggregate
economic growth raises per capita averages, it is members of the party and their
close associates who experience the most gains.

Unlike Vietnam and China, where the military is increasingly separate from
party leadership, military leadership remains integrated with the LPRP. After a
focused recruitment effort, party membership now stands above 190,000, more
than double the party's size in 1995. It remains to be seen whether a younger

generation of leaders will emerge to replace the "revolutionary generation" of the LPRP before the Lao PDR becomes a gerontocracy.

International Aid Community

The Lao PDR government collaborates extensively with the international aid community in pursuing its development policies. International agencies, regional bodies, and bilateral aid programs do not directly control policy but do much to set the policy agenda in Vientiane. A principal international partner, for example, is the United Nations Development Program (UNDP). It ties its efforts in Laos to achieving the UN Millennium Development Goals. Focusing on programs to reduce Laos's poverty rate by half and move the country out of least developed country (LDC) status, the UNDP guides a formalized roundtable process of aid coordination with various UN agencies and the network of embryonic civil society organizations now operating in the country.[11]

Other principal partners with the Lao government include the Asian Development Bank (ADB), through its Greater Mekong Subregion Program, as well as the IMF and World Bank. Over fifty bilateral agencies of OECD countries also help prop up the Lao state. The ADB alone is responsible for seventy-five loans worth over $1.7 billion since 1968. The World Bank is particularly influential in supporting the massive hydropower projects the Lao government is undertaking. Antiglobalization critics angrily indict the World Bank for manipulating Lao authorities and the policy agenda.[12] The critics may have to broaden their scope. In 2015, Laos became a founding signatory to China's new Asian Infrastructure Investment Bank (AIIB), the likely source of loans to fund the proposed high-speed railway connecting China to Southeast Asia.

Lao Abroad

Since 1975, over 300,000 refugees, mostly lowland Lao, have left the country. Ethnic Hmong, Mien, Lahu, and other upland groups recruited by the CIA for its secret war in Laos also compose a large segment of this migrant population. Without US "allies" to protect them, many Hmong and others were subject to genocidal recrimination in the form of chemical-biological toxins falling from Vientiane aircraft in the late 1970s and 1980s. As reported by droves of refugees fleeing into Thailand, whole villages suffered illness and fatal hemorrhaging from "red, yellow, and green gases" dropped from the sky. Disastrous living conditions forced others, including many lowland Lao, to seek refuge as well. Refugees reported forced labor, torture, "seminar camps," and starvation.[13]

After years in Thai border camps, most refugees were resettled in third countries such as the United States, France, and Australia. For decades, a vocal segment of the overseas refugee community lobbied foreign governments with little success to exert greater pressure on the LPRP communist regime. The plight of upland minority groups within Laos and the forcible repatriation of refugees from border camps also have drawn the attention of Amnesty International and other human rights groups.

In 2007, Hmong community leader Vang Pao, a former CIA ally, was arrested at his home in California on evidence of plotting to overthrow the Lao government—an act in violation of US law prohibiting Americans from acting violently against foreign governments that have peaceful relations with the United States. In support of the legendary leader, hundreds of Hmong Americans flocked to the Los Angeles courthouse where Vang stood accused. Vang was eventually released on a $1.5 million bond. The alleged plot of Vang Pao and his coconspirators included smuggling Stinger missiles into rebel areas and hiring US mercenary forces to launch an offensive on Lao government forces. After extended legal wrangling, the charges were dropped. WikiLeaks cables revealed the episode actually improved Lao-US relations.[14] At the age of eighty-one, Vang Pao died in 2011, along with the likelihood of any future rebellions organized from California.

An increasing number of economic migrants from Laos, often undocumented, now work in Thailand as laborers. The wages earned and wealth created by these workers, together with the earnings of overseas Lao in third countries, often find their way back to relatives in Laos. In recent years, remittances from abroad, according to Lao government reports, accounted for as much as 28 percent of household earnings in many parts of Laos.[15] To incentivize its own laborers to stay in the country, Laos raised its minimum wage by nearly a third in 2015. The Lao government has also sought, without great success, to entice wealthy and capable overseas Lao back to the country by offering them government jobs, new homes, and other perks.

Among the Lao abroad is exiled crown prince Soulivong Savang, grandson of King Vattana, the last king of Laos, who died in a reeducation camp following his overthrow in 1975. Soulivong has held meetings with US government officials and pushed for a more aggressive international isolation of Vientiane. Residing in France, the crown prince remains a dim symbol of hope for Lao seeking regime change and restoration of a constitutional monarchy.

STATE-SOCIETY RELATIONS AND DEMOCRACY

Laos, like its neighbors Cambodia and Myanmar, is an example of a state with little capacity to meet the needs of its citizenry or to mobilize its collective strength. Laos does not have a societal group that is independent of social controls and designs of state leaders. The LPRP dominates every aspect of Lao political life, having co-opted virtually the entire administrative class and local leadership. In Laos there is no independent intellectual class capable of competing with the state leaders. The long tradition of student activism seen in Thailand, Indonesia, and Myanmar is almost nonexistent. In Thailand, a 2009 attempt of antigovernment protest by a group of student activists led to arrests and exile. Internet activism, to the extent it exists, is dominated by second-generation overseas Lao who indicate little desire to return to a country they technically never left.

Political institutions beyond the LPRP are feeble or nonexistent. Whereas Thailand is propped up by a long-standing monarchy that helps provide state legitimacy, Laos has had no parallel institution since 1975. Buddhism is receiving renewed government support, but the institutionalization of the *sangha* as a political actor is weak compared to the role of the monastic order in Thailand and Myanmar. Moreover, increasing dependency on financial and technical assistance from international aid agencies and wealthy Asian entrepreneurs fosters patronage and corruption—phenomena of state weakness, not strength. Additionally weakening the Lao state is the absence of skillful or charismatic leaders. Leaders function as party managers capable of repression more than as mobilizers of popular sentiment or political will.

There is no semblance of democracy in Laos, nor has there ever been. The country's communist leadership has not instituted reforms permitting a representative system or civil liberties. Laos can be classified as a politically closed regime. Testimony to the Lao people's view that their government is not legitimate is the fact that since it came into power, about one in ten residents have left the country. Indeed, the regime's insecurity regarding its legitimacy is shown by its refusal to allow any kind of opposition or open elections. The government has experimented with village-level elections, but the activities of interest groups and civil society groups are closely monitored.

According to Freedom House, the Lao government does not censor the Internet, a reality stemming more from lack of capacity than any ideological commitment to free speech. Television broadcasts from Thailand are the public's chief link to the outside world. The dearth of education in the countryside inhibits opportunities for a civic consciousness to develop. Individuals speak out at great risk. A dozen or so have just disappeared. In late 2012, for instance, a well-known democratic activist, Sombath Somphone, mysteriously disappeared after being stopped by police. Questions from foreign diplomats about the whereabouts of the white-haired, University of Hawaii–trained agronomist have persisted for years with no response from Lao authorities. Shui Meng Ng, Sombath's indefatigable Singaporean wife and UNICEF official, travels the world drawing attention to her husband's disappearance and Laos' human rights failures.

Political liberalization, let alone democratization, is a distant prospect for Laos. Strong economic growth since 2000 is creating a fledgling urban middle class, but those benefiting most are those closest to the regime and thus least likely to pressure it to reform. Laos' LPRP rulers maintain a monolithic hold on political power and face no overt political opposition.[16] With regime change an unlikely prospect, greater political transformation may depend on a generational shift in leadership.

ECONOMY AND DEVELOPMENT

Laos is one of the world's poorest countries. With a gross national income per capita of $1,600, and a poverty rate of nearly 27 percent, the standard of living is low. In Laos, only 42 percent of births are attended by a skilled professional compared to 93 percent in neighboring Vietnam. In rural areas, nearly one in three residents lack access to improved sanitation. Electricity has yet to reach most villages beyond the lowland areas and firewood remains the chief source of fuel in the residential sector. Throughout the country the spread of HIV/ AIDS is growing rapidly. Malaria, tuberculosis, and chronic diarrhea are also widespread.

With respect to overall economic policy, LPRP leaders realized after a half decade of communist rule that their agricultural and industrial policies were failing. By the early 1980s, new pragmatic policies were formally set forth at the party's Third Congress. Government control over the economy was loosened, agriculture was decollectivized, and new technologies were introduced resulting in a large crop output. As a result, Laos achieved self-sufficiency in rice for the first time since the revolution. Officials dubbed the reforms *chin tanakan may* (new thinking), Laos' version of the Soviet Union's perestroika and Vietnam's *doi moi*.

The most fundamental economic changes, however, did not begin until 1986 at the Fourth Congress of the LPRP. These changes, called the "New Economic Mechanism," allowed family farms to completely replace the unpopular agricultural cooperatives. Market mechanisms gradually replaced centralized planning. Two years later, Kaysone admitted that the party's previous policies of putting private traders out of business, collectivizing farmers, and nationalizing industry had caused the production and circulation of goods to come to a halt, grievously affecting the people's livelihood.[17] Following this admission, Lao officials accelerated reforms.

New reforms emphasized grassroots economic units including factories, merchants' shops, and construction projects.[18] State land was distributed to individual families on a long-term basis, and consideration was given to making such land inheritable.[19] Reforms also included a new foreign investment code designed to attract outside investment to finance the Lao infrastructure, but the initial results were disappointing. Laos lacked a constitution or a civil code, a fact that frightened off many potential participants. Corruption also discouraged foreign investors reluctant to pay "tea money" to officials. An equally important problem was administrative capacity: Laos demonstrated little absorptive capability that would allow follow-through on investment and aid projects. Laos finally adopted a constitution in 1991 and experienced increased foreign investment and new growth in the mid-1990s. Unfortunately, triple-digit inflation emerged only to be followed by a currency collapse during the 1997 Asian economic crisis. A year later, party leaders dismissed the country's top technocrats for mishandling macroeconomic policy, and Laos experienced a slow return to modest growth in the early 2000s.

Since 2005, the Lao economy has experienced rapid GDP growth, averaging 7.5 percent from 2005 to 2015. Inflation has been moderate, and the kip has stabilized—although Thai baht and US dollars remain in wide use. Foreign investment by Asian companies in textiles, food processing, and low-tech assembly has expanded Laos's once-pathetic industrial sector. Only 6 percent of GDP in 1990, industry now accounts for nearly 30 percent of economic activity. Drawing on financial and technical support from South Korea and Thailand, Laos opened a stock exchange in 2011. Vietnamese investors send more investment to Laos than any other country. And investment from China continues to pour in, totaling upwards of $5 billion.[20] Although much of it is dedicated to natural resources and energy, about a third of Chinese investment lies beyond the commodity sector. Vientiane now features a new Chinese-built sports stadium, a Chinese cultural center, and multiple low-cost shopping malls stocked with Chinese goods.[21] Deterred by Laos's poor rankings on ease of business surveys, Western investors have largely left Laos to Chinese risk-takers.

Tourism, another recent arrival to the struggling Lao economy, currently generates over $600 million per year with over 6 million annual tourist arrivals. The sector stands second only to mining among Laos's top earning industries. In 1995, Luang Prabang, a former royal capital nestled along the Mekong River in the north, was declared by UNESCO as Laos' first World Heritage Site. Six years later, Wat Phu Champasak in the south became its second. Popular backpacker guides lure visitors by describing Laos as "the road less traveled," the home of "Southeast Asia's most pristine environment," "intact cultures," and "the most chilled-out people on earth."[22]

Trade, investment, and tourist dollars are not the only sources of Laos's foreign exchange. Though amounts are not publicly disclosed by the government, many estimates put foreign aid at about 40 percent of Laos's GDP. Since 1989, when the United States granted its first assistance to Laos since the communist takeover with an antinarcotics project, international aid to Laos has gradually expanded to a diverse array of intergovernmental, bilateral, and nongovernmental sources.

Large infrastructure projects also attract official assistance. In 1994, Australia financed the construction of a bridge to Thailand near Vientiane, the first along the six hundred miles of river that form much of the Thai border. Other bridges spanning the Mekong, backed by foreign monies, now connect Laos with road networks in Thailand and Myanmar. More bridges linking Laos with its neighbors are planned as part of the ADB's Greater Mekong Subregion initiative. Due to improved access, Thai food processing and manufacturing companies have been busily relocating factories to Laos and taking advantage of the improved Asian Highway Network that connects Thailand to China through Laos. Mining, a transport-intensive industry, also draws private investment from East Asia and Australia, much to the dismay of environmentalists.

Through assistance from the World Bank and the Asian Development Bank, the Lao government has been pursuing an economic growth strategy built on massive hydroelectric projects, aimed to feed the insatiable power grids of Thailand, China, and Vietnam. Twenty-five-year purchase agreements tied to the projects were a welcome arrival to Laos's cash-strapped government. Even Singapore has negotiated to import electricity from Laos. Controversy surrounding resettlement of displaced villagers, environmental destruction, and the distribution of benefits tied to hydropower draws serious international attention. The construction of the $1.3 billion, 1,070-megawatt Nam Theun 2 Dam, for example, displaced 100,000 people, or nearly one in sixty Lao citizens. At least ten other hydropower dams are in the construction or planning stage. Rumors abound that the government's goal is to construct seventy total dams.

Laos's resource-based economy faces new challenges due to external pressures beyond its control. In 2012, somewhat remarkably, the Lao government suspended plans to build the Xayaburi hydroelectric project on the Mekong after strident complaints from downstream neighbors.[23] Declining global commodity prices and ballooning budget deficits later led Lao authorities to cancel hundreds of state investment projects over fiscal concerns.

Today, about 75 percent of the labor force in Laos remains in agriculture, typically as rice farmers who suffer poor distribution systems and market coordination. Growing food for consumption is the norm in rural Laos, where food markets remain secondary to home production. Moreover, households in rural areas remain large, averaging over six residents, with fertility rates hovering around four births per woman. In much of Laos, nutrition and food security remain concerns. Nearly 40 percent of all rural children are underweight. Among minority upland groups, almost a quarter of all households suffer from food insecurity.[24]

Because of poor governance, ethnic diversity, and challenging mountainous geography, Laos lags far behind its Asian neighbors in education. Although literacy is reported at 70 percent, half of all households lack adults with any secondary schooling; among female adults in the home, an astonishing 71 percent failed to complete primary education.[25] Linguistic chauvinism contributes to the problem. Although 50 percent of Lao citizens speak a minority language, government bureaucrats continue to mandate Lao as the language of instruction for all schools. Consequently, many villagers in minority upland areas "have consciously chosen not to participate in education because they feel it has no relevance to their lives."[26]

At the tertiary level, the country's first university did not open until 1996. A handful of universities outside the capital have since followed, but the country's overall progress in education remains distressing. Due to poor enrollment and retention rates, Laos failed to meet the 2015 Millennium Development Goals in providing universal primary education.

In 2000, the Lao government, in coordination with the United Nations Development Program, set a goal for the country to graduate from least developed country (LDC) status by the year 2020. If realized, Laos would join only three other countries in successfully exiting the UNDP's original 1971 list of forty-one LDC countries.[27] To be eligible for graduation, Laos must show significant progress in at least two of three target areas: per capita income, health and education, and decreasing economic vulnerability. Because only two are required, it is possible that Laos may shed its LDC status even before significantly improving the health and education levels of its people.

FOREIGN RELATIONS

As a landlocked nation, Laos has always had to rely on its neighbors for security. Traditionally, Thailand, China, and Vietnam have had the greatest impact on Lao political affairs because these counties share long borders with Laos and control its access to the oceans. After World War II, however, the United States became the paramount power, with almost total control over every aspect of Lao political and economic life.

Until 1975, the United States played the leading institutional role in Laos. By dominating the policies of the Vientiane administrations and financing the Lao military, the United States became the patron and the Lao government became a client of US interests. To secure the continuation in power of pro-US forces, the United States engaged in a secret war in Laos in the 1960s, which cost $2 billion annually. Covert operations and massive bombing raids over Laos were designed to strengthen the anticommunist government in Vientiane, demolish the Pathet Lao infrastructure, and interdict soldiers from North Vietnam. In the long run, however, none of these goals were achieved.

After 1975, the United States no longer had influence over the Lao government, and CIA-supported allies such as the Hmong were left to defend themselves. Not until 1987 did relations with the United States change, when the two governments signed agreements for crop substitution programs. Laos had agreed to make a "maximum effort" to stop opium trafficking, and in return, the United States removed Laos from its "decertification list" and reopened its aid program. The irony of these events was the previous tacit US support of upland drug running as a means for upland groups to finance their war efforts.

A major source of tension between the United States and Laos concerned some 500 US troops from the Vietnam War classified as missing in action in Laos. The Lao government was bitter about US demands to conduct excavations because it offered no compensation for the thousands of Lao continuing to die every year from miniature land mine bomblets (called "bombies"), full-size land mines, and other unexploded ordnance (UXO) still scattered throughout the Lao countryside. The lasting presence of UXO, the legacy of 580,000 US bombing missions, continues to hinder rural development, rendering thousands of acres of arable land too dangerous to use.

In 2012, US secretary of state Hillary Clinton became the highest-ranking US official to visit Laos since Secretary of State John Foster Dulles in 1955. Secretary Clinton visited an artificial limb center and met with UXO victims even though the United States has yet to sign the International Convention on Cluster Bombs. The official visit, ostensibly to note the scheduled 2013 entry of Laos into the WTO, was viewed as yet another signal to China that it will not be the only superpower active in the region going forward.

From 1975 to the early 1990s, Vietnam was the country with the greatest influence on Laos's foreign and domestic policies. Vietnam had placed approximately 50,000 troops in the country in the late 1970s. Strategists in the West and China feared that Laos and Cambodia might be assimilated into a greater Indochina federation under Vietnamese dominance. Such a confederation never occurred and all Vietnamese troops were withdrawn by 1990. Laos then began to assert a more independent policy by strengthening its relations with Thailand, ASEAN, and China. In recent years, however, Vietnam and Laos have rekindled their relationship. Much is at stake for Vietnam. Hanoi is concerned about the downstream effects of dam building on its Mekong Delta rice basket as well as China's growing influence on leaders in Vientiane. In 2015, Laos signed a zero-tariff trade pact with Vietnam, and the two countries opened talks on a rail link backed with South Korean funding.

Laos's relations with Thailand have been tense since the Pathet Lao took power in 1975. During the 1980s, Thais viewed Laos as a base of support for insurgency. The hundreds of thousands of Lao (and Cambodian) refugees who crossed into Thailand were viewed as an economic burden. In 1987–1988, Laos and Thailand fought a bloody three-month conflict over a disputed border area. Later, as relations warmed, Thai entrepreneurs took advantage of the economic reforms in Laos to set up businesses, and border towns became market centers for Thailand. Since joining ASEAN in 1997, relations between Laos and Thailand have remained stable due in part to ASEAN's principle of noninterference.

Affected by the Sino-Soviet split during the Cold War, Laos improved relations with China after Soviet aid dried up in the late 1980s. Since 1990, two-way trade with its massive northern neighbor has risen rapidly. China is now the top foreign investor in Laos with particular interests in hydropower generation, rubber, and copper mining. Some concessions in these interests have 100-year-lease arrangements.[28] Beyond investment, Laos receives from China consumer products, improved infrastructure, and weaponry.

Although the two countries share an interest in turning Laos into the crossroads of Southeast Asia, some Lao officials have openly registered suspicion about Chinese intentions in Laos and object to plans for a new railway and its expensive price tag.[29] And after plans for a trade zone went awry, Lao lawmakers forcibly closed the "Chinese colony" known as Golden Boten City along the Lao-China border. Having attracted casinos, brothels, lingerie shops, criminal gangs, and sex tourists, the boom-bust town operated in Chinese currency, on Chinese clocks, and with Chinese beer. In the aftermath, investigative reporters proved unable to trace the sources of the estimated $200 million to $300 million lost in the project.[30]

After a fifteen-year process, Laos finally joined the WTO in 2013. Classified as a least developed country, Laos's ascension to the global trading body followed special guidelines. The process required thirty-seven new laws, over fifty decrees, and nine new bilateral treaties before Laos could qualify. Unlike neighbors with port access to the Pacific, Laos remains excluded from APEC and the Trans-Pacific Partnership (TPP).

CONCLUSION

Laos has been the "forgotten country" of Southeast Asia because it is small and lost strategic importance after the Vietnam War. Its total population is far smaller than that of the city of Bangkok. In Laos, politics at the top remains opaque even to its closest observers. The country's leadership is relatively unknown to the world, its military capacity is weak, and social forces in the country are even weaker. In contrast to Thailand and Vietnam, much of Laos has changed little over the past several decades. Though the current mini–economic boom is altering Vientiane, and tourists now dot the streets of Luang Prabang, development in most of the country's towns and hill areas has remained largely static. Meeting its stated goal to exit LDC status by 2020 would be a major achievement for Laos. Such a feat, however, may require China-like growth rates and the success of initiatives that reach Laos's diverse and largely rural populace.

NOTES

1. The Plain of Jars is a common name for the Xiangkhoang Plateau, where in certain areas hundreds of thick, three-meter-tall stone jars lie strewn across the plain. With the jars dating back to 500 BCE, their source and purpose remains a subject of Lao legend and of considerable archaeological debate.

2. Takai Yasuhiro and Thanongsone Sibounheuang, "Conflict between Water Buffalo and Market-Oriented Agriculture: A Case Study from Northern Laos," *Southeast Asian Studies* 47, no. 4 (March 2010): 452.

3. W. Randall Ireson and Carol J. Ireson, "Laos," in *Coming to Terms: Indochina, the United States, and the War,* ed. Douglas Allen and Ngo Vinh Long (Boulder, CO: Westview Press, 1991), 66.

4. Ibid.

5. The most seminal work documenting the difficulties of collectivizing agriculture in Laos is Grant Evans' *Lao Peasants Under Socialism* (New Haven, CT: Yale University Press, 1990).

6. Geoffrey C. Gunn, "Laos in 2006: Changing of the Guard," *Asian Survey* 47, no. 1 (January/February 2007): 184–185.

7. Martin Stuart-Fox, "Family Problems," *Inside Story*, January 19, 2011, http://inside
.org.au/family-problems.

8. "The Future of Laos: A Bleak Landscape," *The Economist* 409, no. 8859 (October 26,
2013).

9. Macalister Brown and Joseph J. Zasloff, *Apprentice Revolutionaries: The Communist
Movement in Laos, 1930–1985* (Stanford, CA: Hoover Institution Press, 1986), 165.

10. Stuart-Fox, "Family Problems," inside.org.au/family-problems.

11. Geoffrey Gunn, "Laos in 2007: Regional Integration and International Fallout,"
Asian Survey 48, no. 1 (January/February 2008): 64.

12. Michael Goldman, *Imperial Nature: The World Bank and Struggles for Social Justice
in the Age of Globalization* (New Haven, CT: Yale University Press, 2005).

13. Jane Hamilton-Merritt, *Tragic Mountains: The Hmong, the Americans, and Secret
Wars for Laos, 1942–1992* (Bloomington: Indiana University Press, 1993).

14. Michael Doyle, "WikiLeaks Cables Bare Secrets of Lao-US Relations," *McClatchy
News*, April, 22, 2011, www.mcclatchydc.com/news/special-reports/article24625492.html.

15. Bertil Lintner, "Laggard Laos Turns Economic Corner," *Asia Times Online*, January
10, 2008, www.atimes.com/atimes/Southeast_Asia/JA10Ae01.html.

16. Bertil Lintner, "Political Dissent in Laos," *The Irawaddy* 8, no. 6 (June 2000): http://
www2.irrawaddy.org/article.php?art_id=1903.

17. *Asia Yearbook, 1990* (Hong Kong: Far Eastern Economic Review, 1990), 161.

18. Ibid., 96.

19. Martin Stuart-Fox, "Laos in 1988," *Asian Survey* 29, no. 1 (January 1989): 81–82.

20. Frank L. Albert, "Laos Approaches the World Stage," CSIS Asia Program–CogitASIA
.com, September 8, 2015, http://cogitasia.com/laos-approaches-the-world-stage.

21. Ibid.

22. Andrew Burke and Justine Vaisutis, "Laos," 6th ed., *Lonely Planet* (August 2007), 4.

23. Jane Perlez, "Vietnam War's Legacy Is Vivid as Clinton Visits Laos," *New York
Times*, July 11, 2012, www.nytimes.com/2012/07/12/world/asia/on-visit-to-laos-clinton
-is-reminded-of-vietnam-war.html.

24. Food Security Atlas for Lao PDR: Human Capital, *World Food Program*, October
20, 2015, www.foodsecurityatlas.org/lao/country/assets/human-capital#section-6.

25. Ibid.

26. Ibid.

27. The three countries are Botswana, Cape Verde, and the Maldives.

28. "The Future," *The Economist*.

29. Albert, "Laos Approaches," http://cogitasia.com/laos-approaches-the-world-stage.

30. Ron Gluckman, "Bungle in the Jungle," Forbes, July, 27, 2011, www.forbes.com
/global/2011/0808/companies-laos-china-economy-gambling-gangsters-bungle-jungle
.html.

7

THE PHILIPPINES

In the quest for political and economic development, the experience of the Philippines is unique in Southeast Asia. The Philippines experienced a longer colonization and greater influence from the West than any country in the region. In many respects, foreign culture was thrust upon Filipinos through four hundred years under Spanish colonization and forty-eight years of American occupation—"four hundred years in a convent, and fifty years in Hollywood," Filipinos sometimes joke. In fact, many legacies from these formative periods persist. The Philippines today faces difficulties that first arose during colonialism: oligarchic politics, personalism, chronic economic inequality, church-state tensions, and a fascination with celebrity. In the Philippines, development and democratization are stymied by the diminished capacity of the political system to cope with the people's demands. The result is more often institutional decay rather than development, and authoritarianism rather than accountability.[1]

The Philippines, with 101 million people, recently overtook Vietnam as Southeast Asia's second-most-populous country. The archipelago includes 7,107 islands. Nine of these islands—including Luzon, the largest and most politically significant—contain 90 percent of the population. Over 170 languages are spoken across the islands, with Tagalog serving as the lingua franca. About two-thirds of Filipinos have some degree of fluency in English, which is widely used in business, government, education, and pop culture. The religious makeup of the Philippines reflects Spanish and US colonial influences, as well as the country's proximity to Muslim neighbors Malaysia and Indonesia. Officially, over 81 percent of the current population is Catholic; Protestant and evangelical groups account for another 12 percent; Islam, at 5 percent, prevails across many of the southern islands.

The Philippines is largely poor, with a gross national income per capita of $3,440. One in four Filipinos lives below the national poverty line. Pockets of wealth and modernity do exist in the urban areas of Manila and other principal cities. Despite political dysfunction, lawlessness, and endemic corruption, the

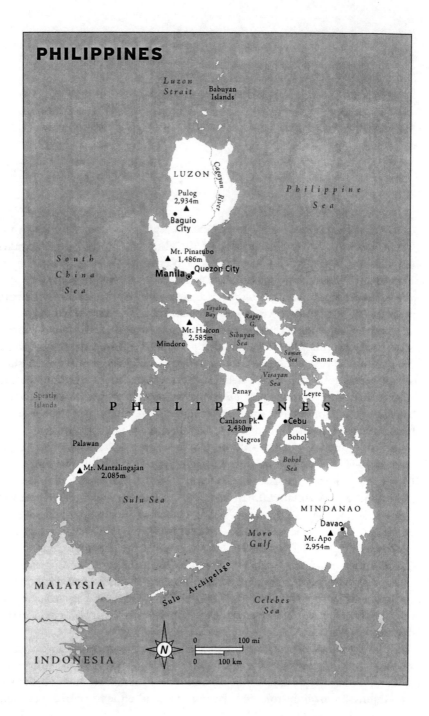

PHILIPPINES

country's economy has experienced modest aggregate growth in recent decades, and a middle class is emerging. A national audience favoring authority grounded in formal institutions rather than personalism exists, but "violence and guile" have tragically operated as the currency of social mobility.[2]

In many respects the experience of the Philippines parallels a Latin American trajectory more than it does Asian political history. The long Spanish and shorter (but also influential) US domination of the Philippines left a mixed legacy. From the Spanish, the Filipinos inherited not only Catholicism but a highly inequitable system of land tenure dominated by a powerful land-owning class. The landed families and the hierarchical society, still powerful in Filipino politics, were rooted in clan warfare and Spanish feudalism. US rule nudged the country's political structures toward competitive democracy, introduced a system of public education that improved literacy rates, and fostered the rise of technocrats, bureaucrats, and entrepreneurs.

The US presence from 1898 to 1946 (a consequence of the Spanish-American War) provoked Filipinos to wage an unsuccessful war against their new occupiers. Politically, occupation helped nurture provincial leaders and a nascent oligarchy at the expense of the masses.[3] It also integrated the Philippine economy into the US economy along colonial lines. The economic relationship between the Philippines and the United States was built on the primary goods produced for the American market, such as tobacco, sugar, and tropical fibers. Sixteen years into the occupation, President Woodrow Wilson pushed the Philippine Autonomy Act through the US Congress—an act supporting a transition to free, democratic government. Full independence was delayed, however, due to squabbling among American politicians, the Great Depression, and Japanese occupation during World War II.

Philippine independence, proclaimed on July 4, 1946, began a period of semidemocratic rule within the context of a continuing oligarchy. A series of democratically elected presidents ruled over a society still pervaded by personalism and *compadrazgo* (godfather-based ritual kinship). The greatest democratic gains, however, were during the four years the country had under President Ramon Magsaysay, who died in a tragic plane crash in 1957. The magnetic Magsaysay, elected on the basis of his clean image and successful crushing of the communist Huk rebellion, promoted civil liberties and enhanced Philippine democracy. His legacy remains larger than his successes in government because he struggled to manage the young postcolonial democracy. Violence perpetrated by the private armies surrounding the nation's elite families continued during his tenure and long afterward.

When Ferdinand Marcos was first elected president in 1965, the Philippines was experiencing economic growth and political stability. The vital Liberal and Nacionalista Parties, despite their fluid, nonideological nature, ensured a lively competition for public office. At the same time, Philippine society suffered from problems that originated during the colonial era, the most salient of which were social and economic inequality, corruption, food shortages, and widespread violence.

In 1969, Marcos became the first president in the postindependence Philippines to be reelected. His reelection was bought in the sense that he gave government funds to local officials who manipulated the vote in his favor. A constitutional provision precluded a third term, so Marcos planned to stay in power by abrogating the constitution and asserting that national crises demanded extraordinary measures. His proclamation of martial law in September 1972 ended formal democratic rule and began a fourteen-year period of authoritarian rule.

A majority of Filipino citizens supported Marcos's initial steps to end the breakdown of law and order, his promise of land reform, and his strengthening of the army against insurrections by communists throughout the archipelago and by Muslim dissidents in the southern islands. This support dissipated as it became clear that Marcos's achievements did not match his rhetoric and that the "temporary" period of martial law was merely a pretext to perpetuate his personal power.

Acting with the wholehearted support of the US government and using his martial law powers, Marcos was both executive and legislator. To give legitimacy to his regime, he instituted referenda, all of which turned out a 90 percent vote in favor of his continued tenure. There were no checks on his self-appointed powers. Press censorship of antigovernment criticism, jailing of dissidents, lack of basic civil liberties, absence of a secret ballot, and control of ballot counting were the methods Marcos used to secure his rule. To each of his twelve closest loyalists who helped him enforce martial law, his "twelve apostles," Marcos gave a gold Rolex watch.

By the mid-1970s, Marcos's so-named New Society initiatives under martial law began to disintegrate due to the rise of lawlessness in the countryside and the realization by Filipinos that the "constitutional authoritarian" government was more authoritarian than constitutional. Growing awareness of a mismanaged economy created new political pressures. Unemployment rose to over 20 percent and underemployment to 40 percent, real income shrank as inflation increased, and corruption reached an intolerable state under crony capitalism, whereby Marcos's friends were placed in charge of business conglomerates despite their lack of business acumen. As conditions worsened, Marcos responded by imprisoning respected political leaders such as his most serious rival, Senator Benigno Aquino Jr.

The "lifting" of martial law in 1981 temporarily improved the image of the New Society but did not significantly change the authoritarian political order. As the regime lost its legitimacy, the Armed Forces of the Philippines became less professional even as the Communist Party of the Philippines strengthened alongside its military arm, the New People's Army (NPA). Economically, Marcos did little more than create monopolies for himself, his family, and political cronies. The country's most profitable exports, such as sugar, coconuts, and to-bacco, were thoroughly under his control, with profits siphoned off to offshore accounts.

In August 1983, after the hierarchy of the Philippine Catholic Church and business leaders had turned against Marcos, and when Marcos's health was known to be precarious, Senator Aquino returned to the Philippines after several years of exile in the United States. Aquino, the single greatest challenger to President Marcos, was dramatically assassinated the moment he stepped out of the airplane that had flown him back to his country. The almost universal belief of Filipinos in the government's complicity in this assassination released long-suppressed grievances. The Marcos regime would no doubt have fallen even without Aquino's martyrdom, for Filipinos already knew that Marcos and his associates were responsible for the country's low vitality, whereas other noncommunist Southeast Asian nations were beginning to flourish.[4]

After Aquino was assassinated, the Philippines suffered disastrous declines in industrial and agricultural production. High inflation and capital flight were accompanied by wage declines and rising unemployment. Severe undernourishment for children in rural areas revealed a growing rich-poor gap. While the other noncommunist Southeast Asian countries boasted high growth, the Philippines posted negative growth rates.

From December 1985 through February 1986, during three remarkable months, a seminal event in contemporary Southeast Asia occurred. It began when Marcos, sensing disarray among his political opposition and bowing to intense pressure from the United States, called for a snap election to be held on February 7, 1986. Marcos gambled, believing he could relegitimize his rule with a new vote. From the moment he announced the elections, the key question was whether the opposition could unite around a single candidate, a question which remained unanswered until the final filing day. Marcos's ability to manipulate, co-opt, or eliminate rival forces finally came to an end with the rise of Corazon "Cory" Aquino, the widow of the martyred Senator Benigno Aquino Jr.

Cory Aquino's genuine reluctance to lead added to her appearance as a sincere, honest, and incorruptible candidate, precisely the antithesis of the president. Educated in the United States, but lacking any prior leadership experience, Aquino emerged as the person around whom the opposition could coalesce. A grassroots groundswell of support culminated in a petition with over a million signatures from Filipinos urging her to run for the presidency. Aquino fashioned an eleventh-hour agreement to run, with a rival presidential candidate, Salvador H. Laurel, as her vice president. For the first time since 1972, when martial law was declared, the opposition had achieved unity.

Candidate Aquino proclaimed a "people's campaign," realizing that she could not match the president in financial or organizational strength. Aquino's campaign speeches stressed her sincerity and honesty while vilifying the president for his corruption and immorality. She cited evidence that the president had lied both about his role as a hero in World War II and about his fortune of several billion dollars in real estate around the world.

Marcos's campaign focused on his experience, including his wartime record, in contrast to his opponent's "naïveté." Marcos tried to stoke fears over the prospect of weak female leadership, suggesting that a woman's place was in the bedroom rather than in the political arena. He stressed his relationship with US president Ronald Reagan, a staunch ally. His campaign had easy access to government money, which he used to raise officials' salaries, decrease taxes, and lower fuel and utility rates. Marcos spent some $500 million from the government treasury on his reelection. In contrast, the opposition spent $10 million, all of it raised from donations.

The voting was marred by fraud committed by Marcos supporters. When the "official" count gave Marcos 54 percent of the vote, the National Assembly—the final arbiter for voting controversies—proclaimed Marcos the winner, but the opposition launched a peaceful crusade of civil disobedience to bring down Marcos and allow the real winner, Aquino, to assume office. The US State Department, official observers, journalists from dozens of nations, the Catholic Church, and most Filipinos agreed that Aquino had actually won the election by a large margin. In an embarrassing statement, President Reagan indicated that Marcos's claim of fraud on the Aquino side deserved equal attention.[5]

As Aquino's civil disobedience campaign took hold, a series of high-profile defections from the president began. Defense Minister Juan Ponce Enrile and Lieutenant General Fidel Ramos, vice chief of the armed forces, defected from the Marcos camp and called for Aquino's ascension to the presidency. Marcos retaliated by threatening to bomb the armed forces headquarters, a move that provoked thousands of Filipinos to surround the building, and some even to lie in the streets to keep the tanks from approaching. The influential archbishop of Manila, Jaime Cardinal Sin, actively encouraged Filipinos to join the demonstrations. This display of unity by students, farmers, nuns, and shop owners became known as "People Power." It was later dubbed the "EDSA Revolution," after the avenue where the core of the demonstrations took place.

Facing off with demonstrators, the tank commanders eventually retreated, with many defecting to the opposition. The United States signaled its support of the rebellion, thereby undermining Marcos's claim that only he enjoyed the confidence of the superpower. On February 25, 1986, Aquino and Laurel proclaimed the people's victory and were sworn in as president and vice president. The next day, Marcos fled the country with his family to live in exile in Hawaii, where he died three years later at the age of seventy-two. Thus, with little bloodshed, People Power had triumphed over a regime that had dominated the political, social, and economic life of the Philippines for twenty-one years. The republic was awash with optimism that a new era in Philippine politics had arrived.

In both the political and economic realms, President Aquino's new administration initially achieved notable gains. Filipinos again could express pride in their country's government after years of corrupt and demeaning leadership. Under a president committed to democratic values and procedures, civil liberties were reinstated, political prisoners were released, free elections were regularized, and governmental institutions were rejuvenated. These gains and others came about through the promulgation of a new democratic constitution approved by over 75 percent of the Filipino people in a February 1987 referendum.

Aquino had raised the people's expectations with promises of reform in all areas of life. Her followers, who affectionately called her "Tita Cory" (Aunt Cory), expected that she would solve the nation's problems single-handedly. Nevertheless, Aquino failed to change the system in a fundamental way. Over her tenure, policy failures became more pronounced and oligarchic rule, economic and social inequality, and the politics of personalism crept back into the system.

Economically, although the Aquino administration achieved modest aggregate growth, it failed to pursue meaningful land reform and ineffectively dealt with corruption allegations against Aquino's own family members. Her Comprehensive Agrarian Reform Program included loopholes allowing her family to retain long-held family land. In fact, at the time it was passed, 169 of the 200 elected members of Congress were leaders of established landowning families or otherwise related to landed elites. Aquino's six-thousand-hectare hacienda on Luzon, named "Luisita," remained farmed by tenants and untouched by her own agrarian reform plan.

In the security realm, after an initial policy of reform and reconciliation with communist NPA insurgents failed, Aquino surprised many by adopting a hard-line counterinsurgency policy that endorsed localized self-defense organizations that essentially functioned as vigilante groups. The move invited international criticism that her government was prone to "serious and unjustifiable" violations of human rights and had "turned the whole of the Philippines into a battlefield pitting civilian against civilian."[6] With questions over Aquino's leadership growing, opponents in the military became bolder. Within four years of assuming the presidency, Aquino survived six coup attempts.

With Aquino's failures, the post Marcos period soon began to breed new disillusionment. A series of internal and external shocks further eroded the economy and confidence in Aquino as president. A horrendous earthquake in Luzon in 1990 was followed by rising oil prices throughout the country due to the Iraqi invasion of Kuwait. Then, a number of destructive typhoons and floods killed hundreds and created thousands of homeless, while also lowering crop yields for farmers. In June 1991, Luzon's Mount Pinatubo erupted after having been dormant for five hundred years—the most devastating volcanic eruption in modern Asian history. Clark Air Force Base, which was situated only about twenty miles from Mount Pinatubo, was buried beneath several feet of ash and subsequently closed down by the United States.

After intense public speculation, Tita Cory decided not to seek a second term. (The constitutionality of a second term was part of the debate.) Seven candidates declared their intention to become president, all but one of whom represented traditional interests. The most notorious of the *trapos*, or traditional politicians (*trapos* is also a Tagalog word for "rags"), was former first lady Imelda Marcos, known worldwide for her 1,200 pairs of shoes. Aquino endorsed her own minister of defense, Fidel V. Ramos, who was subsequently elected in May 1992 by plurality with only 23.4 percent of the popular vote.

Ramos, who was known for his heroism in turning against his former boss, Ferdinand Marcos, proved to be laconic, careful, and deliberate once in power. Facing the same issues Aquino had been unable to solve—a debilitated economy; rising crime and ransom kidnappings; ongoing insurgencies by communists, rightist soldiers, and Muslim separatists; daily electrical brownouts across the country—Ramos adopted an aggressive crisis management strategy. He decisively appointed commissions to tackle each problem, and conditions began to improve over the ensuing months and years. During his six-year term (1992–1998), Ramos became respected as the nation's most effective president to date.

In aggregate terms, Ramos's successes were shown by record growth rates approaching 7 percent, overall growth in exports, and declining rates of absolute poverty. More specifically, he transformed a former US naval base on Subic Bay into an enterprise zone with foreign investment; privatized certain state enterprises, including Philippine Airlines; and pushed through a fast-track mechanism for privatizing power companies, a decision that helped solve the ubiquitous problem of electrical shortages. Although critics and leftists accused Ramos of hewing closely to the neoliberal policy prescriptions of the World Bank and IMF, and of favoring close associates and foreign capital, by the time he left office his popularity was high and the country rested on more solid footing.

Because the constitution allowed for only a single term in office, many of Ramos's supporters pushed for a constitutional amendment to extend his presidency. After massive protests in reaction to this idea, Ramos announced publicly and straightforwardly that he would not seek a second term. Winning a landslide victory in the next election was his vice president, Joseph Estrada (nicknamed "Erap"—the Tagalog word for "friend," spelled backward). A garrulous populist known for his playboy lifestyle of womanizing and gambling, Estrada had built his brand through starring roles in over 100 action films. He was favored overwhelmingly by the rural poor and opposed vociferously by urban intellectuals who viewed him as rude, crude, and boorish.

Estrada began his six-year term of office auspiciously, with a majority in both houses of the Philippine Congress. The 1997 economic crisis had not affected the Philippines as strongly as it had Thailand, Malaysia, and Indonesia, at least partially because the economy was relatively less globalized. As the new millennium began, the Philippines boasted positive economic growth rates, a significant change from negative growth rates caused by recent financial contagion. Estrada's rhetoric favored the poor during his first two years as president, but he did not succeed in producing policies that alleviated the difficulties of the poorer classes.

In 2000, Estrada was accused of gross corruption, and an impeachment trial began in the Senate. Evidence showed that Estrada had been involved in illegal gambling activities and that he had accepted public monies for his private gain. His personal life was condemned, especially regarding his lavish gifts to his minor wives and mistresses. Catholic leaders publicly criticized him for immorality. For many in the poorer classes, however, the trial was initially viewed as the elite's attempt to undermine and overthrow their champion. Nevertheless, as the evidence grew mass demonstrations against him took place.

In January 2001, Estrada's impeachment trial collapsed when the Senate voted eleven to ten to disallow prosecutors from using bank documents as evidence proving his ill-gotten wealth. This act was viewed as a virtual exoneration of Estrada. Hundreds of thousands of Filipinos then emerged to demonstrate against Estrada in what became known as "EDSA II." Officials in the military and government also rose against him until demonstrations forced him to leave Malacañang Palace, the traditional home of the president. The Supreme Court declared that the office of president was vacant and that the vice president could legally assume the presidency. Although Vice President Gloria Macapagal Arroyo had resigned her cabinet post months before to protest the Estrada administration, she nevertheless replaced Estrada.

Estrada was later arrested and tried on charges of plundering $300 million in state funds. He was eventually found guilty and sentenced to life in prison. An official pardon in 2007 by Arroyo kept Estrada from serving his sentence. The pardon was made on the condition that the former president stay out of politics permanently (which he did not).

Under Arroyo, the Philippines continued to reverse the political stability won by Ramos but destroyed by Estrada. President Arroyo, often referred to as "GMA" by the media, was the daughter of Diosdado Macapagal, former president and doyen of the Filipino establishment. A classmate of Bill Clinton's at Georgetown University, Arroyo held a doctorate in economics from the University of the Philippines. She entered office facing a citizenry split over the constitutionality of the overthrow of Estrada. She also confronted an economic malaise lingering from the Asian economic crisis and faced a refurbished military capable of attempting a coup d'état against her.

In July 2003, a rebel faction of the Armed Forces of the Philippines seized a shopping mall and the Oakwood luxury apartment complex in Manila's financial district. They demanded that Arroyo and others in her administration resign, claiming that corruption threatened the country. They also alleged that top military brass had staged bombing incidents on the island of Mindanao to attract more US military aid in the aftermath of the 9/11 attacks. The "Oakwood Mutiny," as it became known, ended hours later and resulted in the arrests of perpetrators and the resignations of officials who had mishandled the affair.

While completing the remainder of Estrada's presidential term, Arroyo publicly declared her desire to stay out of the 2004 presidential elections, only to reverse her decision later. Arroyo ran and won with 39 percent of the vote against a field of weak candidates that included an Estrada ally, a movie star, an anticorruption icon, and a broadcaster-cum-evangelist gadfly. The elections were marred by allegations of rigging and an explosive leak of an election-time conversation between Arroyo and an election commissioner hinting at foul play. Pollsters found that most Filipinos believed the elections were tainted. Calls for Arroyo's impeachment followed and her unpopularity grew.

In 2006, upon the twentieth anniversary of the People Power movement to oust Marcos, Arroyo, citing coup rumors, declared a state of emergency. She deployed the military to Manila streets and barricaded Malacañang Palace with barbed wire. Scheduled marches to commemorate People Power were canceled, and what was to be a celebration of Philippine democracy actually echoed Marcos's own 1972 imposition of martial law.[7] Arroyo eventually lifted martial law three weeks later and arrested suspected political enemies on specious charges. A year later, the leader of the failed Oakwood Mutiny, Senator Antonio Trillanes, audaciously attempted yet another coup with allies during his own court proceeding. Trillanes, who had only recently run for Senate from prison and won, waited in vain during the courtroom fiasco for an uprising that never emerged. A circus atmosphere began to take hold in Philippine politics.

Throughout her presidency, Arroyo maintained power via patronage to politicos, provincial bosses, and the military brass. It is a familiar but dangerous formula in Philippine politics. A corruption scandal involving government communications contracts even drew in Arroyo's husband, the "First Gentleman," who left the country for a year in self-exile. Also revealed during Arroyo's tenure was a secret meeting at the presidential place where bags of cash were handed to House of Representatives members who had been told to first support, then later derail, a "sham" presidential impeachment proceeding in an effort to thwart the possibility of a genuine attempt.[8]

Then, on November 23, 2009, an appalling episode of political violence occurred under Arroyo's watch. A prominent political family in Maguindano Province brazenly engineered the massacre of fifty-eight people in election-related violence. Members and associates of the Ampatuan family, who dominate the province and who share membership in Arroyo's political party, forcibly stopped a large convoy of political rivals en route to the election office. The group was on its way to file candidacy papers for their own nominee, Esmael Mangudadatu, who sought to challenge an Ampatuan family member for the provincial governorship. The perpetrators used high-powered firearms in the assault and then crushed and buried the victims in mass graves using an earthmover. Gruesome images of the incident were widely broadcast. Among the dead were Mangudadatu's wife, his sister, and numerous aides and supporters (including a pregnant woman), as well as thirty accompanying journalists who had come to document the candidacy filing.

In a public move, Arroyo immediately distanced herself from the Ampatuans. She quickly engineered their expulsion from her party and declared a state of emergency in the province. Nevertheless, because the Ampatuan political clan—virtual warlords in Maguindano with a private army of 3,000—had helped GMA secure votes in her previous election, the massacre simply fueled more doubts about Arroyo's integrity.[9] Domestically and internationally, the incident stood as a reminder of just how dirty Filipino politics remained under Arroyo's nine-year tenure. Over time, seventy-nine people faced charges in relation to the incident, but prosecution has been slow. As cases have gone to court, a half dozen potential witnesses have been mysteriously killed and others intimidated.

In 2010, new elections were held for president and Congress. Constitutionally restricted from running for presidential office for another full term, Arroyo endorsed a political ally in her cabinet. Other presidential candidates included a prominent billionaire real estate developer and, remarkably, the former president Joseph Estrada, who had been politically rehabilitated by a constitutional court. For many of the poor, Estrada still symbolized their aspirations better than the alternative choices of family elites.

Another high-profile candidate was Benigno S. Aquino III, the only son of assassinated politician Benigno "Ninoy" Aquino and former president Corazon Aquino. Known as "Noynoy," Benigno Aquino's pedigree, résumé, and life story combined to produce electoral gold. Under Marcos, Noynoy and his parents were forced into exile; he later saw his father dramatically assassinated, watched his mother lead a revolution, and took bullets himself during a failed coup attempt against her (one bullet remains lodged in his neck). He studied economics at Ateneo de Manila University and even took courses from Arroyo prior to her presidency. He worked for private businesses (including Nike Philippines) and served as a congressman for multiple terms. Announcing his candidacy barely a month after his mother died of cancer, he adopted the campaign slogan "If no one is corrupt, no one will be poor."

Victory in 2010 came easy to Noynoy in a plurality vote of 41 percent (among nine candidates). Estrada amazingly came in second, with just over a quarter of the vote.[10] Arroyo's preferred candidate garnered the support of barely 10 percent of the vote, further cementing the failed legacy of Arroyo's presidency. Not finished with politics herself, GMA ran for a congressional seat in Pampanga, winning easily after having lavished her home district with special projects during her presidency.

After his victory, Aquino's supporters quickly updated his nickname to "PNoy" by combining the words "president" and "Noynoy." Among PNoy's first acts was an executive order to establish a truth commission to investigate his predecessor for graft, human rights violations, and other political mischief. The Supreme Court ruled the commission unconstitutional and it never formally emerged. Undeterred, PNoy persisted in alleging corruption against Arroyo and the matter eventually found its way into the criminal justice system. In classic Filipino-style politics, where political expediency trumps all, PNoy welcomed allegations against Arroyo by an imprisoned member of the murderous Ampatuan clan, who claimed Arroyo had engineered vote rigging and project kickbacks in the Ampatuan clan's province.[11]

In late 2011, while hospitalized for a bone ailment, former president Arroyo was arrested. She remained detained at a military hospital for eight months before being released on bail. Facing separate charges of vote tampering, plunder, and graft, she returned to the hospital in 2012 for more care and was then put under "hospital arrest." Charges allege she and nine other officials siphoned $8.7 million from a state charity lottery for personal use and that she also took a $30 million bribe to abort a $327 million telecom deal with a Chinese company. The legal case remained unresolved as of late 2015.

As president, Noynoy Aquino put the country on a more positive track, though chronic problems persisted. To address the country's protracted fiscal deficit, Aquino revamped fiscal management and brought the debt-to-GDP ratio to a thirteen-year low. He also ordered officials to aggressively go after white-collar criminals and tax evaders. In 2012, the first person in Philippine history to be sentenced for tax evasion was imprisoned. Later, the country's Supreme Court chief justice was found guilty of graft and impeached by the House of Representatives, led by Aquino allies. Aquino also took on the Catholic Church over reproductive rights, pushing a new law mandating that health centers provide free contraceptives. Later, after being challenged, the Supreme Court upheld the constitutionality of the law.

Under PNoy, the economy stabilized and investment increased. GDP growth averaged over 6 percent during his presidency and might have been higher if not for a massive 7.2 earthquake in October 2013, which was followed three weeks later by Typhoon Haiyan, a category 5 super-typhoon. The country's competitiveness ranking and credit rating markedly improved under Aquino as well. Of over 170 countries measured, the Philippines' ranking on Transparency International's Corruption Perceptions Index fell 49 spots, from #134 in 2010 to #85 in 2014.

Despite improvements in some areas, public confidence in PNoy began to slip over time due to ineffective antipoverty initiatives, a growing reputation for indecisiveness, and a new spate of government corruption scandals. In 2013, a massive government pork barrel scandal broke that set back many of the gains made by Aquino's anti-graft reforms. Investigative reporters discovered that dozens of elected officials and bureaucrats were abusing a long-standing legislative spending program by funneling millions in state funds to their own pockets through bogus NGOs and ghost projects. Originally designated to assist poor farmers, funds had been grotesquely siphoned off by officials in an elaborate graft scheme organized by a politically dubious businesswoman with a long history of impunity from illegal activity.

Tied to the pork barrel scandal, known locally as the "PDAF Scam," was a slate of twenty-eight elected legislators and over thirty government bureaucrats—a veritable Who's Who of Filipino political and military families (e.g., Estrada, Marcos, Enrile, Gregorio Honasan). Although President Aquino was not directly implicated with the graft, his own policies had actually prioritized the long-standing program. Critics called for Aquino's impeachment. In addition, because many of the involved were Aquino's political rivals, they alleged that the president's real priority was a smear campaign against them. Investigations into the matter were mired in foot-dragging by congressmen protective of their own assets and worried about a wider probe. The Supreme Court later ruled Aquino's accelerated program unconstitutional, and the mastermind behind the scam was put in detention.

Following the PDAF Scam, Aquino found himself on the defensive again when his office organized a January 2015 raid on Moro separatists in the Muslim South, which left forty-four police commandos dead. The episode created a media storm with relatives of the dead police officers publicly expressing grief and confusion. Blame for the failed raid went right to the top and Aquino's poor handling of the debacle raised further questions about his leadership.

With a high-stakes presidential election looming in mid-2016, few observers were surprised when a political split surfaced toward the end of Aquino's single six-year term. In 2015, after five years in Aquino's cabinet, Vice President Jejomar "Jojo" Binay resigned dramatically, charging Aquino with insensitivity, incompetence, and selective justice. In turn, supporters of PNoy labeled Binay a "master *trapo* politician," and viewed the resignation as crass political maneuvering, a means to distance himself from the president. Aquino later endorsed his own interior minister, Manuel "Mar" Roxas, in the 2016 race.

As the new standard-bearer for the Liberal Party, Roxas has been persistently dogged by rivals during the campaign for his pitiful response as interior minister to provide relief and recovery to victims of Typhoon Haiyan in 2013. Disaster aid from Manila following the storm's devastation was slow to nonexistent. What did arrive was disgracefully channeled unevenly to electoral wards where Liberal Party support was strongest.[12]

Joining Binay and Roxas in the 2016 presidential race were the populist Rodrigo Duterte, the crude and imperious mayor of Davao (nicknamed "the

Punisher"), and Senator Miriam Santiago, an accomplished international law-
yer. A fifth potential candidate, Grace Poe, an extremely popular senator with a
progressive record favoring the rights of women and children, fell into legal
limbo over her eligibility to run due to her extended residence in the United
States. The adopted daughter of two famous Filipino film stars, Poe later married a Filipino American and carried dual citizenship before returning to the
Philippines in 2005, when she launched a political career.

With each candidate representing unique constituencies, and most connected to *trapos* families or celebrity patrons, the likelihood of another victory
by mere plurality rather than majority remains high. The probability of PNoy's
successor successfully transcending the country's troubled political culture, by
contrast, remains low, regardless of who wins. Personalism, subornment, fraud,
and guile, ever endemic to Filipino politics, continue to shape events and define
the oligarchic tendencies of Philippine democratic rule.

INSTITUTIONS AND SOCIAL GROUPS

Patron-Client Relations

The Philippine government can be described as clientelist, a form of societal organization in which political life centers on relationships that are largely person
to person, informal, hierarchical, reciprocal, and based on *utang na loob*, an
obligation of indebtedness. Because they are too weak, interest groups, political
parties, the legislature, and other government institutions have been supplanted
by clientelist relationships. Thus, political life in the Philippines has consisted of
constantly changing coalitions of clientele groups that serve both to articulate
mass interests and to ensure government control over the people. At the top,
these patron networks create a type of predatory oligarchy that engages in
"booty capitalism" and suffers from a "guns, goons, and gold mentality."[13]

Overreliance on patron-client networks undermines the importance and
legitimacy of democratic institutions, resulting in the continued decay rather
than development of Philippine politics. Under President Marcos, the clientelist nature of Philippine society was most evident in the president's grant of
monopoly privileges to selected followers. Marcos put the control of numerous
industries in the hands of his clients and assured them of immunity from loss;
when the economy began to collapse and his authority lost legitimacy (after the
assassination of Senator Aquino), Marcos lost control, first over the resources
he used to reward his clients and eventually over the entire society.

During the rise of President Corazon Aquino, Marcos's clientele lost its
source of favors, and new patronage groups emerged. This same pattern followed with subsequent presidents, albeit in a less corrupt manner than with
Marcos. The biggest departure from cronyism was perhaps Fidel Ramos. Even
so, most Philippine politicians find it difficult to ignore these relationships
and thus rely on their own clientele. The tenures of both Estrada and Arroyo il-

lustrate this fact well. More than any president after Ramos, Benigno Aquino III actively pursued an anti-corruption agenda and bolstered the rule of law. Scandals involving elite allies, however, tempered Aquino's successes.

Constitutions

The Malolos constitution of 1899, promulgated by Filipino nationalists, was the first democratic constitution in Asia. It was based on South American and Spanish models and embodied the ideas of liberal democracy, representative government, separation of powers, and a system of checks and balances. This constitution endured only a short time before the United States ended the republic.

The US-sponsored constitution of 1935 provided for a representative democracy based on the US presidential model. Japanese occupiers set up their own constitution in 1943 for the Philippines, but it was viewed as illegitimate and collapsed with the end of World War II. The 1935 constitution was subsequently restored and served the Philippines until 1973. In 1972, Marcos convened a constitutional convention to draft a new constitution based on a parliamentary rather than a presidential model. However, Marcos's declaration of martial law silenced debate on his proposed constitution; a few months later, a constitutional convention approved the new document, which called for a parliamentary form of government led by a prime minister and allowed the interim president (Marcos) to decide when to convene the interim national assembly and, further, to make and execute all laws until he convened the assembly.

Corazon Aquino's People Power victory led to a "Freedom Constitution," a provisional document issued by presidential proclamation. It provided for presidential appointment of a constitutional commission to draft a new, permanent constitution. President Aquino held executive and legislative powers until the commission presented this new constitution, which was adopted in 1987. In the 1987 Constitution, which otherwise contained elements similar to the 1935 Constitution, the powers of the president became more circumscribed. The presidential term was set at six years, with no reelection permitted. To curb the familial patronage of the Marcos years, the president's spouse and all close relatives have been barred from appointment as public officials. The document specifically prohibits political dynasty and imposes a ban on foreign troops or bases in the country without specific legislative approval and popular referendum.

Challenges to the 1987 Constitution have persisted through various pretexts. In clear violation of the constitution, multiple coup attempts by rebel elements within the military have sought to overthrow chief executives. All have failed. Estrada's removal in 2001 is sometimes referred to as a "coup" but represents an ambiguous departure from constitutional practice. It was not the result of a military seizure of power. The removal of the president by the military, during a botched impeachment trial, was an act endorsed by the Supreme

Court. Following the constitution, the court then certified the legal ascension of Vice President Arroyo to the presidency.

Attempts at major constitutional reform have been proposed at times by past governments, including those of Ramos, Estrada, and Arroyo. In many cases, proposals favor the adoption of parliamentary-style government, and unicameral legislature, to reduce congressional gridlock and enhance the policymaking of the executive. "Charter change," commonly referred to as "cha-cha" by Filipinos, is a difficult prospect for sitting governments that are likely to benefit from the changes. President Arroyo campaigned on a pledge of charter change, but Benigno Aquino, whose mother initiated the now twenty-five-year-old 1987 Constitution, publicly announced his reservations about any "cha-cha" under his watch.

The Legislature

In the postindependence period, the Philippine legislature has been both a bulwark protecting freedom and a tool for legitimizing presidential decrees. The 1987 Constitution gives numerous prerogatives to the Congress, including the sole power to declare war, to withdraw presidential emergency powers, and to determine revenue origination and appropriation. Whereas the Marcos constitution of 1973 allowed President Marcos to exercise both legislative and executive powers, the 1987 Constitution clearly separates these powers. It includes a bicameral Congress, consisting of a twenty-four-member Senate, elected at large for six years and for not more than two consecutive terms, and a House of Representatives of not more than 250 members, most of whom are elected from legislative districts apportioned on the basis of population.

The remaining members of the House, 20 percent, are elected through an at-large party-list system with a 2 percent threshold for seat placement. Designed as a functional representation system, the party-list system is organized around "sectors," or parties that represent labor, women, minority communities, and similar groups (excluding religion). Accusations are common that leading parties manipulate the sector-party-list system to gain more support in the House.

Political Parties

The Philippines had a two-party system for most of its early democratic period (1946–1972), when the Liberal and Nacionalista Parties alternately held power, with neither party ever able to get its presidential nominee reelected.[14] The ideological differences between the two parties were negligible. For the most part, the two parties functioned as mobilizers of votes for specific candidates.

Under Marcos, one party dominated the political scene. Marcos's Kilusang Bagong Lipunan (KBL; New Society Movement) was a noncompetitive, authoritarian party devoted to keeping Marcos in power and maintaining the support of the US government. Through his magnetic personality, his dominance of the bureaucracy and the legislative and executive branches, his fraudulent plebiscites and referenda, and his manipulation of nationalist symbols, Marcos controlled every aspect of the party and its program.

In the post–martial law era after 1981, the KBL continued to dominate politics. However, as Marcos's support deteriorated, opposition parties emerged. The most important of these were organized under the United Nationalist Democratic Organization, or UNIDO, a coalition of parties formed in 1979 by Salvador Laurel, who had broken from the KBL. UNIDO, largely an alliance of establishment politicians who had lost out when Marcos took control, was united primarily in its opposition to his domination of the political scene. Thus, it became an umbrella organization encompassing a number of smaller parties under the leadership of Senator Benigno Aquino Jr. and his party LABAN! (Fight!), which he formed as a political prisoner of Marcos. UNIDO coalition parties later formed the core of support for Corazon Aquino during her 1986 presidential run.

Since the early 1990s, the most successful political parties have included (1) the Lakas-Christian Muslim Democrats, the party of Fidel Ramos launched after the EDSA revolution; (2) the center-left Liberal Party, the country's second oldest and the party of both the late Benigno Aquino Jr. before his imprisonment and his son, Benigno Aquino III; (3) the populist-oriented Pwersa ng Masang Pilipino, the party vehicle used by Estrada; and (4) a revived Nacionalista Party, which today bears a reputation of being a pro-business, conservative party. These "mainstream" parties in the Philippines are generic catch-all parties that serve as patron-client political machines for those at the top. Smaller parties tend to be more ideological and issue oriented. In 2009, the center-right Lakas-Christian Muslim Democrats merged with Arroyo's Kampi Party and so remained the largest party in the House following 2010 elections, occupying 37 percent of seats.

For most Filipinos, political parties play little role in presidential elections, which are determined primarily by the general public's attitudes toward individual candidates. At the national and local levels, party politics remains an elite-establishment activity based on patronage and personalism. Wealthy founders and politicians fund parties, and party switching does occur on occasion. The need for coalitions to pass legislation forces alliances and empowers party bosses who wheel and deal for votes.

The easiest path to Congress is as a member of an entrenched political family, typically one with a regional presence somewhere in the archipelago. Established celebrity is another viable path, as evidenced by Joseph Estrada. Ten-time world champion boxer Manny Pacquiao, the most beloved Filipino athlete ever, is already an elected senator and reportedly eyeing a presidential run in 2022. Pacquiao is wildly popular due to his humble origins, a pro-poor image, and a growing record of philanthropy. However unprepared he may be for the position, one would be foolish to discount the possibility that the "Pacman" may one day lead the world's twelfth most populous nation.

The Military

Although long involved with supporting particular candidates for office, the military has never played the dominant role in Philippine politics. In contrast to Thailand's military, the Philippine military has been subordinated to civilian leaders and given the orthodox task of providing external defense and security against domestic subversion. (Marcos exploited this second task to protect his personal interests.) Fidel Ramos is the only president to have been a military general.

During his tenure, Marcos expanded Armed Forces of the Philippines (AFP) to three-and-a-half times its original size at the end of World War II (from 37,000 to 142,000 personnel). Even more consequentially, Marcos increased military involvement in civilian life and transformed its role.[15] He deprofessionalized the military by appointing cronies and fellow ethnic Ilocanos (from northern Luzon) to commanding positions—including his cousin Fabian Ver, appointed as the AFP's chief of staff and later implicated in the planned assassination of Senator Aquino.

A group of reform-minded soldiers who reacted against the politicization of the military and its diminished professionalism later organized into the Reform the Armed Forces Movement (RAM) and led the army rebellion against Marcos following the 1986 elections. Juan Ponce Enrile, a RAM leader, was subsequently awarded the position of minister of defense in Corazon Aquino's government for his role in ousting Marcos.

Despite attempts to reprofessionalize the military, or because of them, Corazon Aquino was constantly threatened by elements within the AFP. Along with other RAM officers, even Enrile eventually turned against Aquino and led coup attempts against her government. In December 1989, seventy-nine people were killed and over six hundred were wounded during such a failed coup attempt. To successfully repulse the attack, Aquino asked the United States to provide air support to AFP forces loyal to the government. US F-4 Phantom jets flying from Clark Air Force Base assisted in immobilizing rebel forces attempting to seize Manila. Aquino's reliance on foreign support did not sit well with many Filipinos. Her move exacerbated anti-US sentiments and complicated later negotiations on the removal of American bases. Ramos and Estrada experienced no military coup attempts but coup rumors persisted under Arroyo's rule, leading to the failed Oakwood Mutiny incident launched by a rebel AFP faction.

The AFP currently boasts 125,000 troops but has suffered from an enduring "institutional rot" due to poor organization and equipment, factionalism, and uncontrolled elements.[16] Regionally, the Philippine army is considered weak.

Depending on the direction that the Spratly Islands dispute takes in the future (see below), the AFP could face the most serious test of its military capacity yet. Rising tensions in the South China Sea led President Benigno Aquino III and top generals to pursue a "Capability Upgrade Program," which produced new contracts and plans to purchase helicopters, aircraft, missile systems, and submarines.

Women

Traditionally, women have played only minor roles in Philippine politics. The rise of Imelda Marcos, Corazon Aquino, and Gloria Macapagal Arroyo to positions of immense power is anomalous rather than a pattern, as all are related to powerful male politicians. Imelda Marcos, who was governor of metropolitan Manila and minister of human settlements until her husband was overthrown in 1986, owed her claim to leadership to her husband's authoritarian rule. Aquino was the saintly widow of Senator Benigno Aquino Jr. Gloria Macapagal Arroyo, the daughter of a Philippine president, spent her teen years in the halls of Malacañang Palace. The rise to power of these women, and others in Filipino political and business circles, is often as much a function of their family name as it is the successful surmounting of the formidable barriers that have traditionally kept women out of power.[17] Comparatively, however, it is worth noting that the Philippines ranks better than other countries in the region in terms of the United Nations' Gender Empowerment Measure. Twenty-two percent of legislative seats won in the 2010 elections are occupied by women, a number twice as high as other elected legislatures in the region.

The Catholic Church

With over 12,000 priests and nuns throughout the archipelago, the largest land holdings in the nation, and control over thousands of parishes, schools, and hospitals, the Catholic Church is a significant political, economic, and social institution. Factionalized among conservative, centrist, and progressive forces, the church has played a crucial role in all areas of Philippine life.

The most politically active leader of the church in the Philippines in the new international era was Jaime Cardinal Sin, archbishop of Manila and head of the centrist faction. Cardinal Sin, who jokingly called his residence "The House of Sin," was a Filipino of Chinese descent with a reputation for good humor. In conjunction with church bishops and clergy, Sin played an important role in undermining President Marcos's administration and in fashioning the compromise that unified the opposition under Corazon Aquino.

In policy matters, church leaders have been outspoken in condemning corruption and other dishonest practices and invariably supporting programs that favor the poor and greater social justice. However, the church has proven reluctant to associate poverty with demographic pressures. Its condemnation of family planning, specifically the use of contraceptives, kept multiple governments from implementing a comprehensive plan designed to improve health standards and reduce poverty. The church's stand against homosexuality and artificial contraception has also affected the availability of condoms and sex education for those most in need. Cardinal Sin denounced an anti-AIDS program proposed by President Ramos that included the distribution of condoms but enthusiastically supported President Arroyo's population program of "natural family planning."

Notwithstanding controversies, the church has emerged as a primary symbol of peaceful change, warning against political excesses by government and opposition groups alike. Cardinal Sin retired in 2003 and died two years later. His successor, Cardinal Rosales, proved to be more politically reticent. The current Archbishop of Manila, the unpretentious Cardinal Tagle, has adopted more socially progressive positions in line with Pope Francis, with whom he is often compared.

Papal visits play a significant role in shaping the Filipino Catholic church, its direction, and the standing of its local leaders. Pope John Paul II's second visit to the Philippines, for World Youth Day in Manila in 1995, produced a then record papal crowd of 4 million. After Pope Benedict declined multiple invitations to visit the Philippines, it took Pope Francis only two years as Pope to visit the archipelago. Surpassing John Paul's crowd by 2 million, over 6 million Filipino Catholics attended Pope Francis's final mass during his historic 2015 visit. The pro-poor Pope stole the media spotlight for days and won hearts with specific visits to victims of Typhoon Haiyan. The papal visit also propelled Cardinal Tagle into the global spotlight, fueling speculation that the Filipino Cardinal, now dubbed the "Asian Francis," might possibly rise to the papacy himself.

Communist Insurgents

With origins in the Soviet-supported Huk rebellion, the revolutionary opposition in the Philippines gained strength in the 1960s but became a meaningful threat to the nation's security during Marcos's rule. The Communist Party of the Philippines, the central organizational unit of the revolutionary opposition, is the largest communist party in ASEAN. The party oversees the New People's Army (NPA), the region's last remaining communist insurgency. The Maoist NPA controls about 5,000 troops spread throughout the archipelago's provinces. At its peak in the 1980s, the NPA had 20,000 loyalists who controlled some 20 percent of the country's territory.

The NPA's strength has come from disillusioned peasants, especially tenant farmers and day laborers, whose hopes for a better life were lifted by Marcos's announcement of a "New Society" and then dashed by unfulfilled promises and expectations. Similarly, the rise of Corazon Aquino initially weakened the NPA until her promises of meaningful land reform and improvement in the standard of living went unmet. Many students, intellectuals, and leftists in the

Catholic Church, inspired by Peruvian Gustavo Gutierrez and Latin American liberation theology, supported the NPA's nationalist struggle against imperialism and poverty as "just violence." Other citizens supported the NPA as the only viable force against the corruption and abuses of rights perpetrated by local dynastic politicians and military units.

Although little outside support is provided to the NPA, it has been able to capitalize on the negative growth of the national economy and on the consequent extreme poverty endemic in many Philippine communities. The nation's interminable economic difficulties make it difficult to resolve the protracted, forty-year guerrilla war. The NPA's political arm, based in the Netherlands, expressed a willingness to meet with the new Benigno Aquino government after years of rejecting negotiations. Peace talks later began in 2011, held in Oslo with Norway acting as a broker. They quickly stalled as the objectives of both sides remain worlds apart. Minor government clashes with NPA troops continue to the present. In four decades, the numbers of deaths linked to the conflict range between 35,000 and 40,000 people.

Moro Islamic Separatists

Fighting primarily for an independent state for Muslims in the southern islands of the Philippines, Moro nationalists launched an armed campaign in 1972. In 1975, the Moro National Liberation Front (MNLF) was formally recognized by the Organization of the Islamic Conference (OIC). Engaging in armed warfare, sabotage, and political violence, the MNLF struck agreements for autonomy under Marcos and Corazon Aquino that were never fully implemented. In 1984, a leadership struggle led to the creation of a second group, the Moro Islamic Liberation Front (MILF).[18] Also in the 1980s, a third group, Abu Sayyaf, formed with the assistance of a brother-in-law of Osama bin Laden's.[19]

In 1996, the Philippine government established the Autonomous Region in Muslim Mindanao (ARMM) as part of a historic peace agreement with the MNLF. Implementation, however, struggled and produced lingering resentment. The conflict with the MILF raged on but conditions changed following the 9/11 attacks and subsequent US war on terrorism, which drew attention to all the groups in the area, their activities, and their affiliations. Abu Sayyaf's alleged connections with al-Qaeda and Jemaah Islamiyah (based in Indonesia) came under great suspicion as the group adopted strategies of kidnapping tourists for ransom to finance their rebellion. Such risky activities belie evidence that Abu Sayyaf acts as a tentacle of the well-financed al-Qaeda.

Eventually, over 7,500 US troops were stationed in Mindanao related to a military offensive to weaken the remaining Moro separatists and Abu Sayyaf Islamists. The use of military pressure was combined with political efforts led by Mahathir bin Mohamad of Malaysia, the OIC, and USAID programs to help reintegrate Moro fighters into civilian life. A reduction in fighting occurred, but local bombings still plagued the area.

In December 2007, an agreement between the MILF and MNLF to put aside their decades-old animosity gave new hope that a political resolution with the Arroyo government was possible.[20] The Arroyo administration signed a controversial memorandum of understanding with the MILF to expand the ARMM into an ancestral homeland with wide-ranging self-government for the Moros. Drawing the ire of many Filipinos, the agreement was viewed by nationalist critics as a violation of the constitution and a threat to the republic. Fighting continued after the memorandum was signed, and Philippine courts eventually nullified the deal.

Under Benigno Aquino III, however, a new framework for peace brokered by Malaysia's prime minister, Najib Abdul Razak, was agreed to in 2012 by Aquino and MILF leader Murad Ebrahim. The agreement will phase in regional autonomy for the Moros by 2016 and include control over local law enforcement and a revenue-sharing arrangement with the central government over natural resources in the area.[21] A more robust peace agreement signed in 2014 in Kuala Lumpur by both sides established further details of "Bangsamoro," the designated name of the region.

One of the sticking points inhibiting prior agreement was the MILF's supposed ties to the more radical Islamist group Abu Sayyaf, an allegation that MILF leaders persistently deny. Aquino, like others before him, refused to recognize Abu Sayyaf as anything but a terrorist group and vowed to crush its estimated 250 remaining members. Approximately 2,000 Islamist terrorists have been captured or killed by Philippine forces since a 2006 offensive was launched with the assistance of US counterinsurgency advisers. Abu Sayyaf, concentrated on Jolo, an island in the southernmost Sulu Archipelago, did not participate in 2012 peace talks and is unlikely to ever compromise with government leaders.

Peace deals with MILF leaders have unfortunately created breakaway Moros rebels who now frequently clash with officials, such as in a failed 2015 raid which resulted in the deaths of forty-four police commandos. After the Islamic State of Iraq and Syria (ISIS) declared a caliphate in 2014, a few rebel groups in the southern Philippines pledged allegiance to ISIS. Though some have ties to Abu Sayyaf, others have been labeled as "criminal gangs" by Philippine military authorities, who claim that "no evidence" exists of formal links to jihadists in the Middle East, and that such gangs are "not really ISIS" but merely "ride on the popularity of ISIS."[22]

STATE-SOCIETY RELATIONS AND DEMOCRACY

The Philippines was once known as Southeast Asia's "showcase of democracy." In terms of the formal institutions of government, that description was accurate. In the postindependence period, up to the time of martial law, the Philippine state appeared strong and the government carried out its functions based on constitutional guidelines, through the separation of powers and adherence to a bill of rights. On the surface, it appeared that the state's capacity was growing and that democratic institutions were consolidating.

Behaviorally, however, the picture was much different. State autonomy and democratic institutions have always been eclipsed by oligarchic inertia in the Philippines. Since the Spanish colonized the Philippines almost 500 years ago, the nation has been ruled by a small number of family dynasties that have controlled both the economic and political spheres through decidedly undemocratic means. From the great haciendas of the Spaniards to the patronage politics of the US period, these dynasties have ruled in a baronial, feudal manner, each controlling a particular area of the archipelago. Even during the country's "showcase" period of democracy, the fundamental forces that determined allocation never changed: intertwined landed wealth and state power. As characterized by one scholar, evidence from the "the highly mythologized Magsaysay period (1953–1957) bear[s] witness to a familiar and long-standing sense that democracy practiced in the Philippines is not quite, not really, well, democracy."[23]

The country's archipelagic nature is partially responsible for the development of this decentralized, dynastic system. Pervasive poverty also helps explain why the poor learn to rely on their wealthy patrons. In the Philippines, dynastic families sponsor the weddings of their laborers and tenants, pay for children's education, and care for the sick, thereby forming a tie of dependency that keeps the poor deferential and loyal. Without strong government institutions, patron-client relations develop to meet the needs of the majority poor.

The dynastic nature of Philippine politics is also due to cultural factors. A Filipino's loyalty is directed first to family, then to close friends, then to the local community, then to personally known political leaders, and finally to distant, impersonal governmental agencies. Although all of these concentric circles of allegiance place emphasis on the personal nature of loyalty: an individual's family and patron family demand the deepest loyalties.[24] In the *compadre* (godfather) system, reciprocity is formed in which the higher-status *compadre* renders material benefits and prestige and the lower-status family provides loyalty, deference, and support. Thus, a candidate for office may be asked to sponsor a marriage or a newborn baby in return for a family's electoral support, and the family then has the right to seek political patronage from its new *compadre*.[25] Politicians are equally desirous of becoming sponsors to ensure a wide base of electoral support.

For democratic consolidation to take root in the Philippines, the formal institutions of government must become more than facades for oligarchic rule. The overwhelming majority of newly elected senators and representatives are members of families who have dominated Philippine politics for centuries. Although the people in charge of the government have changed, and despite various efforts to reform the system, there have been too few fundamental changes in the character of the Philippine political system.

Under Arroyo, a deepened sense of political malaise persisted throughout the Philippines. Benigno S. Aquino III's election restored some optimism, but the overall system of oligarchy remains entrenched, a sort of dysfunctional democracy. Public cynicism extends itself especially to oppositional politics. People Power, once the essence of democratic spirit, is slowly becoming delegitimized as a useful political tool. Each time a popular revolt or elections overthrows a corrupt president (e.g., Marcos, Estrada, Arroyo) a new set of elites takes the reins of power only to extend oligarchic rule and, consequently, disillusionment.[26] This revolving door of elites is referred to as *pulitika*, the "jockeying for position among the old political oligarchy."[27]

In a country where democracy has become synonymous with elections, election races often resemble cheap reality show contests and public evaluations of celebrity popularity. Pop culture icons and infamous figures now commonly join the usual array of *trapos* candidates as representatives of the Filipino people. The dubious list of celebrities elected to prominent offices since 2010 includes multiple TV stars and pop icons; world champion boxer Manny Pacquiao; former first lady Imelda Marcos and her presidential-wannabe son; a convicted rapist; a notorious gangster-warlord and his son, who is a self-identified cocaine and gambling addict facing drug charges in Hong Kong; and fifteen members of the mafia-like Ampatuan clan.[28]

Civil society in the Philippines has grown in the face of oligarchy, but it is overwhelmed by a disturbing degree of violence and lawlessness. Weak state and democratic institutions contribute to a culture of violence and impunity. From year to year, Reporters Without Borders (RSF) ranks the Philippines as one of the most dangerous countries in which to practice journalism. Since 1991, over seventy journalists have been killed and only a handful of cases have been brought to conviction. Political violence in the form of bombings, assassinations, and voter intimidation chronically haunts elections. Over 275 people were killed during the 2004 and 2007 elections, and the 2010 elections were declared by officials as the most violent yet, with one in three municipalities experiencing "ERVIs," or election-related violent incidents. The Global Impunity Index, devised by the Committee to Protect Journalists to measure both fatal violence against journalists and any penal accountability for those murdering journalists, ranked the Philippines the fourth worst in the world in 2015, behind only Somalia, Iraq, and Syria.

Such lawlessness produces other undesirable social phenomena. In spite of government pledges to neutralize them, there exist an estimated 112 private armies in the Philippines employed by politicians to harass and intimidate opponents and their supporters.[29] Some argue that the decentralization of fiscal authority has raised the stakes of local government, compounding the trend toward election violence.[30] Regardless, after sixty years of attempting democratic transition, rather than developing quality democratic institutions, the

Philippines appears closer to consolidating *pulitika* and the wretched practices of political violence, gangsterism, and judicial impunity.

ECONOMY AND DEVELOPMENT

Despite abundant natural resources, strong ties to the United States, and an English-speaking workforce, the Philippines has failed to realize its economic potential. Inequality remains the constant theme of the Philippine economy, even during periods of growth. In the mid-1970s the Philippines was on par with Thailand in terms of annual per capita GNP, about $300. By 2014, the GDP per capita in the Philippines and Thailand had risen to $6,916 and $14,600, respectively, when measured in terms of purchasing power parity.

The Philippine economy has been skewed since the days of Spanish colonialism, which thrust a feudal economic system upon the Filipinos. When Americans refined the Philippines with their neocolonial system, the Philippine economy fell under the control of outside forces, including multinational corporations and a group of fabulously wealthy Filipino families (mostly with Spanish or Chinese backgrounds). Neocolonial relations between Americans and Filipinos were characterized by exploitation rather than cooperation for the mutual good, with the bulk of the profits gained by businesses in the Philippines going to Americans.

The Philippine economy at the end of World War II was in shambles because of the widespread damage in Manila and destruction of basic infrastructure throughout the archipelago. As with most Southeast Asian nations in the 1950s, the Philippines adopted an import-substitution industrialization (ISI) strategy to develop its economy. In essence, the ISI strategy restricted imports of foreign goods to improve the balance of payments and to generate new industries to make the nation more self-sufficient. The United States had already penetrated the domestic Philippine economy, so Americans did not oppose this policy.

Initially, ISI policies worked well in terms of benefiting domestic manufacturing industries, and between 1950 and 1980 the share of manufacturing in the total economy rose from 8 percent to 25 percent, whereas the share of agriculture declined from 42 percent to 23 percent.[31] Manufacturing accounted for more than half the value of Philippine exports in the 1970s, just a decade after accounting for only 6 percent. At the same time, however, every economic indicator showed the Philippines to have the least effective economy in the region. Moreover, only a small group of Marcos-centered industrialists and financiers benefited from this new form of state capitalism, while small businesses and labor groups were weakened. In the agricultural and commodities sector, where most Filipinos were employed, the economy suffered ongoing maldevelopment.

The mixed success of ISI led international agencies such as the World Bank to change their advice and to recommend an export-oriented industrialization strategy for economic development. However, interference by Marcos-tied cronies kept protectionist measures and monopoly controls intact, so the new strategy never worked effectively. In the commodities sector, reform was largely ignored. Marcos had given his best friends monopoly control over the sugar and coconut sectors, which led to their amassing fabulous riches. These riches ended up in Swiss and US bank accounts and in real estate investments throughout the world, a capital flight that subverted the economy into an incurable state.

In the 1970s, Marcos and his sugar barons made a costly bet on global markets by hoarding the commodity only to see the price bubble burst by the end of the decade and render the country's massive sugar stock worthless. In the early 1980s, rising oil prices and the collapse of other commodities resulted in economic recession and acute economic hardship for many Filipinos. Farm prices had dropped so low that starvation became a real threat in the major sugar areas.[32]

Economic growth rates since Marcos reflect participation in Asia's economic dynamism but at a slower pace due to chronic challenges in the Philippine economy. Corazon Aquino and Ramos helped economic growth return to the Philippines only to see it thwarted by dependence on oil imports, inflation, and the Asian economic crisis of the late 1990s. High population growth rates, which persisted well above 2 percent until the new millennium, combined with inefficient use of educational resources, have exacerbated the country's economic woes. Unemployment and underemployment have caused many Filipinos to travel abroad as guest workers in the Middle East, Hong Kong, Japan, and even fellow ASEAN states. Remittances topped $24 billion in 2015, about 10 percent of the Philippines' GDP.[33] Only the overseas workers from China, India, and Mexico send home more money than do Filipino expatriates and guest workers.

For his part, Fidel Ramos focused his presidency on improving the Philippine economy by liberalizing virtually every facet of it, allowing technocrats and the market system to prevail. The 1990s growth period continued until the 1997 economic debacle that began in Thailand caused a devaluation of the Philippine peso. Ramos also failed to address land reform. Estrada's cronyism eroded investor confidence and left the stock market in tatters. Despite Arroyo's political difficulties, economic policies produced improved results initially only to plummet after the 2008 global financial crisis. But around this time, outsourced international customer service (call centers) began to join microchip processing and automotive manufacturing as promising areas for economic growth. Under Benigno Aquino III, the economic growth and the stock market have each recovered, the latter reaching record highs.

In spite of recent economic gains in the Philippines, the country's poverty rate continues to stand in stark contrast to those of its neighbors. During PNoy's administration, income inequality, as measured by the GINI index, has remained unchanged (around 43.0). In fact, by UNDP measures, over 36 percent of employed Filipinos remain classified as "working poor" who live on less than $2 a day. Using the same measure, the combined average of Thailand, Malaysia, and Vietnam is less than 10 percent.[34] In Southeast Asia, only Myanmar and Timor-Leste suffer higher poverty rates.

The Philippines thus remains a society defined by poverty amid plenty. Current trends do not suggest that the country's plague of inequality will change soon. Weak progress on the UN Millennium Development Goals (MDGs) indicates that the country has progressed far more slowly in overall development than similarly populous neighbors such as Indonesia and Vietnam. Lack of progress in reducing poverty is only one area of concern. Since 2000, the child mortality rate in the Philippines has barely declined. Goals to reduce the country's alarmingly high maternal mortality rate (MMR) also failed miserably. In 2000, at the beginning of the MDG period, the Philippines' MMR stood at 124 deaths per 100,000 live births. By 2015, the same figure was reduced to 114 deaths. At current rates, the Philippines will not meet its MDG goal of 52 deaths per 100,000 live births until well beyond 2050. Goals to improve education have also fallen far short. A joint report by the United Nations and the Asian Development Bank identified the Philippines and Myanmar as Asia's worst laggards in making progress toward MDG targets.[35] Looming on the horizon is another economic challenge beyond low development and rising inequality: the fact that the Philippines remains one of the world's most vulnerable countries to global climate change.

FOREIGN RELATIONS

The United States, the Philippines' closest ally, also represents the republic's biggest foreign policy problem. Since the colonial period, the United States and the Philippines have had a "special relationship," a term that aptly describes the close and complex ties shared by the two nations for almost a hundred years. The countries are party to a bilateral mutual defense treaty signed in 1951.

The Philippines, as Asia's most Americanized country, shares a common Christian heritage and the widespread use of the English language. In fashion, music, art, education, and politics, Filipinos often emulate Americans rather than their Asian neighbors. The result has been a love-hate relationship. Many Filipinos look to the United States as their hope and even their future home at the same time that they demonstrate against US interference in their affairs. While under Marcos, a 1972 Gallup poll of 2,000 Filipinos revealed that 60 percent favored making the Philippines the fifty-first American state; only 28 percent were opposed to the idea.[36]

The presence of US military bases on Philippine territory, which continued following Marcos's departure, intensified the conflicting emotions Filipinos felt toward the United States. Though most Filipinos were eager to shed their dependence on US protection, an estimated 3 percent of the Philippine GNP was generated, directly or indirectly, by two principal US bases, Subic Bay and Clark Air Force Base. Over 45,000 Filipinos worked on the two bases where 30,000 US personnel were stationed. At their peak, an estimated $500 million was generated by the bases each year, helping to feed local economies. Other Filipinos viewed the bases as "moral cesspools" where some 16,000 prostitutes serviced US military clients. Around the bases, HIV and other sexually transmitted diseases ran rampant and allegations of misogynist violence were common.

In 1991, after months of negotiations, the Philippine Senate rejected a new bases treaty and requested that the Americans leave Subic Bay. Prior to this decision, the United States had already begun withdrawal from Clark Air Force Base as a result of the destruction from the earlier eruption of Mount Pinatubo. Internationally, the decision lowered confidence in Philippine stability and worsened the image of an already desperate economy. However, for many Filipinos, the long-term gain for the country's psyche was thought to be worth the short-term costs. Shouldering sole responsibility for security and foreign affairs would oblige Filipinos to look more creatively and determinedly for appropriate solutions to their problems. By 1998, under Ramos, the Philippines invited US troops back for a new round of recurring training exercises with Philippine forces.

Post-9/11 agreements between Gloria Macapagal Arroyo and US president George W. Bush resurrected some of the mixed feelings Filipinos had toward the United States. Many Filipinos did not want to turn to the US umbrella yet again, but evidence from the 9/11 Commission Report revealed that al-Qaeda hijackers had met in the Philippines before the attacks. The troubled south took on international dimensions with new fears of international Islamists operating amid Moro separatists, namely the al-Qaeda-linked groups of Abu Sayyaf and Jemaah Islamiyah.

Arroyo offered the Philippines' full support for Bush's war on terrorism, and the United States gradually dispatched over 7,500 troops to assist with fighting rebellion and terrorism in the separatist Muslim south. By 2006, the US State Department had officially declared certain areas of the south as "safe havens for terrorists." Months later, echoing the US PATRIOT Act, the Philippine House of Representatives and Senate passed the Human Security Act to allow wiretapping of suspected terrorists.

Joint exercises are now commonplace between US and Philippine troops, as are sporadic bomb blasts (and kidnappings) claimed by Abu Sayyaf and Jemaah Islamiyah. The Joint Special Operations Task Force–Philippines (JSOTF-P) remains the primary vehicle for US involvement in the area. Operating with a counterinsurgency mission, the JSOTF-P emphasizes technical and humanitarian assistance to the AFP and local populations. US military activity, some of it outsourced to US defense contractors, includes arms sales to the AFP and cash rewards for local informants. Rumors of plans to reestablish a permanent

US base in the Philippines located in the south (expectedly) sparked new controversy.

The Philippines' political and economic ties to ASEAN, Japan, and China also shape Manila's foreign policy priorities. As a founding member of ASEAN, successive Philippine governments have maintained steady support for the body and its goals of regional cooperation. During the Cold War, the Philippines and Japan had cordial relations that have since accelerated in response to China's rise. In 2015, President Benigno Aquino III and his counterpart Prime Minister Shinzo Abe signed a joint declaration of strategic partnership, opening the door for Senate ratification of a visiting forces treaty. The obvious matter bringing Japan and the Philippines strategically together is the ongoing dispute in the South China Sea.

The Spratly Islands Dispute

For Philippine leaders, the Spratly Islands imbroglio is the security flash point of greatest concern (see chapters 4 and 13 for more context on the Spratlys dispute). Philippine interest in the South China Sea—called the "West Philippine Sea" by Filipinos—involves particular territorial claims to several islands as well as maritime jurisdiction over a wide expanse of the sea's resources. Philippine officials define the problem in terms of respect for Philippine territorial rights and sovereignty. For the military, the Spratlys are a matter of national prestige and overall security. The Philippine military is much weaker than its Chinese and Vietnamese counterparts, and diplomatic concessions by past Philippine presidents on the matter have caused the issue to fester in Philippine politics. Chinese claims and actions create a formidable threat to Philippine interests in the Spratlys, even as China stands as the Philippines' largest trading partner.

For all sides, including the United States, the South China Sea dispute is a growing geostrategic concern. In 2011, during the same year that President Barack Obama announced his "strategic pivot" to build a US presence in Asia, US ambassador to the Philippines Harry Thomas publicly stated in Manila, "I assure you, in all subjects, we the United States, are with the Philippines."[37] Philippine leaders interpreted Thomas's remarks as a coded assurance that any Chinese belligerence will be met with a US response. Reaction to this and similar US policy statements, not to mention subsequent diplomatic activity by Secretary of State Hillary Clinton across the region, provoked negative reactions in Beijing and agitated the Chinese public. Officially, however, the United States has stated no position on sovereignty claims in the South China Sea, only that the resolution of the dispute be peaceful and that freedom of navigation in the area be honored.

In 2012, an incident near Scarborough Shoal involving the Philippine Navy and Chinese patrol boats (ostensibly protecting Chinese fishing boats) created a tense two-month standoff between the two countries. Subsequent diplomatic tension, public protest, and military brinksmanship proved just how potentially volatile the Spratlys dispute had become. Both sides saved face by withdrawing due to rough seas and the coming typhoon season. ASEAN's failed meeting in Phnom Penh that same year only embittered all sides further. The Philippines prefers a multilateral and regional approach, whereas the Chinese prefer a bilateral approach to reconcile the conflict.

After a decade of China's continued encroachment in the area, and its seeming indifference to a (non-binding) declaration on peaceful settlement it had signed with ASEAN in 2002, the Philippines decided in 2013 to file a formal case against China with the Permanent Court of Arbitration (PCA) at The Hague. The case claimed China's occupation of features in the Spratly Islands violated existing international law, as did China's exploitation of waters within the Philippines' exclusive economic zone defined under the United Nations Convention on the Law of the Sea (UNCLOS). Complicated by the fact that China refuses to participate in the legal case, the PCA ultimately agreed to rule on the case with full deliberations to take place in 2016. Whatever the results of the case, a final resolution of the Spratly issue remains elusive; the more important question concerns the rising risk that future actions by China, other claimants, or even the United States might somehow spark an actual conflict or interstate war.

CONCLUSION

The contemporary Philippine political system is formally democratic, with structures and procedures conducive to an open polity. Informally, however, the system remains oligarchic, ruled by a self-perpetuating elite of landed families that has commanded the political and economic scene for centuries. Philippine society has not assimilated modern democratic values with traditional ways in a coherent or harmonious manner. Its leaders face constant challenges of legitimacy, allegations of corruption, and threats from the country's military. More tragically, Philippine leaders have rarely met the people's needs. Poverty rates have barely dropped, and the standard of living has deteriorated because of mismanagement and the greed of the country's oligarchic families. The Philippine polity has yet to develop an effective capacity to cope with changing demands and to assert the nation's destiny.

Thirty years have now passed since Marcos's ouster, yet the problems besetting the Philippines remain the same: extensive poverty, structural inequality, corrupt leadership, monopolistic industries, land disputes, and an elite class more concerned with self-interest than the common good. On average, more Filipinos continue to experience a lower standard of living and more limited opportunity than their cohorts in other Southeast Asian countries. The country's endemic problems are not likely to be solved single-handedly by the next elected president, or the one who follows. Truly neutralizing the graft, gangsters, and goons dominating the Philippine system is an impossible task for a single leader. Rather, it is the project of the rising generation who must somehow generate a societal commitment to fundamental changes in Filipino life, including a newfound respect for the rule of law and an unwavering commitment to democratic institutions beyond campaigns and elections.

NOTES

1. David Wurfel, *Filipino Politics: Development and Decay* (Ithaca, NY: Cornell University Press, 1988).

2. John T. Sidel, "The Philippines: The Languages of Legitimation," in *Political Legitimacy in Southeast Asia: The Quest for Moral Authority*, ed. Muthiah Alagappa (Stanford, CA: Stanford University Press, 1995), 165–168.

3. Paul Hutchcroft, "The Arroyo Imbroglio in the Philippines," *Journal of Democracy* 19, no. 1 (2008): 142.

4. William Overholt persuasively argues that, contrary to the established view that the assassination caused the collapse of the regime or even accelerated Marcos's decline, the assassination was a successful stratagem by Marcos to delay the consequences of his regime's political, moral, and financial bankruptcy. See William Overholt, "The Rise and Fall of Ferdinand Marcos," *Asian Survey* 26, no. 11 (November 1986): 1,137–1,163.

5. For a comprehensive look at US Cold War support of Marcos, see Raymond Bonner, *Waltzing with a Dictator: The Marcoses and the Making of American Policy* (New York: Times Books, 1987).

6. Justus M. van der Kroef, "The Philippines: Day of the Vigilantes," *Asian Survey* 28, no. 6 (June 1988): 630.

7. Sheila S. Coronel, "The Philippines in 2006: Democracy and Its Discontents," *Asian Survey* 47, no. 1 (January/February 2007): 175.

8. Allen Hicken, "The Philippines in 2007: Ballots, Budgets, and Bribes," *Asian Survey* 48, no. 1 (January/February 2008): 76–77.

9. "Philippine Massacre Exposes Political Underworld," BBC News, January 21, 2010, http://news.bbc.co.uk/2/hi/asia-pacific/8470726.stm.

10. Completing his full resurrection to political life, "Erap," at age seventy-five, was elected as the mayor of Manila in 2013.

11. Gil C. Cabacungan Jr., "Lawyers Tell Arroyo: Say Nothing More," *Philippine Daily Enquirer*, July 18, 2011, http://newsinfo.inquirer.net/25035/lawyers-tell-arroyo-say-nothing-more.

12. Kate Hodal, "Tacloban: A Year After Typhoon Haiyan," *The Guardian*, October 31, 2014, www.theguardian.com/world/2014/oct/31/tacloban-a-year-after-typhoon-haiyan.

13. Patricio Abinales, "The Philippines in 2009: The Blustery Days of August," *Asian Survey* 50, no. 1 (January/February 2010): 218.

14. One of the best overviews of the evolution of political parties in the Philippines is Luzviminda G. Tancangco, "The Electoral System and Political Parties in the Philippines," in *Government and Politics of the Philippines*, ed. Raul P. De Guzman and Mila A. Reforma (Singapore: Oxford University Press, 1988). Part of the following paragraphs are based on her analysis.

15. Felipe B. Miranda and Ruben F. Ciron, "Development and the Military in the Philippines: Military Perceptions in a Time of Continuing Crisis," in *Soldiers and Stability in Southeast Asia*, ed. J. Soedjati Djiwandono and Yong Mun Cheong (Singapore: Institute of Southeast Asian Studies, 1988), 169.

16. Michael J. Montesano, "The Philippines in 2003: Troubles, None of Them New," *Asian Survey* 44, no. 1 (January/February 2004): 96.

17. Raul P. De Guzman, Alex B. Brillantes Jr., and Arturo G. Pacho, "The Bureaucracy," in *Government and Politics of the Philippines*, ed. Raul P. De Guzman and Mila A. Reforma (Singapore: Oxford University Press, 1988), 180.

18. Michael Leifer, *Dictionary of the Modern Politics of South-East Asia* (London: Routledge, 1995), 162.

19. Simon Elegant, "The Return of Abu Sayyaf," *Time*, August 23, 2004, www.time.com/time/magazine/article/0,9171,686107,00.html.

20. Hicken, "The Philippines in 2007," 78.

21. "Philippines and Muslim Rebels Sign Key Peace Plan," BBC News, October 15, 2012, www.bbc.co.uk/news/world-asia-19944101.

22. "Eight IS Supporters Killed in Philippine Clash," *New Straits Times*, November 27, 2015, www.nst.com.my/news/2015/11/114125/eight-supporters-killed-philippine-clash.

23. Sidel, "The Philippines: The Languages of Legitimation," 147.

24. Linda K. Richter, "Exploring Theories of Female Leadership in South and Southeast Asia," paper presented to the Association for Asian Studies, Chicago, April 1990, p. 7.

25. David Joel Steinberg, "The Web of Filipino Allegiance," *Solidarity* 2, no. 6 (March/April 1967): 25.

26. Coronel, "The Philippines in 2006," 178.

27. Sidel, "The Philippines: The Languages of Legitimation," 147, n. 44.

28. Patricio N. Abilanes, "The Philippines in 2010: Blood, Ballots, and Beyond," *Asian Survey* 5, no.1 (January/February 2011): 163–172.

29. Kristine L. Alave, "Most Violent Elections Yet, Says Comcon Exec," *Philippine Daily Enquirer*, July 4, 2010, http://article.wn.com/view/2010/04/07/Most_violent_elections_yet_says_Comelec_exec.

30. Carlos H. Conde, "Election Violence Escalating in the Philippines," *International Herald Tribune*, May 6, 2007, www.nytimes.com/2007/05/06/world/asia/06iht-phils.1.5583626.html.

31. S. K. Jayasuriya, "The Politics of Economic Policy in the Philippines During the Marcos Era," in *Southeast Asia in the 1980s: The Politics of Economic Crisis*, ed. Richard Robison, Kevin Hewison, and Richard Higgott (Sydney: Allen & Unwin, 1987), 82.

32. Ibid., 83.

33. Felipe Salvosa, "Philippine Remittances: Under Threat," *Financial Times*, July 21, 2015, www.ft.com/cms/s/3/17eaf74a-2faf-11e5-91ac-a5e17d9b4cff.html#axzz42QwyZKPi.

34. Philippines Country Profile, *2015 UNDP Human Development Report*, http://hdr.undp.org/en/countries/profiles/PHL.

35. Coronel, "The Philippines in 2006," 182.

36. "Filipinos Favor U.S. Statehood: Says Poll," *The Age*, May 18, 1972, 6.

37. "Spratly Islands Word War: US Will Defend RP," *Philippine News*, May 9, 2011, www.philippinenews.com/top-stories/2526-spratly-islands-word-war-us-will-defend-rp.html.

8

INDONESIA

Indonesia, with its 256 million inhabitants, presents different challenges in its quest for economic and political development compared to its less-populated neighbors. As an equatorial archipelago stretching as wide as the United States, Indonesia is the fourth-most-populous country in the world. Over one-third of all Southeast Asians live in Indonesia. Eleven major ethnic groups and hundreds of minor ones inhabit 6,000 of the country's 17,000 islands.[1] Amazingly, more than half of all Indonesians live on the island of Java, one of the most densely populated areas of the world. Although 85 percent of the country's population is nominally Muslim, the variety of religious beliefs within this Islamic ambience suggests diversity more than unity. Thus, even as the world's largest Muslim country, Indonesia is continually shaped by geographic, linguistic, ethnic, and social heterogeneity. The population has overcome almost insuperable obstacles in achieving nationhood.

Indonesia experienced a daunting struggle for independence at the end of World War II. Having lived under Dutch control for 350 years and then Japanese occupation during World War II, Indonesians looked for a leader who could forge unity within diversity in the postindependence period. As spokesman for Indonesian independence, leader of the revolutionary struggle against the Dutch from 1945 to 1949, and first president of independent Indonesia, Sukarno became the charismatic "solidarity maker"—destined, it seemed, to forge a "new Indonesian person."

Postindependence Indonesia can be divided into four periods, separated by one- to two-year transition phases: (1) fragile parliamentary governance under Sukarno, 1950–1957; (2) "guided democracy" under Sukarno, 1959–1965; (3) the "New Order" under Suharto, 1967–1998; and (4) liberal democratic reform under multiple presidents, 1999–present. The first period featured numerous political parties, elections, and weak parliamentary government. These Western-style governmental forms—adopted to prove to Indonesians that they could govern themselves in a "modern" democratic manner—did not fit well

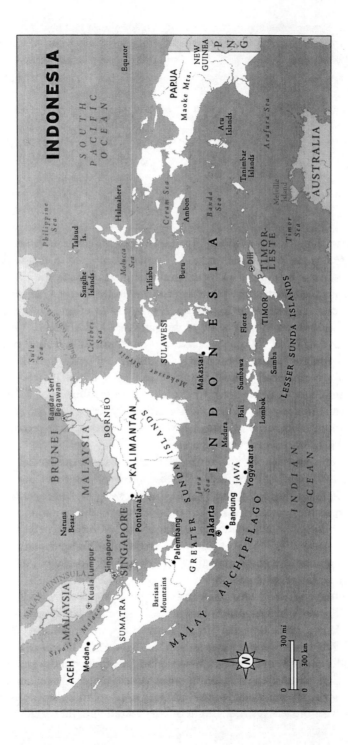

with traditional Indonesian culture, which placed little value on representation, group formation, and majority rule. Sukarno pejoratively referred to democracy as "50 percent plus one" governance. Eventually, Westernized institutions were blamed for the government's inability to meet the people's economic needs.

As liberal democracy floundered, Sukarno moved toward a system based on traditional political concepts, mixed and reformulated to meet goals of nation-building. The essence of "guided democracy" was *gotong royong* (mutual cooperation), where decisions could be arrived at with unanimous approval via collaboration rather than competition. Western-style voting was also replaced by *musyawarah-mufakat*—a traditional method of deliberation-consensus—with Sukarno himself as the ultimate and unchallenged arbiter.

To rally support for guided democracy, Sukarno made nationalism the cornerstone of his new ideology. Nationalism was defined as the submergence of regional and ethnic loyalties in favor of national ones, allegiance to Sukarno, indigenous patterns of governance (free from the mentality of colonialism), and the annihilation of neocolonialism. Loyalty to the greater interest was rooted in *Bhinneka Tunggal Ika*, a Javanese-derived phrase meaning, "We are of many kinds, but one" (sometimes translated as "Unity in Diversity" or "*E pluribus unum*").

Fearful of disunity, Sukarno had brilliantly established *Bahasa Indonesia* (a minority Malay-based dialect) as the new national language upon independence. Although the country was home to over 300 languages, demographic realities rendered Javanese the most commonly used language per capita. Nevertheless, by resisting the temptation to designate Javanese as the national language, and by favoring a minority lingua franca used by coastal traders, Sukarno ameliorated Javanese chauvinism, a force that continually challenges the unity of postcolonial Indonesia.

Sukarno also cultivated the idea of *Pancasila,* a term adopted from Sanskrit meaning "five precepts." *Pancasila,* the declared state philosophy of Indonesia, syncretically embraces the belief in one God, humanitarianism, nationalism, democracy, and social justice. Ambiguously defining each, often in long, fiery speeches, Sukarno's vision of "sociodemocracy" audaciously blended elements of liberalism, Marxism, theism, traditionalism, and modernism. The country's official emblem, the *Garuda Pancasila,* was unfolded by Sukarno as a mythical Hindu bird adorned with a coat of arms symbolizing the principles of *Pancasila.* A decorative ribbon held by the bird's talons declared the state motto.

Where *Pancasila* defined the scope of politics, *Marhaenism* functioned as the centerpiece of Sukarno's economic philosophy. *Marhaenism* targeted the rural experience as a type of subsistence socialism. Deriving its name from an apocryphal Sundanese farmer he supposedly met while cycling, Sukarno used it to emphasize "self-help" as the chief bulwark against "exploitation." By glorifying Indonesia's many small cultivators "who worked for themselves and no one else," *Marhaenism*'s economic ideals thus belied any need for class revolution or organized struggle. It promoted, rather illogically, the development of an atomized but unified rural proletariat of national loyalists—a Sukarnoist dream of content, self-sustaining peasants neither radicalized into class consciousness nor corrupted by individualism or avaricious want.

By embracing *Pancasila, Bhinneka Tunggal Ika, Bahasa Indonesia*, and *Marhaenism*, Sukarno encircled the new regime with his own ideology, goals, and charisma, indistinguishably fusing his persona with the postcolonial state and regime. Recognized and celebrated across the third world for his postcolonial ideology and vision, Sukarno, similar to many of his contemporaries (Mao, Nasser, and Castro), was a one-man political institution.

After he banned most political parties, reduced the power of Parliament, and suspended civil liberties, Sukarno's political course under guided democracy became erratic. He moved ideologically to the left, embracing the Partai Komunis Indonesia (Communist Party of Indonesia or PKI), and then to the right—strengthening the armed forces—when the PKI became too dominant. He tried desperately to balance the demands of numerous groups, including the PKI, Chinese entrepreneurs, students, rural farmers, rightist Muslims, outer-island groups, and the army.

Although guided democracy was initially supported as an Indonesian antidote to failed Western liberalism, deteriorating economic conditions and administrative chaos created disunity rather than erasing it. In practice, *Marhaenism* resulted in rural neglect, a disorganized attempt at state-led nationalization, and a large, informal, free-for-all economy. Conditions of poverty thus worsened. Forever obsessed with foreign exploitation, Sukarno nationalized Dutch and British holdings, expelled 40,000 foreign expatriates, and demanded foreign-held territories in Borneo and New Guinea. As domestic problems deepened, he turned his attention abroad, pursuing a coercive foreign policy known as *Konfrontasi* (confrontation).

Under *Konfrontasi*, Sukarno moved beyond the Dutch and began to target the Federation of Malaysia, Britain, the United States, and the United Nations. Sukarno refused to recognize Malaysia with diplomatic relations upon its 1963 independence from the British and began to engage in guerrilla warfare with the new state over territorial claims. Then in 1964, Sukarno told the US ambassador at a public gathering to "go to hell with your aid," despite Indonesia's dependence on Western military and financial assistance. Thoroughly convinced of a neocolonial plot and irate over international support of Malaysia, Sukarno spitefully withdrew Indonesia from the United Nations, rejecting its aid and antipoverty programs as well.

Sukarno's narcissistic obsession with his own international image exacerbated policy failure on the domestic front—rural neglect in particular. Under guided democracy, Indonesian society deteriorated precipitously. Government corruption turned flagrant, and the cost of living index rose from a base of 100 in 1957 to 36,000 in 1965. Unemployment grew rampant, and hungry peasants migrated en masse, forming a distressed population of urban homeless. Politically, the PKI gained strength, supported by radicalized peasants and stressed urbanites who began to arm themselves with Chinese-made weapons.

Sukarnoism's final ideological piece, *Nasakom*, was perhaps more tactical than visionary. Introduced in the early 1960s, the acronym-slogan embraced a tripod of social values: nationalism, religion, and communism. With *Nasakom*, Sukarno openly embraced the country's communists as part of Indonesia's political future. With this move, the PKI's confidence surged even as revolutionary movements elsewhere in Southeast Asia were gaining strength. Images of the sickle and hammer and pictures of Marx, Lenin, and Mao began to appear proudly in public. Coinciding as it did with rising poverty, a faltering economy, and foreign policy zealousness, Sukarno's shift to the left sparked fear among right-wing military leaders and Western governments, as well as many pious Muslims throughout the archipelago.

On the night of September 30, 1965, in one of the seminal events in contemporary Southeast Asian history, a group of pro-Sukarno dissident army and air force officers launched a purge of their high command, alleging that a CIA-sponsored coup to topple Sukarno was being planned. In a dramatic abduction, six senior generals were murdered and subsequently dumped down a well at "Crocodile Hole" outside of Jakarta. An immediate and successful countercoup then followed, targeting the perpetrators. Within a matter of hours, the coup leaders were captured and the putsch came to an end. *Gestapu,* as it was named, collapsed because the army united against the rebels and the population failed to rise in support of the coup.

The events of 1965 remain surrounded by shadow, rumor, and intrigue. Nebulous circumstantial evidence surrounding the coup suggests possible involvement by American or British intelligence. Some skeptics theorize the whole affair was orchestrated by the CIA and the anticommunist Suharto. Nevertheless, the precise roles of the dissident army rebels, the army generals, the PKI, foreign agents, and President Sukarno himself may never be known; evidence remains inconclusive and contradictory.[2]

What is clear is that *Gestapu* rendered Sukarno politically sterile, tainting his legacy and contributing to the emancipator's ignominious demise. It is also clear that General Suharto, the commander of the Strategic Army Reserve and one of the few surviving generals, assumed command of the army and, within two years, the entire country. The events of 1965 fundamentally changed Indonesia's political structure, decimated the PKI, led to one of the worst bloodbaths in history, and swept into power a military government that ruled Indonesia for thirty years.

In the months following the failed coup, hundreds of thousands of suspected communists and sympathizers were slaughtered by members of the army and anticommunist vigilante groups. This massive slaughter was aimed primarily at Sino-Indonesians, who were despised by many for having a disproportionately large role in the Indonesian economy and who were suspected of being more loyal to their Chinese homeland and communism than to Indonesia. Despite its enormity, the slaughter did not become the focus of international condemnation, perhaps because it occurred during the height of the Cold War and because the new anticommunist government in Indonesia was allied with the United States.

By 1967, Suharto had reduced Sukarno's power, banned the PKI, ended *Konfrontasi* against Malaysia, brought Indonesia back into the United Nations, and taken all power for himself. Suharto proclaimed a "New Order" for Indonesia, ending the twenty-year charismatic, ideological, and ultimately catastrophic postindependence leadership of Sukarno and beginning a period of development-oriented, authoritarian, and stable rule that endured until the Asian economic crisis of the late 1990s. Sukarno, at the age of sixty-nine and under house arrest, died of kidney failure on June 21, 1970.

The first task of Suharto's New Order was to create a stable and legitimate political system with control throughout the archipelago; the second task was to rehabilitate the shattered economy. Suharto used the military to accomplish the first goal, portraying the armed forces as the savior against the communist threat that had existed before the coup. To counter the problems of inflation, corruption, and poor economic growth, Suharto instituted a bureaucratic authoritarian state where power was limited to the state itself, led by the military, his close friends, some Western-trained technocrats, and eventually his family members. Suharto based New Order control primarily on co-optation and bureaucratic repression.

To enhance his nationalist credentials, Suharto mobilized the Indonesian army in 1975 to occupy East Timor, after the territory had declared independence from the Portuguese that same year. He feared that Catholic East Timor would be led by leftists and could become a beachhead for Soviet expansion. In 1976, East Timor became Indonesia's twenty-seventh province, but this was accomplished amid terrible carnage with fully 10 percent of the population killed during the invasion. Over time, Suharto's Indonesia developed East Timor with schools, hospitals, and infrastructure, but most residents continued to reject Indonesian control. Indonesian suppression of East Timorese dissent was brutal and, at times, merciless. In 1996, the Nobel Peace Prize was awarded to two East Timorese leaders, Catholic Bishop Carlos Filipe Ximenes Belo and exiled freedom fighter José Ramos-Horta, for their courageous struggle against Indonesian aggression.

To consolidate power, Suharto also pursued a strategy to depoliticize all potential challengers. He purged the army of pro-Sukarno forces and made it the basis of his own strength. Suharto set up a "political organization" called Golkar (an abbreviated form of *golongan karya*, or functional group), which was administered by officials at every level of government, from national to village. Suharto also restricted political association by forcing four Muslim political parties to merge into one: the United Development Party (PPP). The remaining secular and Christian parties were also forced to merge under the Indonesia Democracy Party (PDI). These two opposition parties, the only ones permitted by law, did not have access to the state resources available to Golkar.

Throughout Suharto's thirty-year rule, political freedom and civil liberties were subject to serious constraint. Journalists self-censored their work or were subject to harassment and detention. Business associations and NGOs operated under close supervision of Golkar's corporatist state. To keep Islamic claims on the state at bay, Suharto embraced *Pancasila* as the New Order's guiding political ideology. Later, as Islam's influence grew outside his control, he sought to co-opt Islam more directly by making a pilgrimage to Mecca and supporting the formation of the Indonesian Association of Muslim Intellectuals (ICMI), an organization loyal to the New Order regime.

Suharto also used elections to prop up his legitimacy for continued rule. Golkar's victories in these elections were guaranteed through institutional arrangements ensuring that Suharto loyalists would maintain control of the People's Consultative Assembly (MPR). The MPR's membership was drawn from elected delegates, the military, and presidential appointees. Serving also as an electoral college, the MPR formally elected the president and vice president for five-year terms. Suharto thus handpicked much of the delegatory body that elected (and reelected) him to office.

Over six general elections from 1971 to 1997, the vote for Golkar never fell below 62 percent and Suharto's claim on the presidency was never challenged. Golkar's electoral success was due to (1) a requirement that all governmental bureaucrats and employees join Golkar; (2) laws that restricted political parties and prohibited a free opposition; and (3) performance legitimacy with respect to improving economic conditions and post-Sukarno political stability.

Suharto was as successful in rehabilitating the economy as he was in stabilizing and legitimizing the political system. Following the advice of a group of Western-educated economic technocrats he had assembled, he cut government and defense spending and reaped revenues from the sale of oil. As a result, inflation was reduced, per capita income was greatly increased, and economic growth maintained a steady pace. Indonesia eventually became self-sufficient in rice, and the availability of food improved. The success of Suharto's economic policy stood in stark contrast to Sukarno's failures. In 1967, when Suharto took full power, per capita GDP stood at $100; at the time of his ouster in 1998, it had risen tenfold, to $1,080. Under Suharto's watch, Indonesia became recognized as a Southeast Asian tiger economy, joining the new international era as a contending emerging market.

Economic growth brought Suharto legitimacy and undercut allegations made by his detractors about the authoritarian nature of his regime. These allegations included accusations of nepotism and corruption for allowing his wife and children to control lucrative monopolies. Critics also pointed to a widening gap between rich and poor accompanying the country's tremendous economic growth. Over time, Indonesian students and intellectuals began to carefully criticize the New Order, push for increased democracy, and resist Suharto's autocratic rule. Human rights issues became central as living standards rose, a vibrant middle class emerged, and more and more Indonesians came to believe that military-dominated governments were anachronistic in an age of democratization.

By 1997, an election year, Indonesia's growing population was younger than ever. To a whole generation of Indonesians, Suharto was the only president they had known. Because of his advanced age, much discussion about the shape that post-Suharto Indonesia might take characterized the preelection period. Golkar (unsurprisingly) won a sweeping victory in Indonesia's general elections to seat representatives in the MPR, thus ensuring Suharto's reelection if he desired to stay in power. Suharto announced his availability for a seventh term even as the country confronted a growing regional economic crisis. By late 1997, Indonesia, following Thailand, faced a loss of investor confidence, capital flight, rising debt, and economic uncertainty.

As the economy soured, criticism of Suharto grew proportionally. The major criticism of Suharto's leadership concerned his family's and friends' domination of indigenous business and industrial conglomerates. More and more areas of the industrial economy—television stations, toll roads, telecommunications facilities, oil tankers—had become controlled by Suharto's children during his rule.[3] Because these monopolies arose through personal contacts with the president, the international business community became increasingly cynical about the economy.

Suharto rebuked foreign criticism and responded to detractors by using coercion, force, or denial. Free speech was continually suppressed as local and international journalists confronted restrictions. Many older Indonesians still remembered the dire poverty and chaos of the former regime and were willing to give the New Order much slack. But with a growing middle class, widespread literacy, and access to radio, television, and the printed media, the new generation of Indonesians was quickly growing into a dynamic force for change. The effects of the Asian economic crisis clashed head-on with Suharto's long-standing performance legitimacy.

With the twin pressures of economic collapse and political crisis bearing down, Suharto fretted, teetered, and balked in making needed policy adjustments during the ensuing months. An initial rescue package from the IMF was announced at the end of October 1997. This package stopped the economic slide only temporarily since new concerns over Suharto's ailing health kept investors nervous. The economy worsened, and Indonesia's currency, the rupiah, dropped to 10,000 per dollar, whereas it had been 2,430 prior to the crisis. Inflation skyrocketed. Job losses increased. Pessimism flooded the archipelago nation. Charges of official corruption, collusion, and crony capitalism became common topics for the media and public.

After twice rejecting the conditions of another IMF rescue package, Suharto, still ailing, finally agreed to a second $43 billion bailout package in April 1998. Conditionality on the massive loan, however, not only cut subsidies on crucial goods that affected everyday Indonesians (cooking oil, paper, plywood, cement, and even imported wheat used for instant noodles) but further exposed the extent to which Suharto's family and tycoon partners controlled the public budget and every major sector of the country's economy. In May, Indonesia erupted when sustained street demonstrations turned violent. Antigovernment protests proliferated, and Sino-Indonesian business owners were attacked, often brutally. The violence drove the rupiah down further, to 16,500 per dollar. Indonesia's thirty-year run of political stability and steady economic growth was over.

Amid the disarray, on May 20, 1998, following ten days of antigovernment demonstrations led by students, Suharto resigned. B. J. Habibie, then vice president, was sworn in as the country's new leader, receiving the military's support. Because Habibie was viewed as a Suharto protégé, he faced the problem of distancing himself from the former president. The politically powerful in Indonesia viewed Habibie as an unpredictable gadfly unsuited for the presidency. While setting forth economic policies designed to resolve the crises of currency devaluation, inflation, and unemployment, Habibie indicated his support for reform and democratization. He called for new elections, free of the party constraints known under Suharto's rule.

Among Habibie's most significant decisions during his short tenure was to hold a referendum in East Timor offering an option of autonomy or independence. The result was an East Timorese majority of 78 percent favoring independence. The transition to independence was made difficult by the Indonesian military's continued oppression and violence against the East Timorese people. Massive intervention from the international community and the United Nations was eventually needed to assist Timor-Leste into its new era of independence.[4]

On June 7, 1999, democratic elections were held for the first post-Suharto Parliament in Indonesia. Some forty-eight parties competed for 500 seats. Habibie, attempting to lead Golkar, had already lost the confidence of the population and received little support. With Golkar down, the elections resulted in a plurality victory for the Partai Demokrasi Indonesia–Perjuangan (Indonesia Democracy Party of Struggle, or PDI-P), led by Megawati Sukarnoputri, daughter of the founding father and first president of Indonesia. Her party won 34 percent of the vote, or 153 seats in Parliament. Golkar won only 22 percent, or 120 seats, while Partai Kebangkitan Bangsa (National Awakening Party, or PKB) won 12 percent, or 51 seats. The PKB was led by Abdurrahman Wahid, leader of the Nahdlatul Ulama (Renaissance of Religious Scholars, or NU), the nation's largest Islamic organization. Other parties won fewer seats.

Ninety percent of eligible Indonesians voted in this first democratic election since 1955. Because the PDI-P won the greatest number of votes, many believed Sukarnoputri would become president. However, she chose not to campaign for the presidency (an office still elected by the MPR). Her gender worked against her, since many devout Muslims indicated they could not abide a female leader, and she was viewed as a secularist among the more fundamentalist. Wahid ran for president and won; Sukarnoputri became his vice president.

President Wahid faced overwhelming crises, none of which he successfully resolved. His tenure as president failed to come to grips with any of Indonesia's modern problems. He proved incapable of running an economy and was ill-suited for the task of recovery. His failing health also kept him from being a vibrant leader. Legally blind and enfeebled by strokes, Wahid came across as a very old person who could not cope with the daily stresses of his position. He often dozed during his own speeches, which were presented by his aide.

Under Wahid, the Indonesian archipelago looked as if it might disintegrate. Separatist movements, which had been bottled up by Suharto, hit Aceh on Sumatra, the Dayak region of Kalimantan, and West Irian Jaya (West Papua) on the eastern end of the archipelago. The resulting instability raised the question of whether Indonesia could reform and stabilize simultaneously. In 2001, after just nineteen months of his five-year term, Wahid was twice censured by the MPR as a prelude to full impeachment. The first rebuke was on February 1 and the second was on April 29. Sukarnoputri's party, PDI-P, supported censure. Wahid was asked to give a response to Parliament, which he did, but it was deemed unacceptable when he claimed the Parliament was acting unconstitutionally.

Finally, on July 22, 2001, the MPR met to debate Wahid's impeachment and to name Sukarnoputri president. The vote against Wahid was 591 to 0. Wahid responded by ordering an emergency rule, which he hoped would postpone or end the move against him, but Indonesia's security forces and the legislature defied him by refusing his orders. Wahid warned that if he were forced from office, many provinces would attempt to separate themselves from Indonesia. But that came to naught, and on July 23, 2001, Megawati Sukarnoputri became president of the world's largest Muslim country. Wahid initially refused to leave the presidential palace but then relented and went to the United States to seek medical treatment.

Megawati Sukarnoputri had not entered politics until the mid-1990s, but rose to prominence after troops attacked her party's headquarters upon Suharto's orders. Raised in a presidential palace, a college dropout, and thrice married (including an annulled two-week elopement with an Egyptian diplomat), she was known to be taciturn, shy, and not particularly savvy regarding politics. She derived much of her support from Sukarno's charismatic aura, but her own style proved far different. "Mega," as she is commonly called, did not share her father's love for theatrical oration or his aptitude for political infighting. Upon assuming the presidency, her task was not to build a new nation but to reform Suharto's corrupt ancien régime. The effort was dubbed *"reformasi"*: an agenda to reform institutions, bring corrupt officials to account, and revive the ailing economy.

Immediately dictating the context of Megawati's rule were the events of September 11, which occurred half a world away only weeks after her appointment. She soon found her country caught in the crosshairs of America's war on terrorism. She rejected claims by Washington that terrorists operated in her country until events proved her wrong. In 2002 and 2003, deadly terrorist bombings targeting nightclubs, hotels, and the Australian embassy rocked Bali and Jakarta. The plotters of the bombings, members of the Indonesia-based Jemaah Islamiyah (Islamic Congregation, or JI), were known communicants with Osama bin Laden's al-Qaeda. Megawati pledged to quell domestic terrorism but on her own terms, largely independent of the United States' antiterrorism framework, which was tainted by deep resentment among Indonesians, who universally condemned the US occupation of Iraq.

The disconnect between both governments grew. The Bush administration viewed Indonesia as a terrorist haven but Megawati, like many Indonesians, viewed US Middle East policy as responsible for her own society's victimization at the hands of chauvinistic Arab-Islamists and extremists. Alternatively, street-level conspiracy theories claimed that Bush agents had perpetrated the local bombings to bring an anti-Muslim war to Indonesia. US-Indonesian relations became more strained than they had been since the Sukarno era of *Konfrontasi*.

Although attending the UN-sponsored ceremony granting Timor-Leste full independence helped Megawati's standing with Washington and Canberra, cold diplomacy defined relations between Indonesia and its principal Western partners. Unlike leaders in Thailand, the Philippines, Singapore, and even Malaysia, who cautiously supported Western antiterrorism efforts, Megawati pursued a more reticent approach. For example, fearing alienation among Muslims and taking care not to speak too strongly against political Islam, she refused to classify JI and similar groups as illegal organizations. At the same time, she apprehended suspects in the Bali and Jakarta bombings and sent them to court, where some received death sentences—although Abu Bakar Ba'asyir, the suspected mastermind and spiritual head of JI, served what eventually became a shortened prison term.

Beyond security issues and terrorism, Megawati's greatest troubles were in managing the domestic economy, controlling ethnic separatism, and delivering on her anticorruption agenda. Under her watch, foreign investment did not return to Indonesia's beleaguered economy at the rate it did elsewhere in Southeast Asia. Displaced workers continued to move into a growing informal sector, and farmers struggled with drought support. Tourism, an early recovery sector, also fell sharply, due to terrorist fears and the 2003 regional outbreak of SARS (Severe Acute Respiratory Syndrome).[5]

In both Aceh and Irian Jaya, Megawati's unprecedented attempts to establish greater autonomy backfired and resulted in further revolt and military suppression. Violent rioting between Christians and Muslims in the Moluccas Islands also erupted in 2004, drawing unwanted international attention. Megawati also failed to bring to justice corrupt officials and military officers of the New Order era, including Suharto himself (deemed too ill to stand trial).

Megawati Sukarnoputri's most significant reform under *reformasi* proved to undermine her own political career. Amid continued economic and ethnic troubles, the sitting president reversed a previous position and supported a constitutional change for direct presidential elections. Subsequently, in October 2004, she lost the presidency to Susilo Bambang Yudhoyono in the country's first direct election of an executive. Yudhoyono, a minister with a military background and security policy experience, pledged decisiveness on *reformasi* where his predecessor had failed.

Weeks later, on December 26, 2004, a magnitude 9.0 earthquake off the Sumatra coast caused the most deadly tsunami in recorded history.[6] Of the twelve countries affected, Indonesia experienced the greatest devastation: 126,804 dead; 93,458 missing; 474,619 internally displaced; and an estimated $5.4 billion in damage, a figure almost equivalent to Sumatra's entire GDP. International sympathy poured in, propelled by the media age and harrowing images of loss and destruction that were broadcast globally. Rescue aid from Asian, Western, and Muslim sources amassed with unprecedented speed and at record levels for a natural disaster. Former US presidents Bill Clinton and George H. W. Bush became special UN ambassadors, to raise funds for recovery, and visited Sumatra. During the early months of 2005, the entire international community was consumed with addressing relief and recovery from the disaster in Sumatra and elsewhere.

Politically, the tsunami was significant, given that areas partial to Aceh's independence movement were among the hardest hit. Multiple countries dispatched military units to take part in a broadly coordinated aid mission. Images of US troops arriving in Aceh, unthinkable before December 26, symbolized the suspension of political concern in favor of humanitarian necessity. In August 2005, Yudhoyono, less than a year into his presidency, was able to reach a disarmament agreement with Aceh's depleted rebels that offered them greater autonomy—the three-decade-old separatist movement that had produced over 15,000 deaths finally concluded. A year later Aceh held its own direct elections, selecting a former rebel leader to serve as provincial governor.

On the other side of the archipelago, untouched by the tsunami, the story in West Papua followed a different track, and Yudhoyono's efforts were less conclusive. West Papuans had been granted greater autonomy in 2002 by the government, including the shedding of the unwanted administrative name Irian Jaya in favor of West Papua. However, rough implementation of the agreement kept tensions festering and separatists hoping for an independence referendum.[7] Given the revenues West Papua's mining resources produce for the country's economy, the likelihood that Jakarta will allow such an event remains low.

Over the course of his presidency, Susilo Bambang Yudhoyono (popularly known as "SBY") skillfully reversed the direction of ailing Indonesia. Although a member of a minority party when elected (Partai Demokrat), Yudhoyono revived economic growth, quelled ethnic separatism, further depoliticized the military, and won praise from the United States and Australia for effective counterterrorism efforts. Using his specialized Detachment 88 force, funded in part by the US State Department, Yudhoyono won credit for capturing Jemaah Islamiyah's top political leader, its top recruiter of suicide bombers, and its chief bomb-maker.

In spite of relative success, Yudhoyono's popularity took some hits during his first term. Indonesia's open political environment, expanding civil society, and free press held the president accountable for failed promises. Much of the *reformasi* agenda remained elusive, and impunity for corrupt officials remained problematic. Ironically, Megawati Sukarnoputri and her PDI-P colleagues were counted among the biggest critics of Yudhoyono and his inability to execute trials against Suharto and New Order tycoons, something they had also failed to achieve when in power.

On behalf of the country, government prosecutors eventually filed a lawsuit against Suharto for embezzling $440 million and for damages of $1.1 billion— by all estimates a drop in the bucket. In a 2004 report, Transparency International estimated Suharto's ill-gained wealth at $15–35 billion and listed him as the most corrupt politician of all time; far ahead of the Philippines' Marcos (ranked second at $5–10 billion) and Mobutu of Zaire (ranked third at $5 billion). In January 2008, with his civil suit pending, Suharto died of organ failure. Neither Sukarnoputri nor Yudhoyono (nor anybody else) would ever be able to claim victory in bringing the world's most corrupt chief executive to justice.

In April 2009, SBY's Partai Demokrat swept parliamentary elections in a major defeat of Golkar and PDI-P, previously the largest parties in the assembly. In an endorsement of his leadership, Yudhoyono's party picked up a remarkable 95 new seats and secured a plurality of 150 of the body's 560 total seats. Indonesia also held its second direct presidential election on July 8, 2009. Yudhoyono, as expected, defeated his two primary challengers: Megawati Sukarnoputri (PDI-P) and Jusuf Kalla (Golkar). Both elections (which neighboring Filipinos envied for their lack of violence and controversy) signaled the decline of Suharto-era parties and the inability of Islamic parties to appeal to more than one in four Indonesian voters.[8]

During his second five-year term, Yudhoyono started strong but finished ignominiously. SBY continued to win praise well into his second term for steady executive management that produced "the most stable period of governance in Indonesian democratic politics."[9] Indonesia enjoyed seven straight years with a "free" rating from Freedom House (2006–2012), and the country's strong economic performance under Yudhoyono sparked new debates about Indonesia's international status. In fact, foreign investors and financial experts began speculating about whether Indonesia should be listed among the so-called BRIC economies (the large producers of Brazil, Russia, India, and China); some suggested it should even outright replace weaker-performing Russia or India.[10] In the immediate years following the global financial melt-down of 2008–2009, no major economy outside of China grew more rapidly than SBY's Indonesia. Even Indonesia's corruption ranking, according to Transparency International, was moving in the right direction, dropping over five years from 143 (2007) to 100 (2011).

As a former minister under the impeached Wahid, Yudhoyono feared the political risks of a small coalition. During his tenure he had judiciously brought into his government six of Indonesia's nine political parties. Such inclusiveness created broad stability but meant spreading positions and patronage, and arbitrating conflict rather than actively leading. Toward the end of his term, SBY's broad political coalition gradually unraveled. To ensure partners never lost face or felt disrespected, Yudhoyono repeatedly relinquished decision-making by cowing to coalition demands.[11] As resources spread and top-down discipline dissipated, Indonesia's patronage networks grew. In his final years, SBY's previous achievements began to be overshadowed by government corruption scandals, growing sectarian unrest, and controversial measures that reduced civil liberties.

In 2012, revelations emerged that senior officials in Yudhoyono's cabinet, including SBY's favored Partai Demokrat protégé, Dr. Andi Mallarangeng, had taken massive bribes from private firms in exchange for government contracts.[12] Subsequent investigations uncovered an intricate web of involved officials and family members. The party's treasurer, for example, not only received kickbacks but attempted to bribe Indonesian judges. He later became the subject of an Interpol capture in Cartagena, Columbia, where he was found hiding under a false identity. Headline news compared SBY's cabinet to old-style New Order graft. The scandal thoroughly damaged Yudhoyono's Partai Demokrat edifice and blew wide open what proved to be two divisive, high-stakes elections in 2014.

The April 2014 general elections for the 560-seat People's Representative Council (DPR) featured twelve contesting parties that split the electorate widely (no party won more than 20 percent of the vote). SBY's Partai Demokrat lost a humiliating 87 total seats with many of the gains going to former opposition parties. A new majority coalition formed in Parliament outside of Yudhoyono's influence. SBY later caved to this new legislative majority when it passed laws scrapping direct elections of local leaders and restoring Suharto-style limits on the activities of mass organizations and NGOs. After public outcry, he belatedly tried to overturn the new elections law by decree, hoping the DPR would some-how ratify it.

The disappointments regarding Yudhoyono's tenure mounted. Over his final years, his government also became indifferent to human rights and exhibited weak responses to Sunni attacks against Christians, Buddhists, and minority Shia and Sufi Muslims. Because of government scandals and democratic reversals, Transparency International reported in 2012 Indonesia's corruption ranking had worsened by eighteen spots in a single year; two years later, Freedom House lowered Indonesia's rating from "free" to "partly free." Democracy in Indonesia was backsliding.

Following April's legislative elections, the July 2014 Indonesian presidential elections proved even more dangerously polarizing. Shaped by old influences, growing cleavages, and money politics, Indonesia's divided electorate flirted with an outcome that could have accelerated the country's democratic slide—a return of Suharto allies to power.

In the run-up to the July 2014 direct presidential elections, constitutional rules required party coalitions to form in order to nominate candidates (because no single party held 20 percent of DPR seats). With SBY's Partai Demokrat in disgrace, two candidates thus emerged around two large party coalitions. On one side was Suharto's son-in-law, Prabowo Subianto, fond of blaming Yudhoyono-era corruption on excessive democracy. A retired special forces general, the well-known Prabowo cultivated a confident, tough-guy image, crafted during numerous violent episodes (labeled "security operations") against East Timorese and Chinese and Papuan minorities. With Napoleonic flare, Prabowo sometimes arrived at campaign rallies in martial fashion, fully booted, stone-faced, on horseback. His primary support came from a "Red and White" coalition of six parties including Islamist groups and remnants of SBY's old coalition, including Golkar. Essentially, Prabowo championed a return to the bureaucratic authoritarianism of Indonesia's past, which (laughably) he portrayed as less corrupt. Because his positions sought to reverse various post-1998 democratic rules and institutions, a Prabowo victory would have been the death knell of *reformasi*. To his supporters, he held potential to become a domineering potentate or Indonesian version of Lee Kuan Yew.

The other side held faint ties to Sukarno's legacy of populist nationalism. Hand-picked by PDI-P's Megawati Sukarnoputri, the second party coalition coalesced around Joko Widodo, a popular local leader with no military background or elite family name. "Jokowi," as he is commonly called, carried a reputation as a pragmatic man of action due to successful stints as the twice-elected mayor of Solo (a large Javanese city) and as the governor of Jakarta.[13] With a low-key personal style, his campaign emphasized nationalist ideals, improvements in public goods, social welfare, and vigorous pledges to end political horse-trading.

Jokowi, the establishment outsider, won the duel with nearly 71 million of 133 million total votes cast, or 53 percent of the electorate. Hopes he would restore Mega's record of *reformasi* swept through his supporters. However, due to earlier DPR elections, it was Prabowo's party that actually led the majority parliamentary coalition, while Jokowi's PDI-P remained in the legislative minority. In fact, in the three months between Jokowi's election and his assuming office, Prabowo cunningly "outfoxed and outgunned" the new president by rewriting legislative procedures to gain control of all important DPR leadership positions. Jokowi entered office lacking a compliant legislature, fully checked by his election rival.[14]

Over his first year, Jokowi found himself managing affairs in a fashion similar to his predecessors, trading off reform goals for stability. Cautiously adopting an accommodating stance rather than confidently confronting opponents, the inexperienced president left critics wondering if the new era was destined to be "business as usual."[15] Concerns rose that Jokowi could do little to sway an opposition bloc to act on his agenda. Even so, the global decline in commodities prices put pressure on Indonesia's lawmakers to come together on broad economic interests. Fears of governmental paralysis were also mollified when the DPR decided to ratify SBY's previous decree retaining direct elections for regional governors and mayors—a post-1998 democratic feature, of course, responsible for Jokowi's own rise.

INSTITUTIONS AND SOCIAL GROUPS

The Constitution

The 1945 Constitution has been the primary legal document guiding contemporary Indonesia since its independence. Although manipulated by both Sukarno and Suharto to suit their respective purposes, the document has retained popular legitimacy. Since the collapse of New Order rule, the constitution has proven pliable to reform and undergone major changes affecting all branches of government. These changes, as part of *reformasi*, have been aimed squarely at addressing past political problems.

Indonesia's current constitution oversees a hybrid presidential and parliamentary form of government. Presidents today are not rulers in the manner of either Sukarno or Suharto. Although it appears to be a presidential system, executive power is now checked by more than just an electorate. The Indonesian legislature is empowered to subject the president to votes of confidence. Elected presidents must also work with elected legislators to formulate policy. Because executives are not necessarily from the largest political party, the legislature may feel no compunction to follow the president's policy agenda. Where the president holds greatest power is in appointing cabinet members, acting as commander in chief of the armed forces, and arbitrating foreign affairs as head of state. As now amended, the constitution states that elected presidents in post-Suharto Indonesia can serve only two five-year terms. To ensure that a president is elected by a majority rather than a plurality vote, Indonesia's constitutionally mandated electoral law employs a run-off system.

The present constitution establishes a 692-member People's Consultative Assembly (MPR) as the highest governmental body in the land. During most of the Sukarno period and all of the Suharto period, the MPR did not function as a free representative legislature. Only since the 1999 legislative elections and subsequent constitutional changes has the MPR begun to serve a democratic function embedded in pluralist, free party competition. Where the MPR formerly elected the president and vice president as an electoral college, a constitutional amendment in 2004 stripped the assembly of such power. Today, the MPR holds powers to pass constitutional amendments and impeach the president (an MPR power Abdurrahman Wahid would attest is indeed functional). Day-to-day legislative activity, however, is handled by the country's recently reformed bicameral legislature, whose combined membership constitutes the MPR itself.

The lower house, the *Dewan Perwakilan Rakyat* (People's Representative Council, or DPR), seats 560 members through national elections in a mixed system of district and proportional representation. Under the constitution, the DPR is the locus of legislative power. A body with regional representation, the 132-seat *Dewan Perwakilan Daerah* (Regional Representative Council, DPD), was recently developed. The DPD cannot revise DPR legislation, but it can formulate legislation related to local autonomy, resource management, fiscal matters, and other issues concerning provincial relations with the central government. Though important, the DPD does not carry the standing or authority of an upper house, such as the US Senate.

Pancasila

As the country's national ideology, *Pancasila* underpins the constitution, supporting the basis of statehood and the ideals of legitimate government. It includes five principles:

1. Belief in one God (embracing religious belief and tolerance vis-à-vis secularism)
2. Humanitarianism (implying civilized society absent of oppression)
3. Nationalism (implying unity amid ethnic diversity, or *Bhinneka Tunggal Ika*)
4. Democracy (defined as consensus-oriented decision-making, or *musyawarah-mufakat*)
5. Social justice (idealized as the economic welfare of all peoples of Indonesia)

To create a defense against Western liberalism as well as Islamic privilege, Indonesia's founders sought to develop an anticolonial political ideology that embodied republicanism and embraced Indonesian aspirations. Few have since questioned its validity, although its interpretation occupies the ideological center of Indonesian political debate. Islamic groups, in particular, are among those who challenge *Pancasila*'s secular dimensions. One such challenge came in 1980 when Islamic groups, the PPP, and a number of retired military figures submitted a petition known as the "Petisi Kelompok 50" (Group of 50 Petition), criticizing Suharto and his administration for using *Pancasila* to undermine political opposition. Predictably, the government-dominated Parliament ignored the petition.[16]

Open to interpretation with changing conditions, *Pancasila* ideology has retained its legitimacy throughout the country's major political transitions. Although no longer required, most political parties embrace *Pancasila* as their official party ideology. In the post-Suharto era, government manipulation of *Pancasila* has given way to increasing public contestation of its meaning and, in some respects, its meaninglessness as materialism, secularism, and globalized values expand.

Although attempts have been made, no other Southeast Asian country can claim the success Indonesia has had in creating and maintaining its own state philosophy. Among Muslim-predominant countries elsewhere, *Pancasila* has arguably proven less divisive than Turkey's secular-rationalist Kemalism, more internationally and domestically legitimate than Iran's theocratic imperative, and more compatible with modernity than the ultraconservative Salafism currently animating antimodern Islamist movements throughout the Muslim world. Many observers vaunt Indonesia as the preeminent model of an Islamic society with functional pluralist democracy. *Pancasila*, which is the often-overlooked ideological core of that model, is among Sukarno's most admirable legacies.

Political Parties

Until the 1999 election, no party was realistically able to compete with Golkar, the official party of the government and the military. Golkar functioned simultaneously as the principal support of the government and as the representative of the Indonesian people. The military originally established Golkar in the 1960s to oppose communist organizations; thus, the party developed a national apparatus down to the village level. The only other permissible parties under New Order rule—the United Development Party (*Partai Persatuan Pembangunan*, or PPP) and the Indonesia Democracy Party (*Partai Demokrasi Indonesia*, or PDI)—were destined to oppositional roles and split Golkar's opponents into two controlled camps.

All of this changed in 1999 when Indonesia held open democratic elections with multiple parties. The biggest plurality of votes went to Megawati Sukarnoputri's Indonesia Democracy Party of Struggle (PDI-P), which garnered 34 percent of votes for the DPR. Golkar won only 22 percent, down over 40 percentage points from the previous election. At the time, the MPR still elected the country's executive. Although Megawati had rights to claim the presidency because of her party's plurality victory, Abdurrahman Wahid managed to win a majority of votes to become president. Sukarnoputri was made vice president. The aftermath of the election was chaotic, but the bigger picture was clear: For the first time in their lives, most Indonesians were able to participate in the political system and freely choose their own leaders. At campaign rallies, in print, and through diverse forms of public and private interaction, Indonesians became citizens able to express their complaints, opinions, and aspirations.

Subsequent legislative and presidential elections—as well as various local, mayoral, and gubernatorial elections (instituted as part of *reformasi*)—have included political parties and candidates from across the spectrum. Dozens of political parties have competed in recent national elections, although current rules demand a party capture at minimum 3.5 percent of the national vote before it can claim DPR seats through proportional representation.

Thus far, the institutionalization of particular parties appears a long way off. With the exception of Golkar, most major parties operate around strong figures, their personalities, and even famous families. Partai Demokrat is associated with Susilo Bambang Yudhoyono, PDI-P with Megawati Sukarnoputri, and now the Great Indonesia Movement Party with Prabowo Subianto. Successful leadership succession within parties and greater levels of trust and confidence from the electorate will be important markers of a more stable party system. Unfortunately, money politics, vote-buying scandals, and voter registration fraud are increasing problems in Indonesia and a cause of disillusionment and cynicism among voters. Such problems do not yet delegitimize election outcomes, but if they remain unaddressed, a loss of faith in democracy could grow. Combined with the country's judicial system, which is also prone to corruption, Indonesia's political parties remain a weak element in the country's democratic development.

Political Islam

As the largest Muslim country in the world, Indonesia has a relatively admirable record of integrating Islam into its secular political system. Political Islam, or the participation in political life motivated by Islamic values, has not produced the degree of instability, conflict, or antigovernment rebellion experienced elsewhere in Southeast Asia. Revolutionary Islam has proven more vexing to governments in Thailand and the Philippines. In these countries, Muslim minorities have been oppressed and have engaged in long-standing, Muslim-based separatist movements. In Malaysia, where large, non-Muslim Chinese and Indian minorities live side by side with a Muslim majority, political Islam has proven more divisive than in Indonesia.

Nevertheless, political Islam does animate Indonesian politics, and the more open period of post-Suharto politics has expanded the range and intensity of its recent involvement. Although religious and sectarian clashes erupt on occasion in parts of the archipelago (sometimes with deadly consequences), a broad-based, organized Islamic revolution on the scale experienced in Iran and Afghanistan is not featured in Indonesian experience. Thousands of varied religious institutions and strands of Islamic expression exist in Indonesia. This Islamic milieu weaves itself into the fabric of Indonesian society in a manner that defies traditional or monolithic characterization. Islam in Indonesia is temporally dynamic and socially contested.

Indonesian Muslims have a reputation for practicing a moderate, if syncretic, brand of Islam. About 99 percent of Muslims in Indonesia are Sunni. The heterogeneity that characterizes Islamic belief and practice in the country is rooted in the division between *santri* and *abangan* cultures within Java as well as other forces of *aliran* (i.e., vertical divisions across society produced by ethno-linguistic differences and identity politics). *Santri*, or pious Muslims, generally represent political Islam, whereas *abangan*, or nominal Muslims, lean toward secular politics and absorb cultural influence from *priyayi* traditions (pre-Islamic, Javanese-Hindu customs and supernatural beliefs). In Indonesian politics the dichotomy between *santri* and *abangan* drives much of political Islam, including much of the Islamic antipathy toward a hegemonic *Pancasila* ideology.[17]

Aliran forces influence how Islam is interpreted and practiced from group to group and region to region. Loyalties in Indonesia have traditionally been to the group first, exacerbating ethnic tensions but mitigating the formation of superior Islamic identity or a single Indonesian Muslim narrative. Because of these factors, Islamic revolution is unlikely to emerge or achieve a hegemonic role in Indonesian political life. Moreover, as Indonesia's rulers could attest, it is not easy to mobilize a diverse population of nearly a quarter-billion people for any cause, be it *Marhaenism*, communism, or some singular Islamic vision.

Since independence, Indonesia's leaders have nevertheless remained cautious about the potential for political Islam to coalesce into a larger political movement with revolutionary aims. By embracing the national ideology of *Pancasila*, radical Islamist aspirations have been suppressed by successive regimes that have embraced Islam's presence alongside the security imperatives of ethnic and religious diversity. Further, state patronage and regulation of Islam have often placed serious parameters around Islamic education and influences from outside Indonesia, especially under Suharto. By demobilizing Islam, Suharto, with an *abangan-priyayi* upbringing, began to co-opt Islam for seeming political gain. Suharto became a *hajji* (pilgrim to Mecca) and supported the creation of the Indonesian Association of Muslim Intellectuals (ICMI). He also developed a purposeful program to send the country's Islamic scholars to study at centers in Europe and North America, thus avoiding the more radical mosques in the Middle East.[18]

In Indonesia today, political Islam's largest role is found not in extremist movements but in political parties and mainstream social associations that champion Islamic values without pressing for the creation of an Islamic state. Prominent political parties include the United Development Party (PPP) and the Prosperous Justice Party (*Partai Keadilan Sejahtera*, or PKS). While both claim Islam as their ideology, neither advocates Islamic republicanism or state-based sharia (Islamic law). Together the PPP and PKS garnered over 16 million votes in the 2014 DPR elections. These numbers are strong but pale in comparison to the more politically significant social organizations, such as Nahdlatul Ulama and Muhammadiyah.

Dating back to the 1920s, Nahdlatul Ulama formed in response to rising European Christian activity, secularism, and communism within Indonesia. During much of the Suharto period, Abdurrahman Wahid served as NU's leader. Wahid formally "removed" NU from politics in 1984 by withdrawing from the Suharto-forced coalition of Islamic parties that composed the PPP. Concentrating instead on the organization's own development, Wahid's NU sought to assist Indonesia's Muslims through the religious and social concerns arising from rapid economic change. Wahid later founded Forum Demokrasi in response to Suharto's creation of ICMI. At the time of Suharto's resignation in 1998, NU was poised to reemerge as a political force with its estimated 35 million members. Though it has thus far resisted the temptation to transform into a political party, NU does throw its support behind Islamic-oriented parties and candidates, such as Wahid himself. Widespread on Java, NU finds support among rural Javanese and in religious schools.

Muhammadiyah and its female organizational arm, Nasyiatul Aisyiyah (Young Women), claim membership of over 30 million. Muhammadiyah's primary goals are religious and educational. It sets up schools to promote Sunni Islam while also educating about democracy and public health. One of its most recent influential leaders, Amien Rais, helped force Suharto's resignation in 1998 and later led the national assembly. Nasyiatul Aisyiyah, founded in 1917, has sought to define women's roles and, more recently, Arabism within Islam. Expressing disdain for fundamentalist Islam, women in Aisyiyah work against extremist ideologies that give little space for women within Islam.[19] The organization has even partnered with USAID to fund health projects and promote family planning with noted success.[20]

At the other extreme from parties and religious associations that engage Indonesian society through legitimate political channels are Islamist organizations that employ violence and terror to advance their chief cause: destroying the republic and creating an Islamic state. Although on the fringe of Indonesian society (socially and numerically), these groups create significant political problems for Indonesia and overall foreign relations. Some groups, such as Laskar Jihad (jihad fighters), instigate communal violence targeting nonbelievers;

others, such as Jemaah Islamiyah (JI), seek international attention by targeting foreign interests.

Movements favoring the creation of an Islamic republic date back to the 1950s; however, the most radical groups in Indonesia formed within the past two decades. Jemaah Islamiyah was formed in 1993. The group was tied to five major bombings in Bali and Jakarta from 2002 to 2005 and later saw its top officials arrested and brought to trial. Yudhoyono, in particular, launched more aggressive efforts to weaken JI than did his predecessors. In 2008, when JI bombers were convicted and executed and the organization was finally declared illegal, few Indonesians came to its defense. It has since renounced violence within Indonesia as a strategy of jihad. Smaller pro-violence jihadi groups, animated by events in Syria, have emerged in Indonesia but thus far have remained on the margins.

Mainstream society within Indonesia, increasingly convinced of the pernicious effects of radical organizations, currently demonstrates a willingness to allow elected officials political space to deal with extremist groups. Bombings in July 2009 targeted two Western hotels and killed nine people, including the two attackers. The architect of these and previous attacks, Malaysian fugitive Nordin Top, was later killed in a raid by Indonesian security forces. In 2010, police raided a Jakarta Internet café and killed one of the last suspects in the 2002 Bali bombings. That same year, the British-based risk analysis firm Maplecroft, designer of the Terrorism Risk Index, removed Indonesia from its list of countries at "extreme risk" for terrorist activity. Because of ongoing Islamist unrest in their Muslim-majority provinces, Thailand and the Philippines are regularly ranked higher than Indonesia on such indices.

Military
For much of Indonesia's postindependence period, especially under Suharto, the military pervasively intervened in politics. Aside from Burma, no other Southeast Asian nation had experienced the same degree of military involvement in day-to-day governance. However, the political role of the Indonesian Armed Forces, or the Tentara Nasional Indonesia, has decreased dramatically in the post–New Order era, although its latent power to act remains strong and should not be discounted given the country's history.

Once the political role of the military was enshrined in state doctrine, its leaders set forth the notion of *dwi fungsi*, or dual function, ensuring for itself both a security and a sociopolitical role in Indonesian society. Through legislation, this dual role legitimated the military's involvement as cabinet officers, governors of provinces, members of the legislative body, and leaders of Golkar. Until Suharto's overthrow, it was impossible to imagine an Indonesian administration without the active participation of army generals. The agenda of *reformasi* includes professionalizing the military and dismantling military *dwi fungsi* by removing generals from their designated seats in the assembly and their spots on corporate boards, where many "soldier-tycoons" amassed great wealth in the 1980s and 1990s. Since 2004, no appointed seats for the military or anybody else exist in the MPR. Today, only elected representatives govern Indonesia's lawmaking bodies, as well as the republic's chief executive office.

STATE-SOCIETY RELATIONS AND DEMOCRACY

The diversity of Indonesia's population and its demographic character make the country difficult to control. This diversity, among other forces, has shaped the process of state building, the autonomy and legitimacy of the state, and the development of civil society and democracy.

Like the Philippines, much of Indonesia experienced a long colonial rule, during which its economy served Dutch interests through the exploitation of Indonesia's people and natural resources. The impact of the Spaniards and Americans on the Philippines was greater than that of the Dutch on the Indonesians, perhaps because there had been powerful indigenous empires in Sumatra and Java before the Dutch arrived, whereas there had been none in the Philippines before the Spanish arrived. The Japanese occupation of Indonesia, while not as devastating as in the Philippines, was an important event. Moreover, Indonesia waged a four-year war against the Dutch, who returned to retake their former colony after the defeat of the Japanese; thus, a revolutionary war led to rebellions and ethnic-based regional struggles between contenders for power.

Sukarno's fusion of his own political charisma and power to build a young state was effective in bringing unity to diversity, but narrower economic and political failures undid his regime. Never fully autonomous from the powerful forces of a military with praetorian ambitions, a communist insurgency, and Javanese societal prejudice, the political legitimacy of Sukarno's young state was fragile. In spite of his successes in leading Indonesia to independence and fashioning a new state ideology (*Pancasila*), a lingua franca (*Bahasa Indonesia*), and a singular economic philosophy (*Marhaenism*), Sukarno ultimately discovered that grand ideals alone were not enough to sustain state legitimacy and personal authority.

Following the *Gestapu* coup of 1965, Indonesian society experienced a major bloodbath when about half a million Indonesians were killed. The violence spread as racial, religious, ethnic, social, economic, and political differences were judged to be sufficient cause for mass killings. What began as a political cleansing to oust communists became an orgy of killing and a breakdown of law and order. The Communist Party of Indonesia (PKI), tallying 3.5 million members (and 23.5 million in affiliated organizations), was virtually annihilated. The ideals and state institutions created by Sukarno collapsed and proved unable to protect vulnerable citizens. His collapsing state was replaced by a repressive military state born from chaos. Gradually, the New Order evolved into a stable state dependent on tight political controls and performance legitimization.

In contrast to the Sukarno era, a strong, autonomous state emerged under Suharto. He brought various groups of people into his ruling circle to create this autonomy. Suharto's oft-celebrated technocrats brought order to the economy and thereby managed to strengthen his claim to power. Even more important, Suharto won the ongoing loyalty of military leaders who consolidated their power around the regime and their access to economic opportunity. Suharto depoliticized and co-opted all institutional and societal forces to maintain and enhance state power. Forever distrustful of politics, Suharto intimidated some societal groups with military coercion under *dwi fungsi*, emasculated others through administrative corporatism, and bought off others by giving them a stake in rapid economic growth. Suharto's troubled legitimacy caused close observers at the time to predict another episode of political tragedy.[21]

Today, all potentially powerful groups are essentially integrated into the polity. The military, once overwhelmingly powerful, is now taking its place as a state-based interest group amid an array of formal and informal pressure groups. The elected legislature is rising in its importance and proving capable of checking the abuse of presidential power (e.g., Wahid's). Even the most prominent societal groups once left out of the system (i.e., political Islam and Muslim parties) are now functioning freely and competing within a democratic constitutional framework. Although the state ideology of *Pancasila* is more openly challenged than in the past, the absence of forced allegiance to it (or prohibition against it) has allowed for its organic development and its own post-Suharto legitimacy.

Vis-à-vis society, Indonesia's state has weakened since the collapse of bureaucratic authoritarianism. Nevertheless, the state is not necessarily vulnerable to hegemonic control by a single group. Here, Indonesia's diversity and growing pluralism are assets to its political development. The current trend embracing constitutionalism strengthens the durability of political order and state capability. The extent to which the diverse set of players in Indonesian politics further legitimate constitutionalism, the rule of law, and sanctioned authority will determine the possibility of a resurgent, strong state. Ethnic groups, political parties, political Islam, Javanese elites, the military, the business community, ruralites, non-Muslims, intellectuals, journalists, and civil society organizations (CSOs) must find consensus in the rules of the game while simultaneously keeping state power at bay and keeping from falling prey to particularistic interests or dominance.

Until 1999, liberal democracy had not flourished in postindependence Indonesia. The one attempt to fashion such a system, which lasted from 1950 to 1957, featured multiple political parties and a parliamentary government. However, that period was a time of great political unrest as the country moved from dependence on its Dutch colonizers to independence. Sukarno, who was president during the transition, paid little attention to necessary day-to-day administrative tasks; nevertheless, the democratic system was blamed for the collapse of the economy and the country's infrastructure. Consequently, Sukarno's notion of a unique, indigenous form of guided democracy was readily embraced as more fitting for Indonesia.

Traditional Indonesian political culture is essentially hierarchical and authoritarian: authorities at the center do not tolerate opposition that will endanger the potency of the state.[22] Sukarno's notion of democracy appeared to fit traditional Javanese value systems in which power is bestowed on one person, usually a sultan. From an Indonesian perspective, therefore, guided democracy was the most effective way to make policy, even if that process is not compatible with Western notions of representative and accountable government.

From a Western perspective, on the other hand, guided democracy ensured the perpetuation of Sukarno's power at the expense of the liberties and openness available under liberal democracy. From this vantage point, real democracy was destroyed not by a traditional culture but by corrupt, power-hungry politicians who established repressive policies and authoritarian institutions to retain their positions. Similarly, Suharto's New Order can be viewed from this perspective as the archetypal authoritarian administration that mouthed the virtues of democracy but practiced the politics of dictatorship.

Rejecting both of these extreme positions, a younger generation of educated officials emerged to suggest that accountability and civil liberties are not exclusive values of the West, and that as Indonesia's population becomes educated, informed, and economically developed, there is no reason why Western democratic institutions cannot be compatible with Indonesian culture. Adding to the demand for a more open society were the numerous CSOs in Indonesia, representing women's groups, trade unions, student organizations, labor, and various causes. Their growth in the 1990s represented rising dissatisfaction with the lack of liberty and the suffocating restrictions under the New Order.

Emerging from the Suharto era, many Indonesians did not want Indonesia to be viewed as having an anachronistic political system in an era of democratization. The transition from Suharto to Habibie to Wahid was chaotic but set the stage for meaningful constitutional reform. The 1999 elections were a watershed development, setting the precedent for open party competition. Significantly, the willingness of Megawati and Yudhoyono to play by the rules and endure political victory or failure without resorting to power grabs, emergency declarations, or extraconstitutional measures is the greatest contribution they could offer to Indonesia's democratic future. The contrast here with Thai elites and the never-dying impulse to turn to the king or the military during political crisis, and the Philippine practice of presidential-military alliances and martial law declarations, is indeed notable.

Across the Indonesian polity, an expectation of constitutionally correct politics is taking root. A broad-based political settlement between state and society appears to have emerged—one grounded in democratic pluralism. As a state, the Republic of Indonesia has transcended serious challenges by ethnic groups, political movements, and undemocratic leaders. Following Sukarno's highly volatile balancing act, Suharto's authoritarian New Order, and a wretched crisis-driven transition, Indonesia's young, constitutionally based regime is showing potential and a will for consolidation. Such a feat, however, must be read against the history of previous regimes and their undoing. Events have overtaken Indonesia's political system before and may do so again in the future. For now, however, state-society relations and the country's democratic institutions appear to be transcending previous threats, including the forces of *aliran* and ethnic separatism.

ECONOMY AND DEVELOPMENT

The Indonesian economy is the largest in Southeast Asia. In the developing world only China, India, Brazil, and Mexico have larger economies when standardized for purchasing power parity. Even as a demographic giant, Indonesia's economic gains in recent decades have rendered the country's per capita gross national income ($3,650) higher than many of its less populated regional neighbors (Philippines, Vietnam, Cambodia, Laos, Burma, and Timor-Leste). Having averaged over 6 percent GDP growth each year from 1965 to 1997, during the Asian financial crisis Indonesia sunk to an alarming negative GDP growth of −13.1 percent. Since that nadir, economic growth has climbed back to a high in 2011 of 6.5 percent. Impressively, Indonesia's economy did not contract during the 2008–2009 financial crisis, and from 2011 to 2014 its economy averaged over 5.7 percent annual GDP growth. However, the global decline in commodities prices in 2015 pushed the country's growth trajectory downward.

Sukarno's "revolutionary" economic system under guided democracy was isolationist and xenophobic, skewed to meet ideological goals rather than the needs of the citizenry. Suharto's New Order economics sought to provide order to replace disorder and rationality to replace irrationality so that economic development would become the yardstick by which the success of his regime would be measured.

For the most part, the yardstick measured steady although not spectacular growth, but it was enough to buy a substantial share of popular support and political stability. The means to this end were a series of five-year plans to improve the public welfare, realize a financial bonanza from oil revenues, follow the advice of economic technocrats, repair the infrastructure, and begin to rely on the private sector for the necessary capital, structural change, and productivity.[23] The technocrats behind the recovery came to be known as the "Berkeley Mafia," a group of Indonesian economists trained at the University of California–Berkeley in the 1950s. Although the results were generally positive, some difficulties were encountered, including widespread income disparity, corruption, and mismanaged industries. Over time, a countertrend developed within the New Order for greater economic nationalism.

The most badly managed company was the government-owned oil industry, Pertamina, which went bankrupt in the 1970s. Led by President Suharto's colleague General Ibnu Sutowo, Pertamina incurred huge debts from lavish spending on useless projects. When oil prices dropped precipitously from $34 per barrel in 1981 to $8 per barrel in the mid-1980s, economic growth in Indonesia fell correspondingly, ending a decade of greatly increased government outlays for education, infrastructure, and communications. The Indonesian economy's dependence on the oil sector in the 1980s was evident in that oil exports accounted for 78 percent of export earnings, and oil revenues accounted for 70 percent of government income at that time.[24] A decade earlier, by contrast, oil revenues had accounted for less than 20 percent of government income.

During the 1980s, policies to promote exports and foreign investment more aggressively replaced the policies of import substitution favored by economic nationalists and characterized by protectionism and heavy government intervention in distributing capital. The success of the new policy was shown by the fact that foreign investment commitments rose more than threefold over a three-year period, from $1.4 billion in 1987 to $4.7 billion in 1989.

Part of the reason for the great increase in foreign investment under Suharto was that Indonesia, like Thailand, became a major assembly area for manufacturers from Hong Kong, Singapore, Taiwan, South Korea, and even the United States. Most investments were in labor-intensive, low-technology industries such as footwear, food canning, textiles, and wood processing, where Indonesia's low wages attracted entrepreneurs from higher-wage countries.[25] In addition, the indigenous Chinese, who have long been active in the economy, were given greater leeway in return for their support of Golkar. Officials and military officers provided Chinese business executives with protection and useful legislation, while in return the Chinese supplied capital and access to profits from their businesses. These Chinese businesspeople, called *cukong* (boss), were resented by Indonesian entrepreneurs, who viewed the *cukong* system as corrupt and exclusive.

In addition to growth tainted with corruption, other paradoxical legacies of Indonesia's rapid economy emerged. Although some new wealth trickled down to allow a small middle class to emerge, the rich quickly became richer. Absolute poverty declined markedly, but many Indonesians continued to live a subsistence existence. Foreign investment flooded in, but pleasing investors and ensuring their confidence came at the expense of labor rights and the local environment.

Although foreign investment leveled off in the 1990s as China and Vietnam became cheap-labor competitors, the cumulative effect of investment left the country vulnerable, as demonstrated by massive capital flight caused by the late 1990s "Asian Contagion." While the collapse of the Thai baht triggered a regional crisis, the depths to which Indonesia sank were a result of the inherent weaknesses of the New Order economy, exacerbated by international exuberance for emerging markets and reckless flows of hot money.

In the years before the crisis, the New Order administration moved in contradictory directions, sometimes supporting market mechanisms and liberalization and other times state intervention and the protection of conglomerates controlled by Suharto's family or cronies. The overall strength of the economy and the high rates of economic growth led to some careless policy choices and regulations, most notably nationalist and protectionist policies Suharto engineered to protect those closest to him.

Hutomo Mandala Putra, known as "Tommy Suharto"—a favored son of the president—benefited greatly from his father's patronage at state expense. He was given rights to produce the "national car," the Timor (which is actually imported from South Korea). Tommy's exclusive tax exemptions and tariff concessions allowed him to sell the Timor at about half the price of competing vehicles. The United States challenged Suharto's support for Indonesia's national car on the grounds that to exempt it from taxes levied against imported cars was unfair. Domestically, many wealthy Indonesians refused to buy the Timor, citing its poor performance as an excuse that often masked their contempt for the family dynasty's use of its economic privileges to attempt to corner one of the most promising markets in Indonesia.

Tommy was also presented with lucrative contracts with the Burmese State Law and Order Restoration Council (SLORC) and was awarded Indonesia's trade monopoly for cloves, a position that provided him with the ability to generate tremendous revenue. His siblings received similarly lucrative contracts. His eldest sister, Tutut Siti Hadijanti Rukmana, held a controlling interest in a company that collected revenues from Java's principal toll roads, occupied a senior post in Golkar, and was being groomed as a potential successor to her father. All of Suharto's six children, in fact, were involved in the nation's primary industries: automobiles, petrochemicals, computers, oil, and satellite communications.

Suharto responded to the national community only when the pressure to do so was particularly great. For example, in 1997 he stepped in to block a ministry recommendation that effectively would have forced parents to buy children's shoes from a company owned by the president's eldest grandson. The issue had been on the front pages of national newspapers since it was made public that the ministry had recommended that all elementary schoolchildren wear identical shoes, to be sold for $10.70 a pair. Indonesia's daily minimum wage at the time was about $3. The shoes were dubbed "national shoes" by the public, in reference to the "national car" being manufactured by Tommy Suharto.

In 1997 and 1998, when emergency packages were negotiated with the IMF, new details of Suharto family nepotism and corruption percolated to the surface. Public disdain for the Suharto family grew. The austerity measures imposed as part of loan conditionality proved painful for not only Suharto's family and associates but also, by consequence, Indonesia's general population.

The IMF viewed the economic edifice Suharto had created as the cause of Indonesia's woes and dismantled it virtually overnight. In large part, the Suharto-tied monopolies, as well as importer arrangements, distorted prices of standard goods and items, not just automobiles, cloves, and satellite communications. The IMF-imposed lifting of subsidies, provoking a further slide of the rupiah, caused shortages and huge price increases on rice, cooking oil, instant noodles, paper, and cement. The economic crisis before the IMF measures, itself severely disrupting, demanded economic stimulus, not austerity. At the time when state capital was most needed to buoy an economy suffering capital flight and loss of demand, and when Indonesia's laid-off workers needed subsidized benefits most, IMF measures forced sudden price volatility and sudden budget austerity, and directed $43 billion in rescue funds to pay off international banks and creditors. Unemployment skyrocketed to 15–20 percent. Protesters turned their rage on Suharto's administration, Chinese businesspeople, and the IMF. Social disruption arose. The performance legitimacy of the New Order collapsed.

The Habibie and Wahid administrations suffered the burden of cleaning up the mess. Habibie's tenure, tainted by his Suharto connections, was dominated by political crisis and East Timor's independence, and Wahid, whom many considered incapable of economic thinking, faced economic conditions that would frighten the most skilled policy managers. Sukarnoputri more capably brought stability to the economy, but it was not until Yudhoyono's presidency that "recovery" became more of a reality than a distant hope.

Yudhoyono implemented a set of economic policies designed to reduce unemployment, provide relief to the poorest Indonesians, and restore confidence in the embattled financial sector. To these ends, he invested in infrastructure development and sponsored cash packages and subsidies on rice and housing for the poorest strata. He also developed a deposit insurance scheme while encouraging the growth of sharia banking. Yudhoyono also withdrew Indonesia from membership in OPEC (the Organization of Petroleum Exporting Countries) in 2008 as the country transitioned to being a net oil importer. The move reflected the growth and dynamism of the domestic economy. The outcome of these reforms and others was generally positive; foreign investment confidence improved, as did perceptions related to business corruption.[26] Indonesia's past reputation as a difficult foreign investment environment began to change. A 2011 BBC survey of 24,000 people across 24 countries discovered that Indonesia was home to the most entrepreneur-friendly culture in the world, ahead of other top countries, the United States, Canada, and Australia.[27]

Despite New Order corruption, severe economic crisis, and years of painful economic recovery, the quality of life of average Indonesians has improved significantly over the past four decades. Life expectancy, under fifty years in 1965, now stands at seventy-two years. Primary school enrollment climbed from 41 percent to 94 percent, and literacy is now at 99 percent. Astonishingly, over a forty-year period when its population grew by 75 million people (the equivalent of two Californias), Indonesia saw its poverty rate lower from 60 percent to 13 percent. In terms of the Human Development Index, Indonesia's value from 1975 to 2014 went from 0.47 to 0.68, a more dramatic swing than that experienced by any other Southeast Asian country or other impressive developers such as China, Mexico, and Brazil.

Nevertheless, although it achieved in some aggregate measures, Indonesia only met four of the eight 2000–2015 UN Millennium Development Goals. Disappointingly, it failed to meet targets related to improving maternal health, access to clean water and sanitation, HIV infection rates, and ensuring environmental stability.

FOREIGN RELATIONS

As in other Southeast Asian nations, the primary goal of Indonesia's postindependence foreign policy has been to sustain the republic's security. Sukarno's means to this end relied on anti-Western nationalism; he was opposed to what he called the "old established forces," or "OLDEFOS," and allied with what he called the "newly emerging forces," or "NEFOS." OLDEFOS included the neo-imperialist nations and their allies, led by the United States. NEFOS, on the other hand, included the "progressive" third-world and communist nations, locked in struggle against OLDEFOS. Sukarno's *Konfrontasi* against Malaysia, which began in 1962 and ended in 1965, was described as a classic example of a NEFOS struggle against an OLDEFOS lackey. Supporting Sukarno's foreign policy against the agents of neocolonialism, colonialism, and imperialism was the PKI.

When his New Order was inaugurated, Suharto ended *Konfrontasi*, banned the PKI, and reentered the international arena with a pro-Western, anticommunist foreign policy. New Order Indonesia's quiet support for ASEAN and the Zone of Peace, Freedom, and Neutrality in Southeast Asia reflected its leadership's lower profile in international relations. During the Suharto regime, Indonesia played only a minor role in international affairs, despite the fact that the nation was the fourth-most-populated country in the world and was of immense importance economically, geographically, and strategically.

The major exception to Indonesia's nonintrusive participation in foreign affairs was Suharto's decision to invade East Timor in 1975. This action exacerbated a vigorous guerrilla insurgency movement, which continued throughout East Timor's annexation. Habibie's decision to allow an independence referendum sparked further violence and, from an Indonesian perspective, resulted in the humiliating presence of international peacekeepers and UN authorities.

Relations between Indonesia and the People's Republic of China improved gradually following two decades of tension resulting from the *Gestapu* coup. As part of ASEAN, Indonesia gradually moved foreign policy closer to that of the other ASEAN countries. Sharing interests in checking Vietnamese power, Thailand and China made accommodations with each other in the 1970s. Indonesia, on the other hand, took until August 1990 to formally establish diplomatic relations with China, ending twenty-five years of hostility. It was not until the presidency of Megawati Sukarnoputri that any significant bilateral efforts were made to expand trade between the two countries. Chinese President Xi Jinping's visit to a 2014 summit in Bali resulted in upgrading the China-Indonesia relationship to a "comprehensive strategic partnership." Still, the United States, Japan, Singapore, and other Asian and European countries have been Indonesia's primary markets and sources of investment to date. Development assistance from the United Nations, the World Bank, the IMF, and bilateral partners has shaped Indonesia's macro- and micro-level economic policies as well, but in 2008 Indonesia was invited to join the G-20, the Group of 20 countries that control 85 percent of world GDP.

Unlike Singapore, the Philippines, and Thailand, which emerged as overt and quiet partners in the United States' post–September 11 war on terrorism, Indonesia proved a more reluctant partner and was instinctively leery of US power and its misuse. Sukarnoputri's government publicly opposed George W. Bush's invasions of Afghanistan and Iraq. Susilo Bambang Yudhoyono later welcomed tsunami-related humanitarian assistance from the United States as well as resources to support counterterrorism within Indonesia. General foreign policy skepticism of the United States' relationship with Israel and its war on terrorism persisted through the end of the Bush administration.

Barack Obama's election in late 2008 opened a new door to improving relations between the third- and fourth-most-populous countries in the world. Only days after the historic election, and before Obama had spent a day in office, President Yudhoyono had already called Obama's foreign policy "refreshing" and proposed a strategic partnership with the United States that included stronger people-to-people relations. Raised partly in Indonesia, Obama, he said, "spoke our language, knew our culture, ate our food, played with Indonesian friends . . . [and] experienced the inner soul of Indonesia."[28] Barack Obama sent Secretary of State Hillary Clinton to Asia in February 2009. Children from the Indonesian school Obama once attended welcomed Clinton with songs and flowers. In a press conference from Jakarta, she celebrated Indonesia's new stability as a Muslim-majority democracy and pledged to work toward a "comprehensive partnership" between the two countries. After two disappointing cancellations, Barack Obama finally visited Indonesia during the 2011 East Asia Summit, which Indonesia hosted.

Home of ASEAN headquarters, Indonesia's regional leadership follows a pragmatic path, although different presidents prioritize Indonesia's role in ASEAN variably. As a non-claimant in the Spratly Islands dispute, Indonesia broadly supports its ASEAN neighbors. In 2010, Yudhoyono's government penned a letter to the United Nations stating that Chinese claims lacked a legal basis and "encroach [on] the legitimate interests of the global community."[29]

After his election in 2014, Joko Widodo returned to Indonesia's tradition of foreign policy independence. Eschewing various multilateral summits and events, Jokowi has emphasized domestic policy priorities, causing some of his ASEAN partners to question his commitment to multilateralism.[30] As commodities markets continued to decline during his first year, however, domestic economic priorities pushed Jokowi outward. With his reform agenda on the back-burner, Jokowi, on a state visit to Washington, DC, in late 2015, met with President Obama and expressed sudden interest in joining the Trans-Pacific Partnership (TPP). He also met with US business groups, hoping to attract more investment to the country's flagging economy.

Internationally, Indonesia's status draws considerable attention among the global Islamic community for its successful economic growth and recent political reform toward political openness. It seeks to foster pan-Islamic unity by offering a moderating voice within the Organization of the Islamic Conference. Its reputation in the Islamic world, nevertheless, took a hit in 2015 for its poor handling of humanitarian relief for Muslim Rohingya refugees forced from Myanmar.

CONCLUSION

In terms of stability, democratic political representation, and civil liberties, Indonesia's political direction today is generally favorable. Although the country is forever challenged by geographic and demographic realities, inertia from its current record of economic growth and democratic institutionalization raises the prospects for continued development. The disruption caused by the Asian economic crisis may have been deeper in Indonesia than elsewhere in Southeast Asia, but a favorable democratic dividend has resulted. From the ashes of Suharto's collapse formed rising expectations for democracy and demands for accountable government. Since his death in 2008, ten years after his regime collapsed, Indonesia has more than symbolically transformed itself into a new political system.

Today, constitutionally correct party activity, lawmaking, and peaceful leadership rivalries are encouraging developments of movement toward democratic consolidation. In Indonesia, political power is now gained, wielded, challenged, and transferred legitimately, and the country is developing the concept of loyal opposition in a plural political framework.[31] Although setbacks related to corruption and curtailed political rights have occurred, they have been broadly condemned. In everyday Indonesian politics, the electorate concerns itself with the rule of law, party competition, and holding elected leaders accountable, in contrast to past concerns about the legitimacy of the state or its regime.

How long the current trend in building institutions of representation and accountability will endure remains an open question, but signs of sustainability are undeniable. Unlike the Philippines (troubled by an entrenched oligarchy), Thailand (prone to extraconstitutional impulses), or Singapore, Malaysia, and Cambodia (controlled by illiberal, hegemonic parties), Indonesia is seeing a growing consensus across society that democracy is desirable and possible. Representative government, parliamentary governance, and open party competition are now ideals embraced by ethnic groups, social classes, mainstream political Islam, and (importantly) the rising generation. Within this new framework of expectations, political winners are afforded legitimacy and political losers demonstrate a willingness to play a constructive, oppositional role. If the political system can be responsive to those receiving the fewest economic benefits, the consolidation of democracy in the world's largest Muslim country may be within reach. Sukarno's vision of *Bhinneka Tunggal Ika* (Unity in Diversity) remains Indonesia's central challenge, but the nascent institutions of the new era of liberal democratic reform show encouraging potential.

NOTES

1. In Leo Suryadinata, Aris Ananta, and Evi Nurvidya Arifin's *Indonesia's Population: Ethnicity and Religion in a Changing Political Landscape* (Singapore: Institute of Southeast Asian Studies, 2003), the authors use the Indonesian government's 2000 Census to identify eleven major ethnic groups: Javanese (42 percent), Sundanese (15 percent), Malay (3.5 percent), Madurese (3.4 percent), Batak (3 percent), Minangkabau (2.7 percent), Betawi (2.5 percent), Buginese (2.5 percent), Bantenese (2 percent), Banjarese (1.7 percent), and Balinese (1.5 percent). Other ethnic groups compose the remaining 20 percent of the Indonesian population. Many scholars believe the 2000 Census underreported Indonesian-Chinese, who compose up to 3 percent of the total population (compared to the 0.9 percent officially reported). Given Indonesia's history of anti-Chinese activity and riots, the ethnic Chinese can also be considered a major ethnic group of Indonesia.

2. For a sampling of views of the *Gestapu* coup, see Benedict Anderson and Ruth T. McVey, *A Preliminary Analysis of the October 1, 1965, Coup in Indonesia*, Interim Report Series, Modern Indonesia Project (Ithaca, NY: Cornell University Press, 1971); Arnold C. Brackman, *The Communist Collapse in Indonesia* (New York: Norton, 1969); Arthur J. Dommen, "The Attempted Coup in Indonesia," *China Quarterly* 25 (January 1966): 144–168; John Hughes, *Sukarno: A Coup That Misfired, a Purge That Ran Wild* (New York: McKay, 1967); Justus van der Kroef, "Origins of the 1965 Coup in Indonesia: Probabilities and Alternatives," *Journal of Southeast Asian Studies* 3 (September 1972): 277–298; Tarzie Vittachi, *The Fall of Sukarno* (New York: Praeger, 1967); and W. F. Wertheim, "Suharto and the Untung Coup: The Missing Link," *Journal of Contemporary Asia* 1, no. 2 (Winter 1970): 50–57.

3. David McKendrick, "Indonesia in 1991: Growth, Privilege, and Rules," *Asian Survey* 32, no. 2 (February 1992): 103–105.

4. See chapter 9 for a more detailed account of Timor-Leste's independence from Indonesia.

5. Rita Smith Kipp, "Indonesia in 2003: Terror's Aftermath," *Asian Survey* 44, no. 1 (January/February 2004): 65.

6. According to the US Geological Survey, the energy released from the earthquake causing the tsunami equaled 474 megatons of TNT or 23,000 Hiroshima-sized nuclear

bombs. See http://earthquake.usgs.gov/earthquakes/eqinthenews/2004/us2004slav/faq.php.

7. Damien Kingsbury, "Indonesia in 2007: Unmet Expectations, Despite Improvement," *Asian Survey* 48, no. 1 (January/February 2008): 46.

8. David G. Timberman, "Yudhoyono's Re-Election: Can SBY and Indonesia Up Their Game?" *East Asia Forum*, July 10, 2009, www.eastasiaforum.org/2009/07/10/yudhoyonos-re-election-can-sby-and-indonesia-up-their-game.

9. Marcus Mietzner, "Indonesia in 2014: Jokowi and the Repolarization of Post-Soeharto Politics," *Southeast Asian Affairs*, edited by Daljit Singh (Singapore: Institute of Southeast Asian Studies, 2015), 117–138.

10. Karen Brooks, "Is Indonesia Bound for the BRICs?" *Foreign Affairs* 90, no. 6 (November/December 2011); "Indonesia Surprises with Surge in Economy," *New York Times*, August 6, 2012, www.nytimes.com/2012/08/07/business/global/indonesia-surprises-with-surge-in-economy.html.

11. Mietzner, "Indonesia in 2014."

12. Andi Mallarangeng, a household name in Indonesia, was a classmate of the author's at Northern Illinois University in the 1990s where they took graduate courses together, including a seminar on Indonesian politics taught by Professor Dwight King. At that time, Mallarangeng was a trenchant critic of Suharto's New Order and Suharto family corruption. As a result of the scandal, Mallarangeng was arrested, tried, and sentenced to a four-year prison term that began in 2014.

13. "Game of Shadows," *Tempo* (English), April 21–27, 2014, 11.

14. John Kurtz and James van Zorge, "Overcoming Indonesia's Power Opposition," *Wall Street Journal*, October 19, 2014, www.wsj.com/articles/overcoming-indonesias-powerful-opposition-1413738676.

15. Liam Gammon, "Jokowi's Year of Living Cautiously," *East Asia Forum*, December 12, 2015, www.eastasiaforum.org/2015/12/12/jokowis-year-of-living-cautiously.

16. Leo Suryadinata, "Indonesia," in *Politics in the ASEAN States*, ed. Diane K. Mauzy (Kuala Lumpur: Maricans, 1986), 127.

17. Leo Suryadinata, *Interpreting Indonesian Politics* (Singapore: Times Academic Press, 1998), 29.

18. Michael Vatikiotis, *Indonesian Politics under Suharto* (London: Routledge, 1993), 127.

19. Pieternella van Doorn-Harder, *Women Shaping Islam: Reading the Qur'an in Indonesia* (Urbana: University of Illinois Press, 2006), 1.

20. "U.S. Lauds Muhammadiyah Role in Indonesia," *Antara News*, April 3, 2006, www.antara.co.id/en/print/?id=1144054753.

21. Mochtar Pabottingi, "Indonesia: Historicizing the New Order's Legitimacy Dilemma," in *Political Legitimacy in Southeast Asia: The Quest for Moral Authority*, ed. Muthiah Alagappa (Stanford, CA: Stanford University Press, 1995), 255.

22. Ulf Sundhaussen, "Indonesia: Past and Present Encounters with Democracy," in *Democracy in Developing Countries: Asia*, ed. Larry Diamond, Juan J. Linz, and Seymour Martin Lipset (Boulder, CO: Lynne Rienner, 1989), 455.

23. Geoffrey B. Hainsworth, "Indonesia: On the Road to Privatization?" *Current History* 89, no. 545 (March 1990): 121.

24. H. W. Arndt and Hal Hill, "The Indonesian Economy: Structural Adjustment After the Oil Boom," in *Southeast Asian Affairs 1988* (Singapore: Institute of Southeast Asian Studies, 1988), 107.

25. *Far Eastern Economic Review*, April 19, 1990, 42.

26. Kingsbury, "Indonesia in 2007," 41.

27. Andrew Walker, "Entrepreneurs 'Most Supported' in Indonesia," BBC.com, May 25, 2011, www.bbc.co.uk/news/business-13547505.

28. Paul Eckert, "Obama 'Experienced Our Soul'—Indonesian President," Reuters, November 14, 2008, http://blogs.reuters.com/talesfromthetrail/2008/11/14/obama-experienced-our-soul-indonesian-president.

29. Ehito Kimura, "Indonesia in 2010: A Leading Democracy Disappoints on Reform," *Asian Survey* 51, no. 1 (January/February 2011): 194.

30. Prashanth Parameswaran, "Indonesia's Jokowi to Skip APEC in the Philippines," The Diplomat, November 13, 2015, http://thediplomat.com/2015/11/indonesias-jokowi-to-skip-apec-in-the-philippines.

31. Kingsbury, "Indonesia in 2007," 39.

9

TIMOR-LESTE

Occupying only half of a small island in the expansive Indonesian archipelago, the 1.2 million people of Timor-Leste (commonly called East Timor)
have drawn considerable worldwide attention in recent decades. Regrettably,
East Timor joined the post-Holocaust, "never again" narrative in 1975 when it
experienced its first spate of politically motivated mass killings at the hands of
Indonesian invaders. The world did nothing to stop the violence then, but it
responded with measured effectiveness in the face of a genocide-style reprise in
1999 and internal chaos in 2006. Although episodic bloodshed has continued
to torment East Timor in the new international era, foreign occupation and
meddling have bedeviled the small island for over 500 years. Timor-Leste's
story, both sad and triumphant, is of a long, painful struggle for political freedom, independence, and unity.

Facing Indonesia to the north and Australia to the south, Timor Island sits
prominently in the Timor Sea. It is home to rugged terrain, timber resources,
and mountains that reach to 9,000 feet. Three times the size of Cyprus in the
Mediterranean, the island is similarly divided into two political entities. East
Timor occupies the island's eastern half; Indonesia enjoys sovereign control
over its western half (excluding a small East Timor–controlled enclave).

The division of the island runs centuries deep. Portuguese friars first arrived
on its eastern flank during the sixteenth century, followed by the Dutch, who
gained control of the island's western reaches. By the late eighteenth century,
East Timor was under full Portuguese control, although it remained only a
minor star in a global empire that celebrated Brazil in the Americas, Mozam-
bique in Africa, and Goa in India.

For centuries, Portuguese rule of East Timor followed a pattern of general
imperial neglect, although Catholicism developed deep roots in many areas of
the island. Only in the late nineteenth century did Portugal establish more direct
control over the East Timorese. The Portuguese dismantled local political influence, abolished local kingdoms, and commanded forced labor in infrastructure

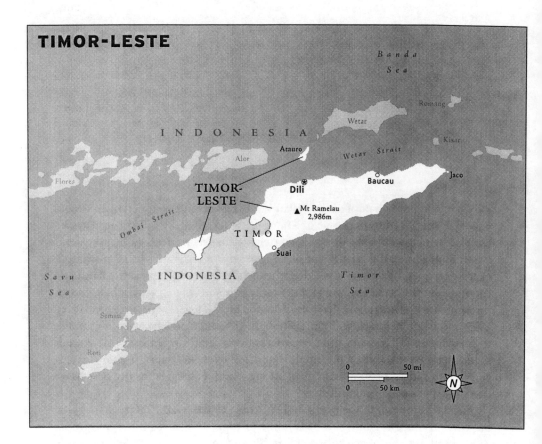

and plantation agriculture. They also put Catholic Jesuits in charge of education and trained up a local political elite of mixed-ethnic "*mesticos* and assimilated natives."[1]

Change did not arrive until World War II, when Dutch and Australian troops, ignoring Portuguese neutrality, overwhelmed the colonists and established East Timor as an Allied military staging ground. Their presence invited Japanese forces, who defeated the Allies in a 1942 battle on the island. As its next occupiers, Japan's warriors brutally demanded submission by East Timor's residents. Tens of thousands were killed, and many islanders were beaten and forced into sexual slavery as comfort women.[2] At the end of the war, Timorese leaders attempted independence but without success. The Portuguese subsequently returned to East Timor for an unwanted three-decade encore of colonial rule.

Independence almost came to East Timor in 1975. In that year, half a world away in Lisbon, a coup d'état led by leftist military officers unleashed widespread Portuguese sentiment to decolonize overseas territories. Timorese aspirants encouraged by these events established Fretilin (an acronym for the Revolutionary Front for an Independent East Timor). Its goal was full independence and statehood. Even as Portuguese administrators experimented with local elections and the planned decolonization of the territory, rival groups claiming leadership of the independence movement sparked a civil conflict. Fretilin forces eventually overcame internal challengers and established control of Dili, the administrative capital. With their plans for an orderly transfer thwarted, Portuguese officials retreated in a messy withdrawal.

On November 28, 1975, Fretilin declared East Timor independent—a "democratic republic." Nine days later, however, shortly after a visit to Jakarta by US president Gerald Ford, Indonesia invaded East Timor, drawing support from some anti-Fretilin groups within the territory. Jakarta's purpose was full annexation and unification of Timor under the Indonesian flag. Decades later, declassified government documents released in Washington, DC, confirmed the Ford administration's knowledge and support of the invasion.[3]

Driven by fears of Fretilin's Marxist orientation, and communist victories in Vietnam, Cambodia, and Laos months earlier, General Suharto's armed forces employed vicious tactics in executing Indonesia's annexation of East Timor. The 35,000 Indonesian "volunteer forces" maliciously attacked Timorese civilians, tortured prisoners, and sprayed chemical napalm on villages to ensure the population's complete submission. During the pacification campaign following the takeover, leftists and refugees were placed in camps or otherwise interned for "reeducation." Out of an original population of 650,000, an estimated 100,000 Timorese (about one in six) lost their lives at the hands of the Indonesian military during the invasion, making it among the worst mass atrocities in modern history in terms of loss of life per capita.[4]

Suharto declared East Timor as Indonesia's twenty-seventh province only months after his forces had occupied it. Although most countries refused to recognize the annexation and condemned Indonesia's actions, Suharto's government experienced only minor international repercussions. The United States and many of its Cold War allies in the region were deafeningly silent on the matter. Australia, a key regional player, formally recognized the annexation as legitimate. By contrast, the United Nations condemned the takeover and granted observer status to Fretilin, inviting its representatives to the General Assembly. However, as with the Palestine Liberation Organization, observer status in the world's premier organization of nations had little effect on dislodging the occupiers or forcing a political settlement.

The ensuing years of Indonesian control of East Timor were marked by continued suppression. Thousands of Timorese resisting Indonesian control were imprisoned or executed. From 1974 to 1999, almost 20,000 Timorese died as a result of armed clashes with Indonesian troops or from extrajudicial killings by occupation authorities; an additional 80,000 Timorese died from preventable illness or starvation.[5] In total, close to one-quarter of East Timor's pre-1975 population died during the twenty-five years of Suharto's occupation. Armed resistance continued during the period, led principally by Fretilin's military wing Falantil (Forces Amadas de Libertação Nacional de Timor Leste). Over time, Falantil weakened and Fretilin turned increasingly to political means, nonviolence, and efforts to raise international awareness of East Timor's plight.

To dampen foreign sympathy and thwart his critics, Suharto closed the annexed territory to outsiders for many years. The tight control of information worked. During the 1980s, the issue of East Timor largely disappeared from the international consciousness.

Suharto's attempt to integrate East Timor with Indonesia failed miserably. Not only did the Catholic population differ from Indonesia's Muslim majority, but there also was too little by way of shared history, language, or culture to bind the disparate populations together. Neither did East Timor's impoverished, battle-scarred populace share in the rapid economic growth sweeping Indonesia. Economic conditions barely improved in the 1980s, with only meager sums of development aid trickling in from Jakarta. Rather than look to Suharto's New Order government, Timorese turned to their local communities and to Catholic leaders for unity and direction.

In 1988, East Timor was finally reopened to outsiders by Suharto. It was a significant shift in policy. Pope John Paul II seized the opportunity to visit a year later, a landmark event that sparked pro-independence demonstrations that were forcibly suppressed by Indonesian security forces. Following the papal visit, a pattern of popular protest and harsh military repression emerged. In 1991, an especially appalling massacre of defenseless protesters occurred at the Santa Cruz cemetery in Dili. Congregating themselves to memorialize the death of Timorese students killed days earlier by security forces, hundreds of young people were suddenly targeted in a vicious melee of bloodshed resulting in 250 dead and countless wounded.[6] Much to the dismay of Indonesian political and military leaders, disturbing video images of the slaughter were smuggled out of East Timor by foreign journalists and broadcasted internationally. Suddenly, East Timor's long saga of occupation drew renewed global attention.

Although never a cause célèbre on the scale of the antiapartheid movement or the ongoing campaign for Tibetan autonomy, East Timor retained a solid core of champions abroad. Throughout the 1990s, numerous international human rights groups stepped up pressure on Suharto's government. The independence movement received a major boost in 1996 when two longtime Timorese leaders, Bishop Carlos Filipe Ximenes Belo and José Ramos-Horta, were jointly awarded the Nobel Peace Prize. The movement also featured an important Mandela-esque face for its cause, that of imprisoned poet-warrior Kay Rala "Xanana" Gusmao, known for his leadership of Fretilin guerrillas and his impassioned prison writings during long years of confinement.

In the end, it wasn't renewed international activism, Nobel-level attention, or Xanana's growing status that triggered events that led to independence. In the new international era, the powerful forces of globalizing markets and Asia's financial collapse put into motion events that ended occupation and Indonesia's claims over the territory. In May 1998, amid the financial contagion rocking Southeast Asia, Suharto's government collapsed in spectacular fashion. Facing unyielding domestic pressure after an IMF bailout helped to expose massive corruption, the once-invincible Suharto resigned in political disgrace. Consequently, East Timor's fate followed a new course.

Only weeks after Suharto's resignation, B. J. Habibie, Indonesia's new president, floated the idea of a "special status" for East Timor. A few months later he announced plans for a UN-supervised referendum where Timorese could choose between "autonomy within Indonesia" or "independence." It was a political gamble. Not only might the vote fall in favor of independence, but offering it could fuel separatist aspirations held by other groups within Indonesia. Smoldering irredentist movements in Aceh and Irian Jaya in particular seemed prone to such trajectories. Undeterred, President Habibie pursued the referendum, believing that Indonesian goodwill on the East Timor controversy could foster international respect for his post-Suharto reform agenda. Desperately enmeshed in Indonesia's worsening economic crisis, Habibie saw East Timor as a mechanism to restore confidence among international observers and foreign investors.

In negotiations over the United Nations' role in the planned referendum, Habibie refused to allow foreign peacekeepers as part of the international mission. The civilian authorities of the United Nations Assistance Mission in East Timor (UNAMET), a $50 million endeavor, carried the mandate to train local officials and educate the public in preparation for the referendum. UNAMET officials would thus rely on local security to see the plebiscite through. For anxious Timorese, Habibie's promised referendum was all that stood between them and independence.

On August 30, 1999, after two disorganized postponements, the residents of East Timor finally went to the ballot box to cast votes on their new political status. The run-up to the referendum was marred by various hostilities and dreadful acts of violence perpetrated by pro-autonomy militias (backed by elements within the Indonesian military). Despite security concerns, the turnout for the referendum was remarkable, surpassing 98 percent of registered voters. The results were equally overwhelming: Nearly four out of five residents (79 percent) voted for full independence.

Reactions to the vote were intense on both sides. Fearful of militias, independence supporters were cautious rather than jubilant. Pro-Indonesia militias, as they had warned, launched a bloody campaign against independence supporters. East Timor suddenly turned chaotic. Enraged thugs attacked civilians with cold brutality. Dili was set ablaze, and disturbing reports of torture and murder surfaced, only to be followed by evidence of mass graves. Fears that political genocide was unfolding grew. Outside Dili, rampaging militias looted and destroyed village after village. Horrific acts of rape and sexual assault accompanied the chaos.[7] Much blame was directed at Habibie and UN officials for failing to plan for post-referendum security. Armed militias even attacked unarmed UNAMET personnel, killing three staffers and exciting fear among the numerous but defenseless foreign personnel. From Jakarta, Habibie first denied the violence was widespread only to later call on the Indonesian military to restore order. Indonesia's generals acted slowly while claiming no responsibility for instigating or participating in the turmoil.

International concern developed further as a refugee crisis mushroomed, sending 250,000 Timorese into Indonesian territory and elsewhere over a matter of days. Among those fleeing were leading independence figures such as Nobel laureate Bishop Belo, who fled to Australia for safety. Alindo Marcal, a well-known Protestant leader, was less fortunate—his corpse was found hacked into pieces in a militia-run refugee camp. In two weeks of postreferendum violence, the death toll had risen to well over a thousand. The extent to which Indonesian generals had armed the local militias or Indonesian soldiers had otherwise participated remained unclear. Most observers believed it was significant.

From his New York office, UN Secretary-General Kofi Annan warned the Indonesian government and its military about "crimes against humanity." He then flew to Jakarta to address the situation personally. Lingering feelings of imperial responsibility reverberated in Portugal. Citizens across Lisbon flooded city streets, forming a six-mile human chain and demanding a forceful international response to end the unrest and killings. East Timor's crisis then grabbed the attention of the UN Security Council but, alas, the United States and China, still reeling from recent events in Kosovo, initially balked at authorizing a coordinated intervention.

As events escalated by the day, a solution surfaced in the form of an Australian-led peacekeeping force. The International Force for East Timor (INTERFET) included troops from Australia, Thailand, Singapore, Bangladesh, Brazil, and other willing countries. Conceding his own ineffectiveness on the matter, Habibie granted permission for INTERFET to enter East Timor. With speed unprecedented in the history of assembling and deploying international peacekeepers, INTERFET troops found themselves in East Timor only five days after their initial authorization. Unwilling to relent, the militias pledged death to all outsiders but soon found themselves overwhelmed by the presence and power of the Blue Berets.

With the violence in check and the refugee crisis under international control, the referendum's results were eventually allowed to follow their intended path to Timorese self-rule. In mid-October 1999, the Indonesian Parliament publicly declared the 1976 annexation of East Timor void. INTERFET was also terminated, replaced by a new UN mission designed to manage East Timor's transition to statehood: the United Nations Transitional Administration in East Timor (UNTAET). In the months that followed, UNTAET successfully governed the country, resettled refugees, and managed elections for a new parliament and president. The UN's highly respected Brazilian-born diplomat Sergio Vieira de Mello functioned during this period as East Timor's chief executive or, as described by his biographer, its "benevolent dictator."[8]

On May 20, 2002, at midnight, Timor-Leste was reborn as a sovereign, independent nation. The nighttime fireworks and celebrations matched the soaring expectations and aspirations of the Timorese people. Present in Dili to memorialize the event were the world's leaders—Kofi Annan, former US president Bill Clinton, and Australian prime minister John Howard. In a show of goodwill, Indonesia's new president, Megawati Sukarnoputri, uncomfortably attended as well. Presiding at the ceremonies was indefatigable freedom fighter and longtime political prisoner Xanana Gusmao, now a free man and the country's first president.

Simultaneous with independence, the United Nations Mission of Support in East Timor (UNMISET) replaced UNTAET to assist the country in early statehood. The new mission included 5,000 security forces and almost 500 foreign advisers. UNMISET, designed to last only one year, stayed three. It expired in 2005 and was replaced by a smaller UN presence of nonsecurity personnel, the United Nations Office in East Timor (UNOTIL).

Timor-Leste's statehood allowed for new opportunities but also created unprecedented challenges. Since its independence, Southeast Asia's newest country has struggled with political infighting, regime instability, and endemic poverty. After a few short years of relative calm, political conditions deteriorated markedly in 2006, less than a year after UNMISET's security forces had left the country. In a sad iteration, political violence returned, and Timor-Leste experienced another round of traumatic street-level chaos, vandalism, mass dislocation, and loss of life. Summoned again to restore peace was an Australian-led peacekeeping contingency, this time under the name Operation Astute. The United Nations followed this event by establishing yet another new mission, the United Nations Integrated Mission in Timor-Leste (UNMIT). Its mandate, originally authorized only through early 2009, included measures to institutionalize democracy with the assistance of civilian advisers and the presence of 1,600 armed UN police officers.

A new round of political hostilities after parliamentary elections in 2007 and a double assassination attempt on the president and prime minister in early 2008 underscored the depth of Timor-Leste's ongoing political fragility. In an encouraging sign, elections in 2012 were conducted peacefully. Later that year, on December 31, the last 1,600 UN peacekeepers left Timor-Leste to secure itself. Absent international security forces, Timor-Leste's *de jure* independence became *de facto* independence.

INSTITUTIONS AND SOCIAL GROUPS

Catholic Church

The most significant colonial legacy of the Portuguese was religion. Ninety-six percent of Timor-Leste's population is Roman Catholic, in contrast to the Muslim presence that characterizes much of the surrounding region. Catholicism in East Timor actually strengthened under Indonesian rule due to *Pancasila's* monotheistic imperative (which required citizens to indicate their religious identification). It was also strengthened by active local leaders, whose work was acknowledged by Pope John Paul II and his decision to visit the troubled island in 1989. As the moral voice of Timorese society and the arbiters of Timorese interests, local Catholic leaders fueled the territory's resistance movement during the preindependence period and continue to shape the country after statehood.

Today, the debate over church-state relations is among the central elements of postindependence politics. Timorese political figures are divided on where church-state lines should be drawn. Prime Minister Mari Alkatiri's proposal to restrict religious education in public schools sparked indignation among church authorities and was ultimately defeated upon the threat of social disorder. Tensions between church leaders and Alkatiri, a Fretilin veteran and religious Muslim, persisted until he resigned under great pressure in 2006. Although Fretilin-led governments did not pursue a socialist agenda while in power, church leaders often characterize party leaders, including Alkatiri, as Marxists.

In recent years, the church has developed avenues for a more forceful role in electoral politics. Church policy disallows bishops and priests from formally endorsing parties or candidates during services, but outside church walls they are encouraged to speak openly about their preferences. State funds have been used to support the church, an action justified, in President Ramos-Horta's words, "as an obligation of the State to the oldest and most credible institution in our Nation."[9]

Independence Leaders

Many of East Timor's most prominent independence leaders continue in pivotal leadership roles in the postindependence period. Having emerged from a seminary-trained class of mestizo elites, intellectuals, and civil servants, these leaders took their cues from the political Left in Portugal during their formative years in the 1970s.[10] Less ideological today than before, veteran independence leaders now jockey for positions in government as partners and rivals hoping to navigate the young country through its seemingly insurmountable challenges.

Chief among Timor-Leste's leaders has been Gusmao, elected as the country's first president (2002–2007), and its prime minister (2007–2015). Known best by his pen name, "Xanana," the journalist-turned-revolutionary found himself atop Fretilin in the early 1980s, following a massive Indonesian offensive that eliminated many of the group's leaders. Xanana then worked with Catholic leaders and Fretilin's rivals to create a broad political coalition and an effective clandestine rebel operation. His legend is part Che Guevara, part Nelson Mandela. When he rejected offers for liberty in exile during his long imprisonment in Jakarta, Xanana became the international face of Timorese courage. Suharto reluctantly honored Nelson Mandela's request to visit Xanana in prison. Strengthened by the visit, Xanana increased calls that Suharto allow for an independence referendum.

José Ramos-Horta, Fretilin's founder, has also bridged the pre- and postindependence eras as a powerful political actor. In what proved to be entirely consequential, he fled East Timor only days before the Indonesian takeover in 1975. While abroad he drew attention to East Timor's plight serving as its observer-representative in the United Nations. Ramos-Horta lobbied governments, legislatures, and human rights organizations in singular fashion to generate international pressure on Suharto's regime. In 1988, he broke with Fretilin to pursue a path of nonviolent resistance. A joint Nobel laureate with Bishop Carlos Filipe Ximenes Belo in 1996, Ramos-Horta served as the country's prime minister (2006–2007) and its second elected president (2007–2012).

Because of his legendary ambassadorial history, Ramos-Horta wields unparalleled moral authority both inside and outside the new country. In 2012, Ramos-Horta was nominated for reelection but refused to publicly campaign out of respect for his opponents who were former Fretilin guerillas. "I cannot compare myself with them," he said in a *New York Times* op-ed. "They have earned the right to lead as much as I."[11] Ramos-Horta then pleaded with the remaining candidates to show greater moderation in their campaigning and tone down their rhetoric for the good of the country. They did. In 2012, presidential power in Timor-Leste was transferred peacefully and Ramos-Horta left Timorese politics to serve as a special envoy for the United Nations. Ramos-Horta was replaced by another heroic figure, former Falantil major-general José Maria Vasconcelos. Known popularly as "Taur Matan Rauk" (Tetum for "Two Sharp Eyes"), the new president is unaffiliated with any political party in the post-2012 unity government.

Mari Alkatiri, also a Fretilin founder, remains another prominent figure. He served a tumultuous four-year stint as Timor-Leste's first prime minister, a position with greater constitutional authority and policymaking power than the president. Interparty divisions and rivalries with Xanana, Ramos-Horta, and Catholic leaders forced him to resign in 2006, but he remains active as a Fretilin party leader in Parliament. He influenced Xanana's 2015 decision to step down as prime minister and magnanimously pledged that he would not seek the prime ministership to open the door for the next generation of Timorese leaders.

Succeeding Gusmao as prime minister is Fretilin Party member Rui Maria de Arujo, a physician fifteen years junior to most of the country's independence leaders. During Suharto's occupation, while pursuing an education in medicine in Indonesia and New Zealand, Rui Arujo had assisted the resistance as a student activist and liaison to Falantil. During stints in Dili he surreptitiously treated rebels in the hills and later worked with the UN. He became the country's first minister of health and served as a state adviser until Xanana's CNRT party nominated him as prime minister to preserve the unity government.

National Parliament and Political Parties

Though weak as institutions, the national Parliament and the country's political parties are important vehicles for political expression and contestation in Timor-Leste's embryonic democracy. The promise of a healthy democracy rests on how well these institutions develop. The extent to which political figures involved in parliamentary politics choose to stay within the bounds of peaceful conflict and favor public over private interests are the crucial questions regarding political development.

These bounds were pushed after the 2007 election when difficulties surfaced in forming a parliamentary government and choosing a prime minister. Fretilin, now a political party, had won the most seats but was unable to find a partner and attempted to form a minority government. The possibility of a unity government of all parties later surfaced, but talks broke down despite President Ramos-Horta's attempts at mediation. Ultimately an alliance government emerged without Fretilin and with Xanana Gusmao, who had recently begun his own party, as prime minister. Fretilin protested the outcome and Dili's streets exploded with angry house burnings and vandalism. This time, however, no deaths were reported.

The sixty-five-member unicameral National Parliament currently seats four of the country's twenty-one parties that contested in the 2012 general elections. A proportional representation party-list ballot determines seat allocation. By law, at least one quarter of all candidates on party lists are required to be women. Fretilin has won nearly 30 percent of the total vote in the past two elections but it is no longer the most influential faction in Timorese politics. Dampening Fretilin's dominance was the party work of Xanana Gusmao, who founded the National Congress for Timorese Reconstruction Party (CNRT) prior to the 2007 national elections. CNRT won 24 percent of the popular vote in 2007 and 37 percent of the vote in 2012. Following the 2012 election, CNRT and Fretilin again engaged in discussions to form a unity government with Xanana as prime minister.

As Xanana's tenure grew longer, charges of nepotism and corruption became more frequent. Questions about his personal integrity chipped away at his once unassailable reputation. Then, after decades of self-imposed exile, the return of Mauk Moruk, a past rival, further complicated matters for Xanana. Moruk had left occupied East Timor in 1984 after a rancorous inner-Falantil power struggle. Resuming past criticism, he labeled Xanana a dictator and alleged he was crafting a new elite power structure. Drawing some support from disaffected Falantil veterans in areas near Baucau, Moruk organized and armed a "revolutionary council." He called for the current government to resign and a return to the 1975 independence declaration. Fearful of new political violence and threats to the state, the unity Parliament authorized security action against the group. Under increased pressure, Moruk eventually turned himself in and was held for about a year.

Although a reprise of guerrilla war that challenged state legitimacy was avoided due to parliamentary resolve, the episode contributed to growing questions about Xanana's leadership. Brewing for some time were also concerns about the next generation of Timor-Leste leaders. Xanana's tight control over appointments of old-guard loyalists had kept members of "Generation '99" leaders on the sidelines.[12]

In early 2015, Xanana Gusmao tendered his resignation as prime minister. Months later, Mauk Moruk was killed in a joint police-military security operation following violent activity by his group. In perhaps two of the greatest non-stories in Timor-Leste's independence, no violent reprisals followed either Xanana's resignation or Moruk's death. Unlike previous episodes, no spontaneous protest or violence erupted, reaction remain muted, and no external force was needed to maintain peace. As old feuds expire, the likelihood grows that the next generation in Timor-Leste will steer political conflict through an institutionalized parliament rather than on Dili's streets. A serious test will occur when the current unity government breaks down and if the democratic concept of a "loyal opposition" is fully accepted by all parties and actors.

STATE-SOCIETY RELATIONS AND DEMOCRACY

Timor-Leste's state is dependent and fragile. Technically sovereign, it can be described as an "infant state"—a state engaged in a needy, agnatic relationship with the international community through its UN parentage. Although sometimes classified as a failed state, Timor-Leste is so new as a political entity that it is difficult to equate it with countries that genuinely experienced a measurable loss of sovereign control, central authority, or capacity for self-governance (such as Somalia, Zimbabwe, or Afghanistan). Not yet having the experience to develop a measurable degree of state autonomy or capacity in the first place, Timor-Leste has been disproportionately dependent on foreign support for its very being since independence.

It was first the United Nations that accreted and concentrated power to manage the polity. In its first decade, virtually all functions of the Timor-Leste state (security, government, social services, and justice) were at one time or another performed by one of nine UN-led operations: UNAMET (1999), INTERFET (1999), UNTAET (1999–2002), UNMISET (2002–2005), UNOTIL (2005–2006), Operation Astute (2006), UNMIT (2006–2012), the East Timor Tribunal (2000–2006), and the Commission for Reception, Truth, and Reconciliation (CAVR) (2002–2005). Essential as these missions were to the country's emancipation and stability, Timor-Leste's future as a fully sovereign state depends on how well it weans itself from UN paternalism. President Ramos-Horta, ever conscious of this fact, vocally encouraged the United Nations to maintain its presence in Timor-Leste for at least a decade to lead the country out of its infancy. After the 2012 departure of the United Nations, Timor-Leste has remained dependent on foreign assistance given the country's low level of development. Politically, Timor-Leste may be decades away from creating a strong state with the autonomy and capability to function effectively.

With respect to the state's legitimacy, questions persist about how willing Timorese are to consent to state authority. The cultural and moral authority of the Catholic Church and particular independence figures remain intact, but a respect for (and submission to) the state and its embryonic political institutions remain questionable. Growing regional divisions between east and west, known locally as the *firaku-kaladi* (east-west) divide, suggest an added challenge to the legitimacy of the state and its territorial integrity.

Institutions of democracy in Timor-Leste are weak and underdeveloped. Indicative of this weakness were the events of 2006, when Dili slid into another episode of political chaos less than four years into its democratic experiment. During a strike over low wages and alleged discrimination, a large number of disgruntled government soldiers from the interior west were fired by Prime Minister Alkatiri. In turn, the soldier-petitioners incited a mutiny of riots, arson, looting, and clashes with local police and military loyalists. Multiple deaths occurred and the homes of certain military officials were set on fire. The risk of general social disorder grew quickly. Xanana Gusmao, then president, added fuel to the fire by publicly indicating sympathy for the soldiers.[13] Echoing earlier incidents, over 150,000 Timorese fled in fear. As the country braced itself for another wave of bloody turmoil, some government ministers and military generals began to distribute weapons to civilians. Only the arrival of yet another Australian-led peacekeeping force was able to bring calm to Dili's streets.

With respect to democratization, the events of 2006 were especially troubling because the political violence could not be blamed on Indonesia, outsiders, or some foreign entity as before. Rather, blame lay within the country, suggesting evidence of a growing regional cleavage and a political culture prone to violent conflict. This fragility was further demonstrated in electoral violence in 2007 and a dreadful episode of political violence the following year. A failed coup in early 2008 included assassination attempts against both President Ramos-Horta and Prime Minister Gusmao. Ramos-Horta suffered serious gunshot wounds to his abdomen requiring extended medical treatment in Australia. Alfredo Reinado, the estranged army major who masterminded the assassination attempts as well as the 2006 mutiny, was killed by security forces during the coup.

Viewed by most as a setback for democracy, hopeful observers saw the death of Reinado as the beginning of the end of any destabilizing rebel movements that threatened democracy.[14] Mauk Moruk's subsequent attempt to dislodge the state in 2013 proved that threats to democracy remained. It is thus far too early to label Timor-Leste's transition to democracy complete. Nevertheless, Ramos-Horta, favoring forgiveness over punitive justice, pointed to a successful 2012 election and economic growth as evidence that "the country is maturing" and that "a new chapter has begun."[15]

In fact, the greatest threat to the consolidation of democratic institutions in Timor-Leste may not be anti-democratic sentiment, authoritarian impulses, or the threat of occupation but rather institutional failure in the needed functions of government. An ethos for democracy is taking root in Timor-Leste, but the country's history is short and its dependence on international support for regime legitimacy remains considerable. Although rated "partly free" in 2015 by Freedom House, the country still fits the definition of what might be called an "ambiguous" regime because of its immaturity.

ECONOMY AND DEVELOPMENT

The UNDP describes Timor-Leste as Asia's least developed country—a country "chained to poverty."[16] Independence has improved economic conditions and overall development but many deficiencies remain. Aside from promising revenues derived from oil extraction in the Timor Sea, the young country enjoys limited economic prospects, especially from a household-level perspective. New autonomy and authority to allocate state resources from oil revenues has spawned infighting because there is little institutional capacity to deliver such allocation. A two-tier oil/non-oil economy has emerged, creating both opportunities and risks.

Subsistence agriculture characterizes the country's economy. Seasonal food shortages afflict much of the island's populace. Almost a quarter of the population depends on food assistance during lean months of the year. Little is produced in the overall economy beyond oil, coffee, and some handicrafts. Manufacturing is negligible. Commercial production of vanilla, palm oil, and other crops awaits more intensive investment before the country's agricultural sector functions profitably in Southeast Asia's trade-based economy. The country is wholly dependent on imports to feed and provide for its population. Without development assistance and oil revenues, the economic situation would be virtually hopeless.

In terms of living standards, no country in Southeast Asia has a higher rate of poverty than Timor-Leste: 49.9 percent (according to 2013 UNDP figures). Its record of overall human development is disheartening. Its literacy rate hovers near 50 percent, the lowest in all of Asia. In rural areas, four in ten Timorese lack access to potable water, and less than one in three women who give birth do so with a medical professional present. A majority of Timorese live in substandard housing and lack access to basic sanitation. When calculated in terms of purchasing power, GDP per capita in Timor-Leste is the lowest in Southeast Asia ($2,228).

Since 2002, the country's oil and non-oil growth rates have risen, especially after 2007, when coffee exports began to generate more revenue. In fact, annual non-oil GDP growth between 2007 and 2011 averaged over 10 percent. As a result, aggregate income figures for Timor-Leste have risen. Evaluating these figures in proper context is important. With a 2014 gross national income (GNI) per capita of $3,210, it may appear the country's population is better off than people in Vietnam and Myanmar, where GNI per capita is much lower.[17] However, non-oil GNI per capita income is actually closer to $810 according to 2013 World Bank figures, far lower than even Cambodia and Laos.[18] The reality is that oil revenues are only marginally improving everyday lives, and structural weaknesses in the two-tier economy remain.

Seventy-five percent of Timor-Leste's GDP is derived from oil and natural gas. Simply stated, Timor-Leste is one of the most petroleum-dependent countries in the world. After hard-fought treaty negotiations with Australia over rival claims, government revenues from oil extraction in the Timor Sea have begun to flow. The oil profits generated by the state are put into a Norway-style sovereign fund, the Timor-Leste Petroleum Fund. This fund, which is managed by government and civil society representatives, has grown dramatically: from $70 million in 2005 to over $16 billion in 2015.

The country dollarized its monetary system in part to mitigate the risk a local currency would create for oil revenues. In 2011, Timor-Leste's Parliament passed a bill allowing a greater share of the fund to be invested in equities, prompting some observers to raise questions about market volatility and finan-cial risk.[19] An active NGO-watchdog in Dili, La'o Hamutuk, believes the coun-try's oil revenues already peaked in 2012. It published alarming projections of declining revenues and expected fund draws over the next decade due to de-clining global prices, production constraints, and yet to be resolved disputes with Australia.[20]

Outside the oil economy, weak private investment currently plagues the Ti-morese economy. Unemployment averages 20 percent across the country and rises even higher in urban areas. Because half of the population is under twenty years old, demographic stress will extend employment pressures well into the future. Prime Minister Gusmao's massive push for new public infrastructure in roads, ports, and electricity is designed to alleviate these problems. The coun-try's annual budget increased from $70 million in 2004 to $1.3 billion in 2011 due in large part to infrastructure initiatives. Indeed, an active state-led eco-nomic program will be needed to develop all sectors of the country's economy. Waiting for private investment to arrive will prove a fool's errand. Timor-Leste's Global Competitiveness Index and Bloomberg Economic Momentum Index rankings are both last in Asia.[21] With a small, poorly educated popula-tion, and a remote island location, the incentives for foreign investment are minimal. Tourist infrastructure remains underdeveloped and years away from allowing the country to realize the full potential of its regional location.

Of course, the greatest risks lie in the oil economy itself. Increasing along-side rising hydrocarbon-driven revenues are the risks of falling into the "oil curse." Common to many small petrostates, the oil curse leads to high-stakes conflict among elites, authoritarian impulses, and corruption. Nevertheless, the opportunity exists for Timor-Leste to learn from mistakes made elsewhere. If political disunity, the temptation for corruption, and inequitable distribution of revenues can be avoided, it is possible that oil wealth will be a blessing to human development, not a curse, if balanced with a stronger non-oil economy.

FOREIGN RELATIONS

As it seeks to wean itself from outside protection, Timor-Leste's relationship with the United Nations remains its most crucial foreign policy priority. Never-theless, the young country's evolving politics is producing a coherent foreign policy agenda and debate. Dili's principal bilateral relations are with Indonesia, Australia, and (increasingly) China. It also desires a healthy relationship with ASEAN.

Among Timorese, relations with Indonesia remain controversial due to past resentments of Suharto's occupation and the postreferendum mayhem in 1999. A bilateral initiative of the two states, the Timor-Leste Commission for Recep-tion, Truth, and Reconciliation (CAVR), was launched in 2005 to smooth rela-tions. For many Timorese who suffered at the hands of Indonesian perpetrators, the creation of a commission smacked of impunity. Xanana, a supporter of the commission, drew the ire of church officials, UNMIT, and international NGOs that questioned the commission's establishment.[22] At the state-to-state level, however, CAVR has allowed current governments to distance themselves from the sins of the past.

Timor-Leste's relations with other major partners reflect an even more forward-looking posture. Its ties with Australia are complex, multilayered, and asymmetrical. Disputes over territorial waters damaged relations after independence, but Australia willingly returned its peacekeepers to Dili in 2006 to quell civil unrest. Certain parties within Timor-Leste fear that Canberra has neocolonial designs to ensure Dili serves Australian interests. Ramos-Horta and Xanana show less concern about this possibility than do Fretilin and Mari Alkatiri, who looks to China and Portugal as patrons. Portugal was only recently overtaken by Australia as Timor-Leste's largest aid donor.

China, a permanent member of the UN Security Council and long sympathetic to Fretilin's objectives, sent troops to support UNTAET and was the first country to establish diplomatic relations with Timor-Leste. While early support of Fretilin reflects Cold War priorities, more recent moves have sought to preempt Taiwan from courting the new Asian country. China's interests in Timor-Leste are more economic than political. Oil and resource hungry, China seeks a partnership with Timor-Leste as part of its grand strategy to secure energy sources. Evidence of a deepening relationship between the two countries includes increasing foreign aid from Beijing; the financing of government buildings, including the construction of Timor-Leste's new presidential palace in Dili; and a $1.6 million seismic study for oil and gas in Timor-Leste's interior.[23] In a reversal of roles, as a show of goodwill, the government of Timor-Leste donated $500,000 to China in 2008 in support of recovery efforts following the massive Sichuan earthquake.

With respect to international organizations, Timor-Leste's key relations are with the Asian Development Bank, where membership was established in 2004, and ASEAN, where membership hopes have been inhibited by a lack of human resources to staff and support ASEAN's many agencies and initiatives. In 2011, Timor-Leste submitted an application to join ASEAN with the support of then chairman Indonesia, but other ASEAN countries believe the young country is far from ready. ASEAN membership for Timor-Leste lies well beyond 2020 according to most experts. WTO membership for Timor-Leste is an even more distant hope, although its partnerships with the IMF and World Bank continue to bring in project-based aid.

FIFA, the world football (soccer) organization, enjoys a strangely active presence in Timor-Leste. Occupying one of Dili's most impressive colonial mansions, FIFA is accused of implicitly supporting a shady program that channels ineligible Brazilian players to Timor-Leste. With seven such foreign players on the national team, tiny Timor-Leste now stands above giant Indonesia in world football rankings and is jokingly dubbed "Little Samba Nation."[24]

Conclusion

The full dignity of independence celebrated by Timor-Leste in 2002 came at a heavy price—achieved after centuries of Portuguese control, three merciless years of Japanese occupation, a thirty-year return of Portuguese rule following World War II, a failed attempt at independence in 1975, twenty-five years of a brutal occupation by Indonesia's Suharto, an independence referendum, a scorched-earth campaign by anti-independence militias, a refugee crisis, a dramatic Australian-led peacekeeping operation, and an ambitious UN mission that governed East Timor's final transition to statehood. Elections, democratic institutions, and membership in international organizations have since followed, but political stability and economic development have remained elusive.

The "never again" narrative, into which Timor-Leste's history is inseparably woven, has recently adopted a new term: *Chega!*, Portuguese for "enough!" or "stop!" The title of a UN-commissioned report on the atrocities committed under Indonesia's occupation, *Chega!* might as well be a mantra for independent Timor-Leste as it seeks full self-governance. Realizing an end to episodic disorder, killing, and refugee flows is requisite for the infant state if it is to experience genuine independence and stability. Political order, elusive today, is the keystone in the delicate bridge that may someday lead Timorese to the economic and human development they so sorely deserve.

Notes

1. Andrea Katalin Molnar, *Timor-Leste: Politics, History, and Culture* (New York: Routledge, 2010), 34–36.

2. Ibid., 36–37.

3. See December 6, 2001, press release from George Washington University's National Security Archive, www.gwu.edu/~nsarchiv/NSAEBB/NSAEBB62/press.html.

4. Michael Leifer, "Timor, East (Indonesia)," *Dictionary of the Modern Politics of South-East Asia* (London: Routledge, 1995), 236.

5. The figures cited here come from the CAVR Report commissioned by UNTAET and the Timor-Leste National Parliament. See www.cavr-timorleste.org/en/chegaReport.htm.

6. Joseph Nevins, *A Not-So-Distant Horror: Mass Violence in East Timor* (Ithaca, NY: Cornell University Press, 2005), 32.

7. Ibid.

8. Samantha Power, *Chasing the Flame: One Man's Fight to Save the World* (New York: Penguin, 2008).

9. Extracted from a campaign speech by presidential candidate José Ramos-Horta, March 23, 2007, Dili, www.pm.gov.tp/speeches.htm.

10. Michael Leifer, "Fretilin (Indonesia)," in *Dictionary of the Modern Politics of South-East Asia* (London: Routledge, 1995), 97.

11. José Ramos-Horta, "Elections to Be Proud Of," *New York Times*, April 16, 2012, www.nytimes.com/2012/04/17/opinion/elections-to-be-proud-of.html.

12. Angie Bexly and Maj Nygaard-Christiansen, "The Lost Leadership of Timor-Leste," *The New Mandala* (April 29, 2015), http://asiapacific.anu.edu.au/newmandala/2014/11/07 /the-lost-leadership-of-timor-leste.

13. Joseph Nevins, "Timor-Leste in 2006: The End of Post-Independence Honeymoon," *Asian Survey* 47, no. 1 (January/February 2007): 162–167.

14. Simon Montlake and Nick Squires, "After Foiled Assassination, Timor Rebels' Sway May Lessen," *Christian Science Monitor*, February 12, 2008.

15. Ramos-Horta, "Elections to Be Proud Of."

16. Nevins, "Timor-Leste in 2006," 163.

17. See Table 1.1 in chapter 1.

18. Timor-Leste Social Assistance, *Public Expenditure and Program Performance Report*, World Bank (June 24, 2013), p. 8, https://openknowledge.worldbank.org/bitstream /handle/10986/16454/734840WP0P126300PER000240June00eng.txt.

19. "Is Timor-Leste's Plan for Oil Fund Investments a Risk Worth Taking?" *The Guardian*, October 24, 2011, www.theguardian.com/global-development/2011/oct/24/timor -leste-sovereign-fund-investment.

20. La'o Hamutuk, "Timor-Leste's Oil and Gas Are Going Fast," Timor-Leste Institute for Development Monitoring and Analysis, Dili, Timor-Leste, April 15, 2015, www .laohamutuk.org/Oil/curse/2015/OilGoingFast15Apr2015en.pdf.

21. Shamim Adam and Ramsey Al-Rikabi, "East Timor Ends First Decade Fighting Oil Curse," *Bloomberg*, May 17, 2012, www.bloomberg.com/news/articles/2012-05-17/east -timor-ends-first-decade-fighting-oil-curse.

22. Jose Cornelio Guterres, "Timor-Leste: A Year of Democratic Elections," *Southeast Asian Affairs 2008* (Singapore: Institute of Southeast Asian Studies, 2008), 369.

23. Ian Storey, "China and East Timor: Good but Not Best Friends," Association for Asian Research, August 15, 2006, www.asianresearch.org/articles/2920.html.

24. "Palestine Protests East Timor's Use of Brazilian Players in FIFA World Cup Qualifier," *Sydney Morning Herald*, October 17, 2015, www.smh.com.au/sport/soccer/palestine -protests-east-timors-use-of-brazilian-players-in-fifa-world-cup-qualifier-20151016 -gkbhue.html.

10

MALAYSIA

Malaysia is in many respects Southeast Asia's most admirable achiever. Though generally classified as an illiberal democracy, Malaysia is more pluralist than Singapore, more politically stable than Thailand, and less corrupt than the Philippines. Malaysia has also more successfully managed ethnic and religious conflict than its geocultural cousin Indonesia. With a population of 30.5 million people and a per capita gross national income (GNI) of $10,660, Malaysia recently achieved newly industrialized country status. It currently boasts a poverty rate of less than 2 percent. Only the citizens of microstates Singapore and Brunei enjoy a higher standard of living in the region. The Malaysian success story is especially noteworthy because of the country's geographic and racial diversity.

Malaysia consists of the peninsula (formerly Malaya) that is connected to southern Thailand, and Sabah and Sarawak on the island of Borneo, several hundred miles across the South China Sea. Today, eight in ten Malaysians live on the peninsula. Less than 10 percent of Malaysia's land is arable. Half of Malaysia's territory remains forested, and in the Borneo regions of East Malaysia lie some of the world's oldest tropical rainforests. Socially, Malaysia's diversity stems from its geography. Home to the famed Strait of Malacca passage, connecting the Indian subcontinent to Pacific Asia, Malaysia's maritime geography has shaped its history, economy, and society.

There is no more powerful force in Malaysian society than communalism, or the division of the country into racial communities: 55 percent Malay, 25 percent Chinese, 8 percent Indian, and the rest smaller minority and migrant groups.[1] The Malays are Sunni Muslim, predominantly rural and agricultural, or *bumiputra* (sons of the soil). Urban centers are attracting more *bumiputra* from the countryside as the country grows wealthier. Most non-Malays are urban and typically non-Muslim, usually employed in industry, manufacturing, and, more recently, finance. Overall, six in ten Malaysians now live in cities. Smaller indigenous minorities, such as the Dayaks, Iban, and Orang Asli of

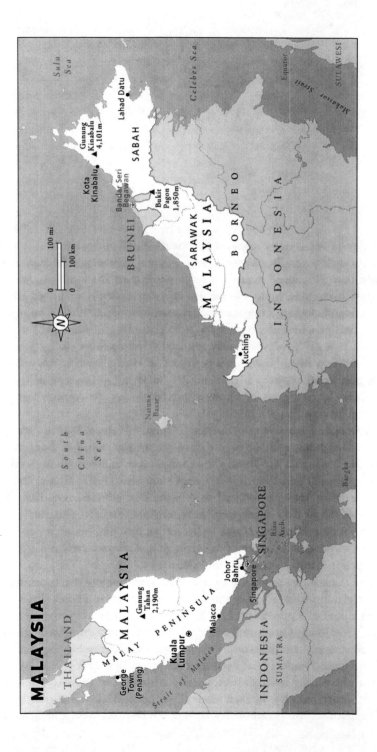

Borneo, remain politically weak and culturally vulnerable to the transformative forces of state and market.

Immigrants to Malaysia from 1860 to 1940 were mostly impoverished workers and peasants from southern China or southern India who came during the British colonial administration to work the tin mines and perform labor the Malays scorned. As with overseas diasporic communities elsewhere, their separateness was reinforced even as they expanded their economic roles. The Chinese in particular became Malaysia's money lenders, middlemen, contractors, and manufacturers. Their primary stress on education and ambition provided mobility so that at present the Chinese are the wealthiest businesspeople in most areas of the economy.

Communalism resulted in the stereotyping of Malaysia's ethnic groups. Historically, Malays routinely viewed the Chinese as aggressive, acquisitive, unscrupulous in business dealings, ritually unclean, and politically suspect. Chinese, on the other hand, saw themselves as hardworking, progressive, competitive, and faithful to their families. To the Chinese, the stereotypical Malay was perceived as lazy and superstitious and without motivation for hard work or personal advancement, whereas Malays viewed themselves as scrupulous in their dealings with others and as more concerned with the quality of human relationships than with material acquisition.[2]

Peninsular Malaysia came under formal British rule in 1874, after decades of control over the key ports of Penang, Melaka, and Singapore. North Borneo (now Sabah) and Sarawak also came under British control in the nineteenth century but were administered separately. Following Japanese occupation from 1942 to 1945, the British reestablished governance. Resistance to British rule emerged from communist guerrillas led by Chin Peng and from anticommunist Malay nationalists led by Tunku Abdul Rahman. The latter group cooperated with British governors, and full independence, *merdaka*, was arranged for peninsular territories on August 31, 1957, under the UN-recognized name the Federation of Malaya. Tunku Abdul Rahman was named prime minister. Within two years of independence, the communist insurgency was neutralized and the defeated Chin Peng fled to Beijing.

By 1963, the newly titled Federation of Malaysia, inclusive of all peninsular states—Sabah, Sarawak, and Singapore (but not Brunei)—was fully formed. To offset the integration of 3 million Chinese from Singapore into the federation, Sabah and Sarawak were brought in to maintain a favorable proportion of non-Chinese in the population. All of these areas shared a common colonial heritage under Great Britain, and all feared that without collaboration, they could not function as viable and autonomous nation-states.

To mitigate ethnic differences, the British arranged "the Bargain" when they relinquished colonial authority. The Bargain included such arrangements as constitutional advantages to the Malays; support for a Malay as head of state, chosen from among the sultans of nine peninsular Malay states; Malay as the country's official language; and Islam as the official religion. Also, the constitution provided special privileges to Malays in land acquisition, educational assistance, and civil service employment.

To meet the terms of the Bargain, the leading Malay, Chinese, and Indian political parties formed a coalition known as the Perikatan (Alliance) with the understanding that non-Malays would prevail in the economic sector while Malays would control the political sector. As long as that formula was accepted by all groups, the Malaysian political system was stable. When the formula was challenged, however, instability threatened, as in 1969 when, following a national election, deadly riots ensued and a state of emergency was declared lasting almost two years.

The original federation itself lasted only two years. It fell apart in August 1965 when Tunku Abdul Rahman expelled Singapore for many complex reasons inextricably bound up with communal problems. Singapore's leader, Lee Kuan Yew, called for a "Malaysian Malaysia"—that is, for a Malaysia with equal participation from all areas and groups. His call opposed and contrasted with Tunku Abdul Rahman's design for a "Malayan Malaysia," with special privileges reserved for the dominant ethnic group. When Lee Kuan Yew attempted to influence the larger area of Malaysia, Tunku Abdul Rahman regarded the attempt as a direct threat to continued political dominance by the Malays.

The May 1969 communal riots were a watershed event in Malaysia's postindependence era, and their immediate cause was the erosion of support for Abdul Rahman's Alliance coalition of parties in the 1969 elections. In the preceding two elections, in 1959 and 1964, the Alliance had won an overwhelming majority of the parliamentary seats. In 1969, for the first time the opposition parties won a majority (51.5 percent) of the votes against the Alliance's 48.5 percent. Although Alliance candidates still controlled a majority in the Parliament despite losing twenty-three seats, the 1969 election showed that the Alliance coalition's capacity to govern was seriously impaired. To celebrate their "victory," anti-Alliance forces marched in the streets of the capital, Kuala Lumpur. Later, on May 13, Alliance supporters paraded, which led to communal tensions reaching the point of provoking mob action that raged for four days and tragically ended in 196 deaths (official count).

The Malaysian government viewed the race riots as a threat to the ethnic Bargain that had been the formula for civic stability. To ensure that Malays retained political power, a state of emergency was proclaimed, Parliament was temporarily disbanded, civil liberties were curtailed, and total authority was granted to a new body, the National Operations Council. The council worked to restore order and sought to return Malaysia to parliamentary democracy. The twenty-one-month period known as the "Emergency" was a time of suspended democracy.

Believing that economic tensions were mainly responsible for the communal riots, Tun Abdul Razak, the new prime minister, proposed the New Economic

Policy (NEP) to promote national unity and a just society, and to attack poverty by "reducing and eventually eliminating the identity of race with economic function." Under the NEP, the rights of Malays were extended by reserving for them a proportion of positions in higher education and certain businesses, and sedition acts were passed that prohibited discussion of such "sensitive issues" as the prerogatives of Malay rulers, special rights for Malays, and official status for the Malay language. In essence, this meant that Malay participation in the economic sphere was to be increased by granting special privileges in terms of business ownership, tax breaks, investment incentives, and employment quotas—a pro-Malay affirmative action program for the majority.

By 1972, parliamentary democracy returned, albeit within the constraints of the sedition acts and the reworking of the Alliance into the Barisan Nasional (National Front), or BN. Tun Abdul Razak established the BN to ensure dominance of the political system by Malays and to preclude upheavals such as the 1969 riots. His party, the United Malays National Organization (UMNO), the lead member of the BN coalition, co-opted most of the opposition parties and won 90 percent of the parliamentary seats in the 1974 election.

When Abdul Razak died in 1976, he was succeeded by Tun Hussein Onn, who, like his predecessors, came from prestigious ancestry and great wealth and had a Western education. He continued BN policies until 1981 when, following a serious illness, he resigned and was succeeded by Deputy Prime Minister Dr. Mahathir bin Mohamad. Mahathir, the first commoner prime minister, with no aristocratic ancestry or family wealth and with a local education in medicine, symbolized the new Malaysian technocrat. His brash and confrontational style was the opposite of that of his refined predecessors.

Mahathir became an articulate spokesman in modern Malaysia's bid to develop economically. His "Look East Policy" argued that Western nations were not appropriate models for Malaysia. He believed that Malaysia should emulate the methods of Japan, South Korea, and Taiwan, all Asian countries whose values were more in tune with those of Malaysia. He also introduced the concept of "Malaysia Incorporated," whereby business and government leaders would work together as in a modern corporation.

In the 1982 parliamentary election, Mahathir and the UMNO-led BN coalition of parties triumphed, winning 132 of 154 seats. Again in 1986, the BN coalition won a landslide victory, winning 148 of the 177 parliamentary seats, but this election marked the beginning of a period of political and economic difficulties. The leaders of the major parties in the BN fell into strife as the country underwent a major recession, which resulted in negative economic growth for the first time since independence.

The major problem was within UMNO, the dominant party of BN and the "political home" of Mahathir (as well as all former prime ministers). Strife in UMNO led to the resignation of high-ranking officials, some of whom joined a faction known as Team B, who then challenged the leadership of Mahathir and his followers, known as Team A. In the elections for the leadership of UMNO in April 1987, Mahathir barely beat his challenger, Team B leader Trade and Industry Minister Tunku Razaleigh Hamzah, when he won by only 43 votes, 761 to 718. In a shocking display of internecine factionalism, Team B officials accused Mahathir of blatant abuse of power, authoritarian leadership, economic mismanagement, and corruption.³ The challenge to Mahathir was especially noteworthy because it is the custom of Malays not to challenge their leaders; it is considered a case of *kurang ajar* (impropriety) to question the leadership.⁴

In response, Mahathir purged Team B members from his cabinet and from UMNO leadership, and he invoked the Internal Securities Act, ordering the arrest of persons critical of government actions. Also, three opposition newspapers were closed, and Operation Lallang was ordered: a sweep by the Malaysian police on October 27, 1987, that took into custody 119 people who had been accused of threatening internal security by provoking communal conflict. All those arrested were members of religious, political, and social organizations that, merely by criticizing regime policies, had qualified themselves as "thorns in [Mahathir's] side."⁵

In still another stunning incident related to UMNO factionalism, the Malaysian high court decreed that since unregistered regional branches had participated in the UMNO elections, UMNO was an illegal organization. Immediately there was a scramble to register a new party with UMNO in its name and to lay claim to the party's considerable assets. After rejecting Team B's applications, Mahathir was able to get UMNO Baru (New UMNO) registered. A dissident faction, again led by Razaleigh, formed a new party, Semangat '46 (Spirit of '46, the year of UMNO's birth), and allied itself with other opposition groups to form an alternative coalition known as Angkatan Perpaduan Umnah (APU), or the United Movement of the Faithful. Subsequently, the Barisan Nasional, led by UMNO Baru, won six of eight by-elections against the APU as well as the national election in October 1990.

Because of high-court decisions against the interests of the BN, Mahathir reduced the power of the courts by taking away their right to judicial review of executive decisions on internal security and matters concerned with the administration and operation of political parties. Ostensibly, this reduction of the courts' power was to ensure that, in case of threat to the nation's security, an executive could move with dispatch rather than having to wait for the cumbersome courts to deliberate. Eventually, at Mahathir's instigation, a specially created tribunal removed a majority of court justices from office.

In early 1989, Mahathir suffered a heart attack and underwent a successful multiple coronary bypass operation. His rapid recovery restored him as the central figure in contemporary Malaysian politics. A strong recovery from economic recession was the principal factor in the overwhelming election victory Mahathir and the multiethnic BN coalition achieved in October 1990. After only a ten-day political campaign, one of the shortest in contemporary Southeast Asian history, he won a two-thirds majority, thus ensuring control over constitutional amendments.

The primary political issue of the 1990s concerned the role of Islam in Malaysian society. Islamization had made inroads into the state of Kelantan, with the state assembly controlled by an Islamic-dominated coalition between the Parti Islam Se-Malaysia (Pan-Malaysian Islamic Party, or PAS) and Semangat '46. Mahathir reacted against the notion of an Islamic state, which he deemed inappropriate for a multiracial society. The issue did not become a crisis at the time because high economic growth rates provided a cushion that softened societal tensions.

In 1992–1993, a social reformation of great significance occurred when Mahathir decided to confront the nation's sultans, the traditional hereditary rulers of most of peninsular Malaysia's states, whose positions were largely ceremonial. The prime minister moved to reduce their power and prerogatives, notwithstanding laws and acts precluding discussion of the sultans' roles. By 1993, Mahathir had thus tamed the bureaucracy, political parties, judiciary, press, and sultans. Through confrontation and co-optation, he had successfully undermined the major forces once competing with him for political power.

The period from 1990 to 1996 was positive for the ruling Barisan Nasional coalition and for its leader, Mahathir. Winning its ninth general election in April 1995, with 64 percent of the popular vote, the BN enjoyed a two-thirds parliamentary majority. In addition, it won control of every state assembly except one (that of Kelantan), and the opposition was left in disarray. Both the Democratic Action Party (DAP) and Semangat '46 were shut out throughout the country. The Barisan Nasional coalition of UMNO, the Malayan Chinese Association, the Malayan Indian Congress, and the largely Chinese Parti Gerakan were united after the election. Malaysians supported the BN because of the strong economy, the disarray of the opposition, and the BN's monopoly of the mass media. At seventy years of age, Mahathir had never been more secure in his position.

As Mahathir's health stayed strong and his international stature increased, few politicians were brave enough to question his preeminence. His main competition came from a former Muslim youth activist and deputy prime minister, Anwar Ibrahim, but Mahathir kept him off balance with intraparty rules that banned confrontations with the leader. Mahathir became Malaysia's longest-serving premier and the only BN chairman to lead his coalition through five successive elections.

Mahathir's international reputation widened after a series of speeches in which he praised the virtues of "Asian values" and condemned "Western values." He often spoke passionately about his nation's sovereignty and, appearing to revel in the role of "West-basher," about the Americans, whom he deemed to be neoimperialist in their desire to control Malaysia and Malaysia's neighbors. In 1996, Mahathir was responsible for backing the construction of the world's tallest building, the Petronas Towers in Kuala Lumpur (eclipsing America's Sears Tower, now called Willis Tower, in Chicago). He built a gleaming high-tech research park, dubbed "Technopolis," and the Multimedia Super-Corridor, linking Kuala Lumpur with an immense new international airport.

In 1997, when the Asian economic crisis hit Malaysia, Mahathir was in his sixteenth year of tenure and in sole command of his country. A new problem arose when the Malaysian ringgit lost much of its value as a result of the Thai currency's devaluation. For the first time, Mahathir was in the midst of a crisis he could not control directly because the crisis was partly caused by inter-national and not domestic factors. His first reaction was to blame outsiders, and he ridiculously pointed his finger at the "Jewish conspiracy" he believed had long wanted to undermine Malaysia because of its predominantly Muslim population. Mahathir later explained that he was referring to only one Jew, Hungarian-born American financier George Soros, whom Mahathir accused of maliciously speculating on the Malaysian currency. Most of the world's press criticized Mahathir for refusing to accept that a large reason for the currency crisis was domestic, and not external.

Since 1991, Mahathir had focused on "Vision 2020," a plan to lift Malaysia into the ranks of developed nations by 2020. The economic crisis blunted his goal, which may explain the depth of his anger and his shocking anti-Semitic accusation. Mahathir emphatically rejected emergency aid from the IMF and, defying economic orthodoxy, imposed capital controls. Foreign investors, stunned by the announcement that their investment funds must remain in Ma-laysia for at least one year, reacted sourly. Although pundits predicted a policy disaster, Mahathir, who accused the IMF of trying to recolonize Asia, eventu-ally won admiration for guiding the country through the turbulent Asian eco-nomic crisis without an IMF bailout.

In 1999, Mahathir dismissed his deputy prime minister, Anwar Ibrahim, for alleged corruption and sodomy. Serious scholars of Malaysia believed that Ibra-him was actually sacked because he was increasingly popular among Malay-sians and a potential threat to Mahathir's continued leadership. The entire issue of trumping up charges against a rival minister proved to be an immense inter-national embarrassment to Mahathir and provided his critics with evidence that Malaysia was no longer a nation of laws, but instead a nation of personali-ties, many of whom were above the law.

Despite the debacle, Mahathir felt confident to set national elections for the Parliament in November 1999, six months before his term was even up. Cam-paigning was minimal, and many topics were banned. The election was an ex-cellent example of electoral politics designed to perpetuate the leading party's power. The short eight-day campaign led to the BN winning an overwhelming majority: 57 percent of the popular vote (down from 65 percent in 1995). Sev-eral provinces voted against the UMNO-led coalition, choosing Islamic parties. UMNO lost nearly half the Malay vote, particularly in Sabah and Sarawak, but the BN maintained Malay support in key peninsular districts and won a majority of the total votes.

Surrounded by yes-men who failed him by pointing out only his successes and not his weaknesses, Mahathir finally stepped down as prime minister in 2003. He left a paradoxical legacy from his twenty-two years in office. Because of his vision and leadership, the nation had enjoyed two decades of ever-improving living standards for all classes of people. With an intolerance of pettiness, disdain for opposition, and fervent commitment to Malaysian sovereignty, Mahathir sidelined rivals while lifting the country out of its third-world status. He embraced strategic alliances with Chinese and Indian elites but also left his UMNO colleagues (and his fellow Malays) as the beneficiaries of a political system stacked in their favor. During his tenure, Mahathir brashly disciplined the bureaucracy, political parties, judiciary, press, and sultans, all of whom once dared to challenge his political power.

Going out in true Mahathir style, the prime minister gave the world some parting thoughts. During a high-profile speech in 2003 at the Organization of the Islamic Conference (OIC), which Malaysia hosted, he claimed that the US invasion of Iraq proved the West's intention to recolonize the developing world. He also claimed that Jews were controlling the world by proxy, adding defiantly that "1.3 billion Muslims cannot be defeated by a few million Jews." Then, as conference host, he turned on his OIC guests and rebuked the Muslim community for its backwardness, deriding its tolerance for religious fanaticism. "Islam is not just for the seventh century," he proclaimed. "Islam is for all times. And times have changed."[6]

Abdullah Ahmad Badawi, a low-key but longtime UMNO minister, replaced Mahathir as prime minister only to struggle to find his own political style and support base. During his initial years as prime minister, a number of official scandals erupted and communalism reared its ugly head with resurgent Malay nationalism. Mahathir's party edifice was crumbling and rallying at the same time. Caught in corruption scandals, UMNO elites came to one another's defense. Badawi's support suffered a blow in 2008, however, when Mahathir left UMNO, pledging not to return to the party until Badawi was relieved of his position.

Mahathir's dissatisfaction with his successor stemmed in large part from UMNO's poor performance in general elections. In the March 2008 elections, UMNO won less than 30 percent of the vote and lost 30 seats in the 222-seat lower assembly. The Barisan Nasional retained power, but with a weaker coalition than Mahathir had ever assembled and a slim 51 percent of the popular vote. The Pakatan Rakyat (PR), or People's Front, a three-party coalition led by Anwar Ibrahim's People's Justice Party, secured 47 percent of the vote. In terms of assembly seats, the PR won 82 to the BN's 140. The first post-Mahathir election had resulted in the BN's loss of its previous two-thirds majority, needed to pass constitutional amendments.

The changes in UMNO leadership caused by Mahathir's departure and election woes opened new political space for democracy activists and opposition groups. Ibrahim, released from prison in 2004 when the previous verdict on the sodomy charge was overturned, reemerged on the political scene. Wan Azizah Wan Ismail, Anwar Ibrahim's wife, was elected by opposition parties as opposition leader. NGOs began to form their own coalitions, and an increasingly vocal Internet community pushed for an end to UMNO's dominance. Facing massive street protests in 2007, UMNO appeared vulnerable for the first time in decades.

Parliament opened in May 2008 with a palpable sense that UMNO's majority was in jeopardy. Pledging to end government corruption, and the privileged position Malay business oligarchs derived from the New Economic Policy, the opposition parties began wooing members to their side, hoping to shake UMNO's grip on Parliament. Facing serious threats, UMNO leaders initially returned to harassing and intimidating their opponents. Activists and antigovernment Internet bloggers found police at their doorsteps and, amazingly, Ibrahim was rearrested, again on specious charges of sodomy.

Subsequent criticism calling for Badawi to resign led the embattled prime minister to offer up a meager package of political reforms. Ultimately, the economic downturn caused by the 2008–2009 global financial crisis brought Badawi down. In April 2009, in an event confirming Malaysia's first intergenerational political dynasty, Badawi was replaced by Najib Abdul Razak, son and nephew of previous Malaysian prime ministers (Abdul Razak and Hussein Onn, respectively).

With UMNO facing unprecedented political pressure, Najib announced a program of reform under the slogan "1Malaysia. People First, Performance Now." It sought to appease the non-Malay voters, as well as many younger Malays, who had abandoned BN. New policy initiatives included reducing NEP quotas requiring compulsory *bumiputra* ownership in private companies and a new government scholarship program based on merit rather than race. Claiming that "Malaysians have reached a high level of maturity," Najib also lifted long-standing emergency decrees, reassessed restrictions on public demonstrations, and repealed the 1960 Internal Security Act, which had permitted indefinite detention without charge or trial.[7]

Though welcomed by some reform advocates, Najib's reforms were not enough; many others interpreted the new Peaceful Assembly law as a vehicle to expand state powers. Angered by ongoing UMNO corruption scandals and Badawi's failed leadership, Malaysia's traditionally apolitical youth were also amid a political awakening by the time Najib came to power. New vehicles of civic expression were emerging in Malaysia: online activity, political blogs, and planned rallies.

Beginning in 2007, under the name Bersih ("clean," in Malay), antigovernment youth and opposition PR figures launched massive rallies and protests organized largely through social media. Later rallies followed, commonly referred to as Bersih 2.0 (2011), Bersih 3.0 (2012), and Bersih 4.0 (2015). Donning distinctive canary yellow T-shirts, tens of thousands of protesters from Bersih (a coalition of over fifty civil society groups) assembled to demand electoral reform, access to government-controlled media, and an end to bureaucratic corruption.[8] Intended to be peaceful and festive, some Bersih rallies have turned violent, with protesters testing public security forces. To disperse crowds, police have resorted to chemical-laced water cannons, tear gas, and excessive force. Over 2,000 detentions resulted from Bersih 2.0 and 3.0. The episodic clashes have emboldened Bersih's resolve to end Malaysia's illiberal electoral authoritarianism; and thus far, UMNO's usual strategies of co-opting, depoliticizing, or intimidating opponents have proven futile.

During his tenure, Najib found himself governing a Malaysia that Mahathir never knew. Not only did Najib face a more troubled global economy, a more active civil society, and a generation of angry urban youth, but political Islam was also strengthening in certain areas of the federation. Resentment among ethnic Chinese over the government policies privileging Malays also reached new levels, with social media offering an important outlet for frustration.

By 2013, it was clear fundamental changes in Malaysia's polity had begun to influence political outcomes. General elections in May of that year produced a shocking result. For the first time in decades, the UMNO-led BN coalition lost the popular vote to the Pakatan Rakyat opposition coalition (47 percent to 51 percent). Saved only by gerrymandered districts that allowed BN to retain a majority of actual seats in Parliament (133 of 222 total seats), BN suffered mass defections by voters in Malaysia's urban areas. Opposition leaders alleged electoral fraud to no avail. Najib responded to BN losses by more ethnic pandering to Malaysia's *bumiputra*, blaming BN losses on a "Chinese Tsunami" rather than his own government's poor performance.

Support for Najib's post-election government took further hits when Najib's cabinet badly mishandled the mysterious 2014 crash of Malaysia Airlines flight 370, caused public uproar by introducing a new goods and services tax, and found itself in a major corruption scandal. Joining international critics in alleging incompetence and dishonesty was the retired, ninety-year-old Mahathir bin Mohammad, never shy about attacking his successors' failures. Known as the "1MDB Scandal," after a state fund first established in 2009, revelations exposed multiple missed payments to the fund's bondholders. In July 2015, $700 million of unaccounted-for funds were discovered in Najib's personal accounts. Evidence raised the likelihood that Najib was either embezzling from 1MDB accounts or at least taking monies from undisclosed Middle East donors for himself. An official probe into the matter was scuttled after Najib removed the attorney general, supposedly for poor health. A deputy prime minister was also sacked for wanting answers from Najib. No longer supported by the majority of its citizens, Najib's UMNO-led BN government grew ever more unpopular.

Even so, UMNO's troubles and election woes did not strengthen the opposition; rather they exposed the Pakatan Rakyat's structural weaknesses. In 2015, pro-Islamic elements within the opposition coalition decided to bolt from the uneasy political marriage with urban Chinese and pro-democracy liberals. Opposition leaders later openly admitted that the Pakatan Rakyat coalition was dead. Astonishingly, the cross-communal coalitions that have long characterized both the BN governments and their foes in the political opposition are beginning to break down. The stability they have helped to foster in Malaysia's multiethnic society may also be at risk.

All signs in Malaysia point to an electorate and party system realigned more strongly along communal lines. If the country's politics continue to trend in this direction, troubled waters lie ahead. To preserve its power, UMNO's illiberal methods may deepen, even with a fractured opposition. Once again neutralized, Anwar Ibrahim, the country's most important Malay figure in the opposition camp, sits in prison stripped of his lawmaker status following failed appeals to overturn a previous sodomy conviction. With or without a unified opposition, Najib's greatest threat remains growing disunity in the Barisan Nasional party coalition itself.

INSTITUTIONS AND SOCIAL GROUPS

Political Parties

Compared to political parties in Thailand, the Philippines, and Indonesia, Malaysia's dominant party, UMNO, the United Malays National Organization, is a highly institutionalized party. Unseating it will be difficult. Every Malaysian prime minister has reached that position because he has led UMNO. Highly institutionalized parties can be dangerous engines of patronage. Ongoing revelations of UMNO corruption render it far from invincible in a system with an increasingly savvy and demanding public. Thus far, however, UMNO's strength as a party remains at the center of Malaysia's competitive authoritarian regime.

UMNO's electoral success is due in large part to coalition building. The Alliance (in the pre-1969 period) and the *Barisan Nasional* (National Front) are coalitions of parties, joined together by the common goals of winning elections and securing societal stability. These goals have for the most part been achieved. Three parties composed the Alliance: UMNO, the Malayan Chinese Association (MCA), and the Malayan Indian Congress (MIC). Representing the three major ethnic groups, these parties accepted the Alliance formula to legitimize the interests of these ethnic groups. The formula required that each group accept the basic societal division: Malays dominate the political sphere, and Chinese and Indians dominate the economy.

When the formula broke down in 1969, the Alliance was transformed into the Barisan Nasional, which consisted of the three Alliance parties as well as a coalition of former opposition parties led by the Parti Islam Se-Malaysia (PAS), or Pan-Malaysian Islamic Party, the country's strongest Islamic party. In all, Barisan Nasional was composed of eleven component parties, but UMNO remained the senior partner, with final say over coalition decisions.[9] PAS was later expelled from BN, but the coalition retained its electoral dominance.

In 1988, a Malaysian court stunned the country when it found UMNO unlawful on the grounds that the delegates sent to the assembly had not been properly chosen. The rapid transformation of UMNO into UMNO Baru (with "Baru" subsequently deleted) was important for retaining the government's legitimacy. For the first time since independence, UMNO was challenged by a formidable party organization, Semangat '46, led by a Malay and strong enough to defeat the BN. Having allied with Razaleigh's United Movement of the Faithful (APU) coalition (which included the PAS), Semangat '46 provided a viable alternative to the UMNO-dominated BN.

However, the APU's strength was found wanting in the 1990 elections, in which some 8 million registered Malaysians voted. Candidates representing the BN capitalized on the issues of economic growth and political stability to achieve another electoral victory. The opposition's focus on issues of human rights, press freedom, lower taxes, and Mahathir's combative personality was not as credible to Malaysia's voters.

The BN also has long enjoyed the advantage of UMNO's access to funds. UMNO has transformed itself into a huge business conglomerate with assets in numerous corporations. Although conglomerates throughout Southeast Asia rely on government patronage, no assemblage of companies owned directly by a political party appears to have benefited from government largesse to the same extent as UMNO's holdings.[10] Neither opposition nor allied parties within the BN have access to such funds. One of UMNO's greatest vulnerabilities, as demonstrated by intermittent scandals, rests in its own missteps in allocating the state budget.

Beyond the APU, there have been other efforts to develop a party coalition to oust the UMNO-led BN. The Barisan Alternatif coalition formed in the wake of Anwar Ibrahim's arrest in 1999. The Barisan Alternatif included Anwar's People's Justice Party, the Islamic-oriented PAS, and the Chinese-oriented Democratic Action Party (DAP). Barisan Alternatif parties, especially PAS, competed well in the 1999 general elections, gaining twenty seats, but the DAP left the coalition shortly after September 11, 2001.

Evolving from the Barisan Alternatif, these same three parties reformed their coalition before the 2008 general election as the Pakatan Rakyat (People's Front, or People's Pact). The coalition's 2008 electoral gains eroded UMNO's control over Parliament, causing the BN coalition to lose its two-thirds majority and the required vote threshold to change the constitution—a key mechanism BN has used to redraw electoral districts in its favor. Even so, past gerrymandering rescued BN when the Pakatan Rakyat won the popular vote in

2013. Had BN-drawn electoral maps not rewarded its own parties disproportionately, the Pakatan Rakyat could have controlled the majority of seats in
Parliament for the first time.

Pakatan Rakyat was not an ideologically cohesive opposition but a tactical
alliance of the People's Justice Party (PKR), the Democratic Action Party
(DAP), and the Pan-Malaysian Islamic Party (PAS). The People's Justice Party's
main goal has been to end preferential policies favoring Malays under the NEP.
Offended by the corruption that preference has bred, the party of Anwar Ibra-
him (its de facto head) and Wan Azizah, his wife (the official leader), is viewed
by some as a viable alternative to UMNO for the federation's leadership.
Anwar, a former Muslim activist, holds acceptable Muslim credentials for most
Malays but his economic leanings have alienated economic nationalists in the
PR coalition.

The Pan-Malaysian Islamic Party is a rising force in Malaysia. With an implicitly communalist platform, PAS is dedicated to advancing conservative
Malay Muslim interests. PAS's platform has included the unrealistic goal of
creating an Islamic state. Some within the party favor sharia-based administration at the state level. PAS enjoyed a brief stint in a government coalition in the
1970s but soon parted ways with the business-oriented UMNO. Although it has
largely jettisoned the objective of transforming Malaysia into an Islamic state,
many moderate Muslims, Chinese, and Indians remain leery of further PAS
gains. Recent changes in the party's leadership reflect a more conservative Islamic orientation. PAS may never dominate Malaysia, but its supporters remain committed partisans, and the party's Malay identity threatens UMNO's
core communal support.

The third party in Pakatan, the Democratic Action Party, is a secular, multiethnic party oriented toward furthering Malaysia's modernity through goals of
social democracy. Advocating a "Malaysian Malaysia," the DAP has resurrected
jargon made prominent decades earlier by Lee Kuan Yew, before Singapore left
the federation. It draws support in urban areas, particularly among Chinese.
While the DAP's platform is somewhat compatible with that of the People's
Justice Party, the three parties of the PR shared little more than anti-UMNO
ambitions.

Despite the PR's 2013 successes, analysts were largely unsurprised that the
coalition fell apart in 2015. Once the fissures between the DAP and PAS cracked
fully open, the Pakatan Rakyat was declared dead. With PAS's disparate policy
objectives and pro-Islamist tilt, a Pakatan Rakyat coalition government would
likely have struggled mightily. Even without Pakatan, PAS remains politically
relevant. UMNO may choose to co-opt PAS to further solidify its growing
Malay communal identity. Whether the bureaucratic, pro-growth establishment in UMNO could endure the Islamist conservatism of PAS in a party alliance remains an open question.

More threatening to UMNO's hold on power than Malaysia's disorganized opposition is the potential collapse of its own party coalition, the Barisan Nasional. Prime Minister Najib's recent troubles increasingly alienate him not only from voters but also from UMNO's elder statesman Mahathir and coalition partners. The consensus approach within BN is breaking down, and disaffected BN supporters in the eastern Malaysian states of Sabah and Sarawak are demanding more from Najib's UMNO-led government. Even Malaysia's typically unobtrusive royal elite have begun to openly criticize Najib.

State Royalty

Malaysia's means of choosing its monarch is unique among Southeast Asia's constitutional monarchies. Nine states have hereditary rulers (sultans) and Malaysia's king, or *Yang di-Pertuan Agong* (Supreme Ruler), is elected from this body (usually on the basis of seniority) for a five-year term. The king, who has ceremonial and religious duties and powers of appointment, can officially delay certain legislative bills (although this power has been circumscribed). The Malaysian king is not held in the same awe as the king of Thailand; nevertheless, he plays an important symbolic role as the head of state.

The sultans' role changed dramatically in 1993 when Mahathir moved to place them under the law. The prime minister's actions were precipitated by an incident in which the sultan of Johor allegedly assaulted a field hockey coach with whom he was displeased. Mahathir lifted the hereditary rulers' immunity from legal action and revoked their right to grant pardons to themselves and their families.

Mahathir's moves were accompanied by daily press reports on the sultans' rampant corruption, philandering, and high living. These reports were shocking to the citizens both because of the extent of the alleged debauchery and because the reports appeared to break Sedition Act regulations forbidding criticism of the sultans. Rural Malays were stunned to read such reports about their sultans, who had long commanded their loyalty and were viewed as their symbolic protectors.

Serving as head of state in Malaysia's federative constitutional monarchy, the people's many rotating monarchs nevertheless bear the global distinction of rarely outlasting the government's prime ministers. Consequently, prominent prime ministers such as Tunku Abdul Rahman and Mahathir bin Mohamad became de facto symbols of the Malaysian state, both inside and outside of Malaysia. Political insignificance is thus the price of a system championing royal fairness.

Federal Parliament

Malaysia's political system is based on the British model, with a bicameral Parliament that elects one of its own members to the prime ministership. The prime minister must sit among the 222 seats in the lower chamber, the House of Representatives (Dewan Ra'ayat) and must command majority support. The upper chamber, the Senate (Dewan Negara), has 70 members: 26 appointed by state legislatures and 44 appointed by the king after the prime minister's recommendation. Senators hold office for six years; representatives serve five years unless Parliament is dissolved sooner than that. Although representation is based on single-member constituencies, a weighting of constituencies in favor of rural areas traditionally enhances Malay representation—in effect almost guaranteeing Malay political power.[11]

The potential of Malaysia's Parliament to alter the course of the federation's politics is significant. Given the fragmentation of political interests in the party system, and the multitude of viable parties (eleven of which hold House seats following the 2013 elections), UMNO could perhaps lose its coalition partners before it loses general elections outright to the People's Pact. Even with a more active civil society than in the past, the locus of political change in Malaysia's future is likely to be found in the parliamentary institution; that is, the electoral politics that determines who sits in it and the coalition governments it creates.

Political Islam

The religious element is central to Malaysians' political party orientations. Parties among the Malay majority are defined largely in terms of their degree of Islamic orthodoxy. Although moderate Islamic parties have been dominant in the ruling alliance, the rise of the conservative Pan-Malaysian Islamic Party in many states and its fickle role as a partner in the parliamentary opposition have been noteworthy developments.

In Malaysia, all Malays are Muslim by legal definition. Islam provides both legal and political privileges to Malays that, if lost, are tantamount to renouncing the Malay way of life. The state's new high-tech national identity cards, or MyKads (which include fingerprint biometrics), prominently list one's race and religion. Traditionally, Malay Muslims did not emphasize distinctions between secular and religious activities. Islam was tightly organized from the village up to the state level; hence, Muslims could be easily mobilized. Following the communal violence of 1969, proliferating *dakwah* (Muslim revivalist groups) made calls for Islamic fundamentalism, promoting rigid codes of conduct and the implementation of Islamic law. Many of these revivalist groups were filled with educated youth, often affiliated with the University of Malaya. Indeed, many of the movement's leaders came to hold radical Islamic ideas from the Arab world while studying in Britain.[12]

In the 1980s, Mahathir sought to defuse the Islamic resurgence by a program of "absorption of Islamic values," but this fanned the contentious flames of communalism. Sentiment for an Islamic state grew as organizations found inspiration from movements in Egypt and Pakistan.[13] Even before the September 11, 2001, terrorist attacks, Mahathir aggressively applied pressure on Islamist fundamentalist groups with international ties. As Washington, DC, launched its war on terrorism following the attacks, Malaysia cooperated with US intelligence to uncover cells of al-Qaeda and Jemaah Islamiyah in the country. Arrests, rumors, and discoveries of terrorist activity fueled anxiety in the region. The Petronas Towers were thought to be especially vulnerable to attack (authorities emptied the towers on September 12, 2001, for example). Terrorist bombings in neighboring Indonesia put Malaysian authorities on full alert about the nebulous threat the federation faced. Mahathir may have railed against Jews and the West in passionate speeches, but he also made no room for terrorists in Malaysia.

Similarly, Prime Minister Abdullah Badawi worked both sides of the Islamist extremism issue. Experienced in state security and antiterrorism as a former home minister, Badawi carried strong Muslim credentials as the son and grandson of Islamic scholars. Advocating a policy addressing fundamentalism's "root causes," Badawi stepped up his government's antipoverty agenda for rural areas following bombings in Indonesia. Standing before the UN General Assembly, he also promoted the concept of *Islam Hadhari* (Civilizational Islam)—that Islam is compatible with both modernity and equitable development.

Domestically, the opposition Pan-Malaysian Islamic Party, which competes with BN's UMNO for the Malay-Muslim vote, has increased its presence in national and state assemblies. Some areas where conservative Islam is predominant have begun to permit underage marriage; others have banned yoga, dark lipstick, and high-heeled shoes. Sharia courts are also on the rise. Sentences of corporal punishment for women involved in extramarital sex and beer drinking spawned international outcry and condemnation from international human rights groups. Under Najib, Malaysia's international reputation as a moderate Islamic society remains intact, but political Islam and fundamentalism are on the rise. PAS, for example, actively advocates that Malaysia adopt *hudud*, strict Islamic laws that include flogging, amputation, and stoning as punishments— a prospect decried by human rights activists. (Unless a perpetrator confesses, *hudud* requires four male Muslim witnesses to prove an offence; women are disallowed as witnesses, even when rape is alleged.)

Notwithstanding recent trends, Islam and modernity have generally evolved to complement each other in Malaysia. Because political Islam is largely moderate and finds expression through the party mechanism and other legitimate political channels, Islamist terrorism in multiethnic Malaysia has thus far remained limited. Malaysia's leaders also gain recognition for dampening the threat of communalism and the dangerous marriage between identity politics and Islamic fundamentalism. Nevertheless, the globalization of Islamist terrorism in the new international era leaves Malaysia exposed to pernicious influences beyond its borders. Small bands of Islamist militants claiming allegiance to ISIS exist in Malaysia, but analysts insist that for now the groups remain "basically merchants" who "use the ISIS flag as a ploy" to attract money from abroad.[14]

STATE-SOCIETY RELATIONS AND DEMOCRACY

Malaysia was granted independence under peaceful circumstances, and it adopted and adapted British governmental institutions; thus, the country emerged from colonialism with a strong and stable political system. Because of the communal character of their society, Malaysian leaders adapted Western democratic structures in an attempt to provide Malays with dominance of the political realm. This required that the principal institutions of the society be merged with the state. This fusion has been both a blessing and a curse to Malaysia's political development.

The clearest example of this close association is the integration of the Alliance (after 1969, the Barisan Nasional) with the state. As in Indonesia, where Golkar was in essence a state institution, the BN (led by UMNO) merged with the state—dominating the bureaucracy, the Parliament, the media, and the courts. This arrangement has set Malaysia apart from Thailand and the Philippines, where political parties are relatively autonomous from the state. If UMNO's control of Parliament is overturned, however, the state could achieve new separation from its long-dominant partner.

One characteristic of strong states is their ability to project their power into the countryside. Through the co-optation of local Malay elites and the provision of roads, financial credit, medical facilities, recreational programs, and other benefits, the Malaysian state has succeeded in tying local power brokers to the central authorities through either UMNO or local-level governmental agencies.

In economic affairs as well, the Malaysian state has asserted its control. No facet of the economy is excluded from governmental intervention, intended to ensure that the goals of the NEP are met and to provide resources to UMNO. The state has co-opted most of those who could challenge it. Indeed, most oppositionists are established supporters of the state, differing only in terms of their desire to replace its political leaders. Thus, the Malaysian state is not subservient to societal forces, such as an autonomous military or insurgency, or to such external powers as a former colonial ruler or present-day international financial institutions.

Malaysia's postindependence prime ministers have also strengthened state institutions as a means to promote political stability, economic development, and ethnic harmony. Malaysia experienced strong leadership from Tunku Abdul Rahman, the father of Malaysian independence, and Mahathir bin Mohamad, the manager of Malaysia's economic success. These leaders did not undermine the state's institutions in a manner similar to that of Ferdinand Marcos in the Philippines, Ne Win in Burma, or Hun Sen in Cambodia.

Thus, as opposed to its neighbors, Malaysia has managed to sustain basic institutions of democratic rule. The major exception, following the 1969 riots, was a temporary state of emergency, but it was carried out less as a coup d'état than as an interlude during which parliamentary democracy could be rebuilt. Unlike in Thailand, Indonesia, and Myanmar, the Malaysian military has not played a major role in politics. In the early years of independence, priority was given to socioeconomic development rather than to building substantial armed forces.[15] Despite significant upgrades in the military's profile in recent years, and new purchases of fighter jets, submarines, and weapons systems, Malaysia's military remains far from being a praetorian force.

The granting of independence by Great Britain was carried out peacefully and was received with some reluctance by Malaysians, who feared their country's viability would be jeopardized without British support. Nevertheless, the Malaysians adopted the Westminster model of governance, including regularized competitive elections, a representative parliament, civilian supremacy, and civil liberties. These adoptions are especially noteworthy because Malaysian elites tend to hold a formalized view of democracy that crumbles when it faces more deeply held values; stability and security, for example, take precedence over democratic values.[16]

Since independence, Malaysia has witnessed an impressive thirteen national elections. Remarkably, UMNO has won them all, and the right to form a government, although sometimes with coalition partners. Over the course of these elections, there have been five orderly successions of power between UMNO elites. Opposition candidates generally win about 40 percent of the votes. In 2013, the Pakatan Rakyat opposition coalition actually won 51 percent of the popular vote but failed to secure a parliamentary majority of seats due to UMNO's past gerrymandering of districts to its advantage.

Despite UMNO's election record, Malaysia is generally regarded as a quasi- or illiberal democracy because of serious limitations on civil liberties.[17] Until it was repealed by Najib in 2012, the country's Internal Securities Act imposed a culture of silence on citizens and prohibited discussion of "sensitive issues." Even after its repeal, newspapers, television, radio, and the Internet are government (read: UMNO) regulated and generally compliant vis-à-vis all communalism issues. Websites, magazines, and newspapers that overstep boundaries can be, and have been, shut down. "Religious freedom" for Muslims in Malaysia includes the criminality of apostasy and, in many states, the criminality of conversion to another religion. In Malaysia's democracy, non-Muslims may not marry Muslims without converting first. Local sharia courts often hold authority over Muslims in such matters of marriage and conversion, and where federal law or state law is silent or ambiguous.

According to the system's defenders, the explanation for the necessity of quasi-democracy rather than full, Western-style democracy is that Malaysia's polycommunal situation is unique. Such a society cannot carry out its affairs in a fully democratic way if one segment of the society must be given special privileges of governance. In the context of communal issues, an election loss or BN-coalition collapse could mean the perceived end of the Malays' primary rights. Emergency rule became necessary in 1969, the argument goes, because Malays and Chinese reacted to that possibility. Many Malay leaders stoke fears that non-Malay control of the country would create chaos.

The rules for Malaysian democracy, which had to be modified after 1969 to ensure that Malay political supremacy would continue, were changed to include opposition parties in the Alliance.[18] Dividing the nation along ethnic lines between those in power and those not in power would only worsen communal issues. To mitigate divisiveness, the Barisan Nasional was created to accommodate a wider range of parties. The BN formula was uniquely Malaysian, reflecting the difficult ethnic sensitivities that have long been at the core of Malaysian politics.

Malaysia's illiberal democracy, or what might be called a competitive authoritarian regime, has been sustained by the continuing strength of the economy, which mitigates extremist demands by the growing urbanized middle class (which favors moderate policies), and by the country's modern history of British-style democratic institutions. Mahathir's emphasis on "Asian values" opposed democratic tendencies, especially regarding the rights to protest and question governmental leaders. Until recently, most Malaysians seemed content with the notion of quasi- or illiberal democracy, which they viewed as appropriate to their values. Nevertheless, the government's treatment of opposition politicians and UMNO corruption scandals are causing many to push for greater civil liberties and fuller democracy.

ECONOMY AND DEVELOPMENT

Malaysia is one of the few success stories of economic development in the third world. With a nominal per capita gross national income in 2014 of $10,600 ($24,715 using purchasing power parity) there has been a clear improvement in the standard of living since independence in 1957. In 1966, only 18 percent of households in a typical Malaysian village had piped water. By 1978, this figure was 71 percent and by 1993 close to 100 percent. Electricity was available to 45 percent of households in 1966; this increased to 79 percent in 1978 and 100 percent by 1987. In 1966, only 4 percent of Malay families owned a television; by 1997, the figure was just under 100 percent. During this period, dirt roads were paved, telephone lines were installed, and mosques were built.[19] By 2014, Malaysia's Human Development Index global ranking was 62 (out of 179), higher than resource-rich countries such as Brazil, Mexico, and Venezuela.

In 1971, by means of the unprecedented New Economic Policy, the Malaysian government initiated an extraordinary twenty-year plan designed to eradicate poverty and eliminate ethnicity as a function of economic prosperity. The plan was meant to change Malaysia's fundamental structures and ethnic divisions by directing the increments of rapid economic growth disproportionately to the Malay sector, without expropriating Chinese assets or weakening the vigor of Chinese enterprise.[20]

The NEP was the government's response to the 1969 riots and the perceived need for a dramatic attack on the ethnic divisions in the economy. According to government data, in 1971 the ownership of share capital was 63 percent foreign, 34 percent non-Malay, and less than 3 percent Malay. The goal was to raise the Malay share of capital ownership to 30 percent and reduce the foreign share to 30 percent, while allowing the Chinese share to rise to 40 percent.[21] The means to this end were tax breaks, investment incentives, employment quotas, and the granting of special privileges in business ownership. The government required all banks to earmark a significant proportion of their business loans for Malays.

The NEP was to end in 1990; however, because the target of 30 percent capital ownership by Malays had not been met (it then stood near 20 percent), the government appointed a commission to design a new twenty-year policy. Other goals were substantially achieved, including the reduction of the poverty level, which had fallen from 30 percent in 1977 to 17 percent by 1987. Many more *bumiputra* Malays were engaged in businesses in which they had formerly been underrepresented. Investments in rural development and agricultural programs increased many times over during the twenty-year NEP.

Like other successful Asian economies, Malaysia's economic achievements are not the result of Washington Consensus policies. Under Mahathir, Malaysia did emphasize market-oriented mechanisms, featuring the privatization of public utilities, communications, and transportation; at the same time it also featured state-owned heavy industrialization and large state-managed holding companies. Mahathir's "Look East Policy" stressed the adoption of the work ethic and other principles followed by companies in Japan and South Korea as well as increased trade with Asian neighbors. The success of these programs led economists to claim that Malaysia had joined Singapore, Taiwan, South Korea, and Hong Kong as Asia's fifth tiger.

Over time, Malaysia became the world's largest exporter of semiconductors and one of the largest exporters of single-unit air conditioners, textiles, and footwear. Manufacturing accounted for 50 percent of total exports by 1990, compared to just 20 percent ten years earlier. These increases in manufacturing output, stimulated largely by export-oriented industrialization, have resulted in a much more broadly based economy. Malaysia's attempt to follow Japan and South Korea in the automobile export industry, on the other hand, failed miserably. (Malaysia's state-subsidized Proton brand became quickly associated with low quality and remains hardly known outside of Malaysia.)

During the 1990s, Malaysia's economic growth rate was one of the highest in the world, averaging 8.3 percent. The country enjoyed low unemployment and inflation rates, along with increases in manufacturing production and foreign investment. However, Malaysia's economic success was mitigated by continuing reports that the percentage of Malays sharing in the new wealth had not increased appreciably, despite the stated goals of the NEP. Hence, in 1991, Prime Minister Mahathir introduced a ten-year new development policy, which sought to achieve 30 percent equity for Malays in the economic system. Mahathir also set forth his ambitious "Vision 2020" goal for Malaysia: developed country status. Such a noteworthy goal would require an annual growth rate of 7 percent during the intervening thirty years.

Despite the country's economic growth trajectory, several challenges emerged, including the need to import migrant labor for plantation work, improving infrastructure, and keeping wages competitive for foreign investment. Most consequentially, the 1997 currency crisis undermined Malaysians' pride in their "miracle" economy and threatened to bring Mahathir's 2020 project crashing down. The crisis meant the new millennium was greeted with nonperforming loans, large debts, rising unemployment, and lower-than-expected economic growth rates.

Malaysia's economy strengthened after the Asian economic crisis, notwithstanding Mahathir's refusal to accept IMF loans. His decision to place controls on capital account transactions went against the decisions of other Southeast Asian leaders. But criticism of the capital controls ended when Malaysia's economy began to flourish again. From 2003 to 2008, Malaysia's GDP growth rate averaged 5.7 percent. After contracting to −1.7 percent in 2009 due to the global financial crisis, Malaysia's GDP growth rebounded to an average rate of over 6 percent. Throughout the global downturn, Malaysia maintained an unemployment rate below 4 percent. By 2012, the World Economic Forum rated Malaysia fourth in the world for protecting investors and twenty-first for doing business overall—ahead of South Korea, China, and all of Latin America. In Southeast Asia, only Singapore ranked higher.

Malaysia's economy today reflects increasing diversity founded on the base of its nationalized oil company, Petronas; manufacturing exports in electronics and information technology; and a natural-resources sector built on logging, rubber, palm oil, and liquefied natural gas. (Malaysia is the world's leading exporter of tropical wood, natural rubber, and palm oil, and the world's second-largest producer of liquefied natural gas.) Small and medium enterprises focusing on textiles, wood products, and services prosper in Kuala Lumpur, Penang, Johor Bahru, and other urban areas. A market capitalization of close to $400 billion shores up the Kuala Lumpur Stock Exchange, one of Southeast Asia's oldest. Malaysia's financial sector is internationally recognized for its efficiency and consistent performance. China's declining demand for commodities and subsequent currency devaluation in 2015 jeopardize Malaysia's natural-resources sector.

In negotiating free trade agreements with the United States (bilaterally) and with China (via ASEAN), Malaysia has forged ahead with a long-term internationalization strategy for its economy. In 2015, talks with Washington and eleven other Pacific Rim countries concluded an agreement for the Trans-Pacific Partnership (TPP). Malaysia's Parliament is likely to ratify the trade deal. Also, with Malaysia seeking to become a financial center for Islamic banking, the country's economic ties to the Muslim world are growing fast. After the United States, Malaysia is Saudi Arabia's largest trading partner, sending it and its oil-rich neighbors in the Persian Gulf furniture, electronics, and construction materials.

FOREIGN RELATIONS

Malaysia has not been an interventionist country, nor has it participated prominently in international affairs since its independence in 1957. During the Cold War, it joined the Non-Aligned Movement but it actively worked to eliminate communist insurgency along its Thai border. Regional cooperation through ASEAN has long been a first priority for Malaysia as a means to enhance both the nation's security and its economic objectives.

Following independence, Malaysia's main adversary was China because of the support the People's Republic gave to communists during the Emergency in the 1950s and because of distrust of Malaysia's indigenous Chinese. Nevertheless, in 1974, Malaysia normalized relations with China, although the domestic communal situation remained a concern in the relationship for decades. Favoring the development of ASEAN, Malaysia adopted a "strategically exclusive" approach to regional security that favors the view that outside powers abstain from interference.[22]

Mahathir was principal spokesman for the ASEAN Free Trade Area (AFTA) and for Asian trade groups, which, he argued, could counter the North American Free Trade Agreement (NAFTA) as well as the European Union. Mahathir also became a spokesman against "Western values," which he viewed as inappropriate for Malaysia and other developing countries. He joined Singaporean leaders and others promoting "Asian values" as a superior alternative to the West's social disorder and moral indifference.

Malaysia supported the admission of Myanmar, Laos, and Vietnam into ASEAN. In 1996, tensions with Singapore increased when Singaporean Senior Minister Lee Kuan Yew made the comment that if Singapore ever was forced back into Malaysia, it would be a catastrophe for Singapore's ethnic Chinese because the Malaysian system was "racist." Eventually, the issue was handled diplomatically, but the disagreement reflected the long-running unease between the two neighbors.

In the new international era, Malaysia's foreign policy focus has been economic. Its strategy for the twenty-first century is built on global trade and investment by enhancing direct links to three of the world's largest markets: the United States, Japan, and China. Under Abdullah Badawi's watch, Malaysia became the United States' tenth-largest trading partner. Japan, for its part, remains one of Malaysia's most important foreign investors and export markets; and Malaysia's trade with China is now experiencing double-digit growth, although the balance is in the latter's favor. The opening of the ASEAN-China Free Trade Zone in 2010 deepened Sino-Malaysian economic ties, and China's appetite for Malaysia's palm oil, as well as its crude oil, continues to grow unabated. One of Prime Minister Najib's first overseas visits after assuming office was to China, the country's former adversary. China reciprocated six months later by sending Hu Jintao to Kuala Lumpur. In 2014, the two upgraded their relations to a "comprehensive strategic partnership" and signed a five-year bilateral trade deal expected to boost trade to $160 billion by 2017.[23]

Growing relations with China have not come at the expense of relations with the United States. President Barack Obama visited Malaysia in 2014, the first official visit by a US president in almost fifty years—an occasion that merited a state dinner with over 600 guests. Months later, Prime Minister Najib found himself playing golf with the US president in Hawaii. Not only do the two countries seek to enhance economic ties through initiatives such as the TPP, but Najib's governments have remained broadly supportive of the US pivot to Asia. In the midst of Malaysia's 1MDB scandal, President Obama returned to Kuala Lumpur in late 2015 to attend the multilateral ASEAN meetings and East Asian Summit. He was noticeably quiet about Najib's alleged corruption.

Malaysia's global significance is now following its economic success. Its delicate position in the relations between the Muslim world and the West reflects its new role. Muslim commentators note that "the entire Muslim world views it [Malaysia] as a successful model of a modern Islamic state."[24] Indeed, of the most successful developers of the Organization of the Islamic Conference's fifty-seven countries (representing 1 billion Muslims), only Malaysia can boast that it is neither a petro-kingdom nor a microstate. Malaysia's increasing economic ties to the Muslim world are also complicating its relations abroad. After China, Malaysia is the largest foreign investor in Sudan's oil industry, drawing criticism that refined Malaysia supports a pariah, genocidal regime. Malaysia's foreign policy, moving beyond Asia-Pacific concerns, is now framed with a greater international dimension.

CONCLUSION

Since 1969, the desire for stability has kept Malaysians from relapsing into destructive identity politics and communalism. The political will of its Malay, Chinese, and Indian citizens to impose order on society found positive expression through political party alliances and by acquiescing to visionary leadership. Symbiotically, rapid economic growth and political order led Malaysia up the development ladder in tandem, hand over hand, foot over foot. By combining market forces, international openness, strong state guidance, and affirmative action policies benefiting the country's poorer majority, Malaysia's leading party, UMNO, and its Barisan Nasional alliance partners engineered enviable degrees of order, development, and equality.

Sacrificing certain civil and political liberties was, of course, a substantial price for stability and success. Mahathir, champion of "Asian values," often offended Westerners by gloating about Malaysia's brand of development, but it is difficult to imagine Malaysia's success in the absence of any trade-offs. As witnessed too often elsewhere, communalism does not generally escape asymmetrical structures of power and inequitable patterns of allocation.

Even as the Barisan Nasional coalition faces unprecedented challenges today from opposition parties, urban protesters, and conservative Islamists, the formula for political success in Malaysia is perhaps more clearly understood than in any other Southeast Asian system: cross-communal alliances with willing Malay, Chinese, and Indian partners underpinned by a Malay-led "fidelity to the icons of indigenousness, protection, Malay unity, dominance, and Islam."[25] Existing institutions have served this formula well, but institutions are human creations that demand guidance and leadership if they are to endure. Malaysia's history suggests considerable risk for leaders who choose to alter this formula or the institutional legacies of Tunku Abdul Rahman and Mahathir bin Mohamad. A realignment of parties along communal lines may pose a real threat to Malaysia's well-regarded stability.

NOTES

1. In the study of Malaysia, the terms "ethnicity" and "race" are widely used to distinguish the same communities of Malays, Chinese, and Indians. In this chapter, both terms are used loosely and are not intended to imply narrower definitions of either term.

2. Milton J. Esman, *Administration and Development in Malaysia* (Ithaca, NY: Cornell University Press, 1972), 20–22.

3. Diane K. Mauzy, "Malaysia in 1987," *Asian Survey* 28, no. 2 (February 1988): 214.

4. Hari Singh and Suresh Narayanan, "Changing Dimensions in Malaysian Politics," *Asian Survey* 29, no. 5 (May 1989): 517.

5. Stephen A. Douglas, "How Strong Is the Malaysian State?" paper presented to the Association for Asian Studies, Chicago, April 1990, p. 2.

6. The full transcript of Mahathir's OIC speech is published by the *Sydney Morning Herald* as "Mahathir's Full Speech," October 22, 2003, www.smh.com.au/articles/2003/10/20/1066502121884.html.

7. James Chin, "Malaysia: The Rise of Najib and 1Malaysia," *Southeast Asian Affairs 2010* (Singapore: Institute of Southeast Asian Studies, 2010); Clara Chooi, "Najib: Government Will Protect, Not Limit Individual Freedom," *The Malaysian Insider*, April 11, 2012, www.themalaysianinsider.com/malaysia/article/najib-government-will-protect-not-limit-individual-freedom.

8. Liz Gooch, "Police Clash with Malaysia Protesters Seeking Electoral Reforms," *New York Times*, April 28, 2012, www.nytimes.com/2012/04/29/world/asia/malaysian-capital -braces-for-rally-by-democracy-activists.html.

9. Zakaria Haji Ahmad, "Stability, Security and National Development in Malaysia: An Appraisal," in *Durable Stability in Southeast Asia*, ed. Kusuma Snitwongse and Sukhumbhand Paribatra (Singapore: Institute of Southeast Asian Studies, 1987), 125.

10. Doug Tsuruoka, "UMNO's Money Machine," *Far Eastern Economic Review*, July 5, 1990, 48.

11. Zakaria Haji Ahmad, "Malaysia: Quasi Democracy in a Divided Society," in *Democracy in Developing Countries: Asia*, ed. Larry Diamond, Juan J. Linz, and Seymour Martin Lipset (Boulder, CO: Lynne Rienner Publishers, 1989), 373.

12. Michael Leifer, "Dakwah," *Dictionary of the Modern Politics of South-East Asia* (London: Routledge, 1995), 83.

13. Ibid.

14. Eunice Au, "Malaysian Militants Plan to Start ISIS Faction in South-east Asia," *New Straits Times*, November 15, 2015, www.straitstimes.com/asia/se-asia/malaysian-militants -plan-to-start-isis-faction-in-s-e-asia.

15. Zakaria Haji Ahmad, "The Military and Development in Malaysia and Brunei, with a Short Survey on Singapore," in *Soldiers and Stability in Southeast Asia*, ed. J. Soedjati Djiwandono and Yong Mun Cheong (Singapore: Institute of Southeast Asian Studies, 1988), 235.

16. A point first observed by James C. Scott, *Political Ideology in Malaysia* (New Haven, CT: Yale University Press, 1968).

17. Ahmad, "Malaysia: Quasi Democracy in a Divided Society," 349.

18. Ibid., 358.

19. These figures come from Marvin Rogers, "Patterns of Change in Rural Malaysia: Development and Dependence," *Asian Survey* 29, no. 8 (August 1989): 767–770.

20. Milton J. Esman, "Ethnic Politics and Economic Power," *Comparative Politics* 19, no. 4 (July 1987): 403.

21. Ibid.

22. Donald Emmerson, *Hard Choices: Security, Democracy, and Regionalism in Southeast Asia* (Stanford, CA: The Walter H. Shorenstein Asia-Pacific Research Center, 2008), 21.

23. William Case, "Malaysia in 2013: A Benighted Election Day (and Other Events)," *Asian Survey* 54, no. 1 (January/February 2014): 62.

24. Abdulaziz Sager, "Saudi-Malaysia Alliance Could Help Reshape the Islamic World," *Arab News*, January 29, 2006, www.arabnews.com/node/279598.

25. William Case, "Malaysia: Aspects and Audiences of Legitimacy," in *Political Legitimacy in Southeast Asia: The Quest for Moral Authority*, ed. Muthiah Alagappa (Stanford, CA: Stanford University Press, 1995), 107.

11

SINGAPORE

The quest for survival, order, and prosperity is a dominant theme of contemporary Singaporean politics. Surrounded by countries hundreds of times larger in area, with populations twenty to fifty times greater, this island city-state is in many respects a speck in a region of giant nations—even tiny Hong Kong is twice its size. As an urban entrepôt with virtually no agricultural base, Singapore stands alone, bereft of the resources and land of its Southeast Asian neighbors.

Singapore's principal resource is its people. Multiethnic and multicultural, Singapore's 5.7 million total residents are about 75 percent Chinese, 14 percent Malay, 9 percent Indian, and 2 percent other minorities. Enjoying a per capita GNI of $55,150, Singaporean citizens are the wealthiest, best-educated, best-housed, and healthiest population in Southeast Asia. Interestingly, only 64 percent of the 5.7 million people actually living on the densely populated island are officially citizens; the remaining 36 percent, nearly 2 million, are nonresident foreign workers or permanent residents.

In 1999, B. J. Habibie, then president of Indonesia, unflatteringly referred to Singapore as a "little red dot," just a speck on the map compared to its massive neighbors. Insulted as they were at the time, Singaporeans began to consider the contemptuous label as a source of pride, symbolic of the republic's remarkable economic success. The country's leaders, prone to strategies of co-optation, embraced the "red dot" label and Singaporeans inside and outside of government now celebrate their new soubriquet with affection.

Ironically, despite its achievements, Singapore has one of the highest rates of emigration in the world. In 1990, about 36,000 Singaporeans lived in other countries. By 2006, over 143,000 émigrés had formally registered with the republic's embassies abroad. A large number of unregistered exiles render the Singaporean diaspora even larger—as high as 192,000 according to one 2012 estimate.[1] It is often Singapore's young and most talented who leave. The primary reasons emigrants give for leaving are advanced education and job

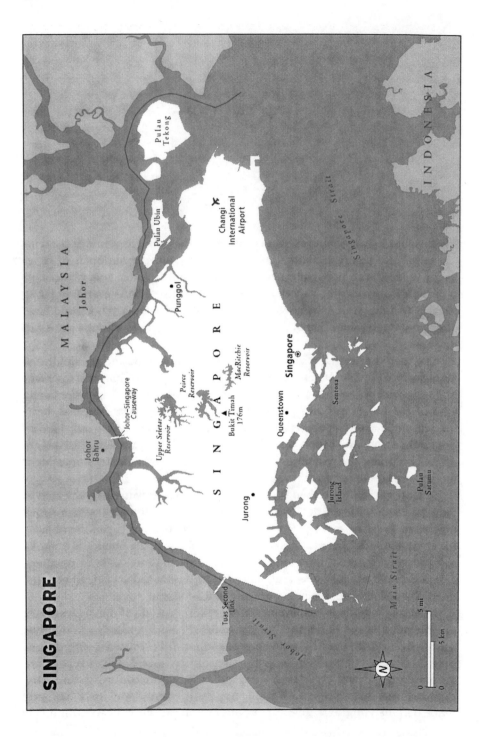

SINGAPORE

opportunities, but for many, the city has become devoid of spirit, heart, and vitality, characteristics that have been displaced by a materialistic coldness symbolized by the nation's ubiquitous rules and prohibitions. According to the country's leaders, emigration threatens Singaporean identity as "the country's talent goes overseas."[2]

No noncommunist society in Southeast Asia regulates its citizens' behavior as much as Singapore. Rules on traffic, street cleanliness, shops and markets, gum chewing, landscaping, and food preparation are strictly enforced by the authorities and rigorously followed by the citizenry. Regulation extends to residential choice. Land poor, Singapore's Housing and Development Board manages a large-scale program housing over 80 percent of citizens in multistory buildings. Since the 1960s, Singaporean authorities have engineered public housing allocations to diffuse ethnic-based residential clustering. Chinese, Malays, and Indians must live amongst each other in government-controlled, but affordable, "housing estates." The government's Central Provident Fund, derived from mandatory payroll contributions, functions as a compulsory savings program that supports the housing program as well as medical care and retirement pensions.

One might expect such bureaucratization would engender corruption. However, less corruption exists in Singapore than in any other Southeast Asian nation. Although a part of the political system, patronage is less salient in political recruitment and policymaking than it is in the systems of Singapore's neighbors. The republic's clean reputation is reflected in Transparency International's annual rankings, where Singapore is regularly listed among the ten least corrupt countries in the world.

To achieve order, Singapore has fashioned one of the world's most effective and efficient governments. Characterized by democratic institutions but within the context of authoritarian order, Singapore's government has been controlled by a single party, the People's Action Party (PAP), since full independence was obtained in 1965. Until November 1990, Singapore had known only one leader, Lee Kuan Yew, who had led the island since 1957. Only two others, including Lee's own son, have ruled Singapore since 1990.

The themes of survival, prosperity, and order have become fused in Singapore to produce a unique style of politics and economic life.[3] The fusion stems from colonial times, when the British controlled Singapore, making it dependent on British economic policies. After achieving limited independence in 1957, Singapore granted Britain control over its external affairs and security matters out of fear of a seizure of power by the communists or external intervention. To achieve full independence, the Singaporean economic system established interdependence in the global economic system, and the country allied with its northern neighbor, Malaya, which complemented Singapore economically.

The concern for survival was the major impetus for the decision by Malaya and Singapore to forge the Federation of Malaysia in September 1963, which included Sabah and Sarawak as well. Tunku Abdul Rahman, Malaysia's founding prime minister, feared that Singapore might become communist, an "Asian Cuba." The solution was to accept the city-state as a member of the federation. From the Singaporean perspective, Malaya's agricultural resources were necessary for their own development. Lee Kuan Yew did not originally believe that Singapore was viable by itself.

The federation lasted only two years. It fell apart in August 1965 because the Alliance government in Kuala Lumpur perceived that Singapore's Chinese threatened the Malays' privileged political position. Lee Kuan Yew had called for a "Malaysian Malaysia," with the implication that all Malaysians, regardless of race, could participate equally in all phases of life. This view was contrary to Tunku Abdul Rahman's belief that a "Malay Malaysia" was in the society's best interest. Unable to reconcile, the parties agreed to remove Singapore from Malaysia. Lee Kuan Yew famously cried in public over the expulsion.

On its own, Singapore faced the challenge of survival in an era of grave tensions, which stemmed mostly from the global Cold War and the *Konfrontasi* threat from Indonesia. Rather than seek a complementary alliance to attain security, Singapore fashioned policies designed to achieve rapid and far-reaching economic development to ensure its sovereignty. By 1969, the government had consolidated the republic's independence, stability, and viability, a consolidation that continues to the present. This success has depended on sustained economic development and the inculcation of values that unify people from diverse backgrounds with an emphasis on hard work and the development of human capital.

When Lee Kuan Yew stepped down as prime minister in November 1990, he sponsored his protégé Goh Chok Tong to be his replacement. Just nine months after becoming the nation's leader, Goh called a snap election to legitimize his administration. Goh needed to step out of the shadow of Lee, who continued in an official capacity as "senior minister." In contrast to Lee's more authoritarian style, Goh used a more consensual approach to governing. He did not yet have a popular mandate and wanted to take advantage of the country's excellent economy to ensure widespread support for the PAP.[4]

The August 1991 election resulted in a decisive victory for the PAP; only four of the eighty-one seats were won by the opposition Singapore Democratic Party. To shore up his administration even more, in December 1992 Goh stood in a by-election and received a significant victory, capturing 73 percent of the vote in his own constituency. There was special poignancy in this victory because in the previous month he had informed the populace that his two deputy prime ministers were both suffering from cancer. The better known of these two was Lee Hsien Loong, minister of trade and industry, the son of Lee Kuan Yew and presumed heir apparent to the position of prime minister. Indeed, many commentators suggested that Goh was only an interim leader until Lee Hsien Loong was ready to assume the top position. The other deputy prime minister diagnosed with cancer was Ong Teng Cheong. Both deputies were immediately treated with chemotherapy and soon recovered.

Indeed, in 1993 both men made remarkable comebacks. Ong Teng Cheong was elected for a six-year term as the country's first executive president in August, and Lee Hsien Loong returned as next in line for the prime ministership. The position of executive president was intended to be subordinate to the prime ministership, and it has not subsequently become more influential. In 1999, S. R. Nathan, a Hindu diplomat and PAP member, replaced Ong as president following an uncontested election.

In 1995 and 1996, both Lee Kuan Yew and Goh Chok Tong engaged in a series of libel suits against their adversaries, winning every case and thus again demonstrating that the Singaporean judiciary has little autonomy from the executive branch. The PAP routinely wins multimillion-dollar defamation awards against political opponents and has even imprisoned some opposition candidates without charge.

In 1995, *New York Times* columnist William Safire described Singapore as a family dictatorship, characteristic of "old-fashioned European totalitarianism."[5] Goh responded with rhetorical shots of his own, and a trans-Pacific debate about "Asian values" played out for months on newspaper editorial pages and in academic circles. Goh, Lee, and others (including Malaysia's Mahathir bin Mohamad) claimed Asian superiority over Western societies, where crime, disorder, and corruption tainted economic success. They argued that a cultural emphasis on order, family, individual sacrifice, and hard work explained Asia's rising status. Critics responded by claiming that rule of law in Singapore was a sham and that "Asian values" justified strong-armed "authoritarian capitalism."[6] During this same time, the formerly impeccable Lee Kuan Yew and his son Lee Hsien Loong were revealed to have received discounts on two exclusive private condominiums. Lee explained that "it is an unfair world," which did little to mollify those who had supported the government's claim to meritocracy.

On January 2, 1997, parliamentary elections were held, but there was never any question about the outcome. The opposition contested only thirty-six of the eighty-three available seats, and the PAP won 63.5 percent of the total votes cast and eighty-one of the parliamentary seats. This strong showing reversed a downward trend that had reduced the PAP vote in 1991 to 59.3 percent. The Singapore Democratic Party lost every seat it had held. The 1997 victory was viewed as a vindication for Goh Chok Tong and his party's economic achievements. Goh interpreted the result as a sign that voters had rejected Western-style liberal democracy; he also saw the outcome as his liberation from the long shadow of Lee Kuan Yew.

Election results in 2001 and 2006 perpetuated PAP legislative dominance, with winning margins of 75 percent and 67 percent, respectively. In 2004, Lee

Hsien Loong took over as prime minister. Goh, credited for sound economic management and for bolstering education and medical assistance during his tenure, stayed on as senior minister. Lee Kuan Yew, ever present, took on yet another new cabinet title as "minister mentor."

The political effects of the 2008 global financial crisis later produced what Lee Hsien Loong described as a "watershed election" in 2011. Problems in the real estate market, rising inflation, and Singapore's worst recession since independence turned a record number of voters away from the PAP. Returning one of its worst election results since 1965, the PAP garnered only 60 percent of the vote. The opposition Worker's Party won six seats in parliament (the PAP retained eighty-one). Somewhat symbolically, after the election, eighty-seven-year-old Lee Kuan Yew resigned from his cabinet post as minister mentor, claiming the time had arrived for a new generation of leaders to guide the country.

In 2013, Lee Hsien Loong's government issued a "white paper" on immigration policy that generated shock waves throughout Singapore. The official report lamented the country's declining birth rate and aging demographic profile. Most alarming to the "Singaporean Core"—those with Singaporean ancestry dating before 1965—the report outlined the government's view that new immigration would be needed to maintain satisfactory economic growth; that by 2030 about half of the country's projected 6.9 million people would need to be immigrants. Spontaneous street rallies followed and social media erupted over the white paper. Singaporeans regularly complain that immigrants push down salaries and erode national identity. Opposition politicians pounced with fresh attacks on the government and called for a freeze on foreign workforce growth. Observers wondered if the PAP's grip on electoral power might be eroding.

Nonetheless, as it had in the 1990s, the electoral dominance of the PAP returned. In a new round of legislative elections held in September 2015, the PAP resoundingly defeated a record number of opposition parties by securing 70 percent of the vote. The opposition seats in Parliament declined and PAP proved resilient. The victory was especially impressive because prior to the poll, ten opposition parties struck a deal to specifically avoid "three-corner fights" in most voting districts. By engaging this strategy, and pitting only one opposition candidate against the PAP's candidate, Singapore's opposition parties sought to avoid taking anti-PAP votes from each other on Election Day. However, the results proved the PAP had little trouble defeating challengers in head-to-head matches.

One possible reason for the PAP's resurgence was Lee Kuan Yew's passing only six months earlier at the age of ninety-one, after a bout with severe pneumonia. Although the official mourning period was for seven days, the outpouring of grief within Singapore continued for months, combined with an inundation of international accolades from world leaders and diplomats praising Singapore's founding father. Under his son's leadership, Lee Hsien Loong's Singapore continues the political patterns Lee Kuan Yew put in motion: one-party dominance, technocracy, meritocracy, and an unapologetic focus on order, security, and material prosperity.

INSTITUTIONS AND SOCIAL GROUPS

Lee Kuan Yew

Few leaders in Southeast Asia have had the impact on their societies that Lee Kuan Yew has had in Singapore. Ho Chi Minh, Sukarno, Suharto, Ne Win, and Norodom Sihanouk had comparable influence, but none ruled a society with as much effectiveness. Lee, who won a Queen's Scholarship to study law at Cambridge, was a brilliant and pragmatic politician with more sustained popular support than any perhaps any other world leader of his day.

By placing highly educated and technically proficient officials in charge of his development programs, Lee relied on his subordinates to establish effective policies free from corruption. By combining select advantages of Western-style democratic institutions with an Asian-style hegemonic political party system, Lee was able to dominate the country's politics and achieve almost universal support and legitimacy.

In the late 1980s, Lee's consummate political skill lost some of its edge as he moved toward authoritarianism and away from open and pragmatic policies. In a series of decisions concerning the jailing of dissident politicians and the restriction of newspapers printing articles critical of his administration, Lee veered from the careful balance he had achieved between civil liberties and order during the previous decades. Lee rationalized the new direction toward tighter order as necessary for the continued stability of the country and as appropriate for Asian culture. Singapore's fiercest critics claimed politics in the city-state had been reduced to loyalty and sycophancy surrounding Lee.[7]

Following his resignation as prime minister in 1990, Lee continued to be the country's most visible statesman as its "senior minister." He traveled extensively, meeting world leaders and advising developing nations on how to achieve their own economic miracle. He stressed the importance of discipline and denigrated Western-style democracy as inappropriate for developing countries. He also gave up his position as secretary-general of the PAP to allow new leaders to develop needed legitimacy.

In November 1991, the Parliament passed the Elected President Act, which provided for a stronger presidency but retained the cabinet, headed by the prime minister. Initially, it was believed that Lee would be nominated for the presidency, but he denied interest in a position he judged too subordinate. When his son, Lee Hsien Loong, assumed the prime ministership in 2004, Lee Kuan Yew preferred to stay on as minister mentor, a cabinet position he kept until the age of eighty-seven. Forever in the shadow of his late father, Lee Hsien Loong, a skilled leader in his own right, has yet to exhibit his father's magnetism or visionary leadership.

Political Parties

The People's Action Party is virtually synonymous with Lee Kuan Yew and his legacy. It has been in power since 1959. More striking than its uninterrupted rule may be that the PAP has won all but a handful of eligible parliamentary seats in every election since 1968, garnering as high as 84 percent of the vote.

The only party ever to provide credible opposition was the left-wing Barisan Sosialis (Socialist Front), which split from the PAP in the 1960s. Since that time, opposition parties have been allowed to function, but none have provided meaningful competition to the PAP. The reasons for the PAP's dominance include the effectiveness and incorruptibility of most PAP politicians, the factionalization of the opposition, and the rigid rules that circumscribe the activities of political parties and opposition groups. These rules were especially important in the late 1980s when newspapers were censored and suspected communists arrested.

Unlike most hegemonic parties, the PAP does not have a large staff to perform research and stage functions.[8] Instead, civil bureaucrats outside the party perform these functions, leaving the PAP visible only before general elections. To ensure its continued dominance, the PAP has prepared for succession through its self-renewal program, choosing young candidates who are more in tune with the electorate. Between 1980 and 2015, the PAP's winning percentage in legislative elections fell below 60 percent only once. Over fifty years following its first victory in 1959, the People's Action Party controls eighty-three of eighty-nine elected seats. So overwhelming is PAP's dominance that opposition parties, such as the Worker's Party and Singapore Democratic Party, consider winning three or four seats an electoral success. Winning six seats, as did the Worker's Party in 2011, was considered a historic success.

Singapore's most visible opposition politician is perhaps Chee Soon Juan, a labor rights advocate and secretary-general of the Singapore Democratic Party. Chee's activities include verbal attacks and publicity events that often allege PAP corruption and undemocratic practices. Legal tangles with all three of Singapore's prime ministers have landed Chee and his activist sister, Chee Soik Chin, in and out of jail and in bankruptcy. Barred from international travel and running for office, Chee Soon Juan draws support from Amnesty International and other rights groups that contend Singapore's leaders restrict political speech and abuse the judiciary to crush PAP opponents.

Legislature

Singapore's parliamentary system is a legacy of British colonialism, even though its practice is much different from that of today's Great Britain. In contrast to the British bicameral system, the Singaporean parliamentary system is unicameral and has presented no meaningful opposition to the administration. Legislators are elected to five-year terms, unless the prime minister dissolves Parliament before the term ends. To enhance legitimacy, voting is compulsory for all citizens, who face fines for failing to vote. Debate persists as to whether or not compulsory voting enhances genuine civic responsibility or creates cynicism and spoilt ballots.

In 1984, to ensure a semblance of bipartisanship, the Parliament provided for three opposition seats to be awarded if opposition candidates did not win at least three in constituency races. These three nonconstituency members (later changed to a possible nine) would be appointed from among the highest-polling opposition candidates as long as they had won at least 15 percent of the votes cast in the constituency.[9] Nonconstituency oppositionists were not accorded full voting rights; they were prohibited from voting on motions relating to constitutional amendments, money bills, or votes of no confidence in the government. The opposition views this provision as tokenism rather than a meaningful commitment to open politics.

Another feature in parliamentary procedures is the "Team MP" scheme. Since the 1988 election, in certain constituencies, the electorate votes for a team of candidates instead of only one candidate. These constituencies are declared Group Representation Constituencies (GRCs), and each is represented by three members of Parliament. No more than half of the total number of constituencies can be GRCs. At least one of the three candidates in a GRC is required to be an ethnic minority (non-Chinese). The team that wins a plurality of the total vote is elected.[10] The primary purpose of group representation is to institutionalize multiethnic politics by ensuring that minorities will be represented in Parliament by getting them elected on the coattails of others.[11]

In another attempt to bring alternative ideas to Parliament, nine distinguished individuals from the community, academia, the military, the professions, and trade unions are now appointed to serve as independent members, or Nominated Members of Parliament (NMPs). Nominated members are technically unaffiliated with any party, but a PAP-dominated committee makes their appointment. Voting rights of NMPs are restricted similarly to those of nonconstituency members. Some NMPs have been active parliamentarians. The only non-PAP-initiated legislation ever to pass the Singapore Parliament came from a nominated member.

Singapore's institutional tinkering to add opposition quotas, ethnic diversity, and independent experts has done little to develop a consequential parliamentary opposition in Singapore. The country's opposition remains effectually powerless to craft meaningful legislation. According to close observers, decades of single-party rule have "reduced the parliamentary function down to passing the annual government budget and making new laws," with elections serving primarily as loyalty tests on PAP leadership and performance.[12] Differences over immigration policy and Singapore's demographic challenges can produce intense public debate, but political cleavage in Singapore's legislature is characterized more by technical policy argument than deep-seated ideological difference.

Foreign Workers and Permanent Residents

As indicated by the controversy surrounding the population white paper released by Singapore's government in 2015, few issues animate Singaporean politics as much as immigration. In 1990, only 16 percent of Singapore's active labor force was composed of foreign workers. That number increased to 35 percent by 2010 (or 25 percent of the total population). Over that same period, the number of nonnative permanent residents in Singapore increased from 3.6 percent to 11 percent. These changes mean that alongside every six Singapore citizens in the city, there already exist roughly three foreign workers and one permanent resident.

One in five foreign workers comes to Singapore to work at the high end of the economy in business, finance, or other white collar jobs. The other four in five arrive via work permits as construction laborers, factory workers or, increasingly, as service workers in homes, restaurants, night clubs, and discotheques. Many nonresident workers are Chinese; others are Indian, Sri Lankan, Indonesian, and Filipino. As Singapore has grown wealthier, meeting demand for low-skill work has led to rapid, though largely legal, immigration. Today, the increased presence of foreign workers animates much of Singapore's Internet chatter and blogosphere. Public debates over job competition, workers' rights, wages, and even the smell of cooking curry have created a new type of social turbulence in the multiethnic city-state.

Although foreign workers are politically powerless in representative politics, NGOs are emerging to address issues related to disadvantaged nonresidents. Advocacy by such groups is beginning to make a difference. For example, a 2013 law established that all nonresident domestic workers be allowed at least one day off each week.[13]

STATE-SOCIETY RELATIONS AND DEMOCRACY

Debate exists about how to best characterize the Singaporean state. Through a Chinese cultural lens, Singapore can be viewed as a "patriarchal state," where traditional elders wield influence over a compliant society. The country is also frequently characterized as a developmental state, due to the state's active management over investment and trade-oriented sectors. Its critics label it an authoritarian state, pointing to its high degree of centralization and power over dissenting voices. The island's own leaders may implicitly see their state in Hegelian terms, as an altruistic state prioritizing solidarity and order over interest-group competition.[14] Debate notwithstanding, analysts agree that Singapore is, if nothing else, a strong state.

Upon first glance, Singapore does not have the requisites for a strong state. Geographically, the country is minuscule and has no important natural resources. Although it boasts the highest per capita income in Southeast Asia, its total GNP is far smaller than that of fellow dragons South Korea, Taiwan, or Hong Kong. Singapore's military is capable of only minor defensive operations.

Viewed in these terms, Singapore would not have the wherewithal to be a strong state.

Nevertheless, using standard criteria, Singapore's state can be considered strong. Its leaders use the agencies of the state to get Singaporeans to do what they want them to do. In no other Southeast Asian society do the citizens follow the state's dictates with the same regularity as in Singapore. Taxes are paid, young men accept compulsory military conscription, and traffic rules are followed. Few autonomous groups compete for influence in the society. Indeed, the state has co-opted the bureaucracy, the military, and interest groups, while the hegemonic PAP—itself a creature of Lee Kuan Yew—has co-opted the state.

In explaining or understanding the high capacity of the state in Singapore, it becomes apparent that the country's small size is a major advantage in strengthening the state. Although Singapore is heterogeneous in the ethnic sense, more important is that its society is quite homogeneous culturally. Singaporeans are urban and largely united in their goals for their society. Living in fewer than 225 square miles, citizens have little room for nonconformity.

Singapore developed a strong sense of the politics of survival due to its wrenching expulsion from Malaysia and its subsequent Cold War experience. The impact of aid and overseas investment during the Vietnam War strengthened the role of the Singaporean state. In the 1960s, when the PAP was factionalized into left-wing and moderate groups, Lee Kuan Yew's victory over the Left was interpreted as a victory over communism and, therefore, as a victory for the survival of the country's capitalist system. Lee justified his "administrative state" as necessary to concentrate power and repress the state's internal and external enemies.

Singapore is the quintessential example of a strong state built from skillful leadership. For many Singaporeans, Lee Kuan Yew *was* the state. His strength came less from charisma or repression than from his extraordinary capabilities to fashion an effective state. The technocrats whom Lee cultivated were among the most educated and skilled in Southeast Asia. Incorruptible and effective, they remain unbeholden to any particular societal groups. Instead, they are integrated into the state through the PAP or the ministries.

The case of Singapore also raises the question of whether a one-party state can be democratic. From a Western perspective, the governmental system of Singapore does not meet the criteria of full civil liberties and competitive choices of leaders. From a culturalist Chinese perspective, the government's paternalistic nature is appropriate, providing, as it does, law and order as well as economic achievement without relying on excessive oppression. Lee Kuan Yew agreed with Sukarno's rationale for guided democracy in Indonesia and has said that Western-style majority rule leads to chaos, instability, dissension, and inefficiency. For Lee's successors, legitimization is sought not through democracy but through performance, which is viewed as a technical matter. In Singapore, the critical factor in politics is the technocratic power of the elite, not the government's ability to ideologically mobilize its citizenry.[15] Techno-crats, not democrats, characterize Singapore's hegemonic electoral authoritar-ian regime.

Singapore is the most disciplined society in Southeast Asia, in part because its citizens fear being fined or punished and in part because these citizens genu-inely believe lawful obedience to be in the public interest.[16] Certainly, the gov-ernment has set forth strict and often ridiculed measures to ensure orderly behavior (such as installing urine detection devices in housing block elevators that, if the rider urinates, lock the elevator door until authorities arrive). Al-though the Chinese heritage is one of discipline for the common good, at the time of independence, Singaporeans behaved no differently from their neigh-bors. The difference is that, since then, the Singaporean state has had the capac-ity to exploit that heritage to help it achieve its aims of survival, economic development, meritocracy, and order. The price it has paid is a lack of mean-ingful popular participation in the affairs of state and a sanitized society that has lost much of its soul.

While building Singapore, Prime Minister Lee argued that in the Chinese tradition there was no concept of a loyal opposition. For example, it was not possible to support an opposition candidate without withdrawing total support from the government. This tradition stemmed from Confucian philosophy, which stressed the principles of centralized authority. Obligation to those in authority was the cement of the Confucian order. As long as the authorities were meeting the people's needs and leading according to moral principles, the ruler was considered to have the mandate of heaven and was therefore deemed legitimate by the public. From this cultural perspective, a strong one-party sys-tem is most conducive to effective rule.[17]

One-party systems can provide policy alternatives if there are differences in opinion among the party leaders. Moreover, if two-way communication be-tween the government and the people is established, the citizenry can assert in-fluence over public policy. In Singapore, a high degree of intraparty factionalism occurs, with varying points of view aired publicly; differences, nevertheless, tend to be issue specific, not ideological. In addition, the PAP has established grassroots organizations, including Citizens' Consultative Committees, de-signed to elicit ideas from the public. These corporatist groups do provide input but do not indicate the development of an autonomous civil society, which the government views as potentially destabilizing. The government's claim to moral authority rests on public recognition of its performance record. Public compliance within this one-party system is rooted in a "broad-based recogni-tion that politics is the business of the government, not the people."[18]

For five decades Singapore's technocracy has provided the republic with ef-fective, but not always accountable, government, consistent with its traditions and history and supportive of the goals of development, order, and merit.

Singapore's capacity to deliver on these goals over time is the fundamental question going forward. Lee Kuan Yew admitted to this fact in 2008 to a large crowd of Singaporeans and international delegates at the World Cities Summit. Speaking extemporaneously, Lee fretted that the island's voters might soon become bored and vote for a "vociferous opposition" out of "light-heartedness, fickleness, or sheer madness." A non-PAP government, he claimed, would ruin the city-state in as little as five years. "When you're Singapore," he clarified, "your existence depends on performance—extraordinary performance, better than your competitors—when that performance disappears because the system on which it's been based becomes eroded, then you've lost everything."[19]

ECONOMY AND DEVELOPMENT

It is impossible to make comparative generalizations about Singapore's economic development because the nation's status as a city-state sets it fundamentally apart from its neighbors. With no agricultural base, Singapore is destined to become increasingly interdependent with the global economic system to ensure its survival.

Singapore is a mixture of capitalist and socialist economics, with emphasis on the former. The PAP leadership inherited a capitalist economic system from the British and has created state institutions to manage key aspects of the economy including housing, transportation, and shipping. Home to the world's busiest transshipment port, Singapore enjoys a geographic location that is its greatest economic asset. Although Singapore typically ranks among the world's most free economies, its government also controls large, state-owned holding companies that invest in manufacturing, communications, and foreign securities markets.

Singapore consistently posts the region's highest growth rates. These growth rates are largely the result of an outward-looking, export-oriented strategy begun after 1965 to accelerate the manufacture of consumer products, reduce unemployment, and obtain needed outside capital. Transport, shipbuilding, ship repair, and manufacturing led the way in Singapore's early economic rise. From 1965 until the 1997 Asian economic crisis, Singapore's annual GDP growth averaged above 8 percent. Since that time, growth fluctuated and then moderated, especially after 2014 as China's demand for commodities tapered. Relatively low rates of inflation and unemployment have accompanied much of this growth.

In anticipation of changes in the world economy, Singapore launched its "Second Industrial Revolution" in 1979, designed to restructure the economy toward high-tech industries. The plan was to manufacture exports of superb quality, win higher salaries for workers, upgrade job skills, and reduce dependence on foreign workers. The economy emphasized automotive components, machine tools, computers, electronic instrumentation, medical instruments, and precision engineering. The inflows of foreign capital that followed reached staggering levels. Foreign investment ballooned from $300 million in 1967 to a stock of over $39 billion in 2010 (ninth in the world).[20]

Not content with the level of economic development, Lee Kuan Yew set forth a controversial program in the 1990s to improve the country's gene pool. He determined that the quality of the people was the most important factor in a country's rapid development, and he arranged a program to encourage the marriage and procreation of the well-educated populace, giving incentives for educated mothers to have more children. Although pro-natal policies haven't resolved Singapore's demographic challenges, government commitments to improve education through high standards and high pay for teachers have rendered Singapore a world leader in human capital development. A 2015 report from the Organisation for Economic Co-operation and Development (OECD) comparing K–12 educational systems in the world's 75 leading countries ranked Singapore number one in the world, far ahead of the United Kingdom (20th) and the United States (28th).[21]

Initially, the 1997 Asian economic crisis did not seriously jeopardize the Singaporean economy, because it was tied into the global rather than just the Southeast Asian economy. However, the worldwide economic slowdown in the United States and Japan that followed proved a challenge for the globalized economy. Singapore slipped into recession, with a –2.4 percent economic growth rate in 2001, a dramatic and significant drop from a remarkable 9.9 percent growth rate in 2000. Singapore recovered in 2002 only to find itself gripped by the Severe Acute Respiratory Syndrome (SARS) crisis that crippled the local economy, closed shopping malls, and devastated its Asian-based tourism sector.

The 2001 recession and economic effects of SARS raised questions about Singapore's export-oriented development model and recent efforts at regional integration. The PAP's answer: to double-down on a knowledge-based economy highlighting financial services and cross-regional free trade agreements. By the mid-2000s, foreign investment in financial and insurance services surpassed manufacturing as the largest sector of foreign direct investment.

Internationally, the country has negotiated over twenty bilateral and regional trade agreements with major economic players in the global economy, such as ASEAN, the United States, India, Mexico, Switzerland, Korea, Panama, Australia, and oil-rich states in the Persian Gulf. It has also pursued closer economic ties with China. China needs assurance that oil will flow freely through Singapore's ports. Two-thirds of the world's oil flows through waters near Singapore each year, and only the port cities of Houston and Rotterdam refine more petroleum. Singapore's most significant activity in trade relations has been as a founding member of the Trans-Pacific Partnership (TPP), a deal signed by twelve countries in October 2015 in Atlanta, Georgia, now awaiting ratification by legislatures.

As a founding member of ASEAN, Singapore supports efforts to further integrate the region's economies. Its economic relations with neighboring Malaysia are of vital significance. Singapore imports nearly half of its water supply from Malaysia, a fact Malaysian leaders frequently cite when relations turn sour. Singapore's investments in Southeast Asian countries are extensive and can invite trouble, such as when Temasek, a public holding company, bought ShinCorp, Thaksin Shinawatra's telecommunications empire—a transaction that helped to trigger the 2006 military coup in Bangkok and left the ousted Thai prime minister awash in legal troubles and Thailand in political turmoil.

The 2008 global financial crisis pushed Singapore into a serious recession and leaders opted for an expansionary budgetary response rather than formulaic neoliberal austerity. Initiatives included a $3 billion jobs credit scheme that subsidized employers' wage bills; a cash subsidy to low-income workers; and an 18,000-jobs expansion plan for the public sector, among other measures. These programs are credited for assisting a quick recovery to growth and showed the flexibility of Singaporean leaders to pragmatically respond to economic stress.[22]

The Singaporean economy is interdependent with the global economic system. With a diversified economy, one of the best infrastructures for transportation in the world, superb medical care, the highest standard of living in all Southeast Asia, a highly educated population, and generally peaceful relations with its neighbors, Singapore's prospects for long-term economic growth remain excellent, although it may never return to the high growth rates of its formative period.

FOREIGN RELATIONS

Singapore did not take charge of its foreign relations until 1965, when the republic was expelled from the Federation of Malaysia. Since then, the basic theme of foreign policy has been survival. As a small city-state with only minimal military capacity, Singapore looked to Western powers and Japan during the Cold War to balance the influence of the Soviet Union and China in Southeast Asia. Unabashedly anticommunist, Singapore helped to support the US war in Vietnam and was a principal advocate for a hard-line policy toward the Vietnamese government as a founding ASEAN member. More recently, Singapore has become a major investor in the Vietnamese economy and sought closer economic relations with China.

Despite its pro-US stance, Singapore often enunciated a policy of neutrality, avoiding embroilment in major power conflicts. Nevertheless, certain issues have strained Singapore-US relations. In 1988, Singapore accused Washington of interfering in its domestic affairs and expelled a US diplomat who allegedly encouraged a high-profile dissident to organize a group of opposition candidates. Bad feelings also arose when President Ronald Reagan removed Singapore from the Generalized System of Preferences. The Generalized System of Preferences had allowed selected goods to enter the United States duty-free, but

Singapore had attained the status of a newly industrialized country (NIC) and was no longer eligible for this benefit.

Relations between Singapore and the United States reached a low in 1994 over the unique case of Michael Fay, an expat American teenager who was sentenced to be caned in a Singapore court for juvenile acts of vandalism. US public opinion polls indicated that most Americans supported Singapore's corporal punishment for the delinquent youth. The Clinton administration campaigned for a pardon for Fay, but Singapore's contemptuous response was to reduce his sentence from six lashes to four.

By the beginning of the millennium, Singapore had achieved its goal of survival. It was no longer threatened by internal insurgency or external intervention, and it was surrounded by large nations that had no capacity or desire to seriously intervene in the republic's affairs. But the events of September 11, 2001, reopened old concerns and caused Singapore's leaders to imagine new ones.

As a porous hub of trade, oil shipments, and transportation, Singapore developed a renewed sense of vulnerability in 2001, which resulted in a warming of relations with the United States. In December 2001, an al-Qaeda sleeper cell with plans to terrorize Western embassies was discovered in Singapore. A year later, President George W. Bush traveled to the republic to sign a bilateral free trade agreement. The post-9/11 United States–Singapore Free Trade Agreement (USSFTA) proved to alter more than just economic relations between the two countries.

During the war on terrorism, Singapore became a vital staging ground for US operations in Afghanistan and Iraq (although it has prohibited the permanent establishment of a US base). Goh Chok Tong even sent a token military unit to the Persian Gulf as part of US secretary of defense Donald Rumsfeld's "Coalition of the Willing." Then, adding to its existing array of F-16s, Apache helicopters, and Harpoon missiles, purchased in the 1990s, Singapore later inked an arms deal with Washington in 2005 worth upward of $1.8 billion. The USSFTA led to the purchase of twelve Boeing F-15SGs and millions of dollars' worth of missiles, ordnance, and other supplies.[23]

In addition to economic benefits and coordination on regional terrorist threats, Singapore's pursuit of stronger cross-regional relations with the United States hedged against an increasingly assertive China. Like its neighbors, Singapore both celebrates and fears China's rise. It is Southeast Asia's largest investor in China, fourth overall behind Japan. The massive Singapore-Suzhou industrial park in Jiangsu Province, negotiated at the highest levels by the two governments, typifies the countries' growing economic relations. Singapore also fits prominently in Chinese President Xi Jinping's plans to create a Maritime Silk Road connecting Asia and Europe through his "One Belt, One Road" strategy. Singapore was also among the first to sign on to China's new Asian Infrastructure Investment Bank (AIIB).

In the new international era, Singapore seeks to interpret China to the United States and the United States to China, even as it plays one off against the other. It is a deft strategy for a small state. Just before signing the USSFTA in 2003, for example, Singapore signed a strategic partnership agreement with China. Subsequently, Singapore embraced the Obama administration's Asia pivot and encouraged the United States to join the TPP, which currently excludes China. Singapore also fears being perceived by its neighbors as an "unrepentant China beachhead."[24] Although fears of communism have long disappeared, uncertainty about a rising China and new threats of Islamist terrorism keep Singapore desirous of a US presence in Asia. By balancing economic and security interests between both powers, Singapore continues its strategy for survival.

CONCLUSION

Singapore's singularity does not always allow for meaningful comparisons with other countries. Indeed, the "little red dot" is an exception in Southeast Asia in terms of culture, ethnicity, geography, state capacity, and level of economic development. Only the less globalized citizens of oil-rich microstate Brunei, with one-tenth the population of Singapore, enjoy such a high income in the region. Singapore's small size notwithstanding, its geographic location remains significant. The city-state is destined to play a role in international trade, commerce, and finance as long as ships need the Malacca Straits to transport food, manufactures, and oil between Asia and the world. New trade agreements with major trading partners are likely to reap economic results in the future for Singapore. Nevertheless, the extent to which Singapore and its PAP leaders can thrive beyond the guidance and mentorship of its paternal founder, the late Lee Kuan Yew, remains an open question.

NOTES

1. Brenda S. A. Yeoh and Weiqiang Lin, "Rapid Growth in Singapore Immigrant Population Brings Challenges," Migration Information Source, April 2012, www.migration information.org/feature/print.cfm?ID=887.

2. Prashanth Parameswaran, "Can Singapore Overcome Its Future Challenges?" *The Diplomat*, July 2, 2015, http://thediplomat.com/2015/07/can-singapore-overcome-its future challenges.

3. Lee Boon Hiok, "Political Institutionalization in Singapore," in *Asian Political Institutionalization*, ed. Robert A. Scalapino, Seizaburo Sato, and Jusuf Wanandi (Berkeley: Institute of East Asian Studies, University of California, 1986), 202.

4. Shee Poon Kim, "Singapore in 1991," *Asian Survey* 32, no. 2 (February 1992): 119–125, and Hussin Mutalib, "Singapore in 1992," *Asian Survey* 33, no. 2 (February 1993): 194–199.

5. William Safire, "Honoring Repression," *New York Times*, July 10, 1995, A13.

6. Christopher Lingle, *Singapore's Authoritarian Capitalism: Asian Values, Free Market Illusions and Political Dependency* (Fairfax, VA: The Locke Institute, 1996).

7. Ibid.

8. Lee, "Political Institutionalization in Singapore," 207.

9. Chan Heng Chee, "The PAP in the Nineties: The Politics of Anticipation," in *ASEAN in Regional and Global Context*, ed. Karl D. Jackson, Sukhumbhand Paribatra, and J. Soedjati Djiwandono (Berkeley: Institute of East Asian Studies, University of California, 1986), 173.

10. Thomas Bellows, "Singapore in 1989," *Asian Survey* 30, no. 2 (February 1990): 146.

11. Lee Lai To, "Singapore in 1987," *Asian Survey* 28, no. 2 (February 1988): 203.

12. Chua Beng Huat, "Singapore in 2006: An Irritating and Irritated ASEAN Neighbor," *Asian Survey* 47, no. 1 (January/February 2007): 208; Cho-Oon Khong, "Singapore: Political Legitimacy Through Managing Conformity," in *Political Legitimacy in Southeast Asia: The Quest for Moral Authority*, ed. Muthiah Alagappa (Stanford, CA: Stanford University Press, 1995), 132.

13. This section draws from Yeoh and Lin, "Rapid Growth in Singapore Immigrant Population Brings Challenges."

14. Terrence Chong, "Why Labels for the Singaporean State Fall Short," *Straits Times*, February 8, 2007.

15. Khong, "Singapore: Political Legitimacy Through Managing Conformity," 132.

16. Donald K. Emmerson, "Beyond Zanzibar: Area Studies, Comparative Politics, and the 'Strength' of the State in Indonesia," paper presented to the Association for Asian Studies, Chicago, April 1990, 28–29.

17. *Asia Yearbook, 1991* (Hong Kong: Far Eastern Economic Review, 1990), 214–215.

18. Khong, "Singapore: Political Legitimacy Through Managing Conformity," 132.

19. Lydia Lim, "5 Years All It Takes to Ruin Singapore," *Straits Times*, June 26, 2008.

20. Figures from the Singapore Department of Statistics and the United Nations Conference on Trade and Development.

21. Nicole Chang, "Global School Rankings," *The Independent*, May 14, 2015, www.independent.co.uk/news/education/education-news/global-school-rankings-interactive-map-shows-standards-of-education-across-the-world-10247405.html.

22. Narayanan Ganesan, "Singapore in 2009," *Asian Survey* 50, no. 1 (January/February 2010): 253–259.

23. Eul-Soo Pang, "Embedding Security into Free Trade: The Case of the United States–Singapore Free Trade Agreement," *Contemporary Southeast Asia* 29, no. 1 (April 2007): 10.

24. Ibid., 22.

12

BRUNEI

Brunei, known formally as Negara Brunei Darussalam (Brunei, Abode of Peace), is on the island of Borneo facing north to the South China Sea. It is divided into two sectors surrounded by the Malaysian state of Sarawak. With a population of only 429,000, and with the second-highest GNI per capita in Southeast Asia ($39,800), only Singapore rivals Brunei in terms of wealth and small size. About 70 percent of the people of Brunei are ethnically Malay, and most of this group works in the public sector. The Chinese community, which makes up nearly one-fifth of the population (but for the most part does not have Bruneian citizenship), supplies most of the nonpublic workforce. Indigenous, non-Muslim ethnic groups who live in the interior regions compose about 10 percent of Brunei's population. Imported laborers from neighboring countries supply additional labor to the microstate. As an Islamic monarchy, Islam is the state religion.

Brunei achieved internal self-government in 1959 when the sultan promulgated the country's first constitution, thereby ending British administration and ensuring that power would be transferred to the ruling dynasty rather than to the people. The British still handled foreign and military affairs, however, until full independence was achieved in 1984. Ironically, the sultan was reluctant to accept independence because he feared his new nation would be vulnerable to attack from its larger neighbors, Indonesia and Malaysia.

Brunei's reluctance to assume full independence also stemmed from the monarch's fear that internal revolts could undermine the royalty's prerogatives. The most threatening incident occurred in 1962 when about a thousand followers of A. M. Azahari revolted. Shortly after attacking royal-owned oil installations, Azahari, who dreamed of an independent federation of Brunei, Sabah, and Sarawak, declared himself premier of Kalimantan Utara (North Borneo). Within two days, the rebellion was crushed by the Bruneian government, supported by Gurkha fighters flown in from British bases in Singapore.[1] The sultan

310

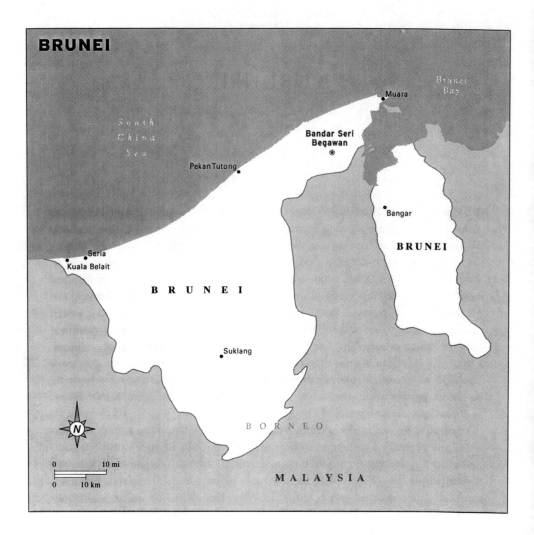

dismissed Parliament and declared a state of emergency still yet to be lifted. (Azahari fled to Indonesia, where he died in exile in 2002.)

Following independence, Brunei achieved political stability and economic development primarily because of enormous revenues from oil and natural gas. These funds allowed the government to establish a cradle-to-grave welfare system (facetiously known as the "Shellfare state") that provided, among other things, free education and health care programs as well as subsidies for rice, housing, cars, funerals, and pilgrimages to Mecca. Moreover, Bruneians enjoy no income tax.

The national ideology of Brunei is *Malay Islamic Beraja* (MIB), which means "Malay Muslim Monarchy." The ideology emphasizes Malay-style Islam, with the monarchy as the defender of the faith and the people. It also discourages Westernization and secularism. All public ceremonies and the school curriculum include MIB teachings.

When the sultan celebrated twenty-five years on the throne in 1992, he strengthened the concept of MIB, drawing from traditional Malay kingship and binding it with traditional Islam. *Malay Islamic Beraja* provides special status for Brunei's indigenous Malays and requires unquestioning deference to the throne. Its purpose is ostensibly to keep unwanted foreign influences out of Brunei.

In honor of his jubilee year (1992), the sultan built a new state mosque on the outskirts of Brunei's capital, Bandar Seri Begawan, at a cost of $30 million. Many Bruneians believed the sultan would establish democratic institutions during the celebrations. Instead, he announced that political parties and elections would remain proscribed and that the monarchy was the proper institution to bring benefits to the people. He tightened internal security, increased defense spending, purchased jet fighters from Great Britain, and announced plans to diversify the economy to lessen the nation's dependence on oil and gas revenue.

In 2004, the sultan revived the moribund Legislative Council, which had not met since before independence. It then passed constitutional amendments to reform the Parliament, including the direct election of one-third of its 45 delegates. Direct elections never followed. Rather, the sultan has since appointed and then disbanded three separate legislatures. He constructed a new parliament building in 2008 and later permitted the indirect election of nine district representatives through peer-based secret balloting.[2] Beyond limited budgetary oversight, legislators function merely as advisers to the powerful sultan. In 2010, the first female cabinet member in the country's history was appointed. In spite of changes, the system is still fully authoritarian, and the country is one of the world's five remaining absolute monarchies.

Brunei made global headlines in 2014 when the sultan announced he would enforce fasting during Ramadan, ban Christmas, and phase in sharia penal code by 2016. Over the next few years Brunei began to institute harsh punishments such as flogging, amputation, stoning, and execution for criminal offenses, drinking alcohol, adultery, abortion, homosexuality, or blasphemy. The move sparked fierce criticism from the United Nations and human rights groups. Some Western celebrities even called for a boycott of the Beverly Hills Hotel, which the sultan owns. Undeterred, the sultan continued phased implementation of sharia law toward his 2016 goal.

INSTITUTIONS AND SOCIAL GROUPS

Sultanate

The sultanate is the embodiment of the state, and Sultan Sir Muda Hassanal Bolkiah—the twenty-ninth ruler in a dynasty that originated in the thirteenth century—is an absolute monarch whose legitimacy derives from his heredity, not from popular elections or accountability to Bruneians. He is the son of Sultan Haji Omar Ali Saifuddien Sa'adul Khairi Waddien, ibn Almarhum Sultan Mohammad Jamulul Alam, who was known as the Sultan Seri Begawan. Brunei's capital, Bandar Seri Begawan, is named in his honor. Although Sultan Seri Begawan abdicated in favor of his son Hassanal Bolkiah in 1967, he attempted to keep ultimate power for himself, so the present sultan was not able to rule unconditionally until his father's death in 1986.

The sultan has ceremonial responsibilities and exercises total control over day-to-day affairs as the nation's prime minister, defense minister, and finance minister. The cabinet is made up principally of members of the sultan's own royal family. There is no dissent from the populace because the sultan has absolute power. He even amended the constitution to include his own immunity from any form of legal prosecution. His power is enhanced by the fact that he oversees the government bureaucracy, which employs an estimated two-thirds of Brunei's total workforce. The hierarchical nature of Bruneian society has made open communication with the sultan impossible for the common people. He is the head of state, head of government, and leader of the faith.

Despite announcements that Brunei would remain free from bourgeois decadence, the microstate loosened up in the 1990s in an effort to attract tourism and Western business elites. Bookstores and movie theaters opened and satellite TV arrived. New Western-style restaurants (including McDonald's and KFC) also appeared. Even hard liquor became available (although the nation is legally dry). In 1996, the American pop singer Michael Jackson presented a free concert for the sultan's fiftieth birthday, although he apparently was asked to swivel less than usual. Wealth brought new social problems to Brunei. A new generation of "bored youth" has emerged, along with graffiti, theft, and the use of inhalants and methamphetamines.[3]

There is no distinction between the state's wealth and the sultan's personal riches. Only four years after independence, the sultan was the richest man in the world, and he remains counted among its richest billionaires (worth about $20 billion). All the state's revenues and reserves are his, and he alone decides what portion goes for state expenditures.[4] The sultan of Brunei resides in a palace forty times the size of the White House, with 1,700 rooms. He rules in the style of classic potentates, albeit with modern tastes. Millions of dollars are spent on exotic collections of art, jewelry, and automobiles, including hundreds of Bentleys, Mercedes-Benzes, and Ferraris. A polygamist—married at one point to three wives (two of whom he later divorced)—the sultan has multiple children born over a forty-year span. Known more as a philanderer than a philanthropist, numerous stories of his activities have undermined his attempt to create an image of a responsible, benevolent ruler. The sultan's attempts to shore up his credentials as a devout Muslim with three separate pilgrimages to Mecca have yet to eclipse his playboy image.

In 1993, Filipino senators investigated reports that some of their country's best-known actresses, models, and singers had engaged in prostitution while visiting Brunei. The senators reported a "high-class white slavery ring." A former Miss USA later made headlines with allegations of sexual abuse by Bruneian royalty. In 2010, Jillian Lauren, a Jewish American teenager who spent 18 months in the royals' orbit, published a jaw-dropping expose titled *Some Girls: My Life in a Harem*.[5] The book, with its graphic content, became a *New York Times* best seller and was eventually translated into eighteen languages.

In 2000, the sultan issued a lawsuit against his brother, Prince Jefri, and about seventy other officials for allegedly having wasted billions of dollars of state funds. The prince was fired from his position as finance minister and cited for particularly gross corruption that included extravagant purchases of planes, yachts, and jewelry, and high-priced sex orgies. The prince entertains a retinue of wives and mistresses and is the father of at least thirty-five children.[6]

Prince Jefri fled Brunei and initially made an out-of-court settlement with his brother to repay losses and change his lifestyle. When he failed to live up to the agreement, a legal case was sent to Britain's Privy Council for further settlement. In full tabloid drama, the Bruneian royal scandal was followed with shock as court documents revealed how both royals had spent billions of dollars on selfish luxuries and services ($900 million on jewelry, $475 million on Rolls Royces, hundreds of millions on a family fleet of jets, and even $3.6 million on badminton lessons and acupuncture). When the court found the prince liable for $8 billion of the missing $15 billion, he fled to France and began to sell off many luxury assets. A 2008 warrant for his arrest from a London judge remains outstanding.

In Prince Jefri's wake is the royal family's latest conspicuous spender, Prince Azim, the third in line to the throne. A paparazzi favorite in London, the younger Prince Azim is known for his legendary birthday parties; for his thirtieth birthday, in 2012, he spent over $100,000 on flowers alone and drew tabloid attention with his guest list of "mature divas" including Raquel Welch, Faye Dunaway, and Pamela Anderson.

The heir apparent to the throne is Crown Prince Al-Muhtadee Billah, born in 1974, three years before his father's third wife. After studying in England,

Prince Billah married Pengiran Anak Sarah, a half-Swiss teenager thirteen years his junior. Their first son, Prince Abdul Muntaqim, born in 2007, is the youngest living person with rights to the world's oldest monarchical line.

Military

The Royal Brunei Armed Forces (RBAF), with about 4,500 members (the strength of a brigade group with support elements), is the smallest military force in ASEAN. This voluntarily recruited, highly paid national defense force represents a state that spends a higher proportion of its budget on defense than any other ASEAN nation.

Since 1962, the RBAF has been augmented by a battalion of British Army Gurkhas paid for by the sultan (the only permanent deployment of British troops in the region). This force helps to ensure that there will be no revolt against the sultan's rule. The RBAF regularly engages in joint exercises with the US Marine Corps, as well as armed forces from Malaysia and Australia. The RBAF also contributed peacekeepers to international operations in Cambodia, the Philippines, and Lebanon. The sultan recently purchased twelve Polish-made Black Hawk helicopters with a capacity to monitor Brunei's 200-nautical-mile Exclusive Economic Zone of the South China Sea.

Political Parties

Brunei has no viable political parties, nor has the government mobilized its own party. The sultan draws support from patrimonialist programs that depoliticize society. Even so, the country's short history is punctuated by failed attempts from actors outside the sultan's circle of patronage to form alternative political parties. The left-leaning, pro-independence Brunei People's Party, for example, briefly held seats in the Legislative Council in the early 1960s but was forced into exile along with its leader, A. M. Azahari, following the 1962 rebellion. The Brunei National Democratic Party, established in 1985, sought to promote a moderate platform based on Islam and liberal nationalism. Its primary goal was to restore parliamentary democracy. When party leaders called for elections and asked the sultan to give up his position as prime minister, they were arrested and the party was forced to disband. In recent years, other parties were also forcibly deregistered including the Brunei National Solidarity Party and the Brunei People's Awareness Party.

STATE-SOCIETY RELATIONS AND DEMOCRACY

Brunei's small size makes governance far easier than in the larger and more diverse countries elsewhere in Southeast Asia. The state has brought virtually all institutions into its fold, leaving no autonomous societal groups to compete with the state apparatus.

There is an essential identity between the state and the person of the sultan. Almost every official, technocrat, and military officer in Brunei is related—

directly or indirectly—to the sultan, his family, and his advisers. These people do not have another base of social control independent of the state. The lack of any mass political base in Bruneian society has reinforced these officials' loyalty to the state. Even the Chinese community is loyal to the state, despite the fact that most Chinese in Brunei are not even citizens. However, their businesses depend on the sultan's continued largesse and support.

The welfare state provides all basic needs of most Bruneians; thus, there is little dissension with the sultan's absolute powers. His lineage and royal aura, and his leadership of Islam in Brunei, further strengthen his position. Moves by groups calling for the formation of democratic institutions, and the relegation of the sultan to ceremonial rather than administrative functions, have failed.

There is no major external threat to Brunei's security today, nor has there been since 1962, when Indonesia supported the Azahari revolt. Since that time no dissident groups have been allowed to grow to the point that they pose a meaningful threat to the regime. Brunei has received considerable aid and support from its former colonial ruler, Great Britain, and the presence of the Gurkhas has strengthened the state by intimidating potential dissidents.

There is no democracy in Brunei. The country's political system is an absolute monarchy with no representative form of government—a politically closed regime. The 1984 constitution consolidated the monarchy's power by suspending parliamentary institutions. The reconvening of the Legislative Council in 2004 allowed for nonelected appointees to participate in some constitutional amendments and policy-level decisions at the sultan's behest. Even if the Legislative Council is reformed with directly elected seats, as the sultan has announced, the capacity of elected representatives to exercise power would be limited at best.

Civil liberties in Brunei include freedom of movement but little else. Journalists must practice self-censorship or risk charges of sedition. Labor rights are circumscribed and abuse of foreign workers by employers is rarely prosecuted. Brunei is perpetually classified as "not free" by Freedom House. The presence of forced labor and prostitution in the sultanate caused the United States to add Brunei to its human trafficking watch list since 2010.

ECONOMY AND DEVELOPMENT

Vast oil reserves make the dynamics of Brunei's economy different from the agriculturally based economies of other Southeast Asian nations. Oil and natural gas are the main sources of government revenue, foreign investment, and employment. Together they account for over 90 percent of total export earnings, 80 percent of government revenue, and nearly 40 percent of GDP. Brunei's revenues from the oil sector dropped significantly as a result of the global financial crisis in 2008. Multiple years of negative or anemic GDP growth followed until prices recovered only to collapse again in 2015. Brunei needs to upgrade aging equipment, and oil dependence casts a dark shadow on Brunei's future. Industry estimates predict that at current extraction rates, Brunei's oil and gas reserves will be exhausted by 2040.[7]

Brunei's top economic priority is therefore to diversify its economy to reduce vulnerability. Long-standing plans to promote pharmaceuticals, cement, chemicals, high technology, and other sectors have thus far failed. Garment manufacturing held some promise but struggled following the abolition of global quotas on textiles. Unsurprisingly, investors have been slow to come to Brunei. A large industrial park aimed at downstream petrochemical industries opened in 2009 but drew only mild interest from some European and Japanese companies.

Brunei's government views ecotourism as a promising alternative to the energy sector. Relatively untouched tropical forests make tourism potentially attractive, but Brunei's remote location renders it unlikely as a tourist destination in a region with many options. Another initiative proposed by the sultan seeks to make Brunei a center for Islamic banking and finance, but the microstate lags far behind Malaysia in this sector. With little promise elsewhere, the sultanate will have to rely on income from its estimated $170 billon overseas assets to compensate for dwindling oil revenue.[8]

A final economic concern is employment. About 40 percent of Brunei's workforce is made up of foreign workers. Brunei's private sector, weak as it is, does not attract the country's own graduates. A rising rate of unemployment among younger Bruneians who are often holding out for better government jobs troubles officials. Increasingly, foreign workers are filling skilled positions in the private sector, adding to the already large base of immigrant laborers. Brunei's dependence on human resources from outside the country shows little sign of abating.

FOREIGN RELATIONS

Just one week after gaining full independence in 1984, Brunei joined ASEAN, strengthening its relationships with former adversaries such as Indonesia and Malaysia. Today, Brunei's foreign policy focuses on security attained through international legitimacy and expanding economic relations. ASEAN membership has been the primary means to that end. Brunei also cultivates relations beyond Southeast Asia with key partners. In 2013, Brunei chaired ASEAN amid growing tensions surrounding the Spratly Islands dispute.

Since independence, Brunei's relations with the United States have been surprisingly close. In 1986, for example, Brunei channeled some $10 million to help the US-backed Contras in Nicaragua after depositing the money in a Swiss bank account; its government confirmed that "His Majesty the Sultan of Brunei Darussalam had made a personal donation to the United States to be used for humanitarian purposes in Central America."[9] This incident became part of US president Ronald Reagan's "Irangate" imbroglio, and it was the first time that most Americans had ever heard about Brunei.

In keeping with the country's generally pro-Western foreign policy, Brunei supported the US-led liberation of Kuwait (an allied sultanate) from Iraq in 1990, as well as post–September 11 efforts at intelligence sharing to target Islamist terrorists. In December 2002, Sultan Hassanal visited President George W. Bush in Washington to personally pledge support for US counterterrorism efforts in Southeast Asia.

Because Brunei is not threatened by any external power, the country has adopted a low-key foreign policy that is more reactive than proactive. Its main concerns are participating in ASEAN initiatives and building its diplomatic missions abroad to ensure trade and investment for the Bruneian economy. Brunei supported efforts to create AFTA, the ASEAN Free Trade Area, and successfully negotiated a free trade agreement with Japan, which imports 90 percent of Brunei's liquefied natural gas. Along with Chile, New Zealand, and Singapore, Brunei played an important leadership role as a founding party to the Trans-Pacific Partnership (TPP), which entered broader negotiations with twelve Pacific Rim countries. After Brunei's imposition of sharia penal codes in 2014, however, some members of the US Congress requested it be removed as a party if the United States were to join the TPP. In spite of objections, the TPP was signed in October 2015 with Brunei at the table; the trade deal awaits ratification.

CONCLUSION

As is true of most other states in the region, there are discrepancies in the explanation of conditions for a strong state in Brunei, whose absolute monarchy is increasingly an anachronism in a world with few absolute monarchies. As the world moves toward open societies and governmental accountability to the people, Brunei continues to more closely resemble a Middle Eastern kingdom. The country's capacity to sustain absolutism results from the great wealth brought in by the sale of oil and its unique cultivation of MIB as a national ideology. In a country surrounded by agricultural societies in which most of the people are poor, the sultan has bought his legitimacy by providing his subjects with all of life's necessities and, indeed, with luxuries. Whether such a system is sustainable beyond the country's finite natural resources is a question Bruneians and others will increasingly ask.

NOTES

1. Justus M. van der Kroef, "Indonesia, Malaya, and the North Borneo Crisis," *Asian Survey* 3, no. 4 (April 1963): 177.

2. William Case, "Brunei Darussalam: An Electoral Feint," *East Asia Forum*, May 26, 2012, www.eastasiaforum.org/2012/05/26/brunei-darussalam-an-electoral-feint.

3. William Case, "Brunei in 2006: Not a Bad Year," *Asian Survey* 47, no. 1 (January/February 2007): 192.

4. D. S. Ranjit Singh, "Brunei Darussalam in 1987: Coming to Grips with Economic and Political Realities," in *Southeast Asian Affairs 1988* (Singapore: Institute of Southeast Asian Studies, 1988), 63.

5. Jillian Lauren, *Some Girls: My Life in a Harem* (New York: Plume, 2010).

6. Seth Mydans, "Brunei: From Oil Rich to Garage Sales," *New York Times*, August 17, 2001, www.nytimes.com/2001/08/17/world/brunei-from-oil-rich-to-garage-sales.html ?pagewanted=all&src=pm.

7. "Brunei: All Pray and No Work," *The Economist*, August 15, 2015, www.economist .com/news/asia/21661040-autocratic-sultanate-turns-more-devout-oil-money-declines -all-pray-and-no-work.

8. Ibid.

9. K. U. Menon, "Brunei Darussalam in 1986," in *Southeast Asian Affairs 1987* (Singapore: Institute of Southeast Asian Studies, 1987), 99.

13

ASEAN

On August 8 every year, Southeast Asia celebrates itself. In Bangkok, Hanoi, Manila, and other regional capitals, "ASEAN Day" is typically marked by a combination of flag ceremonies, marching bands, youth festivals, and aspirational speeches from regional diplomats. In Jakarta, where the Association of Southeast Asian Nations keeps its headquarters, celebrations can be particularly grand. The ASEAN Secretariat Choir often gathers to sing the ASEAN anthem. Cultural shows, fun runs, blood drives, and similar tie-in events are spread throughout the day. At some point, with media crews at the ready, ASEAN's secretary-general delivers a commemorative address while standing regally against a backdrop of national flags and ASEAN's own banner. Regional unity, prosperity, integration, and identity are inevitably touted.

It is unlikely the Cold War–era diplomats who formed ASEAN in 1967 at a golf resort in Bangkok ever foresaw ASEAN Day in its current form.[1] Indeed, only five pro-Western states participated in ASEAN's founding: Indonesia, Malaysia, the Philippines, Singapore, and Thailand. With the Second Indochina War still raging at the time, the thought of region-wide celebrations occurring simultaneously in communist and noncommunist countries was unimaginable.

ASEAN Day, in fact, grew from ASEAN's adoption of a full-fledged organizational charter in 2007. During its first four decades, ASEAN operated by agreement only, without legal personality. The ASEAN Charter, viewed by some as the organization's pivotal achievement, codified the association's principles, rules, and procedures and reestablished the body as a corporate entity.[2] With legal status, ASEAN could now join international treaties in its own name and represent itself in international organizations.

ASEAN's charter also put in motion an audacious political project: the creation of a pan-ASEAN identity. To this end, the charter thus established August 8 as ASEAN Day and enshrined ASEAN's motto: "One Vision. One Identity. One Community." It also proclaimed an anthem entitled "The ASEAN Way," which, sung only in English, speaks of "heartfelt pride," "daring to dream," and "caring to share." In the charter's annexes, drafters meticulously added protocols for the proper use of the ASEAN flag and emblem as well. Henceforth, ASEAN's familiar sheaf of ten amber stalks of bound *padi* (rice) encircled in red and white would no longer be a mere logo but serve as official intergovernmental insignia (analogous to the European Union's circle of stars). Emblazoned at the center of the flag's cobalt blue field, the ASEAN emblem represents all ten states "bound by friendship and solidarity," with colors symbolizing peace and stability, courage and dynamism, purity, and prosperity.[3]

Such symbols are rather lofty for an intergovernmental regional organization whose primary community is comprised of elite diplomats focused on serving the national self-interest of their home countries. To ASEAN's observers, the attempt to develop a single Southeast Asian identity for the region's 650 million residents is a presumptuous enterprise. Many legitimately wonder: What do those who live in Southeast Asia think of ASEAN? Do they identify with its flag or motto? Do they have a sense of an ASEAN identity—of being an "ASEANer"?[4] Outside the association's bureaucracy, does anyone care to sing the ASEAN anthem? More broadly, how relevant is ASEAN inside and outside the region?

As a supplement to this book's country chapters, this final chapter explores regionalism in Southeast Asia and evaluates ASEAN in particular. It is therefore designed as a foundational survey rather than a comprehensive analysis.[5] The survey opens with a look at the origins of regionalism in Southeast Asia and how ASEAN, and the "ASEAN Way" (the held principles of the group), came into being. The chapter then examines ASEAN's record of internal and external relations, inclusive of the association's responses to major regional events and its own multilateral initiatives, which span trade and security. It closes with a general assessment of ASEAN's successes, failures, and prospects.

Regionalism and the "ASEAN Way"

ASEAN's founding in 1967 was not the first major effort in Southeast Asia to form a regional body. The Manila Pact, signed in 1957, created the Southeast Asia Treaty Organization, or SEATO. With organizational headquarters in Bangkok but far-flung membership spanning the globe, SEATO was a misnomer. Led by the United States, SEATO's membership included Thailand, the Philippines, France, the United Kingdom, Australia, and New Zealand. Pakistan was also a member, but quickly lost interest, as SEATO offered little with respect to ongoing tensions between Pakistan and India.

As a security alliance designed for collective defense, SEATO formed out of the confluence of three developments in the region: the arrival of a polarized Cold War, the 1949 founding of the People's Republic of China, and the delayed postwar departure of colonial powers from Southeast Asia. Even though South Vietnam was not party to the treaty, the United States later claimed it as protected territory under SEATO to justify military escalation in the 1960s.[6]

In terms of collective action, SEATO was every bit the paper tiger that China's Mao Zedong alleged it to be. Divergent interests and a willingness of partners to free-ride on US commitments to combat communism rendered the alliance ineffective as collective defense. SEATO was also undermined by the 1962 Rusk-Thanat Agreement, in which the United States pledged unilateral support for Thailand beyond SEATO.[7] In the 1970s, Pakistan and France withdrew support, and SEATO formally disbanded in 1977. That the pact never lived up to its strategic design does not mean it was inconsequential. It construed a "congressional licensing of unilateral US anticommunist military intervention" and "provided the major rationale for a US military role in Indochina."[8] Nevertheless, because of its asymmetric power structure and incoherent geography, SEATO never held the potential to evolve into a multifunctional regional organization.

Two additional attempts at creating regional institutions also predate ASEAN's 1967 founding. In 1961, the Philippines led the formation of a nonbinding dialogue group with Malaysia and Thailand named the Association of Southeast Asia (ASA). The Philippines also attempted to establish Maphilindo in 1963, a pan-Malay grouping inclusive of Indonesia and Malaysia. Both attempts were short-lived due to preexisting conflicts among members over shared borders on Borneo. In fact, Maphilindo died shortly after its birth, when Sukarno dramatically walked out of its second summit due to unresolved conflicts with Malaysia over control of Sabah, an action that rekindled his aggressive *Konfrontasi* policy regime.[9]

Although SEATO's flawed structure and other failed attempts to create a regional body may have opened the door, it was political change in Indonesia that provided raison d'être for ASEAN's formation. Before 1965, the postwar leaders of Thailand, the Philippines, Malaysia, and Singapore remained universally skeptical of Mao's new China, pursued strong anticommunist policies domestically, and sought closer ties with the United States. Indonesia's Sukarno, however, joined Mao in the Non-Aligned Movement, courted Indonesia's communists, and relentlessly harassed US officials. He even withdrew Indonesia from the United Nations. His *Konfrontasi* policies ended only after the *Gestapu* coup event and the rise of Suharto. Together with his foreign minister Adam Malik, Suharto pursued policies of rapprochement with those ill-treated by Sukarno. A window of opportunity then opened for the creation of ASEAN.

The two-page Bangkok Declaration of 1967, which founded ASEAN, committed its five members to the common purposes of promoting (1) economic growth and trade through partnership; (2) peace and stability through the rule of law and adherence to principles of the UN Charter; and (3) social progress through collaboration in research, education, technology, and cultural relations.[10] Although it did not establish collective defense as one of its stated purposes, the reality was in the subtext, given the anticommunist tilt of its five founding members. Without question, the creation of ASEAN should be viewed as the "product of geopolitical circumstances" shaped by the Cold War and "its potential to enhance domestic and regional security."[11]

In 1971, ASEAN member states signed ZOPFAN, a rather inconsequential joint declaration designating Southeast Asia as a "Zone of Peace, Freedom, and Neutrality." The act of pronouncing "neutrality" amid the polarized positions of many of ASEAN's Cold War governments reflected regional diplomatic posturing more than principled commitments to neutrality. Shortly after its reunification in 1975, Vietnam refused ASEAN's offer to sign ZOPFAN, believing the ASEAN organization was a stooge of the United States. In fact, Vietnam responded by proposing its own treaty of "genuine neutrality" that was likewise rejected by ASEAN states.

Of greater diplomatic consequence was the result of a subsequent high-level summit in Bali in 1976. Convened less than a year after the US withdrawal from Vietnam, ASEAN's first official conference reestablished ASEAN as an independent regional organization. It was at Bali that ASEAN partners agreed to its Treaty of Amity and Cooperation (TAC), an enduring political treaty embedded with far-reaching diplomatic language.

Following ZOPFAN, TAC's signatories again renounced the use of force in resolving conflicts, but they also established a code of conduct among members based on the sanctity of national sovereignty and the principle of noninterference. More than any other instrument in ASEAN's long evolution, this code would come to shape ASEAN and the range of its collective action going forward. Over time, adherence to these principles has fostered regional cohesion by allowing governments to conduct domestic policy without having to endure criticism from neighboring states. After TAC was signed and ratified, hallmark text from Article 2 of the treaty—"non-interference in the internal affairs of one another"—became inseparable from ASEAN. Parallel language currently resides in Article 2 of the 2007 ASEAN Charter and remains the subject of tremendous controversy and debate.

It is thus from the Treaty of Amity and Cooperation that the so-called ASEAN Way emerged. The ASEAN Way combines the sanctity of national sovereignty and the noninterference principle with Asian-based procedural norms—namely, intramural consensus, discrete dialogue, nonconfrontational bargaining, and cultural antipathy toward Western-oriented legalism. Creating an important sense of "we-ness," these procedural norms contribute to an ASEAN identity among the region's diplomatic community.[12] However, in addressing regional political problems, the ASEAN Way reduces consensus-dependent decision-making to the least common denominator. Problem-solving strategies emanating from ASEAN are slow to nonexistent. Sovereign actors in ASEAN leave their sovereign equals alone.

Persistent criticism from the international community faults the ASEAN Way for the body's chronic indifference to suffering, violence, and injustice at the hands of disreputable governments in the region. Noninterference in domestic affairs may work to sustain solidarity among the organization's diverse members, but this unity is derived at a very high price: it fosters "reciprocal impunity" that provides illiberal regimes tremendous leeway to act within their own borders without fear of regional condemnation.[13]

ASEAN ENLARGEMENT

Aspirations of a full regional community have motivated ASEAN to expand membership since its creation. In 1984, upon gaining full independence after ninety-five years of British protection, Brunei joined ASEAN before it joined the United Nations. When the Cold War ended in 1989, ASEAN began to open membership to all states in the region. Through its "ASEAN-10" initiative of the 1990s, ASEAN welcomed as full members Vietnam (1995), Laos (1997), Myanmar (1997), and Cambodia (1999).

With respect to ASEAN enlargement, communist Vietnam and Laos joined with less controversy than did Myanmar and Cambodia. Myanmar, still under SLORC, gained membership in 1997 following ASEAN's campaign of constructive engagement, which had been enthusiastically supported by regional business interests. In late 1995, only months after releasing Aung San Suu Kyi from extended house arrest, Myanmar's military leaders signed ASEAN's Treaty of Amity and Cooperation. Soon after, Myanmar's pro-democratic opposition called upon ASEAN governments to recognize its 1990 election victory, to no avail. Singapore's Lee Kuan Yew, an advocate for engaging Myanmar, caustically dismissed Burma's embattled democracy movement by stating that Aung San Suu Kyi should "remain behind a fence and be a symbol."[14] Myanmar's military generals were listening. Myanmar gained full ASEAN membership, hosted its first ministerial meeting in 2000, and then promptly returned Aung San Suu Kyi to house arrest. The international community decried the detention, but from ASEAN states there was silence. In effect, Myanmar's new ASEAN membership granted its military leaders needed political shelter so they could open business deals with regional investors while continuing their suppression of democracy.

As for Cambodia, its planned ascension to ASEAN in 1997 was initially put in abeyance as a result of Hun Sen's coup against First Prime Minister Norodom Ranariddh that same year. After some heated discussion, ASEAN chose to delay Cambodia's scheduled entry and even offered to mediate Cambodia's domestic political conflict. Hun Sen would have nothing of ASEAN mediation and simply leveraged Cambodia's ascension against the ASEAN-10 initiative. In a cavalier manner, he bellowed, "Let ASEAN defeat the formula of the ASEAN-10, let them defeat it. If we don't enter ASEAN, we won't die."[15] In 1999, a year after new elections afforded Hun Sen's political party the veneer of electoral legitimacy, ASEAN quickly granted membership to Cambodia. The ASEAN-10 was complete.

However controversial it was at the time, it is important to appreciate in hindsight that ASEAN's enlargement initiative did provide "a readymade

forum" for Vietnam, Laos, Cambodia, and Myanmar "to return to the international system after decades of self-destructive isolation."[16] With respect to
ASEAN membership, constructive engagement produced the intended results
of amity. Nevertheless, although ASEAN enlargement may have created technical equality among its members, significant development gaps existed between them in reality. Consequently, it became common in ASEAN circles to
refer to the "ASEAN 5" (the founding five) and the "CLMV Countries" (Cambodia, Laos, Myanmar, and Vietnam).[17]

As for Timor-Leste, its leaders formally applied for ASEAN membership in
2011 with the support of Indonesia. Nonetheless, full membership remains
years away. Though its relations with ASEAN countries remain generally
healthy, membership requirements demand more than the young country can
currently provide.[18]

ASEAN's RECORD OF ACTION (AND INACTION)

It is no coincidence that ASEAN's 1976 Treaty of Amity and Cooperation followed communist victories in Vietnam, Laos, and Cambodia in 1975. Cold War
politics shaped regional relations even after US withdrawal from Vietnam. Along
with their rejection of ZOPFAN, Southeast Asia's new communist governments
also rejected an invitation to join TAC. Vietnam's invasion of Khmer Rouge–
controlled Cambodia in December 1978 then rapidly altered ASEAN's threat
assessments, causing Thailand to become instantly nervous with the Vietnamese
troops suddenly positioned alongside its eastern borders. Rallying around their
fellow member, ASEAN states refused to recognize the Vietnamese-installed
government in Phnom Penh and imposed a trade embargo on occupied Cambodia. They also made frequent appeals at the United Nations for Vietnam to withdraw its troops.

Southeast Asia's "Kampuchea question" came to dominate ASEAN politics
for the following decade. ASEAN constructively asserted itself by pushing for
diplomatic talks among Cambodia's competing factions. Although its unity
was stressed at times, the Cambodia issue helped ASEAN come of age as a regional body as it began to exhibit a corporate interest. However, its stern opposition to Vietnam forced ASEAN into unseemly diplomatic support of the
Khmer Rouge. ASEAN-sponsored talks held in Jakarta during the 1980s proved
unable to dislodge Vietnam from Cambodia. In fact, troop removal came only
after the Cold War ended and the reconciliation of the USSR and China, the
respective patrons of Vietnam and the Khmer Rouge. With the full support of
the UN Security Council and eighteen country signatories, a peace plan brokered in Paris finally became viable in 1991.

ASEAN's involvement in Cambodia's affairs represented a willingness of
the body to articulate a unified approach to conflict resolution. Nevertheless, it
is important to emphasize that when Vietnam occupied Cambodia, neither
were yet members of ASEAN. ASEAN justified its interference in the affairs of

non-member neighbors as both prudent and diplomatically consistent with the ASEAN Way. Further, final resolution was brokered by the United Nations rather than by ASEAN.

In striking contrast to Vietnam's occupation of Cambodia, Indonesia's earlier occupation of non-member East Timor drew no serious response from ASEAN. When Suharto's troops invaded Dili in 1975, ASEAN partners chose to interpret Indonesia's seizure as an internal matter. They quickly accepted Jakarta's claim of provincial status for East Timor and then remained aloof for the next twenty-five years of ruthless Indonesian occupation. Even the most dreadful evidence of Indonesia's harsh control, such as the 1991 Santa Cruz Cemetery Massacre, did little to dislodge ASEAN's members from adhering to the ASEAN Way.

When Suharto's New Order collapsed in 1998 and East Timor was granted an independence referendum, ASEAN governments expressed fear that Indonesia, ASEAN's largest partner, might "Balkanize." They also raised concerns that Western states were unduly internationalizing the East Timor issue.[19] It was only after the United Nations became involved, and upon Indonesia's consent, that ASEAN members acted on the issue by offering troop commitments to the Australian-led INTERFET mission. While the episode indicated a willingness by ASEAN to mobilize peacekeeping forces, it demonstrated again that when the situation demands that it take collective responsibility for regional security problems, ASEAN falters. Fearing intra-ASEAN discord, it tends to act only after external powers initiate a resolution process.

Additionally staining ASEAN's historical record is the association's silence when Myanmar's generals brutally suppressed the 2007 Saffron Revolution. As armed troops attacked pro-democracy monks and protesters on a live global media feed, just weeks prior to ASEAN's annual summit, "the ASEAN Way of keeping quiet while turning a blind eye was on full display," reinforcing to the world that its "doctrine of noninterference . . . implied nonresponsibility."[20] Embarrassed by ASEAN's nonresponse, one diplomat from Singapore rather unexpectedly offered bitter criticism of Myanmar's crackdown during a speech at the United Nations. His ASEAN colleagues acquiesced to the unprecedented reprimand of a fellow member, but no action from ASEAN followed.[21]

In 2008, ASEAN acted more reasonably in reaction to Myanmar's inept and callous response in the aftermath of destruction caused by Cyclone Nargis, Southeast Asia's most deadly storm in over 125 years. For one long week following the storm, Myanmar's government refused international disaster relief over fears that foreign aid workers would engage in political espionage. ASEAN Secretary-General Surin Pitsuwan, together with the UN's Ban Ki-moon, deserve credit for cracking through the junta's paranoia. Because of their actions, ASEAN states became important staging areas for aid delivery and dispatched teams of emergency and medical workers.[22] Nevertheless, it is analytical folly to characterize Myanmar's belated acceptance of ASEAN disaster assistance as an indicator that ASEAN's noninterference principle had weakened. ASEAN remained quiet as the junta went ahead with a constitutional referendum just days after the storm, in a process condemned as fraudulent by democratic governments everywhere. If anything, Cyclone Nargis highlighted ASEAN's difficulty in dealing with member sovereignty and showcased the bizarre realities that Myanmar's membership creates for ASEAN.

No claims over sovereign rights have challenged ASEAN unity more than ongoing disputes over the Spratly and Paracel Islands. As discussed in the country chapters of this book, this potentially explosive issue involves four ASEAN claimants: Brunei, Malaysia, the Philippines, and Vietnam. Individually, the stakes of a resolution are high, particularly for the Philippines and Vietnam, where fervent nationalism animates the issue. Yet it is the broader claims and aggressive behavior of China—ASEAN's most significant dialogue partner—that continue to test the limits of the ASEAN Way.

To its credit, ASEAN negotiated with China two successive declarations on the South China Sea, the first in 1992, and the second in 2002, after the CLMV countries had gained membership. These declarations committed all claimants to avoid escalating tensions, to exercise "self-restraint," and to engage in a settlement process built on international law and "peaceful" and "friendly" dialogue. The fatal flaw of both declarations, alas, has been their nonbinding character. Due to objections by China and Malaysia, the 2002 Declaration on the Conduct of Parties in the South China Sea, for example, includes "no enforcement or dispute resolution mechanisms, and no sanctions against those deemed to have violated its provisions."[23]

At ASEAN's annual meeting in 2012, disagreement over the unresolved claims boiled over. Cambodia, as summit host, infuriated ASEAN's claimants by adopting the pro-China position that existing territorial disputes should be resolved bilaterally. Lacking consensus, ASEAN failed to issue a final joint statement for the conference, a diplomatic low point in ASEAN's history of unity. In the months and years following the conference, China stepped up aggression in the disputed areas and hostile confrontations proliferated. Bypassing ASEAN's dialogue approach, the Philippines announced a new policy of "lawfare" (legal warfare) in 2013 and filed a case against China with the Permanent Court of Arbitration at The Hague. China reacted by submitting a position paper to the body contending it held no jurisdiction over the matter.

With tensions rising, ASEAN and China began anew on a binding code of conduct for the South China Sea dispute in 2014. Little progress has since resulted. In fact, with China acting as bellicose as ever, ASEAN produced a joint statement in 2014 expressing "serious concern" over "hostile acts" and "land reclamation" in the disputed area. Nevertheless, the statement stopped short of mentioning China by name. Subsequent promises that a binding code of conduct is nigh remain unfulfilled. One seasoned observer awarded ASEAN a "failing grade" on the matter, adding that the regional body's "flimsy" declarations and statements are doing nothing to inhibit an "atmosphere of growing rancor and mistrust."[24]

Beyond the South China Sea, other territorial disputes have tested ASEAN with similarly disappointing results. ASEAN's impotence to mediate conflict resolution in the Preah Vihear controversy is particularly illustrative. A decades-long border dispute over an Angkor-era temple erupted again in 2008 after a new round of border clashes. Subsequently the governments of Thailand and Cambodia chose jingoistic nationalism and brinksmanship over ASEAN's offer to mediate the conflict. Once cooler heads prevailed, the disputing parties continued to bypass ASEAN, turning instead to the International Court of Justice (ICJ). In a 2002 dispute over the Sipadan and Ligitan Islands, Malaysia and Indonesia also turned to the ICJ rather than use ASEAN for mediation. The same approach with the ICJ was used again in 2008 to resolve the Predra Braca affair, a long-running quarrel over uninhabited islets contested by Singapore and Malaysia. Rhetorically, the ASEAN Way may shun legalism as a Western-oriented construct, but on sensitive matters, ASEAN's own member states repeatedly demonstrate a preference for the definitive mechanisms of international conflict resolution to uncomfortable regional dialogue or compromised positions resulting from intramural consensus.

Southeast Asia's most distressing migration crises in years brought yet more global attention to ASEAN's commitment to inaction. Ongoing social tensions in Myanmar's Arakan region between local Buddhists and Rohingya Muslims have long caused communal violence, apartheid-like conditions, and episodic ethnic cleansing. As horrific images of desperate Rohingya fleeing the region flooded worldwide news feeds in 2015, the international outcry ballooned precipitously. ASEAN reacted with paralysis by rejecting legal sanctuary for the migrants. International pressure finally forced ASEAN members into tentative action. Southeast Asian governments agreed to go after human trafficking networks and to halt the practice of sending migrants back out to sea (an act already in violation of international law). Yet, fearful of offending Myanmar, ASEAN chose to label the refugees as "irregular migrants" rather than call the Rohingya by their ethnic name.

The religious dimension of the Rohingya crisis also produced splits between Muslim-majority states and others in ASEAN. Shocked by Myanmar's complicity in ethnic cleansing, retired Malaysian prime minister Mahathir bin Mohamad actually called for Myanmar's expulsion from ASEAN. In reply, Myanmar's foreign minister found shelter under the ASEAN Way: "As you know, ASEAN doesn't make decisions without consensus," he said. "Therefore it is impossible to expel Myanmar from ASEAN."[25]

As with the regional crises preceding it, the Rohingya crisis ameliorated only after external involvement: the implementation of a UN resettlement program led by the United States in which willing countries took refugees. ASEAN states only agreed to provide "temporary shelter," while other countries (including

Gambia, with a lower per capita GDP than any ASEAN state), opened their doors to desperate Rohingya families. With the world watching, and only two years from celebrating its fiftieth anniversary, ASEAN once again demonstrated its inability to manage regional political crises on its own.

ASEAN-led Multilateral Institutions

ASEAN's capacity to create multilateral fora exceeds its capacity to satisfactorily address the region's political challenges in security, human rights, and democracy. When the new international era arrived, ASEAN doubled down on the ASEAN Way by adding four authoritarian regimes as members and beginning to reevaluate post–Cold War possibilities for institutionalizing regional trade and security. Motivated by both hope and fear, ASEAN sought opportunities to make Southeast Asia relevant in a post–Cold War world. A host of ASEAN-led multilateral arrangements now contribute to Asia's current trade networks and security architecture.

AFTA

The 1990s proved to be a formative period for ASEAN. With the Cold War over, and Vietnam's withdrawal from Cambodia complete, Southeast Asian governments began to focus on business. Lack of progress in the Uruguay Round of GATT (General Agreement on Tariffs and Trade) led leaders in the Americas and Asia to form a nonbinding trade liberalization group of their own in 1989: the Asia-Pacific Economic Cooperation, or APEC. Comprising one-half of APEC's twelve founding members were the six countries in ASEAN at the time. Unlike the broader GATT, APEC would follow voluntary compliance norms rather than strap its members to uniform legal commitments.

From ASEAN's perspective, APEC's transpacific membership placed the United States squarely in Asia's trade management structure. Integrating with American markets was desirable, but fears of neocolonialism lingered. Therefore, in 1992, amid a regional economic boom, ASEAN launched the ASEAN Free Trade Area (AFTA). As much a statement of regional pride as an economic imperative, AFTA rode the global wave of trade liberalization. Having experienced rapid growth through export-oriented policies since the mid-1980s, ASEAN's founding countries pursued economic liberalization in parallel with the ASEAN-10 strategy. AFTA's Common Effective Preferential Tariff (CEPT) eventually led to unprecedented tariff reductions in Southeast Asia.

In creating AFTA, ASEAN's governments achieved three main objectives. First, AFTA represented significant progress on unrealized goals of regional economic cooperation that dated to the 1967 Bangkok Declaration. Second, by reducing tariff rates in hosts of product areas, AFTA sought economic efficiencies while simultaneously making the region ever more attractive to international investors. Third, combined with membership enlargement, AFTA helped 150 million more Southeast Asians from the CLMV countries tap into the region's economic dynamism. New members thus entered AFTA immediately after joining ASEAN but were permitted to tarry under a more gradual schedule of tariff reduction obligations.

Over time, ASEAN successfully lowered tariff barriers and enhanced trade regionalism through AFTA. Although AFTA's tariff reductions have been comparatively deeper than many regional trade blocs, serious structural limitations within ASEAN remain. Southeast Asian economies generate similar types of products, exports, and investments. With few differences, Southeast Asian economies compete against each other as much as they complement each other. Compared to NAFTA or the expanded European Union, ASEAN's membership tends to be more economically homogeneous, with trade profiles sharing similar products, goods, and exports. The region's comparative advantage in trade exists primarily with partners in East Asia, Europe, and North America. Within Southeast Asia proper, fierce intramural competition occurs across many sectors, including agriculture, natural resources, manufacturing, foreign investment, and even tourism.

Indeed, although the volume of intra-ASEAN trade has increased since AFTA's creation, it has been outpaced by trade with partners outside the region by a three-to-one ratio.[26] AFTA's individual members, in many respects, are more economically integrated with trade partners outside the region than within it. Such density in trade volume is not only true for manufacturers but also in services such as finance, technical exchange, education, and tourism. Even in the realm of pop culture and commercialized sports, intra-ASEAN exchange is eclipsed by popular imports such as Japanese anime, K-pop, Hollywood and Bollywood movies, and the United Kingdom's Premier League Football.

ASEAN Plus

The reality of ASEAN's extensive connectivity with global markets, supply chains, and business networks lies behind its aggressive efforts to pursue "ASEAN Plus" arrangements. Following the 1997 Asian economic crisis, greater resolve for pan-Asian economic integration emerged. ASEAN's global relevance today owes much to its continuous efforts to form economic partnerships beyond its own region.

In ASEAN jargon, a "plus arrangement" is any arrangement ASEAN formalizes with an external partner. An ASEAN Plus One (ASEAN+1) relationship is thus shorthand for a relationship ASEAN establishes with a single non-ASEAN partner—it is "plurilateral" rather than "bilateral." For example, ASEAN Plus efforts have led to separate ASEAN free trade agreements with China, Japan, South Korea, and India, as well as with Australia and New Zealand jointly. A Plus One agreement with Hong Kong is set to be finalized in 2016. The extent to which ASEAN members benefit from these Plus One arrangements is unclear, as "empirical evidence . . . remains patchy and limited."[27]

Of greater multilateral significance than ASEAN Plus One arrangements is the ASEAN Plus Three (APT, or ASEAN+3) framework, which includes ASEAN plus China, Japan, and South Korea. The vast flows of trade and investment between East and Southeast Asia that began in the 1980s set the stage for serious intra-Asian dialogue. In 1990, shortly after APEC was put in motion, one of ASEAN's most trenchant critics of Western hegemony, Malaysia's Mahathir bin Mohamad, proposed an exclusively Asian economic grouping. Mahathir's idea, later dubbed the East Asia Economic Caucus (EAEC), was ahead of its time. Initially, Japan and others expressed aversion to such a bloc, but following the 1997 Asian economic crisis, all involved countries enthusiastically embraced the proposal. Due to the Clinton administration's tone-deaf response to Asia's economic woes, and the IMF's one-size-fits-all bailout packages, Asian countries sought common cause. In 1998, regional leaders dusted off Mahathir's proposed grouping and created the ASEAN Plus Three.

As Asia's most developed economic grouping, the APT has made real progress in finance and monetary cooperation. The APT's Chiang Mai Initiative (CMI), finalized in 2000, established central bank coordination to provide needed liquidity through potential currency swaps—a sort of pan-Asian macroeconomic safety net. Though largely unused, the CMI built confidence in a region-wide mechanism to complement other options for short-term liquidity. Later, following the 2008 global economic crisis, APT members expanded the CMI's role, increased its funding, and brought Hong Kong into the fold. Renamed the Chiang Mai Initiative Multilateralization (CMIM), the fund grew to $240 billion, 80 percent of which comes from the non–ASEAN Plus Three countries and Hong Kong.[28] The CMIM arrangement coordinates its own macroeconomic surveillance unit to detect risk and assist decision-making. It also established a new framework for bond issuance to allow the use of local currencies in foreign investments.

The ASEAN Plus Three framework continues to promote new mechanisms to facilitate intra-Asian trade and finance. In December 2005, Malaysia hosted an ASEAN Plus Six meeting entitled the East Asian Summit (EAS). The EAS pledged to remain open to "broad strategic, political and economic issues of common interest and concern."[29] Operationally, the EAS has resulted in coordination on transnational issues such as energy market integration, pandemic disease, and food security. More recently China has completed the creation of an Asian Infrastructure Investment Bank (AIIB), which now issues project loans to recipient countries. ASEAN states joined enthusiastically. Remaining in the shadows is also a long-standing Japan-led initiative to develop a full-blown Asian Monetary Fund.

ARF
In addition to seeking economic integration, ASEAN employs its Asian diplomatic networks to manage its post–Cold War political and security interests.

Aware of the changing role of the United States in Asia, the rise of powers such as China, Japan, and South Korea, and growing relations with India and Australia, ASEAN moved swiftly in the 1990s to develop norm-based multilateral security partnerships in every direction. Lacking the resources of hard power, ASEAN leveraged its Treaty of Amity and Cooperation by inviting willing partners in Asia and elsewhere to accept its norms. Over the next two decades, seventeen new countries entered the treaty, including, most recently, Brazil and Norway.

With twenty countries present, ASEAN inaugurated the ASEAN Regional Forum (ARF) in 1994.[30] Grounded in TAC's norms of cooperative security and strategic inclusion, the ARF encourages security dialogue between ASEAN and other powers with interests in Southeast Asia. Eschewing deterrence-based security and embracing inclusiveness, the ARF's framers designed it to foster confidence-building through routinized dialogue, preventive diplomacy, and trust. For ASEAN, the ARF is a socialization mechanism to encourage "good" behavior among larger powers such as China and the United States.[31]

Because it involves all the major powers, including all five permanent members of the UN Security Council, the ARF is the central node of Asia's multilateral security network. In 2010, in consecutive speeches on the US pivot toward Asia, Secretary of State Hillary Clinton used identical language in Honolulu and Hanoi to describe this developing network: "We view ASEAN as a fulcrum for the region's emerging regional architecture . . . indispensable on a host of political, economic, and strategic matters."[32]

Now in its third decade, the ARF still demands little of participants beyond acknowledging TAC's norms and participating in multilateral dialogue through annual meetings. In fact, countries engaged with the ARF consider themselves "participants" rather than "members." With such limited obligations, the ARF's inclusiveness allows states to sideline the resolution of unsettled issues in favor of dialogue about others. Despite giving lip service to "conflict resolution," the ARF meets only once a year, and it has yet to develop a serious framework for dispute settlement. Because it is prone to issue avoidance rather than painful multilateral engagement, the ARF's meeting agendas commonly focus on less confrontational transboundary issues, such as disaster relief, transnational crime, maritime piracy, and the prevention of oil spills. That North Korea has sent representatives to the ARF since 2000 indicates just how nonthreatening the dialogue-heavy forum has become. As for ASEAN, ever committed to the ARF structure, unified responses to China's actions in the South China Sea, the United States' Asian pivot, or the reality of Japan's remilitarization have yet to emerge.[33] Realpolitik meshes rather poorly with ARF's ideational strategies of social interaction.

Having expanded the ARF to twenty-seven countries, ASEAN's role in broader Asian security is a subject of both admiration and cynicism. Questions about ASEAN and its centrality to the very regional institutions it created are starting to emerge.[34] To some, ASEAN remains the "hub and agenda-setter" of Asia's security network—a "convening power with normative and social leadership."[35] To others, ASEAN's constructivist projects in the security realm, including its nonbinding treaty of amity, are worthy of Nobel Prize consideration for fostering norm-based behavior across the world. Realists and other critics, by contrast, view the ARF as another ASEAN "talk shop," or the butt of a joke, where ASEAN stands for "all sitting, eating, and nodding."[36] Whatever the case, observers agree that ASEAN remains fully committed to multilateral dialogue.

AEC

ASEAN's sustained outward push makes consideration of its internal integration efforts that much more interesting. As ASEAN develops partnerships across the globe, including a liberal array of FTAs (free trade agreements), it expects to evolve into a full-blown economic community, analogous to the European Union. In this respect, its rhetorical antipathy toward Western legalism is observably breaking down. Rather than rejecting Grotian-style modes of integration, ASEAN increasingly mimics the West's legal formalism and preference for binding commitments. In 2007, owing to frustration with member noncompliance on agreements and worn-out language of "promoting" and "encouraging" state action, ASEAN not only codified its charter but committed its members to create a binding ASEAN Economic Community (AEC).

The idea of gradually making AFTA a regional economic community first emerged at an ASEAN summit in 1997. Ten years later, ASEAN formalized an "AEC Blueprint" laying out specific implementation objectives and timelines. The scheduled 2020 launch for the AEC was also moved up to December 31, 2015. The AEC is designed to accelerate trade facilitation by eliminating most non-tariff barriers (NTBs) and creating a single integrated customs process for all ASEAN members. When fully operable, the AEC will permit the free exchange of professional and skilled laborers, liberalize the service sector, and open pathways for even small businesses to integrate with regional supply chains.

The AEC Blueprint also includes safeguards, including "ASEAN-X" arrangements that allow single members or subgroups to exempt themselves from designated liberalization measures in "strategic sectors" such as banking. CLMV countries are also permitted greater flexibility and time to transition to the AEC. Because individual members are left to implement blueprint objectives for their own economies, domestic opposition and friction have inhibited a smooth transition. Only months before the AEC's scheduled 2015 start date, progress toward planned objectives was uneven across countries. Services and investment remained only marginally liberalized, and many NTBs persisted.[37]

The AEC is merely one pillar of three in ASEAN's larger goal of an "ASEAN Community." In preparing for this community, ASEAN reorganized its various organizational entities into a more coherent structure in its new charter. Along with the AEC, the ASEAN Community's two other pillars include the ASEAN

Political-Security Community (APSC) and the ASEAN Socio-Cultural Community (ASCC).

The APSC reorganized ministerial-level dialogue in concert with the ARF and within ASEAN itself through the ASEAN Defense Ministers' Meeting (ADMM). Somewhat surprisingly, the APSC also articulated human rights norms through the ASEAN Intergovernmental Commission on Human Rights (AICHR) in 2009. This body holds serious potential to address deficiencies in the human rights records of ASEAN countries. A complementary effort to draft an ASEAN Declaration on Human Rights also exists in embryonic form. However, ASEAN's new "goal of promoting sovereign-transcending norms of democracy and protecting human rights appears to run directly counter to ASEAN's much cherished norm of non-interference and state sovereignty."[38] To date, the AICHR lacks any real corporate power, and its commissioners consistently ignore the ongoing erosion of political rights and democracy in the region. Instead, they choose to focus less controversially on the rights of the disabled and the safety of women and children.[39]

ASEAN's third pillar, the ASEAN Socio-Cultural Community, fosters regional collaboration in areas such as labor rights, the environment, disaster management, health, education, and the arts. Idealistically, it promotes a "common identity" for the region—an "ASEAN Community that is people-centered and socially responsible."[40] The ultimate success of this pillar hinges on whether ASEAN's new activities come to mean anything in the lives of ordinary Southeast Asians or simply contribute to an ever-expanding ASEAN bureaucracy. When it comes to democratic aspirations, the residents of most ASEAN states are still waiting for ASEAN to become an ally. Aspirations of "one vision, one identity, and one community" have thus far proven unrealistic.

ASEAN AT FIFTY

On August 8, 2017, ASEAN will turn fifty years old. On that day, the Association of Southeast Asian Nations will celebrate ASEAN Day by counting itself among the world's largest economic entities.[41] In 2014, ASEAN's combined GDP of $2.4 trillion already rivaled the United Kingdom's, and it exceeded the GDPs of both India and Brazil. If one factors in the economies of ASEAN Plus partners, the regional bloc's economic significance is even more impressive. ASEAN's Plus One FTA with China, known as ACFTA, or the ASEAN-China Free Trade Agreement, amounts to a combined GDP of $11.9 trillion, surpassed only by the trading blocs of the European Union and NAFTA. With respect to foreign exchange reserves, ASEAN's $766 billion tops the $459 billion combined reserves of the European Union and NAFTA. ASEAN is a legitimate economic powerhouse. None of its members acting alone could exert such influence, but, as a group, ASEAN contributes much to the global economy. It also positively affects regional stability. Since signing TAC, no two ASEAN countries have declared war on each other.

ASEAN's aggressive economic diplomacy unambiguously overlaps with Asia's developing security networks. At stake is not just economic growth and security but the preservation of regional autonomy. ASEAN-led multilateralism includes Western powers, but often at arm's length. Although the United States and Europe participate in ASEAN-led summits, the ASEAN Plus approach places higher value on relations with core Asian partners. Discussions of a Regional Comprehensive Economic Partnership (RCEP) are reviving negotiations for a single economic community made up exclusively of the ASEAN Plus Six countries.[42] Poised to rival the United States–proposed Trans-Pacific Partnership (TPP)—which currently excludes China—the RCEP would include over 3 billion people and be the world's largest trading bloc. Combined with the APT's CMIM and China's own AIIB, an Asian-only FTA would stand to remind Washington that Asian regionalism, at its core, seeks to remain Asian. An Asia-centric institutional architecture for security, trade, and monetary relations is evolving. ASEAN is positioned at its diplomatic center.

ASEAN's successful efforts in forging multilateral economic and security cooperation are, no doubt, a product of the ASEAN Way at some level. However, agreeing to lower tariff barriers and hosting security "talk shops" has proven far easier for ASEAN than ganging up on neighboring governments to condemn unjust, inhumane, and undemocratic policies. Doing the latter is especially difficult in a region where ruling elites must think twice before casting stones at each other. Nevertheless, like regional bodies elsewhere, it is incumbent on ASEAN to raise expectations on its member governments, encourage good behavior, and hold officials accountable when they fall short. Similar to the UN Charter and the Universal Declaration of Human Rights, ASEAN's new intergovernmental charter carries the mantle to act as the conscience for the region, as an agreed upon set of norms and standards from which to measure behavior and progress.

It is unfortunate that ASEAN's new charter recommitted the organization to the principles of noninterference and consensus decision-making, given their proven incompatibility with democratic development and the defense of human rights. While supranational powers for ASEAN have never been on the table, formal recommendations by its own advisory group during the charter drafting process urged ASEAN to shed its consensus norm and adopt majority rule.[43] ASEAN member states emphatically rejected the idea.

ASEAN founders have talked openly about emulating Europe's like-minded political community. "It should be put on the record that . . . our model has been and still is, the European Community," emphasized Thailand's Thanat Khoman, whose signature graces the Bangkok Declaration.[44] Yet stubborn commitment to the ASEAN Way and noninterference in domestic affairs undermines development of democratic norms that are crucial to the European Union's success: good governance, protection of human rights, and political freedom. Moreover, although it is true that noninterference, by definition, does not inhibit democracy where it may organically bloom, ASEAN's record of failing to nourish democratic practices within its own region speaks for itself. The ASEAN Way has done more to cultivate illiberalism than liberal democracy in Southeast Asia.

As noted in Chapter 1, it is distressing that in 2015, Southeast Asia remains less democratic than Latin America, sub-Saharan Africa, Oceania, South Asia, and East Asia, not to mention Europe and North America. In fact, at a regional level, only the autocratic regimes of the Middle East and North Africa surpass Southeast Asia in their suppression of political freedoms and civil liberties. To the extent Southeast Asian leaders have cultivated democracy, they tend to favor form over substance. Many of the region's most consequential political figures in the new international era have been autocrats cloaked in democratic pretense—Lee Kuan Yew, Suharto, Mahathir, Hun Sen, and even the popularly elected Thaksin. As the country chapters in this book demonstrate, rare is the democratically elected leader in Southeast Asia who doesn't attempt to rig the rules to extend his or her rule. Sadly, ASEAN at fifty remains rife with authoritarian variants and politically closed regimes.

Such a critical view of ASEAN is held by many of its greatest supporters. Urging reform and a shift from dialogue to action, one long-standing member of the ASEAN Secretariat argues that "ASEAN needs to reinvent itself."[45] Holding up the African Union as a model as opposed to the European Union, another highly respected observer argues that ASEAN "needs to overcome the persisting 'non-intervention' mindset of its members" by exerting its own "political will" to successfully address regional problems and crises.[46] Even Malaysia's Mahathir concedes that ASEAN's policy of noninterference must be put aside if regional governments fail to address human security.[47]

Doctrinaire adherence to the ASEAN Way not only impedes human security, human rights, and democratization across Southeast Asia, but is also affecting ASEAN's external relevance more generally. In particular, to foster respect from its democratic partners in Europe, North America, and East Asia, ASEAN will need to choose whether it will accommodate undemocratic China or imitate it. As the new international era gives way to a new great-power competition in Asia, ASEAN's famous unity could also weaken before ASEAN establishes a corporate identity on par with more robust regional bodies. As states align with old and new powers, a resurgence of nationalism, bilateralism, and realpolitik could indeed spoil the promised ASEAN Community. In such an environment, ASEAN, like SEATO before it, would hang together as "nothing more than the sum of its sovereign parts,"[48] with members appending themselves to more powerful external actors. The ASEAN political project is not yet this fragile, but the potential exists. In the meantime, its unmet promises and callous approach to democratic norms continue to draw ongoing negative attention.

For all its symbolic importance to diplomatic elites in the region, ASEAN Day goes largely unnoticed by the region's 650 million residents. Each year, the organized events in honor of ASEAN's founding do little to stir emotions or engender patriotic pride among the various Filipinos, Thais, Malays, Javanese, Vietnamese, Hmong, Dayaks, Chams, and hundreds of other groups, including the Rohingya, that make up Southeast Asia's tremendous human diversity. Similarly, the official launch of the ASEAN Economic Community on December 31, 2015, excited few across the region. In Bangkok, where ASEAN began, Thai officials celebrated the new AEC by staging a lantern festival aimed at tourists, and with a tacky ASEAN-themed puppet show complete with ten cutesy characters, one per member state. On the same day in Jakarta, home of ASEAN headquarters, a leading newspaper led its opinion page with the headline, "AEC Launch: Will It Mean Much to Southeast Asians?"[49]

NOTES

1. Thanat Khoman, "ASEAN Conception and Evolution," 1992, www.asean.org/?static_post=asean-conception-and-evolution-by-thanat-khoman.

2. Termsak Chalermpalanupap, "Institutional Reform: One Charter, Three Communities, Many Challenges," in *Hard Choices: Security, Democracy, and Regionalism in Southeast Asia*, ed. Donald K. Emmerson (Stanford: Walter H. Shorenstein Asia-Pacific Books, Research Center Books, 2008), 91.

3. "ASEAN Flag," Association of Southeast Asian Nations, www.asean.org/asean/about-asean/asean-flag. Lyrics and audio of the ASEAN anthem are available at www.asean.org/asean/about-asean/asean-anthem.

4. "ASEANer," is a term akin to how "European" is used in the EU context. It has been employed by ASEAN proponents such as Surin Pitsuwan, former secretary-general of the Secretariat of ASEAN (2008–2012) and in *Reporting Development in ASEAN* (Bangkok: IPS Asia-Pacific, 2013), 113, and is the title of a new regional magazine called *THE ASEANER*, www.facebook.com/THEASEANER/info?tab=page_info.

5. Many events discussed in this chapter are detailed more fully in the country chapters. They are mentioned here only in relation to ASEAN.

6. George McTurnan Kahin, *Intervention: How America Became Involved in Vietnam* (New York: Double Day, 1987), 50, 72.

7. Leszek Buszynski, *SEATO: The Failure of an Alliance Strategy* (Singapore: Singapore University Press, 1983).

8. McTurnan Kahin, *Intervention*, 72.

9. R. B. Smith, *An International History of the Vietnam War*, vol. 2 (New York: St. Martin's Press, 1985), 272.

10. This short list summarizes the seven "aims and purposes" listed in the ASEAN Declaration, www.asean.org/the-asean-declaration-bangkok-declaration-bangkok-8-august-1967.

11. Mark Beeson, *Regionalism and Globalization in East Asia: Politics, Security, and Economic Development* (New York: Palgrave Macmillan, 2007), 217–218.

12. Erik Kuhonta, "Toward Responsible Sovereignty: The Case for Intervention," in *Hard Choices*, ed. Emmerson, 292–313.

13. Donald K Emmerson, "Critical Terms: Security, Democracy, and Regionalism in Southeast Asia," in *Hard Choices*, ed. Emmerson, 23.

14. "Suu Kyi Not Angry with Lee Kuan Yew," *Burma Net News*, June 23, 1996, www.burmalibrary.org/reg.burma/archives/199606/msg00280.html.

15. Frank Frost, "ASEAN at 30: Enlargement, Consolidation, and the Problems of Cambodia," *Current Issues Brief 2 1997–1998*, Parliament of Australia, www.aph.gov.au /About_Parliament/Parliamentary_Departments/Parliamentary_Library/Publications _Archive/CIB/CIB9798/98cib02.

16. Amitav Acharya, "Doomed by Dialogue? Will ASEAN Survive Great Power Rivalry in Asia," *The Asan Forum*, June 29, 2015, www.theasanforum.org/doomed-by-dialogue -will-asean-survive-great-power-rivalry-in-asia.

17. Less frequently, Brunei is grouped with the ASEAN 5 to form the ASEAN 6.

18. Since 1976, Papua New Guinea has held observer status in ASEAN. Its prospects for full membership remain dim due to strong resistance by current ASEAN governments.

19. Alan Dupont, "ASEAN's Response to the East Timor Crisis," *Australian Journal of International Affairs* 54, no. 2 (June 2000): 163–170.

20. Emmerson, "Critical Terms," 27.

21. Ibid., 28–29.

22. Ibid., 51–52.

23. Ian Storey, "ASEAN's Failing Grade in the South China Sea," *The Asan Forum*, July 31, 2015, 3, www.theasanforum.org/aseans-failing-grade-in-the-south-china-sea.

24. Ibid.

25. Luke Hunt, "ASEAN Move on Rohingya, Slow But Forward," *The Diplomat*, June 22, 2015, http://thediplomat.com/2015/06/asean-move-on-rohingya-slow-but-forward.

26. In actual 2014 figures, the intra-ASEAN and extra-ASEAN trade percentages were 24.1 percent and 76.9 percent, respectively. See ASEAN, "External Trade Statistics," table 18, www.asean.org/?static_post=external-trade-statistics-3.

27. Tham Siew Yean and Sanchita Basu Das, "The ASEAN Economic Community and Conflicting Domestic Interests," *Journal of Southeast Asian Economies* 32, no. 2 (August 2015): 195.

28. ASEAN +3 Macroeconomic Research Office, "Contributions," www.amro-asia.org /about-amro/history/country-representation.

29. Joseph Chinyong Liow, *Dictionary of the Modern Politics of Southeast Asia* (London: Routledge, 2014), 150.

30. All ten Southeast Asian countries as well as Australia, Canada, China, the European Union, India, Japan, New Zealand, Russia, South Korea, and the United States.

31. Beeson, *Regionalism and Globalization*, 88–89.

32. Hillary Rodham Clinton, October 28, 2010, Honolulu, Hawaii, www.state.gov /secretary/20092013clinton/rm/2010/10/150141.htm; October 30, 2010, Hanoi, Vietnam, http://iipdigital.usembassy.gov/st/english/texttrans/2010/11/20101101114506su0.5574414 .html#axzz41PfhVwUd.

33. Kuroyanagi Yoneji, "The US-China-Japan Triangle and the Concept of 'ASEAN Centrality': Myth or Reality?" *The Asan Forum*, July 31, 2015, www.theasanforum.org /the-us-china-japan-triangle-and-the-concept-of-asean-centrality-myth-or-reality.

34. Yoneji, "The US-China-Japan Triangle"; Mely Caballero-Anthony, "Understanding ASEAN's Centrality: Bases and Prospects in an Evolving Regional Architecture," *Pacific Review* 27, no. 4 (June 2014).

35. Acharya, "Doomed by Dialogue?"

36. Ibrahim Almuttaqi, "ASEAN's Treaty of Amity and Cooperation: Nobel Peace Prize Nominee for 2015?" *The Jakarta Post*, September 21, 2014, www.thejakartapost.com /news/2014/09/21/asean-s-treaty-amity-and-cooperation-nobel-peace-prize-nominee -2015.html.

37. Tham Siew Yean and Sanchita Basu Das, "The ASEAN Economic Community," 193–195.

38. Joseph Chinyong Liow, *Dictionary of the Modern Politics of Southeast Asia*, 86.

39. ASEAN, *Annual Report 2013–14: Moving Forward in Unity*, 31–32.

40. ASEAN, *Annual Report 2013–14*, 52.

41. All figures in this paragraph come from "ASEAN Integration 2015: A Progress Report," *Bloomberg Briefs*, December 2014, www.bloombergbriefs.com/content/uploads /sites/2/2014/12/asean_integration_2015-optim2.pdf.

42. Evan A. Feigenbaum, "The New Asian Order," *Foreign Affairs*, February 2, 2015, https://www.foreignaffairs.com/articles/east-asia/2015-02-02/new-asian-order.

43. Liow, *Dictionary of the Modern Politics*, 85.

44. Khoman, "ASEAN Conception."

45. Termsak Chalermpalanupap, "Institutional Reform," 92.

46. Acharya, "Doomed by Dialogue?"

47. Hunt, "ASEAN Move on Rohingya."

48. Emmerson, "Critical Terms," 27.

49. A. Ibrahim Almuttaqi, "AEC Launch: Will It Mean Much to Southeast Asians?" *Jakarta Post*, December 31, 2015, www.thejakartapost.com/news/2015/12/31/aec-launch -will-it-mean-much-southeast-asians.html.

Index

CPSIA information can be obtained at www.ICGtesting.com
Printed in the USA
LVOW10s1503090716

495461LV00002B/2/P